Musica ficta

The main purpose of this book is to clarify the meaning and use of the conventions governing the practice of implied accidentals in vocal polyphony from the early fourteenth to the mid-sixteenth century – a problem which has fascinated musicologists for over a hundred years now.

Although musicians of the late Middle Ages and Renaissance had at their disposal everything they needed to notate pitches unambiguously, they did not think it was necessary to write down all accidentals; since some accidental inflections were implied by the musical context, performers made them whether or not they were notated. This practice imposes on modern readers of early music sources, be they editors, performers or historians, the task of supplying all such conventionally implied accidental inflections and the successful achievement of this task depends on a knowledge and understanding of the conventions involved.

Since the practice of implied accidentals can be understood only in a wider context of compositional, notational, and performing practice of the period, the book attempts to throw light on some aspects of these practices as well.

Professor Berger's study represents the first attempt to examine the whole surviving theoretical evidence relevant to the subject and thus lays an indispensable foundation for any future work in this area.

Musica ficta

THEORIES OF ACCIDENTAL INFLECTIONS IN VOCAL POLYPHONY FROM MARCHETTO DA PADOVA TO GIOSEFFO ZARLINO

KAROL BERGER

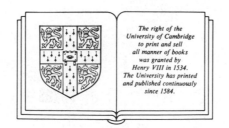

The right of the
University of Cambridge
to print and sell
all manner of books
was granted by
Henry VIII in 1534.
The University has printed
and published continuously
since 1584.

Cambridge University Press

CAMBRIDGE

NEW YORK   NEW ROCHELLE

MELBOURNE   SYDNEY

Published by the Press Syndicate of the University of Cambridge
The Pitt Building, Trumpington Street, Cambridge CB2 1RP
32 East 57th Street, New York, NY 10022, USA
10 Stamford Road, Oakleigh, Melbourne 3166, Australia

First published 1987

Printed in Great Britain at
the University Press, Cambridge

British Library cataloguing in publication data
Berger, Karol
Musica ficta: theories of accidental
inflections in vocal polyphony from
Marchetto da Padova to Gioseffo Zarlino.
1. Musical notation 2. Vocal music –
Europe – History and criticism
I. Title
784   ML431

Library of Congress cataloguing in publication data
Berger, Karol, 1947–
Musica ficta.
Bibliography.
Includes index.
1. Chromatic alteration (Music) I. Title.
ML190.B47   1987   781   86-31750

ISBN 0 521 32871 3

ME

To Anna Maria

Contents

Contents

Note: Throughout this book, the medieval letter notation (Γ, A-G, a-g, aa-ee, ♭=fa, ♮ or ♯=mi) is used to indicate pitches. Italicized capital letters are used when the octave of the pitch is of no concern. Ascending degrees of a mode are indicated by consecutive Arabic numerals beginning with 1 for the final.

Figures

The figures appear by permission of the following: Centrale Bibliotheek, Rijksuniversiteit, Gent (figs 1 and 2); the Music Division, Library of Congress (fig. 3); the Bodleian Library (fig. 5); the Bibliothèque Nationale (fig. 6); the Bayerische Staatsbibliothek (fig. 7).

Preface

Music notation, like other forms of writing, aids memory by means of visual representation of what is intrinsically an aural medium. The development of music notation in Europe shows an increasing graphic control over various aspects of sound and its artistic organization. The problem of how to represent music visually was solved first in the matter of pitch. By the early eleventh century, all graphic signs needed to notate pitch unambiguously had been introduced, so that the principal innovations in music notation made during the high and late Middle Ages and the Renaissance were in the domain of rhythm and meter. However, although musicians of the period had at their disposal everything they needed to notate pitches unambiguously, modern readers of early music sources, be they textual critics, performers or historians, are bedevilled by a persistent problem in reconstructing the intended pitches. This is known somewhat informally as the problem of *musica ficta*.

During the Middle Ages and the Renaissance it was not necessary to write down all accidentals. Since some accidental inflections were conventionally implied by the musical context, performers made them whether or not they were notated. This practice imposes on modern readers of early music sources the task of supplying all such conventionally implied accidental inflections. A successful performance of this task depends on our knowledge and understanding of the conventions involved. The main purpose of the present book is to offer assistance by clarifying the meaning and use of the conventions governing the practice of implied accidentals in vocal polyphony from the early fourteenth to the mid sixteenth century.

It should be self-evident why this is a worthwhile goal. Our understanding of the practice of implied accidentals is a prerequisite for our ability to read, perform and study early music. But the investigation undertaken in the present book will yield some less obvious benefits as well. The practice of implied accidentals can be understood only in a wider context of compositional, notational and performing practices of the period and, consequently, our investigation will need to shed light on at least some aspects of these practices. For example, one of the conventional functions of accidental inflections was to supply cadential leading tones. It is necessary to deepen our understanding of the structure of cadences in order to be able to recognize contexts which called for inflections. The present study will also make new questions and areas of investigation possible. For instance, we will be able to distinguish between conventional and unconventional uses of accidental inflections, a distinction indispensable in studying the development of chromaticism in European music.

Musicologists have been aware of the problem of implied accidentals for more than a hundred years now and, especially in the last forty years, made great progress toward solving it. Our understanding of *musica ficta* has been particularly enriched by Edward E. Lowinsky,[1] Richard H. Hoppin,[2] Lewis Lockwood,[3] Carl Dahlhaus,[4] James Haar,[5] Margaret Bent,[6] Andrew Hughes[7] and Howard Mayer Brown.[8] And yet we are still very far from a generally accepted musicological theory of *musica ficta* and from a commonly employed set of editorial procedures for dealing with written and implied accidental inflections in early music. The problem of implied accidentals remains until this day, in the words of Lewis Lockwood, 'one of the frontier problems of musicology'.[9] The reason why the solution has

[1] See especially 'The Goddess Fortuna in Music, with a Special Study of Josquin's *Fortuna d'un gran tempo*', *The Musical Quarterly*, XXIX (1943), 45-77; 'The Function of Conflicting Signatures in Early Polyphonic Music', *ibid.*, XXXI (1945), 227-60; *Secret Chromatic Art in the Netherlands Motet* (New York: Columbia University Press, 1946); 'Conflicting Views on Conflicting Signatures', *Journal of the American Musicological Society*, VII (1954), 181-204; 'Adrian Willaert's Chromatic "Duo" Re-Examined', *Tijdschrift van de Vereniging voor Nederlandse Muziekgeschiedenis*, XVIII (1956), 1-36; 'Mattheus Greiter's *Fortuna*: An Experiment in Chromaticism and in Musical Iconography', *The Musical Quarterly*, XLII (1956), 500-19 and XLIII (1957), 68-85; 'Foreword', H. C. Slim, ed., *Musica Nova*, Monuments of Renaissance Music I (Chicago and London: The University of Chicago Press, 1964), pp. V-XXI. The work of Lowinsky has played a singularly invigorating role in the history of the subject and if I occasionally take issue with some conclusions reached by him as well as by other scholars mentioned here it is with full awareness that my work would be impossible without these brilliant predecessors.

[2] 'Partial Signatures and Musica Ficta in Some Early 15th-Century Sources', *Journal of the American Musicological Society*, VI (1953), 197-215; 'Conflicting Signatures Reviewed', *ibid.*, IX (1956), 97-117.

[3] 'A Dispute on Accidentals in Sixteenth-Century Rome', *Analecta Musicologica*, II (1965), 24-40; 'A Sample Problem of *Musica Ficta*: Willaert's *Pater Noster*', H. S. Powers, ed., *Studies in Music History. Essays for Oliver Strunk* (Princeton: Princeton University Press, 1968), pp. 161-82.

[4] See especially 'Zur Akzidentiensetzung in den Motetten Josquins des Prez', R. Baum and W. Rehm, eds., *Musik und Verlag. Karl Vötterle zum 65. Geburtstag am 12. April 1968* (Kassel: Bärenreiter, 1968), pp. 206-19; 'Tonsystem und Kontrapunkt um 1500', *Jahrbuch des Staatlichen Instituts für Musikforschung Preussischer Kulturbesitz* (1969), 7-18; 'Relationes harmonicae', *Archiv für Musikwissenschaft*, XXXII (1975), 208-27.

[5] 'Zarlino's Definition of Fugue and Imitation', *Journal of the American Musicological Society*, XXIV (1971), 226-54; 'False Relations and Chromaticism in Sixteenth-Century Music', *ibid.*, XXX (1977), 391-418.

[6] 'Musica Recta and Musica Ficta', *Musica Disciplina*, XXVI (1972), 73-100; 'Diatonic *Ficta*', *Early Music History*, IV (1984), 1-48.

[7] See especially *Manuscript Accidentals: Ficta in Focus 1350-1450*, Musicological Studies and Documents 27 (n.p.: American Institute of Musicology, 1972).

[8] See especially 'Accidentals and Ornamentation in Sixteenth-Century Intabulations of Josquin's Motets', E. E. Lowinsky, ed., *Josquin des Prez* (London: Oxford University Press, 1976), pp. 475-522.

[9] 'A Sample Problem of *Musica Ficta*', p. 161.

eluded us thus far is that scholars working on the problem have never examined systematically the whole available evidence, but have limited themselves to a few individual theorists, composers, sources or works. The practice of implied accidentals stretched over several centuries and over all parts
of Europe with a written music tradition. We cannot exclude the possibility
that the practice evolved in time and differed from place to place. But we
cannot begin to study such chronological and geographical variants before
we acquire a comprehensive picture of the whole practice. Only then will we
be able to distinguish constant elements from variable ones. Otherwise we
shall always run the risk of taking an exception for a rule.

There are two types of evidence relevant to our problem: music theory
and musical sources themselves. We have much to learn from a study of
musical sources, in particular from a comparison of different versions of the
same work, including instrumental intabulations of vocal models. But
much of this practical evidence remains ambiguous if it is not interpreted in
the light of the information provided by music theorists of the period.
Without theoretical evidence we could not be sure that a performer was
supposed to inflect pitches in certain contexts even if the inflections were not
explicitly indicated, we could not discover what these contexts were, and we
would not know how musicians of the period thought about and dealt with
the problem of implied accidentals. The nature of the problem makes a
study of theoretical evidence a prerequisite for an examination of practical
sources.

It is for this reason that a comprehensive study of the entire surviving
theoretical evidence concerning *musica ficta* is attempted in this book. The
evidence examined has been limited only chronologically; I begin with
theorists writing after *ca*. 1300 and stop with those writing *ca*. 1560. The
reasons for the choice of the starting point are first, that the medieval gamut
and the set of concepts and images which it involved and which enabled a
musician to think about pitches and intervals reached its fully developed
state only in the late thirteenth century and second, that the classification of
intervals which underlied the practice of implied accidentals stabilized only
in the early fourteenth century. This is not to say that the practice was
unknown before 1300, but merely that, together with the theory and practice of counterpoint with which it was intimately linked, it entered a mature
and relatively stable phase after that date. The reason for ending the investigation after the middle of the sixteenth century is that by that time the
growing interest of composers in genuine chromaticism made exact notation
of accidental inflections increasingly desirable and thus began slowly to
undermine the practice of implied accidentals. Within the chosen chronological limits, I have attempted to examine the entire surviving evidence to
the extent allowed by the present state of bibliographic control over early
music theory. Relevant theoretical texts may be discovered in the future, but

presently known texts are sufficiently rich and consistent to give us reasonable assurance that we may correctly distinguish the set of ideas commonly shared by musicians from idiosyncratic reform proposals by individual theorists, and that we may describe the historical evolution of this common core of ideas and practices within the studied period. It will be seen that some of these ideas and practices remained constant throughout this period, while others evolved. It will be also be seen that theoretical evidence alone shows no unmistakable geographical variants in the practice of implied accidentals. A future search for such variants will have to be based on the evidence of practical sources.

The most general features of the method followed in the present study have already been indicated. Since what we want to discover are commonly shared conventions, we must distinguish these from a theorist's idiosyncrasies, inventions, reform proposals and the like. The latter may be significant in allowing us to uncover problems with which musicians of the period struggled, but the former will obviously have to be in the center of our interest. In addition, we shall want to distinguish those elements of the set of commonly shared ideas, attitudes and practices which remained constant from those which changed and to describe the historical evolution of the latter.

The book is divided into three parts. Part I ('The content and structure of *musica ficta*') consists of two chapters and attempts to answer the question 'What was *musica ficta*?'. Part II ('The functions and uses of *musica ficta*') consists of five chapters and discusses the question 'Why and how was *musica ficta* used?'. Part III ('Written and implied accidental inflections') consists of one chapter and attempts to illuminate the nature of the practice of implying rather than notating inflections.

Chapters 1 and 2 describe the concepts and images in terms of which musicians of the Middle Ages and the Renaissance thought about and imagined the entire system of steps and intervals they used. An understanding of these concepts and images is indispensable if we are to avoid anachronistic assumptions when dealing with accidental inflections in early music. In the first chapter ('Within the hand'), I concentrate on that part of the total gamut which represented the norm (*musica vera*), in the second ('Beyond the hand'), on the remaining portion of the gamut (*musica ficta*). In each case, in addition to a discussion of relevant concepts and images, I describe the method of writing and reading the steps and intervals, and the content and organization of the gamut. The most important practical result of the discussion is that it enables us to trace the evolution of the content of the gamut and to tell which steps were available at each stage of the evolution. We shall also be able to distinguish those steps which were used only in theoretical experiments from those which were used in practice, and to distinguish within the latter group the normally used accidental inflections from the unusual ones.

The function of accidentals placed at the beginning of the staff is discussed in Chapter 3 ('Signatures'), which includes a correction of a current misconception concerning the effect of a signature on the distinction between *musica vera* and *ficta* and presents a new hypothesis concerning 'conflicting' signatures, while the functions and uses of internal accidental inflections in various types of musical contexts which conventionally required such inflections are considered in Chapters 4–7.

In Chapter 4 ('Horizontal relations') I take up melodic progressions which were conventionally corrected by means of accidental inflections and demonstrate that the prohibition of the melodic tritone was not applied mechanically, but had numerous exceptions. This makes it possible to formulate precise guidelines for the application of the prohibition. The origin and applicability of the 'fa-above-la' rule is also explained here. Once we know how to recognize melodic contexts which had to be corrected by means of accidental inflections, we must find out which inflection to choose when there are alternative ways of correcting the context. It is now possible to explain why flats rather than sharps were regularly chosen to correct such contexts. Finally, theorists allow us to discover what was done when an accidental inflection introduced to correct a melodic progression produced another undesirable progression in turn.

Chapter 5 ('Vertical and cross relations') begins again with the prohibited non-harmonic vertical and cross relations, shows that the prohibition had numerous exceptions, and defines precisely the contexts in which it applied. It will be demonstrated that the prohibition was invoked in practice much less often than hitherto suspected. Also discussed are the problems of how the undesirable intervals were corrected, and what was done when the chosen correction introduced new problems, or when one had to choose between correcting a melodic or a harmonic context.

Chapter 6 ('Contrapuntal progressions') discusses contexts which involve progressions from one vertical interval to another and defines those contexts of this type which conventionally required the use of accidental inflections. Since our ability to recognize such contexts depends on our understanding of cadential structures, I undertake here to define cadential progressions much more precisely than has been done up to this time. The much-discussed problem of whether the lower or upper leading tone to the final was chosen in situations in which both were possible is considered next in the light of new evidence and it is argued that an understanding of the modal context is relevant to the problem. Also discussed is the behavior of the secondary leading tone to the fifth degree above the final and the question of what was done when cadential inflections introduced undesirable relations.

The subject of Chapter 7 ('Canon and imitation') is a family of compositional techniques involving the use of the same complete or incomplete melody more than once in a single work. Techniques of this sort may have conventionally required the use of accidental inflections. They raise the question of whether one tried to preserve exact intervals of the melody at each appearance.

While Chapters 3–7 discussed the functions and uses of accidental inflections regardless of whether these were expressly notated or not, Chapter 8 ('Classes of accidental inflections in early vocal polyphony') addresses directly the problem of unspecified but implied inflections. It is explained here why some accidentals were written down while others were left out. It is also shown that we may distinguish those source accidentals which must have been written down by the author of the musical text (whether the composer or editor of a given version of the work) from those which may have been contributed by the transmitters (scribes, printers) or performers of the work, and that the distinction has important implications both for our ability to read the sources and for future research into the development of tonal language. Finally, a set of general principles and specific procedures which should guide a modern reader (editor, performer) of early music sources with respect to accidental inflections is proposed.

I have been very fortunate in the quality of advice and support I have received while writing this book. It is a great pleasure indeed to be able to acknowledge this help here. I would like to thank particularly warmly Professors James Haar and Anthony Newcomb for their careful and critical reading of the completed manuscript. The book the reader has in his hands would have been much weaker without their expert suggestions, though it should go without saying that such problems as remain are the sole responsibility of the stubborn author. I have also benefited greatly from the comments received from Professor Claude V. Palisca and from stimulating correspondence with Professors Margaret Bent and Howard M. Brown. My friends and colleagues Professors George Houle and William P. Mahrt have been kind enough to participate in my Stanford seminar devoted to the examination of accidental inflections in Dufay's music where the benefits of their practical expertise in early music performance proved invaluable. I have learned a lot from a number of students who patiently but actively participated in several seminars on practical applications of accidental inflections both at Boston University and at Stanford. I am also much indebted to my friend Glenna Houle for excellent advice in matters of style. The staffs at Music Libraries at both Boston and Stanford Universities have been indefatigable in providing me with microfilms and other materials and I am very grateful indeed for their hard work. A large part of my research has been generously supported by a fellowship from the National Endowment for the Humanities in 1980–1. Portions of Chapter 1 appeared earlier in *Musica Disciplina*, XXXV (1981), of Chapter 2(iv) in *Journal of*

Musicology, IV (1985-6) and of Chapter 2(v) in *Revue belge de musicologie*, XXXIX-XL (1985-6); I would like to thank the editors of these journals for their permission to use this material here. I would also like to thank the American Institute of Musicology and Hänssler-Verlag, Colorado College Music Press, and University of Nebraska Press for permission to quote from books they published. Grateful acknowledgements are due to the librarians at the Centrale Bibliotheek of Rijksuniversiteit in Ghent, Bayerische Staatsbibliothek in Munich, Bodleian Library at Oxford University, the Department of Manuscripts at the Bibliothéque Nationale in Paris, and the Music Division of the Library of Congress in Washington for providing me with photographs of materials held in their libraries and for allowing me to reproduce them here. I am much obliged to Ian Rumbold for his expert subediting of the text and to Penny Souster of the Cambridge University Press for her kind overseeing of the transformation of my typescript into the present book. Finally, but most importantly, I could not hope to express my full gratitude to my wife, Anna Maria, the book's first, most critical, but also most supportive reader, for the innumerable arguments we have had over practically every point I make here. Our discussions are the main reason why I have enjoyed writing this book so much.

Part I
The content and structure of *musica ficta*

1 Within the hand

In the course of frequent boasts about the instruction he claimed to have received from the renowned Josquin des Prez, Adrian Petit Coclico gave a convincing outline of the order in which the main subjects of musical practice were studied by an aspiring adept of the art:

He will . . . apply himself to learn . . . the musical hand or scale . . . and soon he will recognize the individual clef symbols; immediately thereafter, he will begin to practice solmization in plainsong or Gregorian chant, and to pronounce musical syllables and their combinations in their order. To these he will add the knowledge of the eight modes . . . Then he will recognize their signs, quantity and values, soon after, the shapes of notes, ligatures, points, pauses; afterwards, the prolations, major and minor, augmentation, diminution, imperfection, alteration, syncopation, at the same time as the beats and certain proportions of utility . . . He will then begin to sing, not only as [the music] is written but also with embellishments, and to pronounce skillfully, smoothly and meaningfully, to intone correctly and to place any syllable in its proper place under the right notes . . . When anyone has learned well those things I have indicated above, he can have also learned counterpoint and composition.[1]

It is likely that Coclico's curriculum corresponds to the normal course of instruction received by a music student not only in the early sixteenth century, but throughout most of the period to be examined in this book. The subjects mentioned by the theorist (the hand or scale, pitch notation, singing of plainchant with solmization syllables, modes, mensural notation, singing of polyphony with text underlay, counterpoint, composition) comprise all the topics commonly discussed in the period's textbooks of musical practice, and their order could hardly be improved upon or even drastically altered, since the successive areas of study presuppose the skills acquired previously. Thus, there can be little doubt that the exposition of the material of commonly used steps was the starting point of instruction.

It will also provide the most appropriate starting point for our investigation. Before we can find out why and how certain steps were used, we have to learn first what steps there were, how they were related to one another, and how they were written down and read. In this respect, we are in a similar position to Josquin's students. In addition, we have to recover the concepts and images in terms of which musicians of our period thought about and imagined the system of steps they used. This is necessary if we are to avoid anachronistic assumptions when dealing with their practice. We shall also want to consider the origin and evolution of the gamut and the associated concepts and images. By showing how these originated, what sort of needs they answered, we shall gain insight into their functions. By showing how the gamut evolved, we shall be able to tell which steps were available at each stage of its development and to distinguish the normally used steps from the unusual ones. These are the questions which will occupy us in the first two chapters of the present book. Like Josquin's students, we shall start in this chapter with the material of the most common steps.

This material of commonly used steps was organized by musicians of the late Middle Ages and the Renaissance into a structure normally referred to as the 'hand' (*manus*) but occasionally known also under other names, such as, especially, the 'scale' (*scala*). The hand was so frequently described, or at least presupposed, by theorists that we may safely assume that it formed the most fundamental conceptual equipment shared by all musicians of our period. Its content and structure may be learned best from Johannes Tinctoris, who devoted a whole treatise (*Expositio manus*, written in or after 1477) to its exposition,[2] using terms frequently employed by other theorists and defining them with precision befitting the author of a dictionary of musical terms.[3]

Some common synonyms of *manus*, such as the already-noted *scala* (used, for instance, in the passage from Coclico quoted above) or *gamma* (used by Tinctoris, among others),[4] clearly indicate that the hand is the direct ancestor of such modern theoretical concepts as the gamut or scale, that is, a set of steps (pitches defined not in absolute but in relative terms, relative, that is, to other steps of the gamut) arranged in an ascending order and representing the tonal material of music. The hand, however, provides more information than the modern gamut, as we shall see shortly.

The hand consists of twenty 'places' (*loca*) defined by Tinctoris as the 'sites' of the steps.[5] The function of the places is to indicate only the order of steps contained in them, but not the intervals between steps. To identify the places, one uses twenty 'letters' (*claves*) of the letter notation.[6] The eight 'low' (*graves*) letters are, in ascending order, the Greek letter Γ (corresponding to G in the modern letter notation) and the letters of the Latin alphabet from A to G (our A to g), while the seven 'high' (*acutae*) letters which ensue are usually the lower-case letters from a to g (our a to g'), and the final five 'highest' (*superacutae*) letters – the double letters from aa to ee (our a' to e'').[7]

Intervals between steps located in places are indicated by means of the six 'syllables' (*voces*) of the hexachordal intervallic series called the 'deduction' (*deductio*), in the ascending order ut, re, mi, fa, sol, la, which are located in consecutive places of the hand, and which form an intervallic series consisting of a diatonic (or Pythagorean minor) semitone preceded and followed by two consecutive whole tones.[8] A step of the gamut is identified by means of a letter and at least one syllable; by locating a syllable within a place, one defines the intervals between the step and the steps surrounding it within the range of the hexachord.

The hand contains seven interlocking hexachords beginning, respectively, on Γ, C, F, G, c, f, g, so that each of its twenty places contains one, two, or three syllables. In order to define intervals beyond the range of a hexachord, one makes a 'mutation' (*mutatio*) within a single place from a syllable belonging to one hexachord to a syllable of the same pitch belonging to another, interlocking hexachord.[9]

Since it is assumed that ut of each hexachord has the same pitch as the syllable of the lower hexachord present in the same place, the pitches contained in the hand include, in keyboard terms, all the 'white-key' steps from Γ-ut to ee-la (modern G to e″) plus the two 'black-key' steps of b-fa and bb-fa (modern b♭ and bb′), which are a chromatic (or Pythagorean major) semitone lower than the 'white-key' b-mi and bb-mi (modern b♮ and b♮′) found in the same places.

In notation, the places are represented by the alternating lines and spaces of the staff, with the place of the lowest letter, Γ, being always a line. One letter (our 'clef') suffices to identify all the places of the staff, of course. Within the regular gamut, an ambiguity as to the desired pitch can arise at only two places, b and bb, since only these contain syllables differing in pitch; in them, fa is a chromatic semitone lower than mi. Because of this, two distinct forms of these letters are used, the 'round b' (*b rotundum*, the ancestor of our ♭, which will be used here) standing for fa, and the 'square b' (♭ *quadrum*, the ancestor of our ♮, which, being the most common medieval graphic variant of this letter, will be used here) standing for mi. As we learn from many theorists, mi is assumed in the places of b and bb unless the round b is implied or expressly indicated,[10] in which case more than one letter is used to define the places of the staff. Characteristically, some theorists refer to ♭ and ♮ as the 'less principal letters' or 'less principal clefs' (*claves minus principales*), to distinguish them from the independent 'principal letters' or 'principal clefs' (*claves principales*) in conjunction with which they are used.[11]

The notation of pitch by means of the staff and clefs (both the 'principal' and the 'less principal' ones) is, of course, in use until this day. It was described for the first time by Guido of Arezzo in a prologue to an antiphoner written around 1030.[12] Radically transforming and improving a device present in an embryonic form already some hundred (and perhaps as much as 170) years earlier in the anonymous *Musica enchiriadis*,[13] a method allowing a spatial representation of the gamut by notating the metaphorically 'lower' or 'higher' steps on the literally lower or higher horizontal 'rows' (*ordines*; the term used by Guido) on the parchment, Guido fashioned the modern staff. To identify the rows, he adapted (and extended to dd) the letter notation he found in the anonymous *Dialogus* written near Milan around 1000 and attributed since the twelfth century to an Abbot Odo,[14] the earliest surviving treatise in which letters (here actually called 'letters' [*litterae*]) from A to aa were used as 'notes' (*notae*) representing the steps of the Greater Perfect System (including the *synemmenon* tetrachord, that is, requiring ♭ in addition to ♮), that is, the gamut transmitted by Boethius, with an additional step represented by Γ added a whole tone below.

But if the notation of pitch by means of the staff and clefs is familiar to us, the conceptualization of pitch in terms of the places and syllables located in them is not, and hence it may be useful to take a closer look at the origin and function of these concepts. In an earlier study, I have attempted to show that one fundamental component of the musical hand, the system of places defining the order of steps located in them, was structurally, functionally, and terminologically identical with the mnemonic system of places defining the order of matters (represented by means of images or notes located in the places) to be taken up in an oration, the system described in classical text-books of rhetoric. The mature hand was an eleventh-century application (almost certainly inspired, and perhaps even achieved, by Guido himself) of the system of places of the ancient art of memory to the purpose of memoriz-ing the gamut.[15]

The introduction of syllables defining intervals between steps was also an eleventh-century development. While the fully mature system of seven deductions seems to have appeared only in the second half of the thirteenth century,[16] its basic elements were again suggested by Guido of Arezzo. In his *Micrologus*, written probably between 1026 and 1028, Guido demonstrated the 'affinities' (*affinitates*) between, respectively, D, E, F, and the steps a fourth below (or a fifth above), by indicating that the intervallic patterns around the corresponding steps were identical so long as one compared the patterns within the ranges C-a and Γ-E (or G-e). The demonstration justi-fied the placing of the same mode at different but corresponding steps, protus at A, D or a, deuterus at B, E or ♮, and tritus at C, F or c.[17] Guido observed additionally that when ♭ was used instead of ♮, G sounded as protus, a as deuterus, and ♭ as tritus.[18] Thus he indirectly suggested one more range within which the intervallic patterns could be compared, F-d with ♭ instead of ♮.

It is worth emphasizing that the system of interlocking deductions and even the very concept of the hexachord or deduction were merely suggested, and not expressly formulated, by Guido, and – what is more important – that the reason why they were suggested was the necessity to resolve the con-tradiction between two independent traditions only recently brought into an uneasy coexistence, the contradiction between modal theory, which recognized only four different finals, on the one hand, and the heptatonic scale, which allowed three additional placements for the finals, on the other.[19] The compromise between these two traditions which Guido suggested remained essentially unchallenged until almost the end of our period when Heinrich Glarean, in his *Dodecachordon* of 1547, proposed the celebrated resolution of the contradiction by increasing the number of the finals. There is a direct causal connection between medieval modal theory and the system of deductions, and it is certainly not an accident that the system gradually lost its vitality once the transformation of modal theory had begun.

The steps which led to the development of the concept of the hexachord have been convincingly reconstructed by Richard L. Crocker.[20] But Crocker's conclusion that his reconstruction 'depends on attributing a greater sense of tonal reality to the relationship of the finals than to the diatonic system'[21] undermines his own argument. Deductions were necessary precisely because the finals were projected upon the diatonic Greater Perfect System, precisely because the relationships of the finals and the diatonic system were felt to be equally 'real'. The deductions mediated between these two realities. Their mediation would have been unnecessary if medieval musicians attributed little tonal reality to the diatonic system and chose another (for instance, the scale of *Musica enchiriadis*) instead. Incidentally, Glarean's solution was to leave the diatonic system intact and to adapt modal theory to it, not the reverse. For him and those who followed him, it was the diatonic system that had a greater tonal reality.

Indeed, one feature of the hand not yet mentioned serves precisely to reaffirm the tonal reality of the diatonic system. The seven deductions do not exhaust the content of the fully developed hand as described by Tinctoris. In addition, the deductions starting an octave apart are considered to have (or be) the same 'property' (*proprietas*) or quality, since they maintain the same relationship with the surrounding deductions. The deductions starting on Γ, G, and g have the property of the 'hard b' (♮ *durum*), since their mi is hard (or sharp) in respect to the fa sung in the same place; the deductions on C and c have the 'natural' property (*natura*), since their steps have the only pitches which are natural in their respective places; and the deductions on F and f have the property of the 'soft b' (*b molle*), since their fa is soft (or flat) in respect to the mi sung in the same place.[22] While the system of the seven deductions is designed to demonstrate that the corresponding steps of different deductions are related in quality, the system of the three properties shows that different deductions of the same property are related in quality. In other words, the deductions serve to demonstrate that the intervallic patterns surrounding the equally-named steps in different deductions are identical within the range-limits of these deductions, and the properties to demonstrate that the intervallic patterns surrounding the equally-named steps in different deductions of the same property are identical without any range-limits. Thus, the properties serve to reassert the equivalence of the steps an octave apart, as if to counteract any possible blurring of this equivalence by the less complete affinities. Already Guido, having discussed the affinities in *Micrologus*, hastened to reaffirm that 'likeness [between steps] is not complete except at the octave'.[23]

In his last surviving treatise, *Epistola de ignoto cantu* of around 1032,[24] Guido introduced his final invention, a method of singing an 'unknown chant' at sight, without the help of the monochord. Instead of reading the steps first on the monochord and then repeating them vocally, the singer should fix the steps in his memory, learning by heart a melody whose consecutive phrases start on consecutive steps of the gamut. Guido provided such a melody for learning the steps from C to a and the text he associated it with could yield the corresponding syllables from ut to la.[25] Whether Guido himself used the syllables to name the steps, let alone to solmizate, must remain a matter of conjecture, but the use of syllables to name the steps of the hexachords starting on Γ and C (that is, a rudimentary solmization and mutation), can be documented already in the second half of the eleventh century.[26]

Thus, the system of deductions can also serve as an aid to a method of sight-singing known as 'solmization' (*solfisatio*).[27] Once the student remembers which syllable or syllables are associated with each letter and can sing the hexachord, he will be able to read any melody at sight by substituting the syllables for the letters and making mutations when the melody goes beyond the range of the deduction. The mutation may be 'explicit' (*explicita*) or 'vocal' (*vocalis*), in which case the singer pronounces both syllables, or 'implicit' (*implicita*) or 'mental' (*mentalis*), when only one of the syllables (usually the second) is actually pronounced, while the other is tacitly assumed, the latter method being, for obvious reasons, generally preferable, especially in measured music.[28] No mutation can be made when there is no common step in a progression from one deduction to another, a sort of progression some theorists refer to as 'disjunct' (*disjuncta*).[29] It should be stressed that the solmization, the method of sight-singing with the aid of the syllables, was a tool designed for beginners. Franchinus Gaffurius and several other theorists leave us in no doubt about this:

Tones which notes indicate are usually expressed in three ways. The first is through solfege, that is, singing the syllable names of the tones . . . This manner of singing is the preferable method of instructing children. The second way is by producing only sounds and tones, and omitting entirely letters, syllables, and words. A skilled singer does this easily . . . The third way is by singing the words subjoined to the notes of a song, as in antiphons and responsories. This manner of singing . . . is the desired goal of the best ecclesiastical singers.[30]

Thus, we should probably not imagine professional singers solmizating in rehearsals but we may certainly expect that they had mastered sight-singing through this method.

The most interesting puzzle about Guido's invention is why he limited himself to only six steps when the gamut – as he repeatedly stressed – contained seven different ones.[31] From the point of view of sight-singing, the limitation was unfortunate since it forced Guido, or rather his successors, to use a highly complex system of interlocking deductions. A heptachord would provide a much simpler aid to sight-singers and it is as easy to learn by heart as the hexachord. We shall never know for sure whether Guido's limitation of the segment of the gamut to be fixed in memory to C-a was connected with the similar ranges he compared in *Micrologus*, but this seems to be the only alternative to thinking that the limitation was an insignificant accident, and – what is more important – the connection was certainly made, if not by him, then by his successors. As we have seen, the ultimate reason behind the creation of the system of deductions was the incompatibility of certain features of modal theory with the gamut. So long as this reason persisted, that is, certainly throughout our period, the system was necessary to demonstrate the affinities and could double as an aid to sight-singing. Even though a simpler system, based on a heptachord rather than the hexachord, could have been devised for the latter function, it was more practical from the standpoint of a student's memory to use a single system in both roles. This is probably why the earliest attempt to simplify the solmization by extending the hexachord to an octave proposed by Bartolomeo Ramos de Pareia in the late fifteenth century, while hotly debated, was not generally accepted. A century had to pass before such attempts started to gain ground.[32] The gradual decline of solmization based on hexachords, like that of hexachords themselves, had ultimately the same reason as that which brought it into being, namely, the evolution of modal theory.

In sum, the hand is the described correlation of the forty-two syllables of the seven deductions with the twenty places and their letters. This content of the hand was commonly represented in a diagram of the type seen in Figure 1. To know the hand means to know all the steps commonly used in music as well as their relationships and to be able to write them down and to read them.

For this knowledge to be fully operative, it is necessary for the student to fix the whole structure firmly in his memory. In particular, if the system of deductions is to be a truly effective aid to sight-singing, the student must be trained to associate automatically particular letters with appropriate syllables. In order to facilitate the teaching and memorizing of the whole structure and especially of individual letters with their corresponding syllables, they were often (though by no means always) inscribed on the finger tips and joints of the inner surface of the left hand from the tip of the thumb down in a spiral course. Since there was no tip or joint left for the last letter, it was inscribed on the same joint as the penultimate letter (the third joint of the

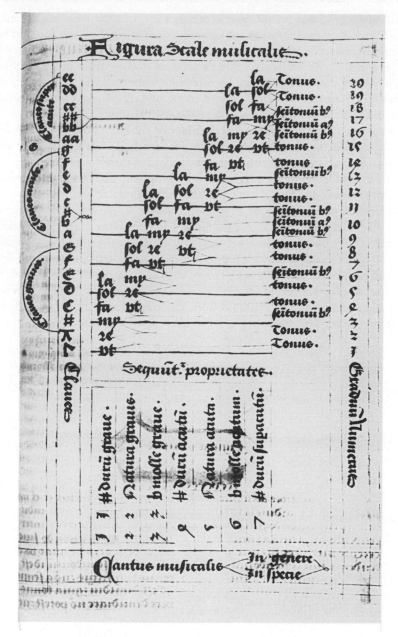

Figure 1. Ms. Ghent, Universiteitsbibliotheek,
70/(71), fol. 108r (1503-4)

9

middle finger), but on the reverse of the hand (a fine point usually mis-understood today, since on the diagrams representing the hand this highest letter appears, for obvious reasons, above the middle finger); see Figure 2. The name of the whole structure derived, of course, from this particular method of representation. (The alternative method of representation, shown in Figure 1, was often referred to as the 'ladder' [*scala*].) The hand-diagram was both a mnemonic and a pedagogical device. The association of a letter and its syllables with a specific place on the hand helped the memory and provided the teacher with a convenient method of demonstrating and practicing the steps and intervals of the gamut. When discussing the question of why the left hand was chosen for the device, Tinctoris characteristically explained that 'the places in that left hand are more easily indicated by the index finger on the right, even though some people most aptly indicate the places on the thumb of the left hand with the index finger of the same hand and the places on the other fingers similarly by the thumb of the same hand; wherefore they may use only one hand, that is, left, in the instruction of this particular kind of lesson'.[33]

The student who has mastered Tinctoris's teaching thus far has mastered the basic gamut, but he is still far from knowing all the steps which may be used in music. The remaining steps will be considered now.

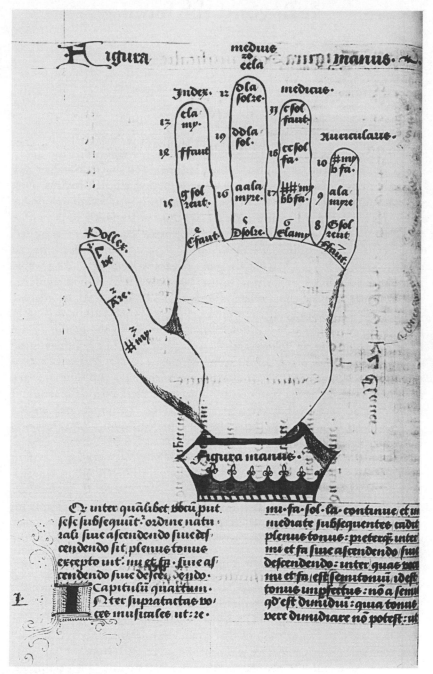

Figure 2. Ms. Ghent, Universiteitsbibliotheek, 70/(71), fol. 108v

2 Beyond the hand

(i) The definition of *musica ficta*

An exposition of the hand provides an indispensable background to any discussion of *musica ficta*. Theorists of the period studied in this book generally identified the content of the hand as the 'true', 'correct' or 'regular music' (*musica vera, recta* or *regularis*) and those steps which could not be found in the hand as the 'feigned', 'false', 'colored', 'conjunct' or 'acquired music' (*musica ficta, falsa, colorata, conjuncta,* or *acquisita*). For Philippe de Vitry, writing in 1322–3 in France, *falsa musica* is 'when we make a whole tone out of a semitone, or the reverse' and he opposes it to *musica regularis*, which clearly implies that it introduces steps not found in the regular gamut.[1] For Petrus frater dictus Palma ociosa, a French author writing in 1336, 'false music is the one which cannot be found in the gamut of the hand'.[2] Prosdocimus de Beldemandis, writing in Padua in 1425–8, calls the steps contained within the hand explicitly *musica vera* and all other steps *musica ficta*.[3] Through the end of our period, theorists continue to make this distinction. Thus, for instance, for Angelo da Picitono 'plainchant and mensural music are divided into true, which can be called real, and feigned . . . . The feigned music is nothing else than the transposition of the notes from the proper place.'[4]

This fundamental identification of *musica ficta* as steps not found within the hand requires further explanation. According to Prosdocimus, 'musica ficta is the feigning of syllables or the placement of syllables in any location on the musical hand where they are in no way to be found – to apply mi where there is no mi and fa where there is no fa, and thus for the other syllables'.[5] Thus, *musica ficta* involves 'imagining' (*fictio*) in any of the twenty places of the hand syllables which are not truly there in *musica vera*. This may, but does not necessarily have to, change the pitch of the step regularly located in a given place. If, in our imagination, we replace the syllables sol, re, ut found at the place of G with mi and the syllables la, mi, re found at the place of a with fa, we will create two feigned syllables (mi at the place of G and fa at the place of a) and two feigned steps (G-mi and a-fa), but only one of these steps will be different in pitch from the true steps located in these places. Since the distance between mi and fa is a semitone, either the pitch of a will remain unchanged and G will be sharpened, or the pitch of G will remain unchanged and a will be flattened. In other words, while it is true that *musica ficta* consists of steps not found within the hand, it is important to realize that a feigned step does not have to differ in pitch from the true one found in the same place. All that is necessary in order for a step to be feigned is that its syllable be feigned.

This understanding of *musica ficta* appears so often in fifteenth- and sixteenth-century treatises that we may safely accept it as the common opinion. 'Feigned music is the putting of some syllable in a place where it is not by itself', says Ugolino of Orvieto, writing in Ferrara in the 1430s,[6] and a century later Nikolaus Listenius, the German author of one of the most successful theoretical bestsellers, explains that feigned music is the one in which 'the syllables are not pronounced in their correct places, just as when ut is sung on E, re on F, mi on G, etc'.[7] Moreover, this understanding of the concept as involving not only steps differing in pitch from those of the regular gamut but also all steps with feigned syllables can be extended back to at least the beginning of our period. A century before Prosdocimus, the conservative Jacques de Liège demonstrated this unambiguously:

The irregular mutation is called 'false mutation' because a syllable is changed into one which is connected with it not truly but falsely. It is also called 'false music' because it proceeds against the regular disposition of the syllables in the gamut. From this it is clear that the descent from mi of b fa b mi by a whole tone and a semitone produces false music because then it is necessary that, when mi is connected in unison, it is changed into sol . . . singing mi sol fa mi.[8]

One more point must be clarified if we are to have a precise understanding of which steps belong to *musica ficta*. From the late fifteenth century, theorists increasingly take notice of the possibility – well explored in polyphonic practice – of extending the range of the gamut. Already Philippe de Vitry observed that the seven steps could be infinitely reproduced in different octaves.[9] Now we find Bartolomeo Ramos de Pareia noting in 1482 in Bologna that one could multiply regular hexachords in infinity.[10] In 1490, the German monk Adam von Fulda attributes the fact that musicians go both below and above the regular range to the influence of Guillaume Dufay, whom he considers to be the inventor of this practice.[11] Similarly, in the first half of the sixteenth century, the extension of the gamut in both directions is attributed to Dufay by Georg Rhau[12] and – in the upward direction only – by Angelo da Picitono.[13] Moreover, around the turn of the century, the Spaniard Domingo Marcos Durán adds deductions on cc and F below Γ to the seven regular ones and considers them part of the true music.[14] He also suggests placing this lowest F on the reverse of the thumb, just as the highest ee was placed on the reverse of the middle finger.[15] The suggested extension of the hand is fully systematized by Stephano Vanneo, whose gamut goes an octave below and above the customary one.[16] The added steps are placed on the back of the hand (see Figure 3). The tip of the thumb remains the place of Γ and the successive steps of the descending octave are placed on the successive joints in the same order in which the ascending steps were placed on the original hand, with the lowest G an octave below Γ placed near the wrist. This lowest octave adds deductions on G, C, and F below Γ. The extension of the gamut an octave up starts with ee located in its normal place (top joint of the middle finger) and proceeds in clockwise order, excluding the places already occupied as well as the finger tips. This highest octave adds deductions on cc, as well as on ff and gg above ee. Vanneo's reversed hand with its added steps and deductions was reproduced by Angelo da Picitono.[17]

This general recognition of the possibility of extending the range of the gamut raised the question of whether all the steps produced by such extensions should be considered as a part of *musica ficta*. Nicolaus Wollick asserted that 'whenever some syllable is adopted in the scale or beyond, if it has such corresponding syllable an octave apart, it is true, and if not, then it will be called feigned'.[18] In his view, in other words, B-fa, for instance, belongs to *musica vera* even though there is no fa at the place of B within the hand, simply because fa is present at the place an octave apart from B, namely, b. Similarly, F-fa or F-ut below Γ belong to true music even though these steps are beyond the hand, because their syllables can be found at the place an octave higher, F, within the hand. This point of view was often expressed by sixteenth-century theorists. Johannes Cochlaeus warned:

But if a syllable of this kind has a corresponding syllable on the octave, it is a true syllable, as when la is sung on D sol re, sol on C fa ut, and fa on B mi, for these syllables are expressly found on their octaves. Thus they are not feigned, since their octaves have the same nature, and are considered as the same.[19]

Vanneo considered it a mistake to regard his disposition of the reverse of the hand as *musica ficta*[20] and derided those composers of polyphony who, when going a step above ee, habitually marked it with a flat in order to indicate that they had left the realm of true music, 'believing, in my opinion, that the final limit of heaven is defined by ee la'.[21] He was faithfully echoed, or rather translated, by Angelo da Picitono.[22] Such views were quite common in the sixteenth century,[23] but they were probably not universally accepted, as one may infer from the fact that they were often expressed as a polemic against the more restrictive view of *musica vera* as containing only the steps and syllables explicitly present in the 'Guidonian' hand and not those implied at the octave. It is, of course, difficult to estimate with any precision the relative popularity of these competing views. Each is consistent in itself, but in an age of the expanding gamut of polyphonic practice the less restrictive view of *musica vera* would seem to have been more convincing and useful. It is also more consistent with the rest of music theory, especially with its clear recognition of the essential similarity of steps an octave apart.

14

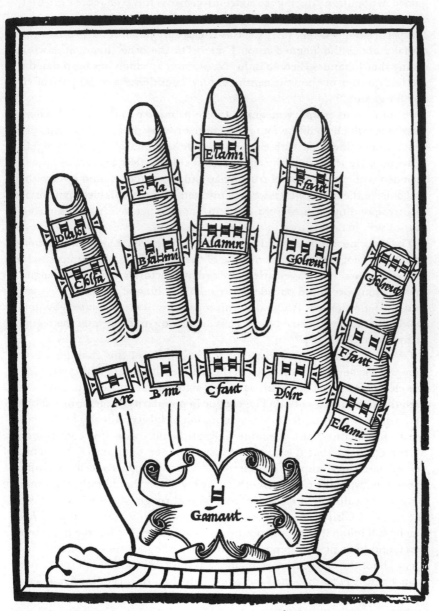

Figure 3. Stephano Vanneo, *Recanetum de musica aurea* (Rome: Valerio Dorico, 1533), fol. 10v

15

Therefore, we are probably justified in believing that the less restrictive view gained in popularity during the sixteenth century. It is even more difficult to estimate whether, and how widely, this view was accepted before the 1490s. I suspect that it was very rare, since as late as 1477 Johannes Tinctoris writes casually about the 'feigned re on Γ-ut'.[24] On the other hand, it is worth noting that Johannes Ciconia in his *Nova musica*, which has been dated to the last quarter of the fourteenth century, considers B♭ to be part of the regular gamut.[25]

In sum, in its primary meaning the term *musica vera* referred only to those steps which could be found within the twenty places of the hand and which were solmizated with the appropriate syllables of the seven regular deductions. In the sixteenth century, a sizeable portion of musical opinion included within the realm of true music also those steps, found both within and outside the hand, which were solmizated with the syllables appropriate to corresponding *musica vera* steps in another octave. All steps outside *musica vera* belonged to *musica ficta*.

The term *musica ficta* could naturally take a derived, secondary meaning and denote not just the steps outside of the hand, but rather music made with such steps. This was clearly expressed in Tinctoris's definition: 'Feigned music is song produced outside the regular teaching of the hand.'[26] A very similar definition of Andreas Ornithoparchus was translated by John Dowland as follows: 'Fained Musicke is . . . a Song made beyond the regular compasse of the Scales.'[27]

Of the various synonyms listed at the beginning of this chapter, *musica falsa* was the one used most often in the fourteenth century and *musica ficta* was clearly preferred in the fifteenth and sixteenth centuries, but both were used throughout our period. The decline in popularity of the former should be attributed to its undesirable connotation of falsity. Already in the early fourteenth century, one encounters dissatisfaction with this connotation. Vitry emphasizes that 'it is not false music, however, but unusual',[28] and he is echoed later by Philippus de Caserta.[29] Marchetto da Padova concludes: 'Therefore, with due regard for others, we say that it should rather and more properly be called colored music than false, through which we taint it with the name of falsity.'[30] Similar arguments against *falsa* and in favor of *ficta* can be still found in some sixteenth-century treatises.[31] That the latter term was found to be more appropriate is not surprising, in view of what we now know about the classical art of memory as the tradition behind the 'Guidonian' hand.[32] *Ficta* suggested more precisely than the other available terms the process whereby the syllables 'truly' present at a given place of the hand were erased as if from a wax tablet and substituted in the imagination by another syllable. The process was analogous to the substitution of regular words with neologisms, or *verba ficta*, of medieval grammarians and it is likely that it is from them that musicians borrowed the term.[33]

(ii) The notation and solmization of *musica ficta*

It will be recalled from the preceding chapter that within the system of *musica vera*, two steps differing in pitch by a chromatic (or Pythagorean major) semitone occured in only two places of the hand, b and bb. The two steps, b-fa and b-mi (bb-fa and bb-mi), were indicated in letter notation by two different forms of the b- and bb-letters, the round form for the lower version and the square one for the higher. In staff notation, a single letter, known as the 'principal clef', sufficed to identify all the places. Since b and bb were not used as principal clefs, the step required at their places was conventionally assumed to be the higher one unless the lower one was implied or expressly indicated by the round b used as the 'less principal clef' in addition to the principal one. The step indicated by the square b was, of course, solmizated as mi and the one indicated by the round b as fa.

Musica ficta extended this possibility of having within a single place steps differing in pitch to other places within and outside of the hand and it adapted the existing notation and solmization accordingly. Fa and mi located in the same place differed by a chromatic semitone, just as they did in *musica vera* at b and bb. The round b was permanently associated with the syllable fa, that is, it indicated, regardless of the place in which it was found, a diatonic (or Pythagorean minor) semitone between this place and the next lower one. Conversely, the square b was permanently associated with the syllable mi and indicated a diatonic semitone between the place in which it was located and the next higher one. Since in *musica ficta* fa and mi could be located in every place, an ambiguity as to the desired pitch could arise anywhere. In any place, a pitch identical with that of a *musica vera* syllable found in the same place was assumed, so that when a pitch differing by a chromatic semitone was wanted, it had to be either implied or expressly indicated by means of the sign of fa or mi. Even before the beginning of our period an anonymous author briefly summarized the basic facts as follows:

False music is said to exist when soft b or square b is placed at a point [place] where it is not customary. There are two indications of false music, that is, soft b and square b. Wherever round b is placed, it is called fa; wherever [there is] square b, it is called mi.[34]

Similar explanations may be found in innumerable treatises throughout our period.[35]

Since the round b means fa and implies a diatonic semitone between the place in which it is found and the next lower one, while the square b means mi and implies a diatonic semitone between its place and the next higher one, it may appear to be possible, in principle, that the round b (or square b) will not change the pitch of the note it accompanies but rather sharpen (or flatten) the step in the neighboring lower (or higher) place by a chromatic semitone. Thus, Ugolino of Orvieto indicated the pitch a chromatic semitone higher than F by preceding this F with the round b located in the place of G.[36] But no far-reaching conclusions should be drawn from such isolated examples. Musicians may have, on rare occasions, used ♭ or ♮ in this fashion, but in reality almost no theorist of the period took this possibility seriously. Their examples and texts indicate that an overwhelming majority of theorists (and, presumably, also musicians) assumed additionally that the round b flattened, and the square b sharpened, the note in the place of which they were found by a chromatic semitone. This assumption did not have to be made explicit simply because it was obvious, since also in their original places, those of b and bb, the round b and the square b changed the pitch of the step within and not outside the place in which they were found. Many theorists, however, did make it explicit. Marchetto da Padova, after having defined the permutation as the change of syllable where the pitch changes although the note remains in the same place, went on to list among the signs indicating permutation the round b to be sung fa and the square b sung mi.[37] Vitry explained that the effect of the round b was to make a whole tone out of a semitone in descent and a semitone out of a whole tone in ascent, while the reverse was the effect of the square b.[38] Another early fourteenth-century theorist, Petrus frater dictus Palma ociosa, stated unambiguously:

Therefore, it should be noted in general that the false music is properly called when the soft b or the square b is located in unusual places. Where ♭ is put, in the same place and under the same step the semitone is lowered beyond the ordinary song, and where ♮ is put, in the same place and under the same step the semitone is raised beyond the ordinary song in unusual places.[39]

Similarly, Johannes Boen explained in 1357 that

the letter b-fa is the sign of the lowering of the note following in the same letter, and b-mi the note of the raising . . . so much as the b-fa lowers, the b-mi raises, since each [does it] precisely by the major semitone.[40]

Many additional examples could be quoted through the end of our period.[41] I shall mention only one more characteristic instance. In a letter of August 20, 1533, which Giovanni Spataro sent from Bologna to Pietro Aaron in Venice, the writer criticized Giovanni del Lago for expressing himself imprecisely, since the latter confused the fa which is only 'imagined' in a given place, in which case the resulting pitch is unchanged, with the fa which is 'signed' by means of the round b, in which case the pitch is lowered.[42] In short, we may conclude that for most musicians of our period, and in most cases, while D (that is, D-sol-re), for instance, has whole tones below and above, D♭ (that is, D-fa) not only has a diatonic semitone below, but also is a chromatic semitone lower, and D♯ (that is, D-mi) not only has a diatonic semitone above, but also is a chromatic semitone higher. (The only common type of exception to this will be discussed in section (iv) of this chapter.)

No natural sign was known or necessary in the common theory and practice of the period, since the square b could be used without ambiguity to cancel the effect of the round b, and the reverse. Boen explained: 'So much as one letter [♭ or ♮] dislocates and untunes the note, so much the following [other] letter tunes and locates [it] back and, consequently, brings [it] back to its proper station.'[43]

We already know that *musica ficta* makes it possible for both the round b and the square b to be located in places other than those of b and bb as the less principal clefs used in conjunction with the principal ones. A less principal clef may be indicated at the beginning of the staff just as the principal one is and then they both are valid for the duration of the staff. The less principal clef has to be indicated in every octave in which it is needed. No justification can be found in theoretical treatises for believing that a less principal clef could be valid in octaves other than its own. Still at the very end of our period, Nicola Vicentino talks about the transposition up a minor third as involving four round b's, while his examples show only three different round b's one of which is doubled at an octave.[44] There is also no trace of any convention as to the order in which such clefs should be written when they cannot be placed vertically one below another.

A less principal clef may also be placed internally on the staff. There is some disagreement among theorists as to how long such an internal accidental remains in force. For Prosdocimus, it applies only to the note it accompanies:

When either of these two signs is applied . . . it ought always to be applied just before the note whose syllable [or pitch] is to be changed . . . whether it be on a line or in a space, for any such sign serves only the note immediately following it (unless the round b is applied at the beginning of some melody as a signature [literally: in the place of the clef], because in that case the b signifies that the whole melody ought to be sung with round or soft b).[45]

For Tinctoris, on the other hand, an internal accidental retains its force so long as the melody remains within the range of the deduction presumably implied by the accidental:

If it [the sign of the round b] is placed at the beginning of the staff, the whole melody will be sung with the soft b. If, indeed, it is placed anywhere else, the melody will be sung with the soft b so long as the deduction which it prefaces will last.[46]

Since the round b means fa, it can imply not only mi but also all other syllables of the deduction. Consequently, Tinctoris seems to reason that instead of mutating unnecessarily, we should try to use these syllables, including the fa itself, so long as the melody remains within the range of the deduction implied by the round b. Both Prosdocimus' and Tinctoris's views are perfectly consistent with the music theory of the period. However, of the few theorists who discuss this problem, all support Prosdocimus' opinion that an internal accidental applies only to the note it accompanies.[47] Consequently, we have to conclude that in this matter, as in several others, Tinctoris attempted, unsuccessfully, to reform contemporary practice rather than to report upon it.

(iii) The square b and the diesis (♯)

The original graphic form of the square b (♮) was, of course, ♭. Various slightly differing forms of the sign can be found in the manuscripts of the period, but these variations do not affect its meaning. In the fifteenth and sixteenth centuries, many theorists indicated that another sign could be used in exactly the same function as the square b. This other sign was usually known as the 'diesis' (*diesis*) and it also existed in a variety of insignificantly differing graphic forms, the most popular of which was ✕, that is, an 'italicized' version of ♯. (♯ will be used here.) In spite of the fact that for so many theorists ♮ and ♯ had exactly the same meaning, these were not insignificant graphic variants of the same sign, but two different signs, since the theorists bothered to distinguish them both by shape and by name. 'Moreover, the sign of the major semitone itself is, according to the ancients, the square b and, according to the moderns, ♯,' says Ugolino.[48] Ramos distinguishes the two signs, but considers them identical in meaning,[49] as does Franciscus de Brugis.[50] Giovanni del Lago confirms that the employment of the diesis instead of the square b is the common usage,[51] and, indeed, the identity of meaning of these two signs is so often assumed or indicated by fifteenth- and sixteenth-century theorists that we have to consider it the norm.[52]

Why were two different signs used if they had the same meaning? Some sixteenth-century theorists want to distinguish between their functions a little and claim that ♮ should be used only in the places of b and its octaves, and ♯ at all other places. Pietro Aaron in his *Toscanello in musica* asserts that the diesis has the same effect as the square b and makes no distinction between the two,[53] but in the later *Lucidario in musica* he criticizes those who sign ♮ at places other than those of B, b, and bb, as well as those who use ♯ at these places.[54] The square b is a 'natural sign' (*segno naturale*), while ♯ and the round b are 'accidental signs' (*segni accidentali*) and should not follow one another in the same place, says Aaron. Consequently, if you want to bring bb back to its natural position, use ♮, if you want to sharpen C, F, or G beyond their natural positions, use ♯.[55] Thus, in Aaron's *Lucidario* we observe an early instance of the transition from the medieval to the modern understanding of these three signs and to the modern terminology in which the 'accidental signs' inflect a step from its natural position and the 'natural sign' brings the step back to it. This modern view, however, presupposes that a musician considers the round b at b and bb as an 'accidental', that is, that he effectively stops thinking about the gamut in terms of the hand, in which these steps are not accidental, and thinks about it instead in terms of the keyboard, in which all the white steps are 'natural' and all the black ones 'accidental'. We shall see later that this presupposition was indeed made by Aaron.

The evolution of Aaron's views on this subject between *Toscanello* and *Lucidario* can be explained as a result of Giovanni Spataro's influence. In one of his letters to Aaron, Spataro criticized a composition with a round b at the clef in which ♯ was placed internally at b. Spataro argued that one should not place one *segno accidentale* (♯) over another (♭). Just as the sign of the round b moves the 'natural hard b' (♮ *duro naturale*) to the position of the 'accidental soft b' (*b molle accidentale*), so also the reverse, the square b, and not ♯, should be used to bring the accidental round b back to the natural position. The ♯ should be signed only in 'natural' positions.[56] Exactly the same arguments and terms reappeared in *Lucidario*. Thus, it is Spataro rather than Aaron who must be seen as the key figure in the transition to the modern understanding of accidentals.

Spataro, in turn, refers to John Hothby, an English theorist active in Lucca between 1467 and 1486, as wanting ♮ used only at b and its octaves, and ♯ at all the other places.[57] This, indeed, is a feature of the notation described by Hothby most fully in his *La Caliopea legale*.[58] Hothby divides all steps into three 'orders' (*ordini*). The steps of the first order require neither ♭ nor ♯ in notation, that is, they correspond to the white keys of the keyboard. The steps of the other two orders correspond to the black keys and they all require either ♭ (second order) or ♯ (third order) in notation. The terms 'natural' and 'accidental' are not used, but the steps of the first order are considered to be the 'foundation' (*fondamento*) for those of the other two orders.[59] Spataro is fully justified in seeing in Hothby an important predecessor. The differentiation of the functions of ♮ and ♯ and the relegation of ♭ to the less fundamental status of an accidental were among the prerequisites if the accidentals were to acquire their modern meanings, and Hothby made these decisive steps. But it has to be observed that, first, neither Hothby nor anyone else in our period fully developed the modern notational system (Hothby's and Spataro's square b is not yet identical with our natural sign) and, second, Hothby, Spataro and Aaron represent the advanced views of a small minority. The great majority of musicians of the period continue to think about the gamut in terms of the hand rather than the keyboard and to treat ♮ and ♯ as fully equivalent. Gioseffo Zarlino's discussion of these two signs close to the end of our period is revealing.[60] They have for him the same effect. To be sure,

moderns, when they wish to write the paramese [♮] in the place of the trite synemmenon [♭], use the sign ♯ instead of ♮, however improper this is. They should use the proper sign rather than an alien one. But actually it does not matter much.[61]

Indeed, we find among Zarlino's contemporaries Loys Bourgeois and Adrian Petit Coclico (to take random examples from beyond the Alps) who use the diesis instead of the square b at the place of b, just as Johannes Boen did 200 years earlier.[62]

Moreover, the ideas of Hothby and Spataro show the way of the future, but they certainly do not explain why the diesis was invented in the first place. The reason could not have been the desire to have a different sign for places other than b and its octaves, since then we should have also found a sign alternative to the round b, and there is no trace of this. For the origin of the diesis we have to look to the writings of Marchetto da Padova.[63]

In the system of tuning in terms of which medieval musicians thought about the sizes of intervals, the whole tone (the difference between the fifth and fourth) was divided into the minor semitone of the diatonic genus (the difference between the fourth and two whole tones) and the major semitone, often identified with the second semitone of the chromatic genus (the difference between the whole tone and the minor semitone), or into two minor semitones and the comma (the difference between the major and minor semitones). The minor semitone could be additionaly divided into two dieses of the enharmonic genus. Marchetto in his *Lucidarium in arte musicae planae* of 1317-18,[64] proposed instead to divide the whole tone into five parts and to call each of these parts a 'diesis', presumably because his 'diesis', like the normal one, divided the minor semitone into two parts. Two 'dieses' produced the minor semitone which Marchetto called 'enharmonic', presumably because it was the smallest of his three semitones. Three 'dieses' gave the major or, for Marchetto, 'diatonic' semitone, and four 'dieses' the 'chromatic' semitone. The 'enharmonic' and 'diatonic' semitones were notated in the same way as the regular minor and major semitones. The division of the whole tone into the 'diesis' and the 'chromatic' semitone, however, required the introduction of a new sign.[65] This new sign, called *falsa musica*, reversed the stems of the regular square b so that the one on the left went downwards and the one on the right upwards: ♯ . (Eventually, it became, of course, our ♯.) Its effect was to sharpen the note it accompanied by the 'chromatic' semitone. For reasons which will become clear when we learn about the difference of functions of sharpening and flattening, no corresponding sign capable of flattening a note by the 'chromatic' semitone was required by the music of the period and, consequently, none was proposed by Marchetto.

In other words, Marchetto proposed to supplement the normal division of the whole tone into the minor and major semitones with another division into the 'diesis', which was smaller than the minor semitone, and the 'chromatic' semitone, which was larger than the major one, and to revise the existing terminology accordingly. His examples make it clear that the new division was reserved for the cadential leading tones, making them sharper than they were in the regular division. Since the cadential leading tone occurred always in the vertical interval of major sixth or major third, it may be that the new division corresponded to the experience of these intervals being very sharp in the Pythagorean tuning. In notation, the two signs indicating the division of the whole tone into minor and major semitones had to be supplemented with another two indicating the new division, but for practical reasons only one of these was introduced, its shape being an adaptation of one of the signs already in existence. In *Pomerium* of 1318-19 Marchetto explained that since the new sign sharpened a note more than the regular square b, this effect should be indicated by a lengthening of the stems of the regular sign, especially the one going upwards on the right.[66] All subsequent graphic variants of the new sign involved such a lengthening. For obvious reasons, Marchetto's term for this new sign, *falsa musica*, was unsatisfactory. He himself preferred the term *colorata* to *falsa*.[67] His successors chose to call it instead the 'diesis', since it indicated the division of the whole tone into the 'diesis' and the 'chromatic' semitone.

Marchetto did not claim expressly to have invented the new division of the whole tone or the new sign. Indeed, some of his remarks seem to indicate that he might have thought he was describing an already-existing practice. Thus, for instance, he criticized 'some' (*nonnulli*) musicians for making no graphic distinction between ♮ and ♯ and, consequently, ignoring their diverse meanings, and he claimed that the name of *falsa musica* was 'commonly' (*a vulgo*) applied to ♯ .[68] It is very likely, however, that he himself introduced these innovations. Some of his successors, at any rate, named him as the inventor, as we shall see presently.

Marchetto's alternative division of the whole tone reappears in various guises throughout our period, in particular, but not exclusively, among the theorists active in his own Veneto region. His most prominent successor at Padua, Prosdocimus de Beldemandis, discussed his ideas extensively, and his polemic against Marchetto was the first large-scale theoretical controversy in Italy and thus opened a tradition of *odium philologicum* which Italian theorists were to cultivate fondly for the next 300 years. Prosdocimus attacked Marchetto's division with the traditional anti-Aristoxenian arguments to the effect that the whole tone cannot be divided into equal parts. Marchetto, in his opinion, was an excellent practical musician, but a miserable theorist.[69] The same arguments were repeated and elaborated in Prosdocimus' most extensive polemic against Marchetto, his *Tractatus musice speculative contra Marchetum de Padua* of 1425.[70] Prosdocimus explained that he wrote his treatise to counter the errors in the speculative theory rather than the practical doctrines of *Lucidarium*, errors which had managed to spread 'throughout Italy and even beyond' (*per totam ytaliam et adhuc extra fore*) among singers rather than theorists, so that the errors produced and disseminated by one Paduan musician would be corrected by another,[71] and he continued to argue at great length the impossibility of dividing the whole tone into equal parts.[72]

But the contagion which spread 'throughout Italy and even beyond' was evidently not stopped by Prosdocimus, since Tinctoris in his dictionary of musical terms of *ca*. 1472-3 reported on conflicting opinions concerning the meaning of 'diesis':

Diesis, according to some, is the same as the minor semitone, according to others, half of this minor semitone. Some want the diesis to be the fifth part of the whole tone, others the third, fourth and eighth.[73]

Tinctoris's own views seem to represent a confused attempt at a compromise between the standard and Marchettan divisions. In his *Liber de arte contrapuncti* of 1477 he assumes the standard division of the whole tone into four dieses (or, rather, *diacismae*, as he prefers to call them) and a comma when talking about the normal minor and major semitones,[74] but he also assumes the Marchettan division into five dieses when talking about the 'chromatic' semitone, since he considers a 'chromatic' semitone, such as the one between f and f♯, to be 'smaller than the others, containing a fifth part of a tone according to some'.[75] This is, of course, a mistake. A little later, he confuses the issue further by stating that when in a perfect concord the lower note is raised a 'chromatic' semitone, this concord will be made too small by one fifth of a whole tone, and when the higher note is so raised, the concord will be made too large by four fifths of a whole tone.[76]

Traces of Marchetto's division are also present in the writings of Franchinus Gaffurius. In his earliest treatise, a compendium of *ca*. 1474 based on various authors and entitled *Extractus parvus musice*, Marchetto's division of the whole tone into five 'dieses' is accepted uncritically.[77] In the late *Apologia adversum Ioannem Spatarium & complices musicos Bononienses* of 1520, however, Marchetto's division is rejected as false and unacceptable to theorists.[78]

Not all theorists concurred with this opinion. Bonaventura da Brescia discussed Marchetto's division in 1489, compared it with the standard one, and, while approving of both, expressed his preference for Marchetto's, which he considered 'very clear and beautiful'.[79] For Pietro Aaron in 1545, the whole tone was normally divided into four dieses and a comma, 'even though some divide it into five dieses'.[80] This appears to be a realistic assessment. Marchetto's division was kept alive throughout our period by some theorists, but it was never universally accepted as the standard division.

This persistent Marchettan tradition reappeared, I believe, in an unexpected (and heretofore unnoticed) metamorphosis in the theory of Nicola Vicentino, who divided the whole tone into five minor dieses and made two such dieses equal a minor semitone, and three equal a major one.[81] Even though in the tuning system advocated by Vicentino the diatonic semitone is major and the chromatic one minor, the resemblance of this division to Marchetto's is unmistakable, since they both substitute the normal division of the whole tone into four dieses and a comma by the one into five dieses, and they both consider the difference between the major and minor semitones to be a diesis rather than comma. Vicentino was very reticent about the sources of his ideas and, consequently, we can be sure neither that the resemblance is not accidental nor that Vicentino was influenced directly by *Lucidarium*. But in view of the continuous survival of Marchetto's division, its influence on Vicentino – whether direct or indirect – is very likely.

Marchetto was prompted by his division to revise the standard terminology and to call his three semitones with the names of the three genera: 'enharmonic' for the smallest, that is, standard minor semitone, 'diatonic' for the medium, that is, standard major one, and 'chromatic' for the largest one. The presence of this peculiar terminology in a theorist's vocabulary is another sign (besides the five-dieses division of the whole tone) that he was affected by the Marchettan contagion. The sources of Prosdocimus' treatise on counterpoint present an intriguing picture from this standpoint. One of the manuscripts containing the first version of the treatise, the version written between 1412 and 1415, uses Marchetto's terms liberally. In the revised version of 1425-8 these traces are obliterated and lengthy polemical passages against Marchetto are added.[82] There is, for instance, a passage which criticizes *Lucidarium* for ignoring what musical authorities understand by such terms as 'diatonic', 'chromatic' and 'enharmonic' and stresses that music theorists recognize only two semitones, the minor and major ones.[83] Marchetto's use of the names of the three genera as the names of the semitones is also criticized by Prosdocimus in his *Tractatus musice speculative*, from which we learn additionally that 'this was one of the chief falsehoods which the said Marchetto propagated throughout Italy and [that] presently this falsehood is so highly esteemed by singers that whoever subscribes to it is considered among singers to be most established'.[84]

The use of the generic names for the semitones was also criticized *ca.* 1458-64 by Johannes Legrense in the context of an extended anti-Marchettan polemic.[85] His criticism was mentioned with approval in 1482 by Ramos de Pareia who used the occasion to attack John Hothby for distinguishing between 'hard' (*durum*), 'soft' (*molle*) and 'natural' (*naturale*) semitones. Hothby must have been influenced by Marchetto, argued Ramos, because no one since Marchetto posited the existence of three semitones.[86] Hothby had, in fact, used the names of the three properties as the names of the semitones within the deductions of these properties. Thus, he called the semitone between B and C 'hard', that between E and F 'natural', and the one between a and soft b 'soft'.[87] Now he defended himself in a treatise devoted to the refutation of Ramos's doctrines, *Excitatio quaedam musicae artis per refutationem*.[88] Hothby claimed that Ramos did not correctly understand 'my fellow-student' (*meum condiscipulum*) Legrense. He stated that what is wrong with Marchetto's theory is not his vocabulary, but his subject matter, that is, his division. It is entirely proper to use the generic names for the semitones, so long as these semitones result from the standard division of the whole tone. In other words, we can call the minor semitone 'diatonic' because it is characteristic of the diatonic genus, the major one 'chromatic' because it appears only in the chromatic genus, and the diesis an 'enharmonic semitone'. The three semitones of Marchetto are incorrect not on account of their names, but because of his incorrect division of the whole tone, and in fact they were never used, but they are semitones, just as mine are, because they are smaller than the whole tone, claimed Hothby. Moreover, Hothby continued, when I talk of some semitones being hard, others soft, and still others natural, I have in mind only the semitones of the diatonic genus and I do not follow Marchetto at all.

Hothby defended himself further in his *Epistola*,[89] where he stressed that it was incorrect to talk of only two semitones, because every interval smaller than the whole tone should be called a semitone, and reiterated most of his other arguments. He additionally explained that while the major semitone was always chromatic and the diesis always enharmonic, the minor semitone could be either diatonic or chromatic, depending upon the genus in which it was found.[90] Moreover, it is even possible to call the natural semitone diatonic, because it falls between two white keys, and the soft semitone chromatic, because it falls between a white and a black key.[91] (We have already observed that Hothby thinks more in terms of the keyboard than in terms of the hand.) And while the hard semitone cannot be called *enarmonico*, it can be called *henarmonico*, because *enarmonico* with *h* means 'joined together in one' (*in uno insieme coniuncto*) and the hard semitone involves the square b which is joined in the same place with the round b.[92] Thus, the minor semitone can be not only diatonic or chromatic, but also 'henharmonic'.[93] The point which clearly emerges from all this quibbling is that all three theorists, Legrense, Ramos and Hothby, rejected both Marchetto's division and his peculiar terminology.

But such rejection could not have been universal, since Tinctoris reports that the major semitone 'is called by many . . . diatonic semitone',[94] that the minor semitone 'is called by others enharmonic semitone',[95] and that 'there is another semitone which is called chromatic'.[96] Among those who used Marchetto's terms was Bonaventura da Brescia whom we have already heard discussing Marchetto's division with approval.[97] In his popular printed treatise, *Breviloquium musicale* of 1497, Bonaventura accepted the three Marchettan semitones without qualification.[98] Bonaventura was not alone in this, as we can infer not only from the popularity of his *Breviloquium* (it enjoyed eighteen re-editions through 1570),[99] but also from the *Quaestiones et solutiones* of an anonymous follower at the end of the fifteenth century who reproduced *Breviloquium*'s opinions.[100] As late as 1555, Pietro Cinciarino, who was familiar with Marchetto's work at first hand, still claims that 'according to Bonaventura and all musicians we have in the hand three kinds of semitone, namely, the enharmonic semitone, diatonic semitone and chromatic semitone, or thus: the minor semitone, major semitone and very large semitone'.[101] Marchettan influence in the mid-sixteenth century is betrayed also by Angelo da Picitono when, in discussing the major semitone, he says that 'according to some learned musicians' it is called 'diatonic'.[102]

The use of the sign of the diesis makes real sense only within the context of Marchettan theory, that is, only so long as the sign has a function truly distinct from that of the square b. We have already seen that the majority of theorists of our period accepted the diesis sign without subscribing to Marchetto's division of the whole tone. In other words, it was common to think of the sign as the exact equivalent of the square b. But we have also uncovered the existence of theorists who accepted Marchetto's division. In view of this persistent Marchettan tradition, it is not surprising that some theorists continued to make a functional differentiation between ♮ and ♯, or at least referred to musicians who did so. The name of the new sign shared a similar fate. No one was happy with Marchetto's name, *falsa musica*, since this term already had a well-established meaning of its own. It was usually called 'diesis',[103] since – as we already know – in Marchetto's theory it helped to divide the whole tone into the 'diesis' and the 'chromatic' semitone. Moreover, it will become clear in Chapter 6 below that the sign was most commonly used in the context in which it did produce the interval of the 'diesis', at least for the Marchettans, namely, as the sign sharpening the leading tone approached from above and resolved upwards. But for the common theorist and musician of the period, 'diesis' was no more than a neutral name for the ♯ sign. Only for the Marchettan minority did it additionally evoke a progression by a fifth of the whole tone.

Once again, it is Prosdocimus who, in his polemic against Marchetto and his followers, provides an indirect testimony that such followers existed. Incidentally, he expresses also his conviction that Marchetto was in fact the inventor of the new sign. (This belief that Marchetto introduced the sign and its name might have been widespread, since it is expressed still in 1538 by Giovanni del Lago.)[104] In one of the interpolations which Prosdocimus added when revising his counterpoint treatise we read:

From what has been said of these signs, the error of those modern writers lies open who in place of square b apply this cross ♯, or, according to the more modern ones, this, ⚡, and call these signs of theirs by the name diesis or falsa musica, following the bad doctrine of the aforementioned Marchetto of Padua. The aforesaid Marchetto was the source of this error.[105]

Similarly, in his *Tractatus musice speculative*, Prosdocimus explained that when a major sixth is required above E, that is, at the place of c, the 'ancients' (*antiqui*) put the square b on the line of this c.

The moderns, however, having no understanding of this, but acting willfully and without reason, put in the place of the square b this cross ♯, and other more modern ones, also acting willfully and without reason, this sign ♯♯. And most of these, especially Italians following the false teaching of Marchetto da Padova, and also many others, call these two signs by the name of 'diesis', not knowing what this name 'diesis' conveys among musicians. For diesis among musicians is a half of the minor semitone . . . And, further, the major part of these moderns, and especially Italians, say, in conformity with the false teaching of their Marchetus of Padua, that the signs are called by this name of 'diesis' only because through those signs an addition of one diesis is made in ascent (which diesis is among their Marchetus and his followers a fifth part of the whole tone), and in descent is made a subtraction of the same diesis.[106]

But, once again, we find that Prosdocimus himself was not untouched by an influence of the followers of Marchetto when we turn to the earlier versions of his treatises. In the original text of his treatise on the monochord he expressly stated that f, which is a major sixth above a, should be marked with the sign of the 'cross' (*crux*) ♯.[107] In the final version,[108] such steps are marked with the sign of the square b. But even in the original version he concluded that 'the cross ought to be written in the form of this square b rather than that of this cross ♯'.[109]

Prosdocimus' campaign against the diesis sign was, as we well know, unsuccessful. Half a century after him, Tinctoris notes that 'there are many people . . . writing this letter [♮] as ♯',[110] that is, making no functional distinction between ♮ and ♯, a common practice he censures, 'for this [♯] is a sign proper to the chromatic semitone'.[111] Thus, it appears that Tinctoris would like the diesis sign to be used only in the function for which it was designed by Marchetto, a position consonant with other traces of Marchettan influence we have observed in his writings. And there must have been a minority of Marchettans persisting in their advocacy of a special function for ♯ still at the very end of the fifteenth century, since Gaffurius observed in his *Practica musice* of 1496: 'There are some who apply this sign ♯ to a note and want it to be lowered a very small diesis, which belongs in the enharmonic genus, for a diesis between two tones is half of a small semitone.'[112] Gaffurius does not realize here that the 'diesis' of the Marchettans differs from the regular one, but the only way to make sense of this sentence is to assume that, in a confused manner, he refers to the Marchettan 'diesis' between a sharpened leading tone and the note a step above from which it is approached.

In the early sixteenth century, the inappropriateness of the name 'diesis' was remarked upon by Spataro:

This aforementioned sign, ♯, was called by my teacher simply 'the sign of the square b' and by brother John Hothby it was called 'the sign of the sloping square b', and this ♮ was called by him 'the sign of the upright square b'. These names are more correct than would be calling this sign ♯ 'diesis', since the name is the result of its effect . . . Therefore, since this sign works effectively just as the aforementioned upright square b does, I say that such a sign will be called more correctly 'the square b' than 'diesis', since, when one says 'diesis', the effect and the name do not correspond to one another, but they do when it is called 'the square b'.[113]

In the 1550s, Ghiselin Danckerts criticized Vicentino for calling ♯ 'diesis' on similar grounds, pointing out that the sign indicates a semitone and not a diesis.[114] (Indirectly, this suggests again the Marchettan background of Vicentino's theory.)

We have seen that most theorists who thought at all about the origin of the diesis sign connected it with Marchetto and his division of the whole tone. In the sixteenth century, however, another, considerably more fanciful, theory explaining the sign appeared. Stephano Vanneo suggested that it is the sign of the minor semitone, which for him is identical with the major diesis (hence, presumably, its name). Since, for Vanneo, the minor semitone consists of two minor dieses, and the minor diesis of two commata, and since the comma can be marked with one stroke (/), the minor diesis can be signed with two strokes (//), and the minor semitone with four (✳).[115] Vanneo's reason for associating the sign with the minor (rather than major) semitone is parallel to Marchetto's reason for associating it with the 'diesis' rather than with the 'chromatic' semitone: the sign is used to sharpen the cadential leading tone approached from above and resolved upwards, that is, to produce the interval of the minor semitone.[116] (The full significance of this last fact will be appreciated once we learn about the normal function of ♮/♯ in the music of the period.) As usual, Vanneo was faithfully followed by Angelo da Picitono,[117] but not only by him. Also Danckerts observed that the diesis, which is a half of the diatonic semitone, since it consists of two commata, can be marked by two strokes, whether parallel (// or ⑊) or crossed (✕), and that, consequently, the minor semitone, consisting of two such dieses, can be marked by four strokes (✳), and he explained that the minor semitone is normally marked by such a sign in a descending motion, that is, as a sharpened note approached by step from above.[118] It might be mentioned here that Zarlino also marks the diesis with a cross (✕), but believes that he is the first to do so.[119]

(iv) The expanding limits of *musica ficta*

The definition of *musica ficta* as the realm of steps not contained within the hand prompts the question of whether there are any outer limits to the multiplication of steps beyond the hand. The simplest way to approach this question is to ask another one: may the two accidentals, ♭ and ♮/♯, be applied in all the places of the hand as well as to all the new steps resulting from such applications, or is there a limit beyond which one cannot go on inflecting steps by means of the accidentals?

We have seen that an accidental always signifies a syllable (♭=fa, ♮/♯=mi). In addition, an accidental usually means that the note in the place of which it is found should be inflected by a chromatic semitone. But, in exceptional cases, it is conceivable that an accidental will not inflect the note in the place of which it is found, but rather the neighboring note (as happens, for example, when Ugolino of Orvieto uses the round b at G to sharpen F), or that it will not inflect any note at all (for instance, when the musicians derided by Stephano Vanneo place a flat at ff simply to indicate that it is beyond the range of the regular gamut). It follows that the only primary and absolutely indispensable function of an accidental is to indicate the syllable and that only secondarily does an accidental also indicate an inflection. But, if the primary function of an accidental is to indicate whether the step which it accompanies is fa or mi, it makes no sense to apply the round b to a step which is already fa, or to apply the square b or diesis to a step which is already mi. In other words, the signs of fa and mi may be applied only in those places of the hand which do not contain these syllables already. These should be the outer limits for the application of accidentals. Since within the hand, ♭, c, f, and all the flattened steps are already fas (for simplicity's sake, I am limiting the discussion to the a-g octave for now), it would be redundant to apply the round b to them, and since a, ♮, e, and all the sharpened steps are already mis, it would be equally redundant to apply the square b to them. In the a-g octave, only a, d, e and g may be flattened, and only c, d, f and g may be sharpened. The logic of the hand dictates that the largest conceivable gamut will contain sixteen different pitches in an octave.

It would appear that we have discovered the outer limits of *musica ficta*. We know, however, that at some point musicians began to go beyond these limits and that eventually it became possible to flatten and sharpen all the seven uninflected notes within an octave and even to use double flats and sharps. I will now attempt to describe the stages through which the expansion of the chromatic gamut in music theory proceeded and to explain the changes in thinking about the gamut which accompanied each new conquest.

The question of whether the round b can additionally inflect a step which is already fa, or the square b a step which is already mi, was not discussed at any length before the early sixteenth century. The sole exception I am aware of is the mid-fourteenth-century Dutch theorist, educated at Oxford and perhaps Paris, Johannes Boen, one of the more original of the writers on music of his time. In his *Musica* of 1357, Boen discussed in detail the effects of ♭ and ♮ and concluded that 'it is impossible to place together two major semitones one after another',[120] giving as an example the progression 𝄢 ♮ ♭ ♭, 'where the middle and the final [notes] are completely equal, since that second letter b-fa cannot dislocate the following note beyond its nature more than by the major semitone of the first substitution; . . . therefore, the second letter b-fa is placed in vain'.[121] Clearly, Boen did not consider a double flat or sharp to be possible. Just before the quoted passage, however, he offered lengthy speculations on the ways to notate three consecutive minor semitones or a comma in which he presented examples of, for instance, the square b truly sharpening a or ♮ and the round b truly flattening c.[122] Thus, for Boen, double flats or sharps were unthinkable, but a flat truly inflecting c or f and a sharp truly inflecting a, ♮, or e were possible. This suggests that Boen thought about these problems not so much in terms of solmization syllables (in which both a flattened step and c, for instance, are already fa and, consequently, cannot be additionally flattened) as in terms of the actual visual appearance of the staff notation (in which the note marking b is preceded by the round b, while the note marking c is not and, consequently, the latter can be additionally flattened, while the former cannot). Consequently, even though he did not conceive of double flats or sharps, he apparently believed that any note could be preceded by a single flat or sharp without redundancy.

Boen did not stop at this, however, but went on to inform us that the 'ancients' (*antiqui*) believed, in effect, that a note with a minor semitone below (that is, fa) could not be flattened, and a note with a minor semitone above (mi) could not be sharpened, which means that

one may not put the letter b-mi in the letter [place] b-mi or in e-la-mi or in their octaves . . . unless the letter b-fa had preceded in the same letters [places], in which case it is permitted in order that the effect of the preceding letter b-fa be cancelled through the letter b-mi . . . One may not put the letter b-fa in c-fa-ut or in f-fa-ut or in their octaves . . . and one may not put the letter b-mi in a-la-mi-re.[123]

In other words, the 'ancients' followed the logic of solmization syllables rather than that of staff notation. To be sure, 'the modern usage allows the said letters [♭ and ♮] in the letters [places] beyond the nature of the manual monochord',[124] but it would be rash to conclude that the moderns permit f, say, to be flattened, or e to be sharpened, since in the remaining portion of his discussion Boen clarifies that what he has in mind is a gamut in which, in the a-g octave, a, d and e could be flattened and c, d, f and g could be sharpened,[125] that is, a gamut still fully within the limits dictated by the logic of solmization syllables (and even omitting one possible step, namely, g♭). The only difference between the 'ancients' and the 'moderns' is that the former would not flatten d once they had decided to sharpen c (because the note with a minor semitone below should not be flattened), while the latter allow c♯ and d♭ to coexist in one gamut.

In sum, Boen's discussion seems to indicate that the logic of solmization syllables, which dictated that the round b (or square b) could not additionally inflect a step which was already fa (or mi), was in general force at his time and earlier and that his own thinking in terms of the staff notation, which allowed any note to be preceded by a flat or sharp, was a sign of his independence and originality and did not reflect the common opinion.

It appears that, except for Johannes Boen and one other theorist to be mentioned shortly, no one in the fourteenth century challenged the limits of the sixteen-step gamut. An indication that these limits ceased to be invulnerable already in the early fifteenth century comes in *Parvus tractatulus de modo dividendi monacordum*, which the Paduan theorist Prosdocimus de Beldemandis wrote in 1413 and revised between 1425 and 1428.[126] Prosdocimus introduces his monochord describing first the steps of *musica vera* and explaining that 'the feigned music has to be put between two unseparated letters which sound a whole tone apart so that one has a semitone in the same place'.[127] He goes on to explain that, since the whole tone cannot be divided into two equal parts but only into a major and a minor semitone, the feigned steps cannot be placed in the middle between two such letters but must be located either so that the minor semitone is lower, as some musicians propose, or that it is higher, as others advocate. Since there are twelve undivided whole tones within the *musica vera* gamut, each division introduces twelve feigned steps, the former ab, db, eb, gb, their octave equivalents, and Bb (which, unlike b and bb, does not belong to *musica vera*), the latter c♯, d♯, f♯, g♯, their octave equivalents, and A♯ (since the whole tone A-B, unlike a-♮ and aa-♮♮, is undivided and, we should add, since A, unlike a and aa, is not already mi). Prosdocimus declares both these systems defective, showing that they lack steps which are necessary in practice, and proposes a third gamut combining the previous two. What results is, of course, the sixteen-step gamut. However, noting that there is both Bb and A♯ between A and B, Prosdocimus allows additionally analogous division of a-♮ and aa-♮♮ whole steps, that is, he adds a♯ and aa♯ to his gamut, even though 'these two feigned steps . . . occur most rarely in any song'.[128]

In other words, Prosdocimus both testifies to the reluctant acceptance of a♯ and aa♯ among the steps of *musica ficta* by at least some musicians since at least the early fifteenth century and explains the process which allowed these musicians to rationalize the existence of such steps by analogy with the low octave in which nothing prevented the feigning of A♯. Such acceptance, however reluctant, represents the first crack in the supremacy of thinking about the accidentals primarily in terms of the syllables and the beginning of the shift toward thinking primarily in terms of the inflections they produce. Such a shift was not very difficult to make, since the accidentals did in fact usually indicate inflections. We have seen that already Boen was capable of making this step. At the same time, the acceptance of a♯

promoted the tendency to think of ♭ as yet another step dividing the whole tones of the gamut, identical in status with other such 'black-key' steps, and to think of the whole gamut in terms of the monochord or keyboard, rather than in terms of the hand.

We have seen that Prosdocimus' reasoning resulted in a gamut in which every whole tone of the 'Guidonian' system except for those between ♭ and c and between ♭♭ and cc was divided into a minor semitone, a comma, and another minor semitone. But since ♭ was as much a *musica vera* step as was ♮, sooner or later someone was bound to attempt a similar division of the ♭-c and ♭♭-cc whole tones. Indeed, we do find such a monochord, attributed to a certain Nicolaus de Luduno, in a fourteenth-century manuscript from Martin Gerbert's monastery of St Blasien.[129] The monochord is represented in a diagram in which every step of the full gamut gets a horizontal line or space. The appropriate lines and spaces are marked by the letter-names of the *musica vera* steps from Γ to ee on the left-hand side, and by the letter-names of the *musica ficta* steps and an indication whether a given feigned step is a minor semitone or a comma higher than the preceding one[130] on the right-hand side. The gamut is identical with that of Prosdocimus in that the whole tones are divided by a minor semitone, a comma, and another minor semitone, but while Prosdocimus chooses to divide the a-♮ and aa-♮♮ whole tones, Nicolaus divides instead the whole tones ♭-c and ♭♭-cc. It is characteristic that in the diagram ♮ and ♮♮ appear both among the steps of *musica vera* and, since they divide the whole tones, also among those of *musica ficta*. Nicolaus' division avoids the troublesome a♯ and aa♯, but introduces the equally troublesome c♭ and cc♭ instead.

Nicolaus, however, appears to have had no followers. Prosdocimus' legitimation of a♯ and aa♯ by analogy with the already legitimate A♯, on the other hand, was such an obvious step that it was accepted by at least one other early fifteenth-century theorist, Ugolino of Orvieto, in the 'Tractatus monochordi' appended to his *Declaratio musicae disciplinae* completed in Ferrara during the 1430s.[131] Ugolino clearly follows Prosdocimus, beginning with the gamut of *musica recta*, dividing all of its undivided whole tones into semitones (with the minor semitone either below or above the major one), and, finally, combining both divisions. But, even more than Prosdocimus, he is uneasy about a♯, aa♯, and even A♯, since he includes them in his 'perfect division of the monochord' (*monochordi perfecta divisio*; that is, the one combining the two earlier divisions),[132] but, inexplicably, omits them in the division which should introduce the minor semitone above the major one, using B♭, ♭ and ♭♭ instead.[133] In short, while the seventeen-step gamut became possible for at least some of the early fifteenth-century musicians, we have to believe Prosdocimus that the seventeenth step, *A♯*, was still a great rarity.

It should be noted in passing that the step appears also in the monochord described by the Parmesan astronomer, mathematician, physician and musician Giorgio Anselmi in his treatise of 1434.[134] Anselmi starts with a four-octave diatonic gamut (without any flats, not even ♭ and ♭♭), divides each whole tone by a flat step (that is, in effect adds in each octave A♭, B♭, D♭, E♭, G♭), and then – without clearly noting that a different division is involved – by a sharp step (that is, in effect adds in each octave A♯, C♯, D♯, F♯, G♯). (The steps are not named explicitly, but they can be inferred from the described tuning process.) I have suggested previously that the seventeen-step gamut reflects thinking in terms of the keyboard and it is significant that Anselmi concludes his discussion by stating that what he has described is the tuning of the organ.[135] Anselmi's discussion is somewhat confused and, like his whole treatise, represents the interests of a speculative rather than a practical musician, but it deserved to be mentioned here, if only because it was considered sufficiently important to be annotated and corrected later in the century by the eminent Milanese theorist Franchinus Gaffurius, to whom the manuscript containing it belonged.[136]

Signs of a reluctant acceptance of a♯ continue to appear during the second half of the fifteenth century. An anonymous Italian *Tertius liber musicae* copied in 1464 presents and discusses a diagram (see Figure 4) consisting of six regular hexachords (that is, all the hexachords of *musica vera* except the one on Γ) and ten irregular ones, of which six are the hexachords of 'false' (*falsi*) steps (on D, a, ♭, d, e♭, aa) and four of steps 'extracted from the false ones' (*extracti de falsis*; on E, F♯, ♮, e). The resulting gamut (with 'false' F♯, c♯, e♭, f♯, aa♭, cc♯ and with 'extracted-from-the-false' G♯, a♯, d♯, g♯) contains a♯ in one octave, although the diagram obscures its presence, making it appear on the same level as (that is, equivalent to) ♭, just as it obscures the presence of d♯ and g♯, making them appear equivalent to e♭ and aa♭ respectively. Also Franchinus Gaffurius, whose familiarity with Anselmi's treatise has been mentioned, considers a♯ a conceivable though useless step when, in his first original treatise, *Theorica musice*, written probably in 1479, he argues in favor of dividing the whole tone between a and ♮ with ♭ rather than a♯.[137]

We have observed that the conceivability of a♯ depended on the extent to which the hand lost its grip over the imagination of musicians and other images, in particular that of the keyboard, came to supplant it. An additional symptom of this development can be seen in the references to ♭ and ♭♭ as steps of *musica ficta* rather than *vera* which appear sporadically in fifteenth-century treatises. When Henri Arnaut de Zwolle, a doctor at the court of Philip the Good of Burgundy, describes *ca.* 1440 the tuning of a clavichord, he starts with the white-key steps, then adds the black-key ♭, calling it 'ficta', and then continues to add the other four 'ficta' black-key steps.[138] In the context of the present discussion, it is, of course, particularly appropriate, as well as understandable, that someone concerned with a key-

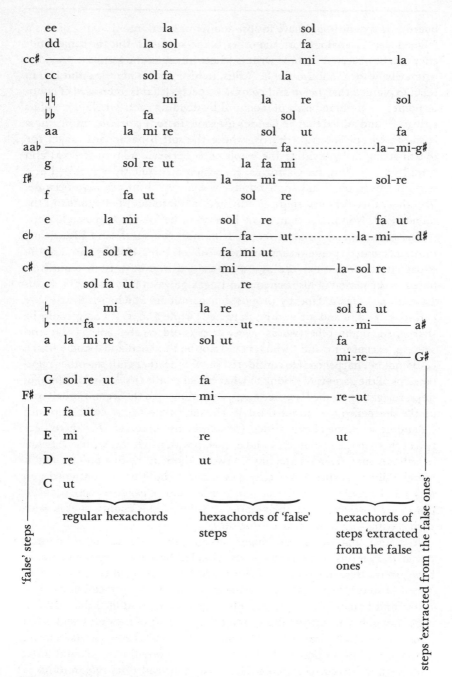

Figure 4. Anonymus, *Tertius liber musicae* (1464). Ms. Venice, Biblioteca Nazionale di S. Marco, lat. VIII.85 (=3579), fols. 84v–85r (transcript)

board instrument would have to slip, sooner or later, into thinking of ♭ as a feigned step by analogy with the other black-key steps. But the same tendency can be observed in those writers whose image of the gamut is provided primarily by the monochord. Gaffurius, in his *Practica musice* published in 1496, explained that '*fictae* and *coloratae* species [that is, intervals] of counterpoint . . . are found on a monochord by dividing each [whole] tone of its strings',[139] and added that 'in Guido's diatonic *Introductorium*, *musica ficta* is shown by one interval, that is, where the soft b hexachord makes the fourth string fa by dividing the whole tone between A-la-mi-re [= a] and b-mi [= ♮]'.[140] Thus, for Gaffurius, ♭ – which he explicitly recognized as a step present in the 'Guidonian' hand – was a step of *musica ficta* because, like the other feigned steps, it divided a diatonic whole tone of the monochord. No wonder that, as we have seen, he found a♯ a possible step.

The seventeen-step gamut received its most systematic and historically most influential presentation in the work of John Hothby, an English expatriate in Italy since the 1450s, whose writings have been tentatively dated to the period of his residence in Lucca between 1467 and 1486. In his *La Caliopea legale*, Hothby proposed a gamut in which, within the a-g octave, a, ♮, d, e and g could be flattened, while a, c, d, f and g could be sharpened, or, in other words, every step could receive both a flat and a sharp, except for c and f which could not be flattened and ♮ and e which could not be sharpened. He considered only ♮, together with the other regular steps of the gamut, to belong to what he called the first 'order' (*ordine*) of steps, relegating all the flattened steps, including ♭, to the second 'order' and all the sharpened ones to the third.[141] Hothby proceeded to call a step with a diatonic semitone above 'prince' (*principe*) and observed that there were two of those in the first order, ♮ and e. A step with a diatonic semitone below he called 'count' (*comite*) and named two of those in the first order, c and f. Hothby did not explain explicitly why c and f could not be flattened and why ♮ and e could not be sharpened, but he made clear that these prohibitions were connected with their status as 'princes' and 'counts', that is, with their having a semitone above or below.[142]

It is clear that Hothby no longer thought about the use of accidentals *primarily* in terms of the hand and its syllables, because otherwise he would have given ♭ the same status as ♮ (he would have put them both in the first 'order' of steps), he would have included a among the 'princes' of the first 'order' and ♭ among its 'counts', and he would have prohibited the sharpening of not only ♮ and e, but also a, and the flattening of not only c and f, but also ♭. It is equally clear that he did not think about these matters in terms of staff notation (as Boen did), because then he would have allowed a flat and sharp to precede every note. He thought instead *primarily* in terms of the keyboard, with the white keys representing the first 'order' of steps and the black ones the second and third, and with only ♮ and e (or c and f) having a diatonic semitone above (or below) in the first 'order'. This agrees with our earlier observations about Hothby's tendency to think about the gamut in terms of the keyboard rather than the hand. Hothby's way of thinking, however, certainly did not represent the universally accepted view of the late fifteenth century. His younger contemporary and fellow-expatriate in Italy, the Spaniard Bartolomeo Ramos de Pareia, still discussed accidentals in terms of solmization syllables and still made it clear that the round b (or the square b) had no real effect when applied to a step which was already fa (or mi).[143]

In the first half of the sixteenth century, the most systematic exposition of the entire conceivable gamut was attempted by Pietro Aaron in the last part of his *Trattato della natura et cognitione di tutti gli tuoni di canto figurato* of 1525.[144] Aaron declared that in every place of the hand one could put all the six solmization syllables.[145] This, in effect, was merely another way of saying what we already know, namely, that one could have mi and fa in every place. Moreover, the principle was ambiguous and could result in a variety of gamuts, but Aaron's attempt to derive all the syllables in all the places from the feigned fas placed where the hand had mis suggested that the gamut he most likely had in mind was the one in which all accidental steps were flat (that is, with feigned ab, db, eb, gb, within one octave).

Aaron's exposition became one of the subjects discussed in the letters which Giovanni Spataro of Bologna exchanged with him and Giovanni del Lago.[146] (Spataro needed two correspondents in Venice, because he was rarely on speaking terms with both of them at the same time.) Spataro's understanding of Aaron's text was identical with the one suggested here, namely, he took it to result in a gamut with all the 'black-key' steps flat. On October 30, 1527 Spataro wrote to del Lago criticizing Aaron for producing a gamut with flats only and ignoring the sharps entirely.[147] He returned to this matter in a letter of January 4, 1529, also addressed to del Lago, repeating the same criticism.[148] In December of 1530 and perhaps even earlier, Aaron must have written to Spataro in his own defense, explaining that the gamut he in fact had had in mind included sharp steps as well as the flat ones. Aaron's letter or letters did not survive, but we learn of its arguments, as well as of the fact that they failed to convince Spataro, from the latter's answer of January 30, 1531[149] and from another of February 8, 1531[150] where he repeated that Aaron should have used the sharps expressly in his exposition instead of having ambiguously implied them. Spataro's critique was cogent: if Aaron truly wanted a gamut which contained sharp steps, he failed to make his intentions clear in the *Trattato*. Aaron accepted the critique and revised his exposition of the gamut in which all the places of the hand contained all the solmization syllables accordingly in a separately published supplement to the *Trattato* which appeared anonymously and without a title in Venice in 1531 under the imprint of Bernardino de Vitali, the *Trattato*'s publisher. This time the exposition clearly implied the seventeen-step gamut, just like the one of Hothby. Aaron confirmed his advocacy of the seventeen-step gamut in his last two treatises, *Lucidario in musica* of 1545[151] and *Compendiolo di molti dubbi, segreti et sentenze intorno al canto fermo, et figurato* published after 1545.[152]

Spataro was clearly gratified with the results he had achieved with Aaron. On October 24, 1531 he wrote to Aaron:

Many days have already passed since I received a letter from Your Excellency with which was included a most learned, subtle, and worthy newly printed little treatise which demonstrated elegantly and with best and true proofs how in each of the places of the Guidonian hand may be found each of the six official names . . . Bartolomeo [Ramos] aimed only at producing so many places of the Guidonian hand signed [with the accidentals] as was useful for the division of the whole tones into two semitones of the monochord and organ used in his time and . . . Your Excellency thought more profoundly and subtly since you wanted every whole tone of the said instruments to be divided in such a manner that below and above appear the major and the minor semitone with the difference of the comma falling between them . . . In no way . . . has Your Excellency left the order of the truth demonstrated by Brother Johannes Hothby, but . . . you have written much better and more clearly than he.[153]

Similarly, in a letter of October 30, 1533, Spataro wrote to Aaron that the perfect division of the monochord requires that every whole tone be separated by two 'black-key' steps, one distant by the minor, the other by the major semitone from the adjacent 'white-key' steps,

as was demonstrated by Brother Johannes Hothby in his *La Caliopea*. This truth, my honored Brother Pietro, was faithfully approved by Your Excellency in this treatise of yours where you teach how to find the six official names in every position of the Guidonian hand.[154]

It is worth noticing how these discussions of the seventeen-step gamut, ostensibly undertaken in terms of syllables and places, slip into the invocation of the monochord and organ. This seems inevitable precisely because Aaron's principle that one should have all the syllables in all the places of the hand (which is another way of saying that one should be able to put mi and fa in every place of the hand where they are not naturally found) can be accommodated by various gamuts, the largest of which is the sixteen-step one.

Since, as is very well known, Spataro spent much of his life defending various doctrines of his revered teacher, Ramos, against numerous detractors, not the least of whom was Hothby, it is amusing to see Spataro, in the letter in which he greeted Aaron's Supplement with such enthusiasm, siding for once with Hothby rather than with Ramos on the question of the full gamut. The irony of his position was not lost on Spataro, since he concluded his letter remarking ruefully that the Bolognese musicians with whom he had discussed Aaron's Supplement, 'laughing, said that they truly believed that my sense had become childish, since they had never found me say that my teacher was inferior to any other musician except at the present time'.[155] We have seen that on the question of the limits of the gamut Ramos was uncharacteristically conservative and that it was Hothby who most clearly and, thanks to Spataro, most influentially defined the furthest limits conceivable to a fifteenth-century musician. But in the first half of the sixteenth century these limits were moved still further and Spataro played a key role also in this process.

Spataro's interest in the problem of the gamut's limits might have been originally stimulated by Adrian Willaert's much discussed chromatic puzzle 'duo' (or, rather, quartet) *Quid non ebrietas*, a motet written between 1515 and 1521 and most likely in 1519, the tenor and cantus of which seem to end on a seventh (E-d), but in fact end on an octave since the E is meant to be read as if it were preceded with a double flat.[156] While the theoretical controversies surrounding the piece in the sixteenth century, controversies in which Spataro took an active role, centered on the issue of the temperament required for its proper rendition, the fact that the last note of the tenor implied what we would think of today as a double flattening was never in doubt. Willaert may well have been the first musician to conceive of such a possibility, and the implications of his piece for the development of the gamut were no less far-reaching than its implications for thinking about temperament. Since within the framework of the hand and its syllables a double accidental is meaningless (a note which is already fa, that is, which already implies a certain intervallic pattern around itself, cannot be made 'more' or 'double' fa in any sense), Willaert's implication of a real double flat, as well as the common acceptance of this implication by those of his contemporaries who were able to resolve the composer's puzzle, shows to what extent thinking about accidentals primarily in terms of syllables was already undermined in the early sixteenth century. At the very least, it shows that for some musicians an accidental was now primarily a method of indicating an inflection and only secondarily a sign of fa or mi.

Spataro discussed the piece in a letter of September 9, 1524 addressed to Aaron.[157] In the letter he talked about accidentals not in terms of syllables but only in terms of inflections which they effect:

Musicians instituted only two signs through which the naturally considered sounds may be removed from the proper place. These signs are ♯ [and] ♭. The former, ♯, removes the natural sound by the major semitone up, the latter, ♭, effects the reverse, that is, it removes the sound from the natural place by the major semitone down.[158]

When accidentals are discussed in such terms, it becomes possible to stipulate that an accidental could be applied to a step twice and inflect it twice as much as normally. In fact, we find Spataro writing about the sign ♭ producing 'twice its effect'.[159] Spataro considered the piece in terms of the Pythagorean tuning and, consequently, criticized the composer's experiment as mistaken, but he had no trouble understanding and accepting Willaert's fundamental idea that a double accidental might be possible. Incidentally, it should be pointed out that neither Willaert nor Spataro indicated such a double accidental expressly. They had neither a graphic sign nor a name for the double flat.[160]

The problem of double accidentals is related to the question of whether one can flatten c or f and sharpen ♮ or e, and the latter problem was also discussed by Spataro at length. In both cases what was at stake was the decision of whether the primary function of an accidental was to inflect (in which case it would make sense to think of, say, double flats or c♭) or to change the step into fa or mi (in which case double flats or a flat on c, for instance, would be redundant). Once again, Willaert's 'duo' may have been an important catalyst of the interest in the problem, since it contains a notated c♭ and an implied F♭. These notated and implied flats are meant to lower c and F by a semitone and are so understood without any difficulty by Spataro in his comments on the piece.[161] Moreover, Edward E. Lowinsky pointed out a letter of May 14, 1521[162] showing that 'three years previous to his study of the duo he [Spataro] recognized only one possibility of placing a flat before F and C, namely when these tones had been sharpened before and had to be restored to their natural positions', as an indication that 'Spataro's conviction that the tones C and F can be flattened . . . is certainly a consequence of his study of Willaert's duo.'[163]

In 1533 such inflections became a subject of a protracted polemic involving Spataro in Bologna and Aaron and Giovanni del Lago in Venice. The specific questions discussed were the beginnings and ends (uts and las) of the hexachords containing F♭, c♭, ♮♯, E♯, and the location of the mi of the hexachord which has its fa on ♮.[164] Del Lago sent Spataro his answers in a letter of August 15.[165] He argued that a flat will make F, for instance, a comma lower than E (since a flat lowers a step by a major semitone and the diatonic semitone between E and F is minor, the difference between the two being a comma) and that, since the comma is not used in musical practice, a flat on F should be avoided and, for similar reasons, c♭, ♮♯ and E♯ should also be avoided.

Several points should be made about this argument. First, for the theorist, the syllable-indicating function of accidentals is no longer primary, since they will flatten or sharpen even those steps which are already fa or mi. Second, his prohibition does not extend expressly to a♯, that is, his position resembles that of Hothby. Third, just as with Spataro's arguments against double flats, it is not the possibility of such signs which is denied, but only their practicability within the premises of the Pythagorean tuning system, that is, the argument falls with the acceptance of equal temperament.

Del Lago's views were essentially identical with those of Spataro; both theorists believed that the primary function of an accidental was to inflect, even when it was applied to a step which was already fa or mi. Only Spataro's insatiable appetite for quibbling can explain his lengthy criticism of del Lago's position in a letter addressed to Aaron on October 30.[166] For our purpose, it suffices to note that, just like del Lago, Spataro believed that F♭ and c♭ will be a major semitone lower than F and c and that ♮♯ and E♯ will be a major semitone higher than ♮ and E[167] – he referred to Willaert's *Quid non ebrietas* to support this claim[168] – but, unlike del Lago, he argued that such steps might legitimately be used.[169]

But not all musicians agreed. In a letter from Venice written on June 3, 1538, del Lago upbraided Piero de Justinis for notating in one of his motets an incomposite melodic tritone between ♭ and e with the sign of diesis preceding the e.[170] It is clear that Piero used the sign in the old-fashioned sense, that is, merely as the sign of mi, and did not intend to sharpen the e but rather to prevent its flattening by singers (there is a simultaneous natural E in the bass). For del Lago, however, the sign invariably moves the step it accompanies a major semitone up. But, while he considered Piero's use of the sign incorrect, he had no difficulty in recognizing Piero's intentions in an analogous case. This suggests that Piero's traditional usage was still current, probably even normal, in the late 1530s.

Aaron, who had been the recipient of Spataro's letters on the subject in 1533, discussed it in print in his *Lucidario in musica* of 1545.[171] On the question of whether it is possible to place the sign of ♭ on C or F and the sign of diesis on ♮ or E, he said:

Therefore, wishing to imagine the sign of ♭ on C . . . it might perhaps occur to you what has occurred to others who believed that, when the musician or composer produces in his musical actions the figure of the soft b or of diesis, this note is not moved from its proper place but remains stationary and that such signs are as if redundant. However, to escape from this error, know that such syllable or note fa put in C with the said sign ♭ is removed from there and is no more there where it found itself previously, but below ♮ by the interval of the comma.[172]

Not surprisingly, Aaron's position is essentially the same as Spataro's or del Lago's. But it is noteworthy that still in the mid-1540s he feels compelled to defend his view against the more traditional one, according to which a flat does not lower C, for instance. We may infer that the latter view was still quite widespread at the time. While Aaron has no doubt that a flat inflects C or F and a sharp ♮ or E, he concedes that such inflections imply hexachords the steps of which cannot be found on contemporary keyboards and are distant from the usual ones by a comma. It is for this reason only that he concludes that these four inflections should not be used.[173]

Let me summarize the results of this section: I have been trying to establish the outer limits of *musica ficta*, the limits beyond which one could not go on inflecting steps by means of accidentals, and I have suggested that such limits were dictated by the terms in which musicians of our period thought about the gamut. So long as the controlling image in terms of which the gamut was conceived was that of the hand, so long, that is, as a musician thought about accidentals primarily in terms of syllables ($\flat$ = fa, $\natural/\sharp$ = mi), he was likely to assume that the flat (or sharp) could not additionally inflect a step which was already fa (or mi) and that, consequently, in the a-g octave, his gamut would allow no more than sixteen different pitches, namely, the eight steps of the 'true' gamut plus the flats only at a, d, e, g and sharps only at c, d, f, g. Boen's solitary mid-fourteenth-century discussion of the problem confirmed that his predecessors and contemporaries indeed made such an assumption, even though his own thinking in terms of staff nota-tion allowed any note to be preceded by a single, but not double, accidental. We have seen many indications that this traditional, syllable-oriented view, limiting the gamut to no more than sixteen different pitches in an octave, retained its vitality, like the hand itself, through the end of the period dis-cussed here. Otherwise it would be impossible to understand such phenomena as, for instance, Prosdocimus' and Ugolino's clear discomfort with the step of a$\sharp$ they propose, or Spataro's, del Lago's and Aaron's lengthy discussions of whether one may really flatten c and f and sharpen a, $\natural$ and e. That the sixteen-step gamut remained a staple of basic music instruction can be seen, for instance, in Martin Agricola's fairly typical *Rudimenta musices* of 1539, where the sign of mi is allowed on C, F, G and d and the sign of fa on a, d, g and e.[174]

At least since the beginning of the fifteenth century the limits of the sixteen-step gamut were challenged by the introduction of non-redundant $A\sharp$ in every octave, not only in the lowest one. The resulting seventeen-step gamut was advocated in Italy by theorists from Prosdocimus to Aaron. The introduction of a$\sharp$ broke the barriers which had up till then limited the gamut, since it implied that the primary function of an accidental was to inflect and that the syllable-indicating function was derived or secondary. If you could truly sharpen a, there was no reason why you could not truly sharpen or flatten any other step, or even apply an accidental several times in a row. There were, strictly speaking, no longer any limits beyond which an application of an accidental would be inconceivable. From now on, the potentially unlimited universe of *musica ficta* was limited only by practical considerations.

It appears that during the fifteenth century no one proposed to go beyond the gamut of seventeen steps. The seventeenth step, $A\sharp$, made its appearance in the two higher octaves thanks to the analogy with its legitimate appear-ance in the lowest octave. The new step promoted the tendency to think of $\flat$ and $\flat\flat$ as steps identical in status with other 'black-key' steps and to think of the whole gamut less in terms of the hand and its syllables and more in terms of the monochord or keyboard. This controlling image of the keyboard accounts, in turn, for the limitation of the gamut to seventeen steps only, the limitation which evidently resulted from the desire to provide all the 'white-key' steps with a diatonic semitone above and below, that is, to make them both mi and fa. The shift from the controlling image and terminology of the hand to those of the keyboard in imagining of and thinking about the gamut is noticeable in many theoretical texts of the fifteenth century, but it reaches its clearest and most influential expression in the writings of Hothby, whose thinking on the gamut was to guide Spataro early in the next century and, through Spataro's mediation, also Aaron.

Two conquests remained to be made in order for the gamut of practical music to reach its fullest state conceivable within our period (and, for that matter, until our own century): the acceptance of non-redundant single flats on c and f and non-redundant single sharps on ♮ and e as well as the acceptance of double accidentals. These conquests presupposed that, in addition to assuming that the main function of accidentals was to inflect rather than to indicate the syllable of the step, one began to think about the gamut in terms of the staff notation rather than the keyboard. Both these conquests were suggested in Willaert's 'duo' and theoretically elaborated in Spataro's private correspondence with del Lago and Aaron in the 1520s and 1530s, correspondence at least in part provoked by the piece, as well as in Aaron's published treatises of the 1540s. While all three theorists understood that the twenty-one-step gamut (in which all the notes could be flattened and sharpened) was possible, only Spataro argued (perhaps more for the sake of argument than out of a real conviction) that it could be used in practice. The other two rejected it in practice because of the problems it created if used within the premisses of the Pythagorean tuning system. And Willaert's implied double flats were conceivable for Spataro (the only one of the three to discuss them), even though he thought them also im-practicable in the Pythagorean tuning system. Thus, with the breaking of the barriers imposed on the expansion of the gamut first by the hand and than by the keyboard, the new practical checks on the potentially limit-less proliferation of accidentals were established when the tuning system was considered.

Because of these practical checks, in the mid-sixteenth century the seventeen-step gamut was still the largest possible gamut of musical prac-tice, even though additional steps were conceivable to speculative theorists and even experimented with in pieces which, like Willaert's 'duo', have to be understood as the continuation of music theory by other means.[175]

A different, and incompatible, view of the content of *musica ficta* has recently been presented in Margaret Bent's imaginative and important paper on 'Diatonic *Ficta*'.[176] Bent offered a hypothesis explaining 'how what we call pitch was conceptualised in the fourteenth to sixteenth centuries' by musicians concerned with 'vocally conceived, contrapuntally based polyphony'[177] and argued that their notion of pitch was radically relative, that is, that their definition of any given pitch was completely independent of any fixed pitch standard and depended solely on the pitch's intervallic relations with other pitches in its immediate vicinity. (To avoid unnecessary misunderstandings, the reader should keep in mind throughout this discussion the specific senses in which the following terms are used in this book: a 'step' is a pitch defined not in absolute but in relative terms, relative, that is, to other steps of the gamut; a 'frequency' is a pitch defined in relation to a pitch-standard; a 'pitch' is a generic term which may cover either a step or a frequency.) Now, the idea of the relative notion of pitch can take two versions, a weak and a strong one. In the weak version, all that is asserted is that a system of steps used by musicians is independent of an absolute pitch-standard, that is, that it is in no way affected by being tuned higher or lower in relation to such a standard. That musicians of our period (and long thereafter) would think about steps of the gamut they used as being relative in this sense can hardly be doubted. So far as I know, this has long been the commonly accepted view among musicologists. Bent, however, is not satisfied with this weak version of the relative notion of pitch and claims in addition that the musicians' understanding of a step was independent not only of an absolute pitch-standard, but also of a relative standard established (more or less freely) at the beginning of the composition by the singers. The identity, definition and understanding of a step depended, in her view, solely on its relations with steps in its immediate vicinity and would not be affected even if its actual frequency changed (moving, for instance, a semitone or two lower) in the course of the performance of the work. Or, to phrase the same claim differently, within a single performance of a single piece, the same step could be expressed by different frequencies. (What is meant here, and throughout the following discussion, are frequency differences of at least a semitone, not the tiny sliding of pitch in a purely vocal performance because of cumulative comma adjustments.) It is this strong version of pitch relativism that constitutes the truly original contribution of the paper and has to be identified as the essence of Bent's hypothesis. All other significantly new ideas presented in the paper (in particular, its understanding of chromaticism which leads to its claiming diatonic status for Willaert's 'duo' and for the so-called 'secret chromatic' repertoire;[178] its view of the relationship between instrumental intabulations and their vocal models;[179] and its conception of tonal coherence[180]) depend on this hypothesis and stand or fall with it.

One cannot but admire the boldness and imagination with which Bent has formulated the problem and the brilliance of her arguments; just as

Edward E. Lowinsky's classic *Secret Chromatic Art in the Netherlands Motet*,[181] hers is without any doubt one of the truly indispensable interventions in the history of our topic. Her hypothesis is most valuable, since it forces us to think about the late medieval conceptualization of pitch with utmost precision. I am afraid, however, that it is untenable. Everything that we know about how musicians of our period who were concerned with vocal polyphony thought about pitches indicates clearly that, for them, the identity of any step encountered in the course of a composition depended not only on its relations with immediately surrounding steps, but also on its relations with steps heard since the singing of the work had begun. Let us take an imaginary example of a voice in a polyphonic composition which in the original notation (in which not all accidental signs had to be written out) starts and ends with G, but which in our transcription would have to start with G and end with G♭, because the operation of conventional contrapuntal rules (which will be discussed in Part II of the present book) forced the lowering of pitch by a chromatic semitone at some point in the course of the composition. On Bent's account, we moderns notice, and perhaps are bothered by, the change of frequency between the beginning and end of the work, because our notion of pitch (just like our notation) depends on the pitch-standard established at the beginning of the piece. For early musicians, she would claim, the change of frequency would be of no importance whatsoever, since their notion of pitch did not depend on such a standard:

There is no absolute pitch G or G fa, even assuming that we know what the frequency of G was at the beginning of the piece. If a new G is established by correct moment-to-moment operation of the contrapuntal rules which are the common property of the composer and the singer, the singer no more needs to keep track of where he was in relation to the original frequency of G than he would need to keep in mind what the original value of a semibreve beat was at the beginning of a piece which has required him to apply a series of proportional relationships.[182]

Similarly, in her discussion of an Obrecht example, Bent correctly points out that only our assumption of 'frequency stability' within a single piece makes us object to beginning the piece on F and ending it on F♭.[183]

It is questionable, however, whether the assumption of 'frequency stability' within a single piece is only ours. A competent early musician would not only be perfectly aware of the fact that the *frequency* of G at the end of our imaginary example is different from the one at the beginning, but, more crucially, he would also think of the two G's as being two different *steps*. Bent's account depends on two misunderstandings. One source of the confusion lies in her not keeping constantly in mind that, as I have explained in Chapter I above, for an early musician 'G' (or any other letter name) is not the full name of a step, but merely the name of a 'place' (*locus*) for a step.' The full name of a step consists not just of a letter, but of a letter combined with a syllable.[184] The first step in our imaginary example would be thought

45

of as being not just G, but G-sol (or, depending on the context, G-re or G-ut), while the last step would most likely be thought of as G-fa (or, in any case, as a step belonging to a different hexachord than the first one). If the identity of the last step depended solely on its immediate predecessors (on steps occurring after the lowering of frequency by a chromatic semitone), as Bent's hypothesis would have it, early musicians would have no reason to think of this step as being G-fa, as belonging to a different hexachord than the first G. But what we have learned above about how early musicians solmized and thought about steps leaves no doubt that they would in fact think of the last step as being G-fa (or, in any case, would assign it a syllable from a different hexachord than that of the first G). To be sure, the singers would not need to keep track of where they were in relation to the original step. But the correct moment-to-moment operation of the solmization and mutation rules would automatically ensure that the last pitch would not only have a different frequency than the first, but that it would also be a different step. That is, for the singers, the name and identity of the last G depended on the names and identities of all the steps sung, all the hexachords and mutations taken, since the beginning of the work. And this shows that their understanding of pitch, while independent of an absolute pitch-standard, did depend on a standard established at the beginning of the performance of the work. While it is true that, within a single performance of a single piece, the same frequency could express different steps, the reverse is most emphatically not the case: identical steps (that is, steps sharing identical syllable, identical hexachord and identical place) could not be expressed by different frequencies.

The second source of the confusion lies in Bent's mixing up the singer's performance of the melody with his understanding of it, in her deriving conclusions concerning the singer's understanding of the music from his way of reading it. She is, of course, entirely justified to assert that, in reading his part, the singer does not need to keep track of where he is in relation to the original frequency of G; all that he needs to do is to get consecutive intervals as demanded by the notation and compositional rules right. But her hypothesis is not only about how vocal parts were read. It is also about 'how what we call pitch was conceptualised', that is, how musicians thought about (applied concepts to) pitches. Now, the singer of our imaginary example might indeed read his part mechanically, caring only to get from one correct pitch to the next. And, for all we know, he probably would not even use solmization syllables when rehearsing his part. But if he were asked what the first and last steps he sung were, he would call them, for instance, G-sol and G-fa, respectively, and would consider these to be two different steps. And this, as we have seen, shows that his *understanding* (as opposed to his *reading*) of a step was dependent on its relations with steps heard since the singing of the work had begun.

46

Willaert's 'duo' (a crucial example in Bent's paper)[185] points to the same conclusion. Here, again, Bent is right to observe that, in order to read the tenor part correctly, the singer needs only to follow the notation and the elementary rule prohibiting melodic leaps of imperfect fourths and fifths. And, again, she forgets that there is a difference between reading a part and understanding it. Just as in the imaginary example above, in Willaert's 'duo' the singer of the tenor part does not need to keep track of where he is when he sings the final E in relation to the original frequency E would have if it were used at the beginning. But if he wants not only to sing the music, but also to understand it, he must realize that the E-fa at the end is a very different pitch (different both as a step and as a frequency) from the (assumed) E-mi or E-la at the beginning, and he must know exactly how different it is, that is, he does have to keep track of where he is. Otherwise, he would miss the whole point of Willaert's paradoxical composition in which the tenor's final E is meant to sound a perfect octave below the soprano's final d. If Bent's hypothesis were correct, Willaert's singers might be able to read his piece, but he himself would have no reason to write it.

Moreover, we should be under no illusion that, since what we want to find out is how vocal polyphony of our period was *sung*, we need not bother with the question of how it was *understood*. In fact, understanding would have to have direct consequences for performance, at least in some cases. The singers' understanding that Bent's solution for the Obrecht 'Kyrie' mentioned above involves ending it with (our) Fb, that is, F-fa a chromatic semitone lower than the F sung throughout the piece, would doubtless influence their choice of whether to follow this solution, or to choose another, ending with (our) F, that is, F-fa of unchanged frequency. If they believed (as Obrecht's singers were most likely to believe) that a *ficta* Fb a chromatic semitone below the *vera* F-fa-ut lay beyond the limits of what was practically possible, they would have opted for a less radical solution.

Observe further that under Bent's hypothesis many phenomena described above (in particular, those features of early theory which indicate that the gamut had limits) become incomprehensible. For instance, it becomes impossible to understand why Spataro and his correspondents worried whether one might really flatten c and f and sharpen a, ♮ and e (without the assumption of 'frequency stability' within a single piece, the very question could not arise), or why simple sixteenth-century music primers allowed the sign of mi only on *F, C, G* and *D*, and the sign of fa only on *B, E, A, D* and *G*. And we cannot dismiss all these phenomena as representing thinking in terms of the monochord and thus being irrelevant to the scale of vocal polyphony; on the contrary, the problems and gamuts mentioned in the preceding sentence are clearly discussed in terms of letters and syllables of the hand or scale of vocal polyphony. All these considerations lead to the conclusion that it would be rash on our part to renounce the idea of 'frequency stability' within a single piece (as opposed to an absolute pitch-standard shared by more than one piece) when thinking about early vocal polyphony.

(v) The common and the unusual steps of *musica ficta*

In the preceding section I have attempted to establish what was the largest possible content of *musica ficta* at various points within the period studied here. It remains now to find out whether all the possible steps of *musica ficta* were considered to be equally useful and usual, or whether it was generally recognized that some of the steps were more common than others.

It appears that in the fourteenth century there was no such generally agreed upon way of limiting the gamut for practical reasons. A musician active in Paris *ca.* 1375 characteristically stated that 'various musicians have set down various numbers of *coniunctae* [that is, irregularly placed hexachords]; for instance, some say there are seven *coniunctae*, others eight, and still others more'.[186] He went on to advocate a gamut with *musica ficta* flats on a, d, e and g and sharps on c and f, that is, a gamut with all the flats of the sixteen-step one, but missing two sharps (on d and g).[187] His choice of steps was, on his own admission, just one of the several current in his time, but, curiously enough, the same choice of steps was made by Adam von Fulda in his *Musica* of 1490. Adam explained his choice saying that 'the soft b may be put in all [the places] in which fa is not put locally; similarly, the hard b may be put in all the letters [places] in which fa is put locally'.[188] In other words, Adam (and perhaps also the late fourteenth-century author) combined the principle which produced the full set of flats (place fa wherever in the hand there is no fa) with another which limited the possible sharps to two only (place mi wherever in the hand there is fa). Justification of the latter principle will become apparent in a moment.

A consensus concerning the practical selection of steps considered to be most useful began slowly to emerge during the fifteenth century. It took the form of a gamut containing twelve rather than the sixteen theoretically possible steps within an octave. The reason for the limitation of the number of steps to twelve only is easy to surmise. Twelve was the largest number of steps possible within an octave if one wanted to avoid the musically useless and troublesome commas in one's practical gamut, or – what amounts to the same thing – if one wanted to avoid split black keys on one's keyboard. The five black-key steps regularly chosen were – in addition to Bb – $C\#$, Eb, $F\#$ and Ab, that is, the normal twelve-step gamut contained three flats and two sharps. An early description of this gamut appears in an anonymous Italian treatise of *ca.* 1400,[189] but it is only in the texts from the second half of the fifteenth century that the gamut begins to appear regularly and that explanations for this particular choice of the five black-key steps can be found.

A mid-fifteenth-century German text of Anonymus XI describes a gamut which, in addition to the steps of *musica vera*, contains Bb, Eb, F#, ab, c#, eb, f#, and aab.[190] The choice of the feigned steps is explained there by the desire to produce whole tones of the natural gamut's semitones and the reverse. Within the a-g octave, the semitone between a and b can be expanded to a whole tone either by ab or by ♮, the semitone between ♮ and c by b or by c#, and that between e and f by eb or f#. Since the resulting feigned steps – ab, c#, eb, f# – (plus b of *musica vera*) also divide all the whole tones into semitones, the twelve-step gamut is sufficient.

Since every semitone of the natural gamut is solmizated mi-fa, it follows that the expansion of the semitones suggested by Anonymus XI involves having fa in every place which in the hand has mi, and mi in every place which in the hand has fa. This was the form which the explanation of the normal twelve-step gamut usually took. It was explained by the desire to have fa wherever in the hand there was mi, and the reverse. The reason for this desire, in turn, is not hard to find. As we shall soon find out, one of the fundamental rules governing the use of *musica ficta* steps was the prohibition of singing mi against fa on a vertical perfect consonance, that is, the prohibition of vertical augmented and diminished fourths, fifths, octaves, and other potentially perfect consonances which, when augmented or diminished, would have to be solmizated with mi against fa. Such intervals were to be brought back to perfection so that they would be solmizated with mi against mi or fa against fa. But, in order to be able always to avoid singing mi against fa, a musician would have to have at his disposal a gamut which contained mi in every place which already included fa and the reverse or, in other words, if mi against fa was to be avoided, it was necessary to be able to feign mi on every step which was fa (that is, to feign mi on *C* and *F*, thus producing *C#* and *F#*) and fa on every step which was mi (that is, to feign fa on *A* and *E*, thus producing *Ab* and *Eb*). In short, the normal twelve-step gamut with black-key *Bb*, *C#*, *Eb*, *F#* and *Ab* was the most economical answer to the requirements of the *mi-contra-fa* prohibition. (I have mentioned above that the gamut of Adam von Fulda combined a full set of flats with only two sharps, the latter resulting from the principle which required mi wherever in the hand there was fa, the justification of which should be clear now.)

The gamut, as well as the usual rationale for it just described, appeared regularly in musical treatises from the last quarter of the fifteenth century through the middle of the sixteenth century. It was advocated, for instance, by Bartolomeo Ramos de Pareia in his *Musica practica* of 1482.[191] Having explained the meaning of the signs of the round b and square b, Ramos continued: 'But singers mark the whole tones or semitones with those signs elsewhere, not only at *paramese* [that is, ♮], for they say [that] wherever fa is found without mi, there mi is to be made, as in b-fa-b-mi [and] the same

49

also where mi [is found] without fa, which many call feigned music.'[192] This principle that every step sung mi (or fa) in *musica vera* should be fa (or mi) in *musica ficta* results, as we have seen, in the twelve-step octave with feigned *Ab, C♯, Eb, F♯*, in addition to the regular *Bb*. (To be exact, Ramos lists the feigned steps without the lowest *Ab* and the highest *eeb*: 'Therefore, according to them [that is, the singers], that soft b will be located in five places, namely, in B, E, a, e and aa . . . but that ♮ or that ♯ in C, F, c, f and cc.')[193] We have observed earlier that Anonymus XI explained the same gamut by the desire to produce whole tones of the natural gamut's semitones and the reverse. There is, of course, no conflict between Anonymus XI's and Ramos's explanations; they are, rather, complementary. Ramos himself follows the above discussion of the feigned steps with the observation that they make a semitone out of every whole tone and the reverse.[194]

Ramos defends his gamut against a certain Johannes de Londonis (whom we can perhaps identify as John Hothby) 'and other less experienced ones'[195] who say that 'just as both signs may be placed in b-fa-b-mi, so also in other places where there is neither fa nor mi',[196] who argue, that is, in favor of the sixteen-step gamut in which the sign of fa appears in every place which is not already fa and the sign of mi in every place which is not already mi. 'It can scarcely be denied,' says Ramos 'that it may be done thus, but I do not think to grant that it should', because 'if the whole tone is divided by the already-named steps into two semitones, the remaining superfluous ones are made to no purpose, since this is allowed . . . so that we may have a whole tone and semitone at any step.'[197] In other words, the sixteen-step gamut is conceivable, but for all practical purposes the twelve-step one will suffice.

Elsewhere Ramos notes that the black key between G and a is made by 'some less discerning of the practitioners'[198] into G♯, which he thinks is a useless step even if *ab* is also present.[199] He also criticizes his friend, Tristanus de Silva, for introducing *Gb*.[200] These remarks indicate that even if Ramos's gamut represents the most common twelve-step selection from the total universe of the conceivable steps, not all musicians wanted to limit themselves to twelve steps and some of those who did may have preferred G♯ to *ab*.

Ramos presents his gamut in the form of a 'composite hand' (*manus composita*) with hexachords on F below Γ, Γ, A, Bb, C, D, Eb, F, G, a, b, c, d, eb, f, g, and aa.[201] The adjective 'composite' implies a combination of the hexachords of the regular hand (on Γ, C, F, G, c, f, g) with those of the hand transposed a whole tone down (on F below Γ, Bb, Eb, F, b, eb, f) and those of the hand transposed a whole tone up (on A, D, G, a, d, g, aa). This interpretation is confirmed by a diagram presenting seven regular hexachords in the center as the 'natural series' (*ordo naturalis*) and the same hexachords placed a whole tone lower on the left and a whole tone higher on the right as the 'accidental series' (*ordines accidentales*).[202] This combination of three hands Ramos calls the 'perfect hand' (*manus perfecta*): 'Therefore, after the addition of the *coniunctae* [that is, irregularly placed hexachords], it is called the "perfect hand", since it is all properly divided by semitones.'[203]

Ramos was not alone in thinking about the normal twelve-step gamut in these terms. Bonaventura da Brescia in his *Brevis collectio artis musicae . . . quae dicitur 'Venturina'*[204] of 1489 deemed the hand of Guido to be imperfect and insufficient for the purposes of singing either plainchant or polyphony and described a 'perfect hand' consisting of three hands, the regular one and its transpositions a whole tone down and up.[205] Bonaventura's use of such terms as *manus perfecta*, *manus composita*, *ordo naturalis* and *ordines accidentales* makes his direct dependence on Ramos more than likely.

The idea of the 'perfect hand' also appeared in the 'Opusculum' with which Franciscus de Brugis prefaced an antiphonary printed in Venice in 1503–4.[206] Franciscus again began with the insufficiency of the 'Guidonian' hand and went on to describe his perfect hand, 'not only for the singers but also for the organists, lutenists and others',[207] consisting of three 'series' (*ordines*), the 'natural' one (*ordo naturalis*), by which he meant a potentially infinite series of white-key steps, the 'soft' one (*ordo mollis*) which transposed the natural one a whole tone down, and the 'hard' one (*ordo durus*) which transposed the natural one a whole tone up.[208] At this point it might appear that the perfect hand of Franciscus differed from that of Ramos and Bonaventura since its natural series lacked ♭ and ♭♭ and, consequently, its soft series would lack a♭ and aa♭, but Franciscus' diagram of the three series made it clear that he wanted his soft series to include also a♭ and aa♭,[209] and he expressly stated that he added a hexachord on E♭ so that the whole tone G-a might be properly divided.[210] Thus, his perfect hand differs from Ramos's only in that it assigns ♭ and ♭♭ not to the natural, but to an accidental series. Its total gamut, however, is identical with that of Ramos and Bonaventura. And also Franciscus' rationale for the gamut is the same as that of his predecessors. Additional steps, such as D♭, are undesirable, since they produce commas in relation to the already-existing steps and a comma cannot be sung.[211] As it is, the hand provides mi wherever in the 'Guidonian' hand there is fa and the reverse, which allows musicians to avoid all mi-against-fa dissonances.[212] Consequently, 'every perfect musical instrument should be so divided'.[213]

The twelve-step gamut described by Ramos represents the most common selection of the black-key steps encountered in treatises of the last quarter of the fifteenth and the first of the sixteenth centuries. Giovanni Spataro, in a passage quoted in the preceding section of this chapter, expressly confirmed that Ramos's gamut was representative for keyboard instruments of his teacher's time.[214] He also criticized Giovanni del Lago for his excessive reliance on 'these verses which he [del Lago] says were assigned by the ancients which demonstrate that one should sign this sign b in the natural A, ♮ and E, and that this ♯ should only be signed in the natural C and F',[215] thus indirectly indicating the normative character of the gamut at least for the musicians of the past. Indeed, in a letter dated on the last day of February, 1520, del Lago described to Giovanni da Legge 'the familiar *coniunctae*, that is, those used in polyphony',[216] as containing our five black-key steps.[217] Similarly, Spataro, in a letter of October 30, 1527 addressed to del Lago, confirmed that the black keys of used instruments are not all flat, but include c♯ and f♯, since 'there are certainly two *coniunctae*, namely, one of the round b which is signed with this sign b in every place where naturally one finds mi, and the other is called the *coniuncta* of the square b which is signed with this sign ♯ in every place where naturally falls fa . . . as my teacher wrote and as is affirmed by every learned man'.[218] Del Lago repeated this formula for the normal twelve-step gamut in very similar words in a letter to Spataro of August 15, 1533.[219]

Not surprisingly, in the first half of the sixteenth century, the twelve-step gamut with black-key Bb, C♯, Eb, F♯ and Ab was described as the normal one and explained by the desire to have fa for every mi and the reverse particularly often, but not exclusively, in simple, introductory textbooks of music. In Spain it was discussed in Domingo Marcos Durán's *Lux bella* which had three editions between 1492 and 1518.[220] In Italy, in addition to its frequent appearance in letters of Spataro and del Lago, it was described by Stephano Vanneo in *Recanetum de musica aurea* of 1533.[221] But the strongest evidence for its continuing popularity is provided by numerous texts of German origin, by, for instance, Sebastian Virdung's description of keyboard in *Musica getutscht* of 1511,[222] Nicolaus Wollick's *Enchiridion musices* of 1512,[223] Andreas Ornithoparchus' *Musice active micrologus* of 1517,[224] Georg Rhau's *Enchiridion utriusque musicae practicae*, which appeared many times between 1517 and 1553 and which states that 'in feigned song fa should be noted chiefly on a and E, and mi on F and c',[225] and Hermann Finck's *Practica musica* of 1556, which states that 'it [feigned song] has two signs, the round b in the hard-b places and the square b in the soft-b places, of which the former designates b-fa, the latter b-mi'.[226]

But if the twelve-step gamut with the black-key Ab, Bb, C♯, Eb, F♯ was the norm in the second half on the fifteenth century and survived in many textbooks through the 1550s, the evidence grows from the second quarter of the sixteenth century on that the standard black-key step between G and a (and their octave equivalents) was now G♯ rather than ab. The competition between ab and G♯ was under way already in the later fifteenth century, since we have heard Ramos arguing against 'some less discerning of the practitioners' who introduced the key of G♯, separately or concurrently with that of ab. Ramos explained that their reason for introducing G♯ was to provide the major sixth going to the octave in the discant moving against the tenor's progression from B to A, that is, to provide the leading tone for cadences on A.[227] Clearly, for at least some of his contemporaries, the desire to have the lower leading tone for A-cadences outweighed the wish to provide for all possible mi-against-fa contingencies.

An uncertainty as to which of the two steps is the more useful one may be read from Arnolt Schlick's *Spiegel der Orgelmacher und Organisten* of 1511.[228] Schlick is not particularly concerned with the question of how to name the black key between G and a (he refers to it, characteristically, as 'fa in a-la-mi-re after sol [that is, ab] or G#',[229] just as he refers to the black key between D and E as 'fa in E-la-mi after re [that is, Eb] or D#, however you call it',[230] but he wants to explain how it should be tuned.[231] He tunes the step so that it is closer to ab than to G#, but he tempers it sufficiently to make it serviceable, if harsh, as a leading tone in A-cadences. He notes, however, that there are people who think otherwise and, instead of making the step accord with c and eb, as he recommends, make it agree better with E and ♮ in order to have an even purer leading tone in cadences on A. But, adds Schlick, 'I have talked a lot about it and asked for instruction the most experienced and best-known speculative and practical musicians, who in our time have had and still have my admiration, and I found that many agreed with me.'[232] Schlick's remarks show, then, that, by his time, even those musicians who, like Schlick himself, wanted ab on their keyboards demanded a serviceable G# as well and that some were ready to sacrifice ab altogether in favor of G#.

And, indeed, descriptions of the twelve-step gamut with G# instead of ab become increasingly common. The gamut appears, for instance, in the popular Spanish text of Gonzalo Martínez de Bizcargui, *Arte de canto llano et de contrapunto et canto de órgano con proporciones et modos*,[233] which enjoyed numerous editions between 1508 and 1550. Martínez specifically notes that ab, which may be necessary when approached from Eb (that is, in order to avoid the tritone), is lacking on the organ, but may be sung.[234] It follows that even though he is aware of the usefulness of both ab and G#, he would recommend to an instrument builder eager to avoid a split key to choose G# as the more necessary of the two. Another Spaniard, Juan Bermudo, explained in his *El arte Tripharia* of 1550[235] that the five black keys within each octave of the commonly used monochord result from the rule providing a fa for every mi and the reverse, except for the black key between G and a, which is G# instead of ab,[236] but he noted that what is true for the organ does not have to be the case for the voice or for another instrument.[237] In Italy, the twelve-step monochord with G# was described by, for instance, Pietro Aaron in *Toscanello in musica* (Bk II, Ch. 40), which appeared in several editions between 1523 and 1562.[238] In his *Lucidario in musica* of 1545,[239] Aaron noted that while it would be useful to have an organ with each whole tone divided into two minor semitones separated by a comma, the actually existing organs had only b, c#, eb, f#, g# and lacked, for instance, ab or d#,[240] and he added that those who considered the lack of ab

53

to be of little importance since it could be substituted by G♯ erred, because even such a small difference of the comma would introduce a discord if the step were to be used simultaneously with c.[241] Other Italian writers of the period who described the twelve-step keyboard with G♯ as the norm include Giovanni Maria Lanfranco (*Scintille di musica* of 1533)[242] and Gioseffo Zarlino (*Le Istitutioni harmoniche* of 1558).[243] It should be added here that surviving practical evidence suggests that in keyboard music G♯ was preferred over A♭ already in the late fourteenth century: the pieces preserved in the Robertsbridge fragment require a number of g♯s and those in the Faenza Codex a number of G♯s and g♯s, while neither repertoire calls for A♭s.[244]

The foregoing discussion established that if a musician made a choice of the normally used steps from the total pool of the conceivable ones, in the fifteenth and sixteenth centuries he was most likely to limit his gamut to only twelve steps within an octave and thus to avoid commas and split keys. His choice would be dictated by the desire to provide fa for every mi and the reverse, and thus to be able to avoid all mi-against-fa dissonances, but already in the late fifteenth century there were those who were ready to sacrifice a♭ in favor of G♯ and thus to obtain the leading tone for cadences on A, and their number increased during the next century to the extent that by its second quarter at the latest G♯ and not a♭ represented the norm. With these facts in mind, it is not difficult to guess what happened when a musician decided to allow some commas and split keys after all. Since both a♭ and G♯ answered clear musical needs, they would have been a likely choice for a split key. Since G♯ was added to the normal twelve-step gamut as a leading tone, one might want to add the other missing black-key leading tones as well, that is, d♯ and a♯. The latter being, as we have seen, something of a rarity and a late-comer to the gamut, however, the former would clearly have the priority.

Indeed, what we know about keyboard instruments of the sixteenth century, or at least about Italian harpsichords of the period, fully supports this picture. They had, at most, three split black keys in an octave, for a♭/G♯, e♭/d♯ and b/a♯, and only very few experimental keyboard instruments went beyond this.[245]

A similar picture emerges from theoretical literature as well. In *De harmonia musicorum instrumentorum* written in 1500, Gaffurius described a 'mixed genus' (*permixtum genus*) which divided the diatonic whole tones with a♭, b, c♯, d♯, e♭, f♯, g♯,[246] that is, a choice of steps which suggests the 'normal' twelve-step gamut plus d♯ and g♯. Aaron, in *Toscanello in musica*, described the twelve-step keyboard with G♯,[247] but observed that, in order to have also d♯, the black key of e♭ had to be split, and added that organists 'more often wish to have the minor third from C-fa-ut than the major third from b-mi, because the latter is seldom used'.[248] His Bolognese correspondent, Spataro, stated in an undated letter addressed to Aaron that d♯ was found on very few monochords, but might be played on a lute or sung.[249] It is not an accident that, as we have seen, in *Lucidario in musica* Aaron singled out ab and d♯ as the steps lacking on contemporary organs. The most specific information on our subject was provided in Aaron's last treatise, the *Compendiolo* published after 1545.[250] He confirmed there that the black key between G and a was G♯, but ab could be obtained by adding another key, and, similarly, the black key between D and E was Eb, but if one wanted to have a major third above B, one had to add another key distant from Eb by a comma, 'as one sees in some instruments in Italy'.[251]

We have seen that the enriched fourteen-step gamut added to the normal twelve-step one the two missing leading tones and I have explained why the addition of one more leading tone, a♯, was less urgent and, consequently, why the keyboards described by sixteenth-century theorists did not normally go beyond two split keys. I know of just one theoretical document the gamut of which, if realized on a keyboard instrument, would require the third split key, b/a♯. The anonymous Italian *Tertius liber musicae* copied in 1464[252] offers the normal twelve-step gamut plus g♯, d♯ and a♯ diagrammatically represented as equivalent to aab, eb, and b. If applied to a keyboard instrument, the gamut would produce three split black keys (aab/g♯, eb/d♯, and b/a♯), but the form of the diagram seems to imply that aab, eb and b represent the norm while g♯, d♯ and a♯ are exceptional, being – together with G♯ – 'extracted from the false', that is, feigned steps of the second rank. Let me repeat, however, that the gamut of *Tertius liber musicae* remains an isolated curiosity in our period.

In sum, in the preceding section of this chapter we established that from the early fifteenth through the mid-sixteenth century the largest possible gamut of practical, as opposed to theoretical, music contained seventeen steps within an octave (in keyboard terms, seven white-key and ten black-key steps, or seven white and five split black keys). In the present section we have learned that during the fifteenth and early sixteenth centuries a musician who wanted to limit the realm of 'black-key' steps would most likely want to avoid commas or split black keys and would consequently choose the five 'black-key' steps which were required by the mi-against-fa prohibition (*Ab, Bb, C♯, Eb, F♯*), with *Ab* being from the late fifteenth century on gradually supplanted by one of the missing cadential leading tones, *G♯*, so that by the second quarter of the sixteenth century the latter and not the former represented the norm. If some split black keys were to be tolerated, they would involve the other two missing leading tones, that is, they would be – in addition to *Ab/G♯* – *Eb/D♯* and *Bb/A♯*, in decreasing order of frequency of use.

Part II
The functions and uses of *musica ficta*

3 Signatures

We know already that the 'less principal clefs', the signs of the round b and square b, may be placed not only internally in the course of a melodic line, but also at the beginning of the staff, in which case they are valid for the whole length of the staff. In order to avoid the historically justified but clumsy expression 'less principal clefs placed at the beginning of the staff', I will call such signs here either by the neutral appellation 'accidental signatures' or by their modern name, 'key signatures', since – as will become apparent in a moment – the latter name is in most cases appropriate also for the period discussed in this book. The question to be discussed in the present chapter is what the function of accidental signatures was.

The answer to this question is simple, predictable, and supported by massive evidence from the beginning to the end of our period: one used an accidental signature when one wanted to transpose a melody to a different location from the one it would have if notated without the signature and to retain all of its intervals unchanged, that is, to retain its mode. This is why one is justified in calling it a 'key signature'.

Marchetto da Padova, in his *Lucidarium in arte musicae planae* (1317-18), shows examples of the same first-mode melody untransposed, that is, without any accidental signature, and transposed a fourth up, that is, with a ♭-signature, and comments on the examples as follows: 'A mode so transposed will be called "proper with regard to composition", since it is formed of its proper melodic species, but "improper with regard to location", since it is located on a pitch other than its proper one.'[1]

Johannes Tinctoris, in *Liber de natura et proprietate tonorum* (1476), presents the standard teaching concerning the four finals (D, E, F, G) and explains that these are called 'regular' (*regulares*) finals.[2] 'However,' he writes, 'these tones can finish in all places by other rules, coming about through true or *ficta* music, either within or without the hand, and then they have been called irregular.'[3] Having explained the difference between the regular and irregular finals, Tinctoris discusses in detail and with many examples the irregular finals of each mode.[4] He shows that modes 1–4 and 7–8 may be transposed a fourth up with ♭ and optional ♭♭ in the signature, a whole tone down with ♭, E♭, and optional B♭ and e♭ in the signature, and a major ninth down with B♭, E♭ below Γ, and optional B♭ below Γ and E♭ in the signature (the optional accidentals appearing in the signature only when the corresponding step is in fact used in the melody).[5] The examples of modes 5-6 behave somewhat differently for the obvious reason that the regular (that is, untransposed) melodies in these modes may be notated without any accidental signature, or with a ♭-signature if the integrity of melody or counterpoint requires it, as Tinctoris explains earlier in the treatise.[6] As a result, he now shows how to transpose these modes a fourth up using ♭ and optional ♭♭ in the signature (as well as an internal e♭ if necessary), a fourth down with no accidental signature, and an octave down also with no accidental signature (but with an internal B♭ if necessary). The first of these transpositions is, of course, identical with the one presented for the other modes and takes as its point of departure untransposed versions of modes 5-6 notated without accidental signatures (but with an internal ♭ used when necessary). The other two transpositions are new. The one a fourth down takes as its point of departure regular modes 5-6 notated with a ♭-signature, and the one an octave down regular modes 5-6 notated without an accidental signature (but with an internal B♭ used when necessary). Tinctoris also makes clear that transpositions to many other places are possible, provided the intervallic species of the regular modes remain intact: 'Therefore, many other irregular places are within the hand and without, in which our eight tones can finish because of the agreement which they have to the regular ones.'[7]

Also in the sixteenth century the function of accidental signatures was clearly to make modal transpositions possible.[8] In comparison with Tinctoris, however, most sixteenth-century theorists are unequivocal concerning the regular (untransposed) modes 5 and 6 with the final on F and state that, unlike the other regular modes, these two are notated with ♭ in the signature. Andreas Ornithoparchus' 'Rules of Solfaing' (that is, solmizating; 'De Solfizatione regule') in his *Musice active micrologus* of 1517 include the following:

The First, He that will *Solfa* any Song, must above all things have an eye to the *Tone*. For the knowledge of the *Tone* is the invention of the Scale, under which it runnes.

The Second, All the *Tones* runne under the Scale of ♮ *Dure*, excepting the fift and the sixt.

The Third, To have a Song runne under ♮ *Dure*, is nothing else, but to sing *Mi* in *b fa* ♮ *mi*, and *fa* in a *flat* Scale. . . .

The Fift, Every *Solfaer* must needs looke, whether the Song be regular, or no; for the transposition of a Song is oft times an occasion of changing the Scale.

The Sixt, Every Song ending in the *Finals* [that is, on D, E, F or G], is regular, and not transposed.'[9]

In other words, the choice of the 'scale', whether the one of the square b (that is, without an accidental signature) or the one of the round b (that is, with ♭-signature), depends on the mode of the song, modes 1-4 and 7-8 using the former, modes 5-6 the latter scale, unless they are transposed, since a transposition most often involves the changing of the scale, that is, of the signature. This appears to be the common sixteenth-century position on the scale used by modes 5 and 6,[10] but there are some dissenting voices as well. Johannes Aventinus, in a section of his *Musicae rudimenta* of 1516 which has the telling heading 'Against Some Common Errors' ('Contra errores vulgi'), says:

No mode, in its simple form, has b flat, because no figure of the octave (since they are the proper system of the modes) has it. However, it happens to every mode that, with an addition – so to speak – it may have b flat. It especially happens to the sixth.[11]

Pietro Aaron, in his *Trattato della natura et cognitione di tutti gli tuoni di canto figurato* of 1525, attests that almost all pieces in modes 5 and 6 are notated with a ♭-signature since the integrity of melodies in these modes often requires the use of ♭, even though the proper forms of these modes are thereby distorted.[12] Thus, in their various ways, theorists reflect the tension between the theoretical tradition according to which the intervallic species proper to the untransposed modes 5 and 6 use the square b and the practical reality in which most pieces in these modes are notated with a ♭-signature.

It should be mentioned that the accidental signatures normally discussed by theorists of our period are the ones involving the use of the round b. A signature with a square b seems to be inconceivable to a great majority of our theorists. Glarean, in his *Dodecachordon* of 1547, writes:

From this some writers have transmitted the general rule, that every song can have, on the fifth above the final key, a *confinalis*, which they call *finalis*. But certainly this is not true in any mode, for everywhere the fourth opposes it. However, here is a genuine rule, and one more to be depended upon: A song in any mode can be concluded on each fourth key above the final, because of the fourth, if indeed *fa* is on the *b* key.[13]

Clearly, the idea that one could transpose a mode exactly also a fifth up by using a f♯-signature does not occur even to this particularly systematic mind.

We can only speculate why this is so; since a signature with a square b is inconceivable to so many of our authors, it is unlikely that we shall find them explaining why it did not occur to them that one could use it. We know that an accidental signature was used when one wanted to transpose a mode, that is, to transpose a diatonic octave-species. If only one accidental was to appear in the signature, this had to be either *B*♭ or *F*♯; accidentals placed elsewhere would only destroy the diatonic series. (And, similarly, if the signature was to contain two accidentals, the second round b would have to be placed at *E* and the second square b at *C*, etc.) Now, a possible explanation of why the ♭-signature was commonly used and the f♯-signature was not may be that, as we have learned above, in notation, in the places in which both mi and fa could be found, mi was assumed unless fa was implied or expressly indicated. Another possible explanation could be that the step

♭ was already available within the hand, while with f♯ one moved into the realm of *musica ficta*. Yet another possible explanation may lie in musicians' tendency (to be explored in Chapter 6 below) to use sharps mostly to inflect cadential leading tones and often to neglect even to think of such sharpened leading tones as mi-steps. The reluctance to think of a leading-tone f♯ as f-mi might explain the reluctance to use the f♯-signature; a signature accidental transposes a mode only because it affects the hexachordal system. These circumstances may account for the fact that flat signatures were the first to be regularly used. They offered, however, no real resistance to the use of the square b in the signature once transpositions began to be explored in a more systematic fashion by musicians.

In fact, by the middle of the sixteenth century some theorists became aware that sharpened steps might be involved in modal transpositions just as well as the flattened ones. Juan Bermudo, in *El arte Tripharia* of 1550, explains that any mode may be transposed a whole tone up with the use of F♯ and C♯, a fourth up or a fifth down with B♭, a fifth up or a fourth down with F♯, a whole tone down with B♭ and E♭, and a minor third down with F♯, C♯, and G♯.[14] Since Bermudo's organ contains two flats (B♭ and E♭) and three sharps (F♯, C♯, G♯),[15] it is easy to see that his list includes all the transpositions possible on it. An example of a three-part composition with signs of the square b in the signature is offered by Heinrich Faber in his *Ad musicam practicam introductio* of 1550.[16] In *Le Istitutioni harmoniche* of 1558, Gioseffo Zarlino devotes a chapter to the subject of the 'transposition of the modes' (Bk IV, Ch. 17: 'Della Trasportatione delli Modi') and presents there examples of a melody in mode 1 transposed a whole tone down and notated with ♭, B♭ and E♭ in the signature and the same melody transposed a whole tone up and notated with f♯, F♯ and c♯ in the signature.[17] Earlier in the same work, Zarlino talks about compositions transposed by signature accidentals a whole tone down and up and offers two polyphonic examples of the former type, but – significantly – none of the latter.[18]

While an accidental placed at the beginning of the staff transposes the mode, an internal accidental does not. This is a lesson we can draw from the well-known musical dispute which took place in Rome between 1538 and 1544 and was described during the 1550s by Ghiselin Danckerts.[19] During a rehearsal of a work which, according to the composer and many others, was in the second mode and was not transposed, a bass added a flat in the place of B as the signature in his part, while a tenor argued that those B's in the bass part which were to be flattened should be marked by internal accidentals, the part as a whole remaining without an accidental signature, since B♭ was not sung ordinarily in this part but merely accidentally. The judges, distinguished singers of the Papal chapel, ruled in favor of the tenor and Danckerts concurred, explaining that in an untransposed composition in the second mode there can be no flat in the signature, since this would destroy the species of the fourth which is proper to this mode and that flat at B can be introduced only accidentally (that is, internally) wherever required.

But what the dispute shows in addition is that as late as *ca.* 1540 some musicians (our bass) could be most casual and pragmatic about signature accidentals and write them into their parts without considering the conflict with signatures of other voices and without considering the modal implications of their additions. This suggests that, at least in some cases of 'conflicting' signatures, the accidental signature of a voice other than the fundamental voice of the polyphonic complex, that is, usually the tenor, might have had a function different from the normal one of indicating a modal transposition. The discussion of the function of such 'conflicting' signatures, however, has to be postponed until the end of this chapter.

Now that we know what the function of accidental signatures was, we may ask why would anyone want to transpose a mode? A few consistent answers are given by some sixteenth-century theorists. Glarean in *Isagoge in musicen* of 1516 points out that the transposition of modes 1 and 2 a fourth up frequently practiced by polyphonic composers helps them to keep the lowest part, which frequently sounds the octave with the tenor, within the gamut of the hand,[20] and he repeats the same information and explanation in *Dodecachordon*.[21] Another reason for transposing, practiced in particular by singers of chant, implies Glarean, is the wish to avoid steps of *musica ficta*.[22] Ornithoparchus brings out similar reasons,[23] and so does Lanfranco: 'Transposition in plainsong is not made, however, unless to avoid false [feigned] notes; in figured [polyphonic] music, in order to have more space for consonance or by will of the composer.'[24] Another reason for transpositions is mentioned by Zarlino: an organist and other instrumentalists accompanying a choir may have to transpose in order to allow the singers to sing at a comfortable pitch.[25] In short, polyphony is transposed by composers in order that the total range of the composition may be comfortably accommodated in notation (that is, within the range of *musica vera*) and by performers (instrumentalists accompanying singers) so that the ranges of the parts may be comfortably sung.

An accidental signature makes a modal transposition possible because it changes the placement of semitones in the diatonic series, that is, it transposes the series. But what exactly does it transpose, the diatonic series (the series in which semitones are separated alternately by two and by three consecutive whole tones), or the hand (the system of seven hexachords)?

Since notation without an accidental signature implies not the hand, but merely the diatonic series (if there is no sign at the place of b-fa-b-mi, the hard b is meant there), it might follow that a signature transposes the diatonic series and not the hand. This conclusion is, indeed, corroborated by sixteenth-century theory. Theorists' terminology may on occasion obscure this fact. Many sixteenth-century theorists refer to the notation without a signature as representing the 'hard hand' (*manus dura*), the notation with ♭-signature as representing the 'soft hand' (*manus mollis*), and the notation with more than one flat in the signature as representing the 'feigned hand' (*manus ficta*). Others use the term 'song' (*cantus*) or 'scale' (*scala*) instead of 'hand' in such contexts. But all these terms, 'hand', 'song' and 'scale', refer here to a system of interlocking hexachords starting alternately a fifth and a fourth one above the other and not to the system of interlocking hexachords which we call the 'Guidonian' hand. We may take Ornithoparchus' explanations to be representative:

Therefore the industrious Musicians have devised Two Scales, in which every Song doth runne, and is governed: and hath ordayned, that the first should be called ♮ durall of the ♮; the second, *b moll* of *b Flat* . . . Therefore generally a Scale is nothing else, but the knowledge of *mi* and *fa*, in *b fa* ♮ *mi*, and in his Eights . . . The Scale ♮ Durall is a Progression of Musicall Voyces, rising from *A* to ♮ sharpely, that is, by the *Voyce Mi* . . . But the Scale *b moll* is a Progression of Musicall *Voyces*, rising from *A* to *b flatly*, that is by the Voyce *fa*.[26]

There follows a diagram in which the hard-b scale is shown to consist of hexachords on Γ, C, G, c, g (that is, all the hexachords of the hand except those on F and f) and to involve no 'less principal clefs', and the soft-b scale to consist of hexachords on F below Γ, C, F, c, f (that is, the hexachords of the hand minus those on Γ, G, g and plus the one on F below Γ') and to involve the 'less principal clef' of the round b placed at B, b and bb.[27] A little below follows the description and diagram of the third, 'feigned' scale.[28] This one consists of hexachords on E♭ below Γ, B♭, E♭, b, e♭ and b♭ and requires the 'less principal clef' of the round b at A, E, a, e, aa and ee. (There is no ♭ at E below Γ or at B, b and bb.)

This is the standard sixteenth-century doctrine. Some theorists prefer the term 'hand' or 'song' to 'scale',[29] some may present a 'feigned scale' with just B♭ and E♭ at the signature instead of Ornithoparchus' B♭, E♭, and A♭,[30] but the central point remains: in the minds of these theorists, an accidental signature does not transpose the 'Guidonian' hand, but merely the diatonic scale conceived in terms of interlocking hexachords alternately a fifth and fourth apart. This conclusion is in accord with the process we have observed in the preceding chapter, the erosion of the primacy of the hand toward the end of our period. Until *ca.* 1500, however, an accidental signature very likely transposed the hand; this is suggested by the transposed hands discussed in Chapter 2(v) above.

But regardless of whether a key signature transposes the diatonic scale (the system of interlocking hexachords alternately a fifth and fourth apart) or the 'Guidonian' hand (the system of seven hexachords), the question remains whether the steps of the transposed system were thought to belong to 'true' or to 'feigned' music. The question is of considerable practical importance, as will be seen in the following two chapters. For the sixteenth century, the very terminology gives a clear answer to our question: a signature of more than one flat produces 'feigned scale'. But if we assume that at some point before 1500 a key signature transposed the 'Guidonian' hand, the question arises whether such a transposed hand was considered to be *musica vera* or *ficta*. What is at stake in particular is the status of *E♭* when there is *B♭* in the signature, the status of *A♭* when there are *B♭* and *E♭* in the signature, etc. If a transposed hand represented *musica vera*, these steps would have to be considered to be 'true' by analogy to ♭ and ♭♭ in the untransposed hand.

The assumption that a transposed system represents *musica vera* and that, consequently, *E♭* under a *B♭*-signature, for instance, is a 'true' step was made by Carl Dahlhaus in 1968 and, independently, an elaborate hypothesis of considerable practical importance was erected on this largely unexamined assumption by Margaret Bent and Andrew Hughes in 1972.[31] The assumption, however, is incorrect. Musicians of our period thought of a system transposed by means of a signature as representing *musica ficta*, not *vera*. '*Recta* transposition,' claims Bent 'is supported by Ugolino's discussion of a "double hand where all the solmisation name[s] of *musica recta* and *musica ficta* are set out" and "another hand of *musica ficta* and *musica recta* starting a fifth below Γ, on C, equivalent to the first hand except for its low pitch".'[32] Ugolino's discussion, however, proves an exactly opposite point. The theorist simply shows all the hexachords contained in each 'double hand' (*duplex manus*). The first 'double hand' consists of hexachords with uts in the places of F below Γ, Γ, B, C, D, E, F, G, b, c, d, e, f and g. The second 'hand' consists of hexachords starting in the places of C below Γ, D below Γ, F below Γ, Γ, B, C, D, F, G, b, c, d, f and g. One may most plausibly interpret the first of these 'double hands' as combining the regular system of seven hexachords with the same system transposed a whole tone down (that is, with hexachords beginning on F below Γ, B♭, E♭, F, ♭, e♭, f) and adding hexachords on D and d. The other 'double hand' may be seen to combine the regular system of seven hexachords with the same system transposed a perfect fifth down (that is, with hexachords beginning on C below Γ, F below Γ, B♭, C, F, ♭ and c) and add hexachords on D, d and D below Γ.[33] The theorist's words make it perfectly clear that he would consider a transposed hand to represent *musica ficta*, not *vera*, since he talks of his 'double hands' as combining steps of *musica recta* and *ficta*:

Therefore, we devise a double hand where are placed in order all the syllables of *musica recta* and *ficta* . . . We devise another hand of *musica ficta* and *recta*, a fifth lower than Γ and beginning on C, equal to the first except for being lower.[34]

Similarly, when the author of the late fourteenth-century Berkeley treatise describes a gamut combining the regular system of hexachords with the same system transposed a whole tone down and up, he calls the transposed hexachords *coniunctae* and makes it clear that these are considered *musica ficta*.[35] Additional evidence showing that fifteenth-century musicians did not differ from sixteenth-century ones in thinking of a system transposed by a key signature to represent *musica ficta* rather than *vera* is provided by Tinctoris, who refers to an example notated with a signature of two flats as 'feigned music'.[36] Elsewhere, the theorist calls Γ notated with a signature flat at B as 'feigned re on Γ ut'.[37] If music notated with a key signature remained 'true', Tinctoris would not have called this step 'feigned'. In short, there is no reason to believe that *E♭* under a one-flat signature, or *A♭* under a two-flat signature, were ever considered to belong to *musica recta*.

Our discussion has thus far disregarded the question of 'conflicting' or 'partial' signatures, an issue which has been given much attention in musicological literature:[38] why did musicians of our period often notate different voices of their compositions with different accidental signatures? In his 1953 study of 'Partial Signatures and Musica Ficta in Some Early 15th-Century Sources', Richard H. Hoppin discovered a remarkable degree of correlation between key signatures differing by one flat and voice ranges differing by a fifth and proposed as a 'reason for the widespread use of partial signatures' the contention 'that partial signatures are an indication of pitch levels lying a fifth apart, which in turn imply the use of two modes simultaneously or of the same mode in a transposed and untransposed position'.[39] Hoppin's discovery is most valuable, but it can in no way be taken for an explanation of the phenomenon. Once we have established the correlation between key signatures and voice ranges, we still have to explain *why* different signatures were used. To say that the use of different signatures implies the use of different modes or different transpositions of the same mode may well be correct, but again it explains nothing, since we still do not know *why* it was desirable to use different modes or transpositions in such cases.

A plausible hypothesis concerning this question will emerge, I believe, when we reflect on what we know about the usual functions of internal accidental inflections (functions to be discussed in Chapters 4–7 below) and suggest that differences between signatures might have been designed to fulfil some of these very functions. It would, then, follow that the functions fulfilled by differences between signatures were the ones involving more than one voice. In the notation of the period, the parts were written separately (either in separate areas of an opening in a choirbook or even in separate partbooks) rather than vertically aligned in score and, consequently, the accidentals which musicians were most likely to miss were the ones needed because of vertical relations arising between different voices. Thus, one less flat in the signature of an upper voice, or one more flat in the signature of a lower voice, would indicate that the fear of a vertical imperfect octave was less in this case than the fear of a vertical imperfect fifth. Hoppin's discovery of the frequent correlation of differences between signatures and part ranges can be easily explained in the light of this hypothesis, since vertical imperfect fifths are most likely to occur between parts the ranges of which are a fifth apart. In his last article on the subject, Hoppin made a passing remark which came very close to my view of the matter: 'Perhaps the relationship between conflicting signatures and part-ranges a fifth apart was adopted because . . . it made diminished fifths impossible.'[40] Incidentally, it should be noted that once we see the function of 'conflicting' signatures in fulfilling *conventional* uses of accidental inflections, our explanation cannot be falsified by an occasional piece in which 'conflicting' signatures are used even though there is no need for them, since the explanation has to do more with what a musician of the period might have expected in general than with what was in fact there in a given piece.

Similarly to the explanation offered here, it might also be claimed that the lack of flats in the signature of an upper voice or voices facilitated the use of leading tones at some cadences. This last contention was, indeed, the centerpiece of Edward E. Lowinsky's explanation of 'The Function of Conflicting Signatures in Early Polyphonic Music' in his 1945 study of the matter: 'The main reason for the use of different signatures in different voices of a single work turned out to be a very simple and practical one: the types of cadence or, rather, the harmonic progressions of which the cadences are the most pronounced exponents.'[41] The hypothesis is plausible and can well coexist with the one presented here. I am inclined to think, however, that the prohibition of vertical imperfect fifths was a much more common reason for 'conflicting' signatures than the wish to facilitate proper treatment of cadences. For one thing, Hoppin refuted the centerpiece of Lowinsky's explanation effectively when he pointed out that new signature-combinations supposedly caused by the change in cadential formulas in fact antedated this change and that, consequently, the old cadences could explain neither the old nor the new signature-combinations, 'since it is just those old cadences that still dominate the harmonic structure of the pieces using the new signatures'.[42] Second, it should be pointed out that the need for cadential inflections was more easily discovered from the perusal of a single voice than the need to correct a vertical discord, since a cadence involved characteristic melodic–rhythmic formulas. Finally and most importantly, as we shall see presently, the only theoretical discussions relevant to the problem of 'conflicting' signatures which I have been able to find suggest that the function of such signatures was to assist in avoiding mi-against-fa discords and do not mention cadences at all.

John Hothby, in *Spetie tenore del contrapunto prima*, gives an example of a tenor with two counterpoints designed to show how one can avoid mi

66

against fa by adding or withholding the sign of the round b (see Example 1).[43] It is clear that, given the tenor, the flats, including the signature flat, are needed in the lower counterpoint, but not in the upper one. Hothby comments:

In the second counterpoint, one should put no soft b, since there occurs no fifth or octave or either mi against fa or fa against mi. But in the first low counterpoint, the soft b is placed several times to regulate such counterpoint, so that one does not hear either fa against mi or mi against fa.[44]

Example 1

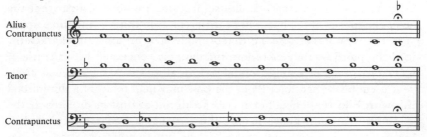

It does not occur to the theorist that the signatures of all parts have to be consistent with the signature of the tenor. He treats the signatures of the parts other than the tenor just as pragmatically as one would treat any other accidental, adding them when they are necessary to avoid mi against fa, omitting them otherwise.

A well-known passage dealing with 'conflicting' signatures occurs in Aaron's invaluable 'Supplement' to *Toscanello*:

The carelessness of other composers should be objected to when they inconsiderately use the signature of *b molle* in one part only of their song, especially in the low part. I say that such a practice is denied and not allowed, nor to be considered by a true musician. When they wish to hold to this ill-conceived notion, they believe themselves excused precisely by the progressions which happen frequently from the note b-mi grave, which makes an imperfect fifth with the tenor. This consideration is pointless and vain, since two difficulties result from it. The first is that every species becomes changed and varied from its natural order, such as from Γ-ut to D-sol-re. What is shown as a ditone becomes a minor third or semiditone, so that proceeding also from D-sol-re to b-mi and from b-mi to Γ-ut, the syllables become re la, la fa, and fa re, when they were first ut sol, sol mi, and mi ut. These species are contrary to all those which appear in the soprano, tenor, and contralto. They do this especially in songs in the seventh and eighth tone. The second difficulty is that the octaves and fifteenth will not sound justly together, so that you must first take care to correct this with similar processes and species. If you wish then to keep your intention described above for the said b-mi, show the ♭ in all the other parts, and every progression and consonance will be without error; they will sound concordant and sonorous together, whereas they were dissonant before.[45]

Aaron's criticism of the practice of combining various signatures in one work is easy to comprehend: he represents the generation of musicians which was early enough to be still familiar with the practice, but sufficiently advanced along the path to 'simultaneous' composition to find the practice obsolete. For us, particularly significant are the reasons which, he claims, motivated those who did use 'conflicting' signatures. They used the signature of the round b in the bass in order to avoid frequent diminished fifths between B in the bass and F in the tenor. This, again, is fully consistent with my hypothesis: one more flat is used in the signature of the bass than in that of the tenor in order to avoid diminished fifths between the two voices. Aaron's arguments against the practice are also significant. He objects, first, that the intervallic species of the bass will be different from those of the three upper parts, that is, will represent a different mode. The argument is characteristic of the post-Josquin generation, increasingly concerned with the use of intervallic species of a single modal pair in all parts. Aaron's second argument is eminently sensible: B♭ in the bass may help to avoid a diminished fifth with F in the tenor, but it will create mi-against-fa discords at the octave and fifteenth above if only the bass has a ♭-signature. Together, Aaron's arguments show not only what the function of 'conflicting' signatures was, but also the likely reasons for the eventual abandonment of the practice. The practice made some sense (provided one had reasons to be more concerned with vertical non-harmonic fifths than with vertical non-harmonic octaves) in the earlier age of 'successive' composition, of complete, functionally differentiated parts successively added to the voice (usually the tenor) which defined the mode of the whole. It was unsuited to the new age of 'simultaneous' composition which minimized the functional differentiation of individual parts and, consequently, encouraged musicians to think about the mode of the whole in terms not of a single part, but of the species used in all parts.

Aaron mentioned 'conflicting' signatures also in his *Trattato della natura et cognitione di tutti gli tuoni di canto figurato*:

> Some other [compositions] appear with the sign mentioned above [that is, ♭] in the bass, and some others in the tenor. I say that such order is neither allowed nor convenient in a composition or song, except when it is considered and applied with artifice, as the excellent Josquin has observed in the 'Patrem' of the Mass *De Virgine Maria*, and similarly the divine Alexander in many of his songs.[46]

Once again, the theorist disapproved of 'conflicting' signatures, except in such special circumstances as a canon at the fifth below in which the lower voice had to use one more flat in the signature than the upper one if the intervals of the 'guide' were to be preserved exactly. Indeed, the 'Credo' of Josquin's *Missa de Beata Virgine* offers an example of just such a canon with an implied ♭-signature in the derived lower voice.[47]

In short, it is likely that the main function of 'conflicting' signatures was to provide an automatic insurance against vertical imperfect fifths, and it is possible that they also served to provide automatically leading tones in upper parts at some cadences. It is easy to reconcile this with what we learned earlier, namely, that the function of a key signature was to produce a modal transposition, once we recall that the period in which 'conflicting' signatures flourished was the period of 'successive' composition in which individual parts fulfilled different functions, so that it was sufficient for one part to be the mode-defining voice. From Tinctoris through the end of the sixteenth century, most theorists considered the tenor to be the principal modal voice, the part defining the modality of a polyphonic whole, but it is possible that in some genres, styles or textures another voice (for instance, the cantus in a fifteenth-century chanson) could have this role.[48] This suggests that we should think of 'conflicting' signatures as being signatures of voices other than the mode-defining one, and the term will be used here in this sense from now on. In a piece with different signatures in different voices, the function of the signature in the mode-defining part was to effect a transposition of the mode, while differing signatures in other parts should be considered to 'conflict' with that of the mode-defining one mainly in order to ensure perfect fifths against it.

4 Horizontal relations

(i) The prohibition of the tritone and diminished fifth

'Concerning musica ficta, these rules must be noted, the first of which is this: that musica ficta is never to be applied [placed] except where necessary, because in art nothing – least of all a feigning – is to be applied without necessity.'[1] Prosdocimus de Beldemandis's first rule of *musica ficta* indicates that one does not introduce feigned steps at a whim but only when it is necessary to do so. This view is echoed by other fifteenth-century writers. Ugolino of Orvieto, for instance, states that 'we do not use feigned music unless through a thoroughly compelling necessity'.[2] Thus, we may legitimately ask which musical contexts necessitated the use of feigned steps. In this chapter, I will consider melodic progressions of this sort.

The most numerous references to a melodic progression which may require a correction by means of a feigned step concern the tritone. The injunction against the melodic tritone is voiced by practically every theorist from the beginning to the end of our period. Jacques de Liège, writing *ca.* 1321-5, informs us that

ancient musicians, considering that the diezeugmenon tetrachord [that is, ♮-c-d-e], in its disjunction from mese [that is, a], presents songs with many stumbling-blocks because of the dissonance of tritone between ♮ and F, added to other tetrachords the synemmenon tetrachord [that is, a-♭-c-d], that is, the song through the soft b, so that the authentic and plagal tritus, that is, the fifth and sixth modes, may proceed through the [perfect] fourth above its proper final step which is F.[3]

In other words, already the practitioners of *ars antiqua* were bothered by the tritone which in the untransposed diatonic system arises between F and ♮ and used ♭ to avoid it. Moreover, according to the same author, the soft b may be used in modes 5 and 6 throughout (that is, presumably, as the signature) and in modes 1 and 2 occasionally; it is very rare in the other four modes and should be employed particularly cautiously in modes 7 and 8 since it changes them into modes 1 and 2.[4] Jacques' remarks suggest that, while the tritone is to be avoided, the modal context of such a tritone has to be taken into account. A tritone with the final seems to be most offensive. On the other hand, it also seems that a correction of the tritone which affects a structurally important step creating either a non-harmonic relation with the final (♭ against E in the deuterus) or transposition (tetrardus becoming the transposed protus) is not desirable. Hence the frequency of ♭ in various modes: it is normal in tritus, occasionally used in protus, very rare in deuterus, and especially rare in tetrardus.

A similar, but more detailed, picture emerges from the anonymous *Quatuor principalia musicae* of 1351 which Coussemaker attributes to Simon Tunstede.[5] The text allows us to see more clearly what is involved in the concept of the 'tritone':

> Therefore, according to those experienced in this skill, when someone has begun to lead the melody in low letters through the natural property [that is, within the range C-G] and makes a mutation on G or on a, if he had ascended to c or d or e before descending to F, he should sing through the square b. And this rule has to be understood in all modes, both in low and in high letters . . . Furthermore, if the mutation is made in the aforementioned place and after the mutation one descends to F before ascending to c or d or e, it is necessary to sing the soft b in b . . . Excepted are the deuterus, tetrardus, and their plagal forms, in which the soft b will not enter. And what has been said of the low letters, should be understood also of the high and highest ones.[6]

Two facts concerning the tritone emerge from the above text. First, the tritone offends not only when it is direct, but also when it is indirect, filled in by all or some of the intervening steps. Second, the tritone does not offend when it is properly 'resolved': if one ascends from F to ♮ (in any octave) and then continues to ascend further, the tritone may stand; if, however, one does not continue, but descends back to F, the tritone will have to be corrected by means of the soft b. It is probably legitimate to speculate that the reason why the tritone does not offend in the former case is that the non-harmonic, *augmented* interval (the tritone) has been properly resolved by a diatonic semitone to the next *larger* consonance (the perfect fifth).

Once again, the modal context is relevant. Pseudo-Tunstede's views in this respect are very similar to Jacques'. The observation in the quotation above to the effect that one does not correct the tritone in the deuterus and tetrardus is qualified below, at least so far as the deuterus is concerned:

> A song of the deuterus admits the soft b very little. The plagal of the deuterus, however, uses sometimes the soft b, for when the ascent will be from the low letters, as was said earlier in connection with the protus, one should sing through the soft b. Or when there will be a descent from the high letters down to a or to G, and from these an ascent to b, and from this a descent to F before an ascent to b, one should sing through the soft b in b.[7]

Another fourteenth-century author who compiled his *Tractatus de contrapuncto* in Paris in 1375 provides us with a similar, if less detailed, picture:

> Note that whenever one ascends from (or from below) F-fa-ut [F] to b-fa-b-mi [♭/♮], indirectly or directly, or when one descends to F-fa-ut before ascending to C-sol-fa-ut [c], he ought to sing fa on b-fa-b-mi (by ♭), unless the song should end on G bassus [G].[8]

That is, the tritone F-♮ has to be avoided regardless of whether it is direct or indirect, ascending or descending, unless ♮ is followed by c or the mode is tetrardus.

Of the many fifteenth- and sixteenth-century theorists who talk about the necessity of avoiding the tritone,[9] I will single out only those whose discussions clarify the problem further. A rich source of information is provided by Tinctoris's *Liber de natura et proprietate tonorum* of 1476. Tinctoris tells us that one uses the soft b in modes 5 and 6 when one wants to avoid the tritone,[10] but adds:

It must be noted too that the tritone must be avoided, not only in these two tones, but also in all the others. Hence this rule is generally observed, that in any tone if after an ascent to B-fa-B-mi acute [that is, b/♮] there is sooner a descent down to F-fa-ut grave [F] than an ascent to C-sol-fa-ut [c], it is sung uniformly by soft b.[11]

And, indeed, he follows this remark with examples in all eight modes.[12] It follows either that the taste has changed since the fourteenth century and that the modal context of a tritone is now irrelevant, or that we have to understand the fourteenth-century theorists discussed above as indicating the relative frequency with which ♭ is likely to be required in various modes rather than offering a general dispensation from the injunction against the tritone if it occurs in the tetrardus. I am inclined to think that the latter is the case simply because even Tinctoris discusses the problem in a chapter devoted to the tritus, thus indirectly suggesting that it is more likely to occur in modes 5 and 6 than in the others. We will probably get closest to the musical reality of the period if we try to integrate what Tinctoris says with the information provided by the earlier theorists as follows: the tritone should be avoided in all eight modes, but the modal context of the tritone has to be considered to the extent that one should create neither a non-harmonic relation with the final of the deuterus nor a transformation of the tetrardus into the transposed protus through an over-insistent use of ♭.

Tinctoris clarifies also that the tritone may be either direct or indirect, ascending or falling, and that 'while the human voice may possibly use a tritone in scalewise progression [that is, an indirect tritone], to use it, however, in a leap [directly] is either difficult or impossible'.[13] His examples of indirect tritones show that these have to be neither fully filled in (♮-a-F) nor filled in with steps moving in one direction (♮-G-a-F).[14] All this helps us to understand what falls under the concept of the 'tritone' and what sort of tritones are more likely to be found tolerable, if for some reason one cannot avoid them.

I have speculated that the reason why an ascending tritone F-♮ followed by c was found tolerable was that the perfect fifth was experienced as a fitting 'resolution' of the augmented fourth. Tinctoris's mention of the falling tritone invites us to speculate further and to suggest that, for the same reason, the tritone ♮-F followed by E would be found tolerable. One bit of indirect evidence for this conclusion is what we have learned from earlier theorists concerning the relative rarity of ♭ in deuterus and its frequency in tetrardus: perhaps one used ♭ so rarely in modes 3 and 4 precisely because the progression from ♮ to F was likely to be followed by E and, conversely, one commonly used ♭ in modes 5 and 6 since the descent from ♮ to F was unlikely to be followed by E there.

Tinctoris's remark quoted above to the effect that a direct tritone 'is either difficult or impossible' to sing does not necessarily have to be taken to mean that one must avoid a direct tritone even when it is properly resolved. In his *Musica practica* of 1482, Ramos explains a solmization practice which he says is improperly called by his contemporaries 'disjunction' (*disiuncta*) which consists in transferring from one property to another without a mutation, for instance, reading the skip from c to F 'fa-fa' (rather than 'fa/sol-ut'). 'The direct tritone,' he continues 'always causes disjunctions, so that when one skips from F to c with the single note ♮ in between, one says "fa" in F and "mi" in ♭/♮ and follows with "fa" in c; and this is called "disjunction", since this "mi" neither follows nor depends on that lower "fa".'[15] The example indicates that even a direct melodic tritone can be tolerated and sung provided it is properly resolved. Similar evidence is provided by handwritten examples on the margin of the Parma copy of Nicolaus Burtius' *Florum libellus* of 1487, examples which accompany the discussion of the use of ♭ to avoid the tritone.[16] One of these shows an unresolved tritone corrected by means of ♭, the other shows the progression F-♮-c left without any corrections. On the other hand, Franciscus de Brugis, in his 'Opusculum' with which he prefaced an antiphonary published in 1503–4, says: 'But if after the third whole tone there follows the minor semitone, the tritone may be sung when it is not simple [direct].'[17] Similarly, Giovanni del Lago, in a letter of August 6, 1533 addressed to Fra Nazaro, says: 'But the immediate, or incomposite, tritone is, on account of its harshness, by itself unsingable, that is, it cannot be sung . . . But the mediated, or composite, tritone is on occasion singable.'[18] Clearly there were musicians (perhaps a majority) who would avoid all direct tritones, even if resolved.

Franciscus offers also some interesting comments on situations in which the tritone F-♮ is not followed by c immediately, but only after some intervening notes, specifically, if after ♮ one preceeds to a, ♮, and only then to c.[19] In such situations, the note before a should be ♭, provided that a is repeated and especially if there is a rest between these two a's; but if there is only one a, one should use ♮. Thus (and these are Franciscus' examples) one should use ♮ in the progression F-G-a-♮-a-♮-c, but ♭ and ♮ in F-G-a-♭-a-rest-a-♮-c. A general rule which may be derived from these comments is, it seems to me, that the resolution of the F-♮ tritone to c may be postponed by the lower-neighbor figure a-♮ (or perhaps even by any ornamental figure) without making the tritone unacceptable, unless there is a rest (or, more generally, a sense of punctuation in the flow of the melody) before the note of the resolution is reached. Furthermore, we learn from Franciscus that such musical punctuation can work both ways: not only does it annul the effect of a resolution, as we have seen above, but also it can annul the effect of a tritone when it occurs somewhere between ♮ and F.[20]

Similar considerations are offered by Gonzalo Martínez de Bizcargui in his *Arte de canto llano* which appeared eleven times between 1508 and 1550. Among several exceptions to the rule that one should avoid the tritone, Martínez mentions the one which allows to leave the tritone F-♮ or ♮-F intact if one cadences on a.[21] The example with which he illustrates this exception is puzzling, since it indicates that Martínez uses ♮ in contexts like the following one: F-G-a-♮-a-rest-F. (The 'rest' is really a breath-mark at the end of a word.) If there were no F at the beginning of the phrase, Martínez's example and exception would agree with what we have learned from Franciscus: the punctuation after a makes the tritone ♮-a-rest-F inoffensive. But it is puzzling that he overlooks the tritone with the preceding F. Perhaps this is simply an oversight.

Martínez's second exception allows the tritone if more than four notes intervene between ♮ and F, since then the tritone loses its force.[22] And his third exception allows us to understand why ♭ was rarely needed in tetrardus: for cadential reasons, F is often sharpened in modes 7 and 8 and when it is, ♮ does not have to be flattened in progressions like this one: ♮-a-G-F♯-G.[23]

Related observations were made by Pietro Aaron in his *Toscanello in musica*, which appeared four times between 1523 and 1562. Aaron discusses situations in which the rule that 'three consecutive tones one after the other should always be mollified and tempered when they do not reach the fifth note'[24] may be broken. The very way in which he formulates the rule deserves our attention, since it suggests that just as an ascending tritone F-♮ may be resolved by c, so the descending ♮-F may be resolved by E. Apart from this, however, there are several situations in which the rule may be broken, according to Aaron. One of these occurs when, by the rules of counterpoint, F is to be sharpened as the cadential leading tone.[25] Here Aaron's observations correspond to those of Martínez discussed above. But Aaron adds one subtle point: if ♮ not only descends to the cadentially sharpened F, but also is reached in a progression from a natural F (that is, in F- . . . -♮- . . . -F♯-G), then ♮ should be flattened, in spite of the resulting diminished fourth ♭-F♯.[26]

We have learned from Franciscus de Brugis that the resolution of the F-♮ tritone to c may be postponed by the lower-neighbor figure a-♮ without making the tritone unacceptable. In a late work of his, the *Lucidario in musica* of 1545, Aaron gives an example of an acceptable tritone which suggests that the resolution may be postponed even further: F-a-♮-a-G-a-c.[27]

One may probably conclude that the resolution of ♮ to c may be postponed by a few notes, presumably of ornamental or structurally less important character, and avoid the temptation of defining more specifically how many or which notes these can be.

Another point discussed in *Lucidario*[28] is worth mentioning here. In the progression e-d-c-♭-a the tritone is tolerable, since it is followed by the perfect fifth. This is preferable to flattening e, since this would produce a diminished fifth e♭-a. Of course, it would be best to use no flats at all. Aaron's remarks support my suggestion that the descending tritone may also be properly resolved downwards to the perfect fifth.

Aaron also thinks that indirect tritones with more than one note intervening between F and ♮ may be treated *ad libitum* by singers and either be corrected or left intact.[29] While many theorists gave us the impression that an indirect tritone is less offensive than the direct one, Aaron is more tolerant of indirect tritones than other writers.

By 1555, Nicola Vicentino will express even more tolerant views in his *L'antica musica ridotta alla moderna prattica*.[30] The tritone, says Vicentino, is tolerated by composers and singers only in indirect form, since it is too harsh when sung direct. However, this leap will occur occasionally in compositions, even though it is difficult to sing, since it is very useful when one wants to set words which have an astonishing effect; the ascending tritone, namely, is lively and shows great power, while the descending one is very funereal and sad. With constant practice one will be able to sing it, says Vicentino, because 'if the said tritone is sung when indirect, why could it not be sung direct with practice?'[31] This is the voice of the spokesman for a new stylistic ideal, eventually to be called the 'second practice'. But what is said on the traditional 'first practice' (the prohibition of the direct tritone, the toleration of the indirect one in certain, here unspecified, contexts) generally agrees with what we have learned from Vicentino's predecessors. The most important codifier of the 'first practice', Gioseffo Zarlino, said, in fact: 'The tritone, semidiapente, and others like them must not be used, however, despite the fact that certain moderns write them and justify the progressions as chromatic.'[32] Thus, both Zarlino and Vicentino reflect in their writings the recent birth of an alternative style allowing the new way of handling the tritone and much else.

The prohibition of the melodic tritone is a constant feature of musical practice from the beginning to the end of the period discussed here. While individual theorists may add specific observations which allow us to understand the prohibition better, the theory as a whole does not present a picture of an evolving practice, but, on the contrary, one of a generally uniform way of handling the problem. Consequently, one is justified, I think, in summarizing as follows what we have learned thus far without paying attention to chronology or geography.

The melodic tritone is prohibited regardless of whether it is ascending or descending, direct or indirect (that is, filled in with notes remaining within the range of the tritone, for instance, with G's and a's if the tritone is F-♮, regardless of their number or direction). There are exceptions, however, to this general rule. The tritone may be tolerated if it is properly resolved to a perfect fifth, up in the case of the ascending tritone (for example, F- . . . . -♮-c), down in the case of the descending one (♮- . . . . -F-E). Moreover, the resolution may be delayed by a few notes (a's and G's again). A syntactic interruption, that is, anything which produces a sense of punctuation in the flow of the melody, cancels the effect of both the tritone and the resolution. Even an unresolved indirect tritone loses its force and does not have to be corrected if it is filled with many notes (more than four, according to Martínez). On the other hand, there is disagreement as to what one does with direct tritones: many theorists think that they should always be corrected, some that they should be corrected only if unresolved. The tritone has to be avoided particularly often in the tritus (because it arises there in relation with the final) and fairly commonly in the protus. On the other hand, ♭ is rare in the deuterus (because it produces a non-harmonic relation with the final) and particularly in the tetrardus (where, unlike in the other modes, the consistent application of ♭ destroys the modal identity, transforming the tetrardus into the transposed protus).

I have found no direct evidence concerning the question of how to handle tritones which are strictly speaking not resolved, but are embedded in perfect fifths, that is, in progressions like c-♮-a-G-F or E-F-G-a-♮. We may speculate, however, on the basis of what we have learned about the handling of the tritone in various modes, that the way in which such progressions were treated may have depended on the relative structural weight of the notes involved. The more important structurally the notes forming the tritone (important by virtue of representing structurally central steps of the mode, or notes of the underlying simple counterpoint rather than those of the embellishing diminished one), the more offensive the tritone was probably found, and vice versa. Thus, the decision whether to correct the tritone in the progression c-♮-a-G-F, say, probably depended on whether it was the tritone (♮-F) or the fifth (c-F) which was structurally emphasized, the tritone requiring correction only in the former case.

It is at least possible that similar ideas governed the decision whether the tritone has been properly resolved or not in such contexts as F- . . . . -♮-c. Here, again, the decision might have depended on the relative structural importance of the notes involved; c might have been felt to provide an insufficient resolution if it was structurally much less weighty than ♮. We are, admittedly, on speculative ground here, but the speculation is, I believe, well founded in musical realities of the period. There can be no doubt that musicians of the fourteenth, fifteenth and sixteenth centuries made distinctions as to the relative structural importance of notes in their music, distinctions based on the differentiation of the underlying simple consonant counterpoint and the embellishing diminished counterpoint which is the fundamental feature of contrapuntal theory and practice of the period, as well as on the hierarchy of steps within a mode (once modal concepts started to be applied to polyphony). Consequently, it is plausible to assume that musicians found tritones involving structurally important notes to be more offensive than those involving less weighty notes, and that they found a resolution by means of a note at least equally important to the offending one to be more satisfactory than a resolution by means of a structurally less weighty note. Should this assumption be correct, it would be clear that musicians of our period would have to make their decisions concerning a given context (decisions, that is, as to whether to correct a given tritone or not) not mechanically, but in a way which would have to involve an understanding of the relative structural weight of notes, an understanding based on contrapuntal and, at least in some cases, also on modal considerations.

One of the melodic 'rules of *musica ficta*' most frequently invoked by editors of early music directs that a note above la (that is, a) should be sung fa (♭). It cannot be emphasized too strongly, however, that, with some qualifications to be mentioned shortly, this is not a separate rule, but merely one of the ways in which the prohibition of the tritone was formulated. In his *Tractatus plane musice* written in 1412 and revised in 1425-8, Prosdocimus de Beldemandis explains that one cannot continue ascending above la on E without a mutation of la into mi (and nothing but mi), so that on the following F there will be fa, which must be sung on F in order to avoid the tritone which would otherwise arise above C.[33] He continues: 'For similar reasons it was necessary to mutate la found in a into mi, if we wanted to ascend from F to ♭/♮ without the tritone.'[34] The same mutations recur an octave above.[35]

Clearly, considerations of this sort eventually gave rise to the pseudo-rule of 'fa above la', according to which in the untransposed system one flattens ♮ in the upper-neighbor-note figure a-♮-a (that is, when one does not proceed to ascend to c which resolves the tritone). Some musicians remembered that one does it only in order to avoid the tritone, others sang a-♭-a regardless of whether there was F before or after it or not. Johannes Cochlaeus, in his *Tetrachordum musices* of 1511, gives an example of a piece in the first mode transposed to G with written-out E♭ in the bass which can be justified only as a 'fa above la'.[36] In another example, this one in mode 4, he expressly marks ♮ at b♭/♮♮ even though there is no f before or after it in order to prevent 'fa above la' which would mar the counterpoint there (and perhaps also in order not to have ♭♭ in the fourth mode, even though there is no e in the vicinity).[37] For Cochlaeus, the fa-above-la rule has clearly become independent of the tritone prohibition. His contemporary and compatriot Georg

Rhau, on the other hand, in his *Enchiridion utriusque musicae practicae* which appeared in many editions between 1517 and 1553, having informed his readers that all modes except 5 and 6 use the 'scale of the hard-b song' (*scala cantus* ♮ *duralis*), that is, the one without a key signature, continues: 'In songs of the first and second mode, when one proceeds beyond la only to the next step, one always sings fa, if the song soon returns to F; if, however, it ascends a third or fourth above a, then one sings mi in ♭/♮.'[38] Rhau, like many others, singles modes 1 and 2 out for attention precisely because it is in these modes that the tritone F-♮ is most likely to require a correction (the tritus having a ♭-signature anyway). But, unlike Cochlaeus, he understands that the fa-above-la rule is simply another way of talking about the tritone.

Both Cochlaeus and Rhau have their followers in the sixteenth century. In 1533, Stephano Vanneo formulates the rule succinctly and without any reference to the tritone: 'Where, however, there will be still one note above la, it will be called by the name of fa.'[39] Almost the same words are used by the immensely popular Nikolaus Listenius in 1537: 'If any note will go beyond the step la by so much as one interval, it will be sung as fa, without mutation, especially in a song of the first and second modes.'[40] A similar formula is provided also by Loys Bourgeois[41] and by Heinrich Faber,[42] both in 1550, by Coclico in 1552,[43] and by Hermann Finck in 1556.[44] (Note, incidentally, that for most of these theorists the solmization of fa above la did not involve a mutation.) On the other hand, Rhau's understanding of the fa-above-la rule as applicable only when one wants to avoid the tritone is shared by Agricola in 1528[45] and Angelo da Picitono in 1547.[46] The whole situation was neatly summarized by Aaron in his *Lucidario* of 1545:

Not a small amazement is certainly produced in me when I consider the heedlessness of so many who, wanting to give precepts in the popular music, envelop the understanding of those who know nothing in thousand errors, since they claim thoughtlessly as a strict rule that this note or syllable which will be above the note called la, will always be pronounced fa, through which inane opinion they lead a new disciple to a false understanding . . . It will not be necessary in such contexts to consider the sweeter [that is, ♭] or the harder [♮], except when there arises the interval of the tritone, in which case you will have to pronounce the syllable fa above the syllable la . . . since in plainchant one does not sing through the soft b for another reason than to sweeten the tritone.[47]

And he reaffirms below: 'The note above the syllable la should not always be called and pronounced fa.'[48]

In sum, there are many in the sixteenth century who apply the rule of 'fa above la' indiscriminately, but knowledgeable musicians remember that the rule is merely a spin-off from the prohibition of the tritone. I can discover no geographical or chronological criteria for either preference. Nor does it seem possible to find out whether the indiscriminate application of the fa-above-la rule was practiced before 1500; I could find no evidence for this.[49] Whether we will want to apply the rule independently of the tritone prohibition when editing or performing sixteenth-century music will depend on whether we will want to follow the most enlightened musical opinion of the period or rather imitate what seems to have been an unsophisticated but fairly common practice. An examination of source accidentals may help us to decide what is appropriate for a given repertoire.

The tritone is not the only melodic interval which should be avoided. Also the diminished fifth may require a correction. From the late fifteenth century on, theorists discuss the prohibition of the diminished fifth scarcely less often than that of the tritone. It is uncertain, but seems likely, that the prohibition was followed by earlier musicians as well, and that theorists had not mentioned it only because they felt that discussions of the tritone covered the whole problem adequately. The fact that the diminished fifth was prohibited throughout the period when it occurred vertically (see Chapter 5(i) below) also suggests that the prohibition of the melodic diminished fifth was in force long before theorists bothered to discuss it.

The diminished fifth and the tritone are the only non-harmonic relations (diminished or augmented intervals) which can arise in the untransposed system and they are often discussed together. Hothby expressly forbids both in *La Caliopea legale*,[50] and so do many others.[51] Ramos's discussion of these two intervals is particularly interesting:

There is, nevertheless, another quantity in which the octave may be divided, which almost does not differ in sound, namely, the tritone and the imperfect fifth which is called the diminished fifth, as B-F and F-♮, since the distance between B and F is as large as the one between F and ♮ and the difference does not matter to practical musicians, but it does to theorists who explore the difference of the semitone. Nevertheless, when it is direct, it is no less discordant in sound than the tritone itself . . . Still, we say expressly 'when it is direct', since, when it proceeds by intervening steps, it is sweet and playful, both in ascending and in descending motion, as in F-E-D-C-B and in reverse B-C-D-E-F. But the song should not rest on F when it ascends, but it should turn back to E. And so when it descends, it should turn back to C.[52]

For Ramos, the difference of size and sound between the diminished fifth and the tritone is more theoretical than practical; both are equally dissonant and, presumably, both should be equally avoided. But just as the *augmented* fourth is tolerable when properly resolved by a semitone *outward* to the perfect fifth, so also the *diminished* fifth does not offend when it is indirect and resolved by a semitone *inward* to the perfect fourth. The principle of the resolution is the same with both intervals.

Similar information may be inferred from Zarlino:

He [the composer] may at times, but not often, also use the semidiapente melodically when it is suitable to the meaning of the text, so long as he keeps within the natural diatonic steps of the mode on which the piece is founded . . . [There follows an example which contains these progressions: f-e-d-c-♮-c; ♮-c-d-e-f-e.] He should not use it, however, where chromatic steps are involved, even when it is intended to produce a consonance, for such steps were devised to contribute to good harmony and not to destroy it. [There follows an example which contains these progressions: g-f-e-d-c♯-d; E-F-G-a-♭-a.][53]

Once again the tolerable diminished fifths are indirect and properly resolved. Zarlino additionally prescribes that only diatonic steps of the mode should be involved in such progressions, excluding chromatically raised or lowered steps even when they function as cadential leading tones (as they do in his examples).

Just as with the tritone, so also with the diminished fifth it is not entirely clear, but likely, that only the indirect ones may be tolerated. Giovanni Maria Lanfranco, for instance, explains how to correct both types of intervals, but adds that this is not always done when the intervals are indirect.[54] Similarly, Glarean says of the diminished fifth that it 'is not allowed as a leap in a song, but as continuous movement either in ascent or in descent',[55] and a little later says of both the tritone and the diminished fifth that 'these are almost never used in a leap'.[56]

(ii) The method of avoiding the tritone and diminished fifth

Since the tritone and diminished fifth are the only non-harmonic relations which may arise in a diatonic series, we may turn now to the question of how they should be corrected. Since in an untransposed system these relations will occur only between F and ♮ (and their octave equivalents), it is evident that they might be corrected either by flattening ♮ or by sharpening F. Now, in view of this fact, one is astonished to discover that throughout our period one theorist after another discusses the problem as if the possibility of using F♯ did not even exist. The conclusion is surprising, but supported by massive evidence and hence inescapable: in the untransposed system, one corrects the non-harmonic relation by means of ♭, not F♯. In a transposed system, one acts accordingly, always using the flat, not the sharp: if there is one flat in the signature, one corrects the non-harmonic relations (*B♭-E*) by flattening *E*, if there are two flats in the signature, one corrects them (*E♭-A*) by flattening *A*, etc.

It would be tedious to do more than list the relevant evidence in a note,[57] singling out for discussion only a few texts. When Gaffurius discusses the division of the whole tone into semitones, he explains that it is more convenient to have the minor semitone below the major one, that is, to use flat black-key steps.[58] One of the reasons is the tritone, which one never corrects by means of a sharp step: 'But wherever and whenever it will happen that a whole tone will have to be divided in order to take away the harshness of the tritone, in no way will it ever be permitted to put the major semitone before the minor one [that is, to use a sharp black-key step].'[59] One cannot be more explicit than that. The only situation in which F is sharpened rather than ♮ flattened we have already encountered: both Martínez and Aaron told us that if for cadential reasons F had been sharpened, ♮ does not need to be flattened. This is clearly not an exception to the general rule, because the sharp is used here not to correct the tritone but to produce the leading tone.

I have found, however, three texts which seem to provide exceptions. One of the manuscripts which transmit Hothby's *La Caliopea legale* adds to the general discussion of the tritone and diminished fifth an observation that these intervals may be corrected by either ♭ or F♯, namely, if F comes first, one uses ♭, and if ♮ comes first, one uses F♯.[60] One of the examples which illustrate this observation employs F♯ as a leading tone in a cadence on G, which means that what Hothby has in mind is clearly not an exception to our rule, but a situation also described by Martínez and Aaron and mentioned a moment ago. Another example, however, employs f♯ independently of any cadential progression: ♮-d-f♯-e-d-♮. Another real exception seems to be offered by Bonaventura da Brescia in his *Breviloquium musicale* of 1497.[61] Bonaventura explains there that whoever wishes to perfect the diminished fifth between B and F can do it by using a feigned step of F♯, while E-♭ is perfected by the natural step of ♮. It should be observed, however, that the passage in question occurs in the context of an explanation of the sizes of intervals and it may be that what Bonaventura does there is not practical advice on how to improve a melody, but merely a clarification of the difference between the diminished and perfect fifths. Finally, there is this intriguing clause in Lanfranco's explanation of the respective functions of the signs of the round b and diesis: 'Just as the soft b is used in songs of the square b in order to avoid tritones, so the diesis, *with which one may also sweeten the harshness of the tritone*, is practiced in any order to create sweeter consonances.'[62] Lanfranco thinks that the signs of the round b and diesis serve different functions: the former corrects the tritone, the latter has uses which will be discussed in detail later. But he adds in the clause which I have italicized that one may also correct the tritone by means of the diesis sign. This is the only passage I have been able to find which unambiguously contradicts the rule that one corrects the tritones and diminished fifths *exclusively* with flats, and yet even this passage implies that flats are *normally* used for this purpose. Thus, we may at most conclude that Lanfranco allows sharps to be used to correct non-harmonic intervals only in exceptional circumstances. It may be that the exceptional circumstances he has in mind are precisely the ones described by Martínez and Aaron, namely, a descent from ♮ to F in which ♭ does not have to be introduced, since the following cadence on G requires the sharpening of F. In this case, also Lanfranco's passage would turn out to offer no real exception to the rule. But in any case, in view of the fact that an overwhelming majority of theorists mentions only flats when explaining how to correct non-harmonic melodic progressions, it seems likely that if sharps were used at all in such circumstances, they were used only exceptionally.

Since no theorist addresses the question of why flats were preferred to sharps when one wanted to correct the non-harmonic relations, I can only offer some speculations on the matter. It is likely, I think, that the modal context of the offending intervals was relevant here. Theorists frequently discuss the use of the soft b in various modes. We have already heard Jacques de Liège expound at the beginning of the fourteenth century the doctrine which will remain standard throughout our period: ♭ is very common in tritus, in which it may be used throughout (that is, presumably, in the key signature), since it corrects a non-harmonic relation with the final there; it is used occasionally (accidentally) in the protus; it is rare in deuterus (since, as we learn from other theorists, it produces a non-harmonic relation with the final), but at least it does not destroy the mode there; it is used most sparingly in the tetrardus, since it changes it into the protus.[63] What theorists tell us about the use of the soft b in various modes will allow us to understand why only ♭ was used to correct non-harmonic relations.

As we already know, ♭ was most commonly used in the tritus where the non-harmonic relations with the final were particularly jarring. The sharpening of the final instead would disrupt the mode even more than the offending tritone did. The protus was the second most common modal context in which ♭ was used. The regularly placed final of the protus was d (in the untransposed system), the irregularly placed one was a (again in the untransposed system). The fact that the sixth step above the final was different in the regular and irregular protus did not particularly vex musicians of our period, Glarean's attempted reform of 1547 and Zarlino's acceptance and popularization thereof in 1558 notwithstanding. Consequently, the use of ♭ in the regular protus did not affect the modal identity of the melody but merely changed its regular sixth step into the irregular one. The use of F♯, on the other hand, would transform the untransposed protus into the transposed tetrardus. Turning to the deuterus now, we recall that ♭ was rarely used there, since it introduced a non-harmonic relation with the final. It should be noted, however, that ♭ at least does not affect the modal identity of the deuterus (since there is no separate mode with the final on ♮ in the untransposed system), while F♯ does, transforming it into the transposed irregular protus. And finally tetrardus: it will be recalled that the use of ♭ was avoided in it altogether precisely because it transformed the untransposed tetrardus into the transposed protus. On the other hand, it was not felt that the use of F♯ affected the identity of the mode, provided F♯ was introduced as a cadential leading tone, since, otherwise, the regular use of F♯ in the tetrardus would make it indistinguishable from the tritus, whose theoretical fourth step above the final was flattened more often than not, as we know. Thus, the only context in which F♯ could be introduced without changing the mode was that of the tetrardus, and there only as the leading tone. Consequently, it makes sense that the one case in which the use of F♯ was at all considered by the theorists explaining how the non-harmonic relations were to be corrected was precisely the cadential progression ♮- . . . . -F♯-G in the tetrardus.

Another answer to our question is implied by Margaret Bent's and Andrew Hughes's claim that, when having to choose which note to inflect, medieval musicians would normally prefer a step of *musica vera* over one of *musica ficta*.[64] '*The primary rule for applying accidentals is that* musica recta *should be used rather than* musica ficta *where possible*,' emphasizes Bent.[65] Were this claim justified, it would follow that, when confronted with the choice of using ♭ or F♯ (and other things being equal), we should choose the former, since ♭ (unlike other 'black-key' steps) belongs to *musica vera*. But in fact it is not at all certain that '*recta* preference' ever governed medieval musicians. Bent and Hughes base their claim on frequently encountered theoretical statements to the effect that, in the words of Prosdocimus de Beldemandis's first rule of feigned music, 'musica ficta is never to be applied except where necessary'.[66] Statements of this sort may be interpreted to suggest a preference for *recta* over *ficta* steps, but they may also be taken to mean simply that one should not use accidental inflections (most of which do involve feigned steps) willfully or arbitrarily, but only when these are necessitated by conventional considerations, such as the need to avoid non-harmonic relations or provide cadences with proper leading tones, that is, considerations discussed in Chapters 4–7 of the present book. To be sure, Prosdocimus himself (but not necessarily other theorists referred to by Bent and Hughes) comes out in favor of *recta* preference, since, to the frequently encountered 'first' rule of *musica ficta* quoted above, he adds another rule which seems to be his own and which would be redundant unless he had *recta* preference in mind: 'The second rule is this: that musica ficta was invented exclusively for the sake of coloring some consonance that could not be colored except by musica ficta.'[67] But it is interesting to observe that even Prosdocimus forgets about *recta* preference when he considers the question whether one inflects the lower or upper voice when one is forced by necessity to 'color' a vertical consonance.[68] Thus, it is by no means certain that the preference for 'true' over 'feigned' steps governed choices made by musicians of our period.

But the main problem with the *recta*-preference rule is that it can explain only choices made in music notated without key signatures. If we try to use the rule to explain why fa-steps were preferred to mi-steps when one wanted to correct non-harmonic relations, we get an answer which seems to be convincing in the untransposed system, but breaks down as soon as we consider what happens in music notated with accidental signatures. As we have learned, there is ample evidence that also in the latter case one uses the flat step rather than the sharp one to correct a non-harmonic relation. Bent and Hughes assumed that an accidental signature transposed the whole hand and that such a transposed hand was considered to be *musica vera*, thus making one flat over and above those in the signature (for instance, E♭ in a melody notated with a B♭-signature, or A♭ with a B♭/E♭-signature) into a *musica vera* step. As I demonstrated at the end of Chapter 3, however, this is not the case: musicians of our period did not think that a system transposed by a key signature represented *musica vera* and regarded E♭ in a system with B♭-signature or A♭ in a system with B♭/E♭-signature to be steps of *musica ficta*, just as they were in the untransposed system. It should be recalled here that Tinctoris introduces his example of how the tritones between E♭ and a in music with a B♭/E♭-signature can be both avoided and tolerated with these words: 'Further, it must be known that, not only in regular tones and true music but also in irregular tones and fictitious music, we ought to avoid the tritone and to use it by the ways given earlier as in the above quoted examples.'[69] There can be no doubt that he wants those tritones in his example which should be avoided to be corrected by means of a♭ and his words make it clear that this a♭ belongs to *musica ficta* rather than *vera*. And yet, if the choice of the step with which the tritone was to be perfected was governed by the preference for a *musica vera* over a *musica ficta* step, Tinctoris would have corrected his tritones by means of E♮, which belongs to *musica vera*.

Moreover, we have an explicit proof that even in the untransposed system the choice of the note to be inflected when perfecting the tritone was not governed by the preference for a true over a feigned step. Bonaventura da Brescia informs us that the tritone can be found in four places of the hand, F-♮, ♭-e, f-♮♮, and ♭♭-ee, and that the first and third of these are perfected by a true step, ♭ and ♭♭, the second and fourth by a feigned step, e♭ and ee♭.[70] If the criterion of choice were the preference for a true over a feigned step, one would have obviously corrected the latter two tritones by means of ♮ and ♮♮.

Thus, the Bent–Hughes theory offers no convincing explanation of why flats were chosen to correct non-harmonic relations in both untransposed and transposed systems. The explanation offered here, on the other hand, works equally well in both systems. The function of a key signature is to transpose a mode and all the considerations we have discussed in connection with the untransposed modes will remain valid for the transposed ones as well, with the role of B♭ in the untransposed system being taken over by E♭ in a melody notated with a B♭-signature, by A♭ in one notated with a B♭/E♭-signature, etc.

(iii) The non-harmonic relations introduced by
internal accidentals and the method of avoiding them

Returning now to the untransposed system, the use of B♭ to correct a tritone or diminished fifth between *B* and *F* may introduce new non-harmonic relations besides those we already know, namely, the diminished and augmented octaves and their octave equivalents including the chromatic semitone, as well as the already-known tritone and diminished fifth between new steps, namely, B♭ and *E*. All of those are also undesirable.

Theorists regularly prohibit the diminished octave[71] and the chromatic semitone,[72] often in the same passage in which also the tritone and diminished fifth are banned. While the prohibition of the imperfect octave became a regular feature of theory only in the sixteenth century, it seems likely that it was practiced long before. The fact that throughout our period the imperfect octave was prohibited when it occurred vertically favors this conclusion.

Glarean states, furthermore, that while the tritone and diminished fifth 'are almost never used in a leap', the diminished octave 'must be avoided entirely'.[73] The prohibition of the chromatic half step, on the other hand, while very strong, seems to be somewhat less than absolute, as these words of Gaffurius indicate:

This [progression from ♭ to ♮, or the reverse] is a difficult and very dissonant movement, and according to musical scholars, it should be avoided with all possible ingenuity . . . The dissonant movement of such a permutation . . . must only be used when it is absolutely necessary because of the arrangement of the notes.[74]

Also Aaron declares, in *Lucidario in musica*, that the major (that is, chromatic) semitone 'is not sounded by itself, even though some have such a false opinion,'[75] and, elsewhere in the book, gives an example:

We have often considered an incorrect opinion of some composers who write in their works on a single line or in a single space two breves or semibreves of which one will be sharpened and the other will proceed naturally. And this is to be understood in all the steps or places where the signs of the square b will reign, that is, in C, F and G, as the example clearly shows.[76]

There follows an example which includes this progression (see Example 2). Aaron explains that according to the rules of counterpoint the second g in the cantus has to be sharpened as the cadential leading tone and the first one has to remain natural or else a non-harmonic relation with the tenor's c will result.[77] This produces the undesirable chromatic semitone, which could have been easily avoided by the composer if the first breve of the cantus were aa.

Example 2

Cantus
Tenor

The same point is illustrated by a very similar example in Ramos's *Musica practica*[78] and, indeed, it appears that the line of musicians criticized here for their use of the chromatic half step extends all the way back to Marchetto da Padova. In his *Lucidarium*, Marchetto exemplified one of the two ways in which he divided the whole tone into two semitones 'in order to color some dissonance such as a third, a sixth, or a tenth as it proceeds to some consonance'[79] by very similar contrapuntal, cadential progressions without indicating that there is anything wrong with them (see Example 3).[80] The

Example 3

other division of the whole tone into two semitones is exemplified by another set of progressions and also here one gets the impression that Marchetto considers such progressions to be perfectly respectable (see Example 4).[81] While

Example 4

for Marchetto these two sets of examples involve two different pairs of semitones, most musicians of our period studying these examples would correctly conclude that this theorist allows the melodic use of the chromatic half step in polyphonic music, provided there are good contrapuntal reasons for doing so.

And, indeed, Marchetto's tolerant attitude toward the chromatic semitone comes clearly across again when he explains the concept of 'permutation':

Permutation is a change in the name of a solmization syllable or note where the pitch
changes although the note lies in the same position on the staff. It is used when a
whole tone is divided, for the sake of consonance, into a diatonic semitone and an
enharmonic one [in standard terminology, these are the chromatic and diatonic
semitones, respectively] or into a chromatic semitone and a diesis [in standard terminology, these are again the chromatic and diatonic semitones, respectively] (or vice
versa), as here [see Example 5].[82]

Example 5

It should be noted that also here Marchetto invokes specific contrapuntal
reasons (which I will discuss later) as a justification for using the melodic
chromatic half step.

Between Marchetto and Zarlino, several theorists mention the possibility
of an occasional use of the chromatic half step, always stressing its rarity.
Hothby, for instance, informs us that the composite chromatic whole tone,
consisting of a major and a minor semitone, is never used in plainchant, and
rarely in polyphony.[83] And Zarlino says of the chromatic half step: 'Although
this semitone is not used in making melodies in the diatonic genus, it is
nonetheless occasionally employed by composers.'[84]

In sum, the prohibition of a direct imperfect octave is absolute, while that
of a direct chromatic half step is strong, but less than absolute. It may be
introduced if its use is justified by contrapuntal rules, and if it is properly
resolved to fill the whole tone (as in the examples quoted above), which in
most cases means if it is followed (and only rarely if it is preceded) by a diatonic semitone going in the same direction. Theorists tell us nothing about
indirect imperfect octaves. Presumably, just as with the tritone and
diminished fifth, the more notes intervene, the less offensive they get. On
the other hand, we learn something about what could be called an 'indirect'
chromatic half step from Hothby, who tells us, like so many others, that if
the tritone between F and ♮ is followed by c, ♮ may be left unflattened,
but only

provided the ♮ of the first [order; that is, in Hothby's peculiar terminology, ♮] is not too close to A of the second [♭], because then there would be a discord between ♮ and ♭, and vice versa. And the hearing will be the judge of whether they are too close or not. But they may not be closer than with only one step intervening between them.[85]

Thus, also in this case, the more notes intervene between the two which form a chromatic semitone, the less offensive the latter.

Let us recall that the 'new' non-harmonic relations just discussed (the imperfect octave and its equivalents) have been introduced into the untransposed system by the use of *B♭* to correct the 'original' non-harmonic relations between *B* and *F* and disregard for the time being chromatic semitones produced by contrapuntally (cadentially) motivated sharps. Assuming that these 'new' relations have to be corrected (and we already know when they have to), it is practically self-evident that the only way they may be corrected is by means of another *B♭*. The use of *B♮* instead would have recreated the original non-harmonic relation which was corrected by *B♭* in the first place. If this were the standard practice, sooner or later we would have encountered a theorist who would have informed us that a tritone or diminished fifth may be left uncorrected, if its correcting produced an imperfect octave in turn. No theorist tells us this, however. On the other hand, some theorists tell us expressly that the diminished octave, just as the tritone and diminished fifth, is to be corrected by means of a flat.[86]

This, however, is not the case with the new tritones and diminished fifths produced by the introduction of an internal *B♭*, the ones between *B♭* and *E*. An interesting comment on the matter is provided by Domingo Marcos Durán, who observes that when one ascends from E to ♮ and returns to F, one has to choose between keeping a perfect fifth and having to put up with a tritone, or getting a perfect fourth but falsifying the fifth.[87] Durán thinks that the former choice is preferable, but he notes that some musicians do otherwise and err. Note that it does not even occur to Durán that one could correct both offending intervals by flattening both ♮ and E; the idea that one flat step could lead to another at a place a fourth or fifth apart in a kind of a 'chain reaction' is alien to him. Similarly, it does not occur to him to solve the problem by means of F♯. Durán's observations make sense if we connect them with what we have learned about the relative rarity of ♭ in deuterus: it is in modes 3 and 4 that the situation discussed by the theorist is most likely to occur and that his decision to keep the fifth E-♮ which defines the modes perfect would be found persuasive by many musicians. The following conclusions may be derived from Durán's discussion. First, when a correction of a non-harmonic relation between *F* and *B* gave rise to another non-harmonic relation between *B♭* and *E*, one dealt with the problem neither by flattening the *E* in a kind of 'chain reaction', nor by sharpening the *F* in a reversal of the normal practice of using only flats to correct non-harmonic melodic relations. Second, we may probably legitimately speculate that the decision whether to flatten B in such contexts or not depended on the functions and relative structural weights of the notes involved; if the E-B relation was understood to be structurally more important than the F-B relation, B was likely to be left natural, and the reverse.

The problem is further illuminated by Pietro Aaron in his discussion of the circumstances in which one should not correct the tritone. One of these occurs when one proceeds from F to ♮ and then leaps down to E: 'I say that you are forced to choose between two evils the least inconvenient, which will be to say the proper mi in the said b ♮ acute [that is, to leave ♮ unflattened], although it is a lesser error to sing the imperfect diapente than a tritone.'[88] The imperfect fifth may be a lesser error than a tritone when it occurs all by itself, but evidently, when we have to choose between the two, it is more important to preserve the perfect fifth than to correct the tritone. In Aaron's three examples illustrating the problem, the tritone is filled in by step, while the fifth is direct. It is thus likely that his categorical choice in favor of the perfect fifth results from the fact that he finds a direct non-harmonic interval more difficult to sing. He says, in fact: 'If he [the singer] sings fa in the b-mi acute [that is, if he sings ♭], he cannot descend correctly to the proper pitch of the note mi [E].'[89] We have already found many theorists to feel that an indirect non-harmonic relation is more tolerable than a direct one. Just like Durán, Aaron does not even consider the possibility of a 'chain reaction' whereby one flat step leads to another: F-♭-E♭. Similarly, it does not occur to our theorist to deal with the discussed problem by means of a sharpening of F. Thus, Aaron's text supports fully the first conclusion we have derived from Durán. As for the second conclusion, it should be enriched to include Aaron's suggestion that an indirect non-harmonic interval is easier to sing than a direct one.

The first conclusion derived from both theorists, namely that when a correction of a non-harmonic relation between F and B gave rise to another non-harmonic relation between $B♭$ and E, one did not proceed to flatten E in a kind of 'chain reaction' involving steps a fourth or fifth apart, but rather left the original problem uncorrected, has an obvious bearing on Edward E. Lowinsky's celebrated theory of 'secret chromatic art' concealed in a small group of Franco-Flemish motets of mid-sixteenth-century, since the practice postulated by Lowinsky involves to a very large extent precisely such 'chain reactions'.[90] Like most attempts to reconstruct a secret society or practice, Lowinsky's theory is, in principle, unfalsifiable. To a sceptic pointing out that the surviving theoretical evidence makes the use of implied flats applied to a chain of descending fifths or ascending fourths an unlikely practice, a believer can always respond by convincingly demonstrating the existence of precisely such chains in a few early sixteenth-century musical experiments.[91] At this point the decision will turn on whether one finds the claim of a similarly experimental status of the 'secretly chromatic' repertoire plausible or not. It has to be stressed, however, that the existence of 'chain reactions' postulated by Lowinsky may be convincingly demonstrated in very few (probably no more than two) musical experiments designed to illustrate theoretical points concerning the content of the gamut and the tuning system, but, if we are to believe our theorists, has no place in everyday musical practice.

Lowinsky presented two examples from music theory designed to show that 'chain reactions' were a normal practice, one from Nikolaus Listenius' *Musica* of 1537 (see Example 6)[92] and another from Matthaeus Greiter's *Elementale musicum iuventuti accommodum* of 1544 (see Example 7).[93]

Example 6

Example 7

Listenius' example, he claimed, 'offers what amounts to clear and irrefutable evidence of the technique of secret modulation'[94] and, similarly, Greiter's example 'corroborates the principle of "secret chromaticism" to the effect that, once one note – "the code note" – has been shown in need of being raised or, mostly, flattened, a chain of melodic and harmonic progressions involving the intervals of the fourth or fifth often supported by motif transposition is used by the composer to enforce – without writing the accidentals – a modulation logical and convincing in its harmonic and melodic evolution'.[95] This interpretation of the examples ignores, however, the function they have in their treatises. Both Listenius and Greiter offer a brief and extremely rudimentary exposition of *musica ficta* and illustrate it with one monophonic example of *cantus fictus*, that is, of a melody using feigned steps. Such an example has to contain a few accidentals, either in the signature or internally. If a theorist chooses to place the accidentals internally and to use – as most such examples do – the most common flat inflections, it is difficult to imagine how he could avoid making the impression that he is exemplifying the technique of 'secret chromaticism'. Durán and Aaron, on the other hand, tell us what musicians in fact did when confronted with musical contexts offering the possibility of introducing 'chain-reaction' flats. Their evidence speaks against 'secret modulation' as a feature of regular practice, but, of course, does not exclude it in an occasional case of a musical experiment.

It follows from the above discussion that in the untransposed system most melodic non-harmonic relations will be corrected by means of $B\flat$. And since, in a melody notated with a key signature, all of the above non-harmonic relations as well as the ways of correcting them will be regularly transposed, it follows, more generally, that in correcting melodic intervals one uses normally always the 'next flat', that is, $B\flat$ if there is no key signature, $E\flat$ in a $B\flat$-signature, $A\flat$ in a $B\flat/E\flat$-signature, etc.

It follows further that the non-harmonic relations discussed thus far are the only ones which can arise in diatonic melodies; all other augmented and diminished progressions will have to result from internal accidentals introduced for some other (as yet undisclosed) reasons. References to such other progressions are most infrequent in theoretical literature. We already know that in the cadential progression ♮- . . . -G-F-G in the tetrardus ♭ is not used since F has to be sharpened as the leading tone. Aaron, in his discussion of this progression, specifically mentions that one should not both flatten ♮ and sharpen F, since the undesirable diminished fourth would result.[96] A few theorists mention another undesirable progression, the diminished third, or two consecutive minor (diatonic) semitones.[97] But these references are most unusual; the only non-harmonic melodic progressions regularly discussed by theorists are the tritone, diminished fifth, imperfect octave and chromatic semitone, that is, those that can arise in the diatonic series or which result from the introduction of the single flat designed to correct them. Thus, it is clear that in so far as the use of accidentals in melodic contexts is concerned (and, as we will find out in the next chapter, not only in melodic ones), theorists of our period are interested almost exclusively in the uses which serve to preserve diatonicism free of all augmented and diminished intervals.

It should also be evident that the two notes which form any one of the offending intervals may be solmized mi-fa or fa-mi. Some theorists refer to the forbidden melodic progressions in terms of these syllables, the implication being that mi-fa or fa-mi on these intervals will produce a forbidden progression. Rhau is quite explicit and provides these verses on the subject: 'Concerning the fourth, fifth and octave, avoid the leap spreading to mi from fa, or the reverse. When such a leap is spotted by you, lead it from mi to mi, [and] from fa – advantageously – to fa.'[98] Also Giovanni Maria Lanfranco tells us that 'mi against fa has no sonority or natural progression either at the fourth or at the fifth, and less at the octave', [99] meaning melodic intervals in this context. In short, the forbidden melodic progressions involve potentially perfect intervals solmizated with mi against fa. The expression 'mi against fa' (*mi contra fa*) is far more common, however, when vertical relations are discussed, and it is to these that we must turn now.

5 Vertical and cross relations

(i) The prohibition of mi-against-fa discords

In the preceding chapter I examined melodic progressions which necessitated the use of feigned steps. In the present one, I turn to vertical and cross relations in counterpoint which may have called for the use of such steps.

The vertical relations which were most commonly prohibited throughout our period were exactly the same as those we encountered in the preceding chapter, the tritone, the diminished fifth and the imperfect octave. For obvious reasons, the prohibition was usually expressed as the prohibition of 'mi against fa' (*mi contra fa*) on perfect consonances. Near the beginning of our period, Philippe de Vitry explained that when the tenor sings mi on b against the discant's fa on f, the resulting fifth will not be a consonance and will have to be corrected.[1] Another early fourteenth-century author, Petrus frater dictus Palma ociosa, provides the same information[2] and adds that octaves should also be kept perfect, by means of accidentals if necessary.[3] The reason why neither Vitry nor Petrus mentions the tritone is that they discuss two-part counterpoint in which the fourth is not a consonance at all and, consequently, does not occur in simple, note-against-note writing which uses consonances only, while in diminished counterpoint it is treated as a dissonance. In fact, Petrus mentions among the dissonances used in florid counterpoint both the fourth and the tritone.[4] The status of the fourth in counterpoint of our period is peculiar in that, unlike that of other intervals, it depends on the context: by itself, the fourth is a dissonance; when supported by a third or fifth below, it becomes a consonance. Consequently, the fourth can be used as a consonance only in counterpoint for more than two parts. Since most treatises of the period were limited to elementary instruction in simple two-part counterpoint, the mi-against-fa rule most often prohibited expressly only imperfect fifths and octaves. It is obvious, however, that in simple counterpoint for more than two parts mi against fa had to be avoided also on the fourth when this was meant to be used as a consonance. And, in fact, those theorists who went beyond two-part counterpoint did expressly include the imperfect fourth in the mi-against-fa prohibition.[5]

Petrus' text raises questions which we will be able to answer only as we accumulate the evidence: does the prohibition of mi against fa apply to the

93

fourth, fifth and octave unconditionally, regardless of whether they are meant to be used as consonances or as dissonances (in which case Petrus' inclusion of the tritone among the dissonances used in florid counterpoint would be a mistake); or does the prohibition apply to them only when they are meant to be used as consonances (in which case Petrus' failure to include the diminished fifth and imperfect octave among the dissonances used in florid counterpoint would be an oversight); or does it apply unconditionally to the fifth and octave, but to the fourth only when it is meant to be used as a consonance (which would be wholly consistent with Petrus' text)?

Philippus de Caserta (or whoever authored the late fourteenth-century treatise which goes under his name) states in his *Regule contrapuncti* concerning the unison, fifth, octave and twelfth that 'we may never make mi against fa, nor fa against mi, of the aforesaid consonances'.[6] We have here an early example of the standard way in which our prohibition was phrased. Once again, the fourth is not mentioned, since Philippus discusses two-part counterpoint. Another standard expression which occurs in the treatise and which is regularly associated with the mi-against-fa prohibition throughout our period concerns the use of *musica ficta* steps in order to correct mi against fa. Such use is said to be 'because of necessity' (*causa necessitatis*) and distinguished from the use 'because of beauty' (*causa pulchritudinis*) to be discussed in the next chapter.[7]

Early in the fifteenth century, Prosdocimus de Beldemandis presents the prohibition among the rules of counterpoint (where it naturally belongs and most often appears) and gives it a general form which implicitly includes the fourth (since this can be used as a perfect consonance in counterpoint for more than two parts): 'In perfectly consonant intervals we ought never to place mi against fa or vice versa, because we would straightway make the perfectly consonant intervals minor or augmented, which forms are discordant.'[8] Since the rule appears among the rules of simple counterpoint, it may be that it does not apply in diminished counterpoint provided such intervals are treated like discords. Prosdocimus returns to the same problem in the final section of his counterpoint treatise, reformulating it this time as a rule of *musica ficta* and neglecting to mention the tritone for the same reasons as his predecessors did:

The sixth and last rule, for understanding the placement of these two signs, round b and square b, in counterpoint, is this: that these signs are to be applied to octaves, fifths, and similar intervals as it is necessary to enlarge or diminish them in order to make them good consonances if they earlier were dissonant, because such intervals ought always to be major or consonant in counterpoint.[9]

The same rule can be presented either as a rule of counterpoint or as one concerning the use of feigned steps. In both forms, the rule recurs regularly in fifteenth- and sixteenth-century treatises.[10]

But when it is phrased so generally, it is still not clear whether it applies unconditionally or only in simple counterpoint, that is, only when the fourths, fifths and octaves are intended to be used as consonances. Since most of the early counterpoint treatises, even those which – like Prosdocimus' – make the distinction between simple and diminished counterpoint, present only the most rudimentary instruction in simple counterpoint for beginners, it is not surprising that they do not address, let alone clarify, this issue. For this we have to wait for authors willing to explore the art of counterpoint in more depth. No one in the fifteenth century did this more profoundly than Johannes Tinctoris and, consequently, it is his counterpoint treatise of 1477 that contains some interesting early information on the question which interests us here.

The penultimate chapter of the second book of *Liber de arte contrapuncti*, in which the use of dissonances in the diminished counterpoint has been explained, proclaims in its title 'that discords which they call false concords [that is, the perfect consonances augmented or diminished by a chromatic semitone] must be completely avoided'.[11] Thus, Tinctoris would clearly banish such intervals from counterpoint altogether, and not only from simple counterpoint. But the text of the chapter shows that Tinctoris's opinion was not shared by his contemporaries:

Continuing, any one who has a clear head must easily understand that whatever we have said about the permission and arrangement of discords is not [to be understood] in relation to those discords which others call false concords. Indeed, we ought to avoid the false unison and the false diapente, and false octave and any other false concord caused either by the lack or overabundance of a major semitone, for this is the reason it is taught by masters to their students from the beginning that they do not introduce mi against fa in perfect concords. Nevertheless, I have discovered the opposite most frequently among many, many composers, even the most famous, as with Faugues in his *Missa Le serviteur*, with Busnois in his chanson, *Je ne demande*, and with Caron in one chanson which is named, *Hellas*, just as is seen here [see Example 8].[12]

Tinctoris often attempts to reform the practice of his contemporaries. For us, the passage, and in particular the examples, are interesting precisely to the extent that they tell what sort of mi-against-fa discords would be tolerated by 'many, many composers, even the most famous' in the late fifteenth century. The diminished fifth between A and E♭ on the penultimate breve in Faugues, the diminished twelfth between E and ♭♭ on a breve in Busnois, and two diminished fifths between E and ♭, one on the first minim, the other on the penultimate semibreve in Caron were all intended by the composers and would be left uncorrected by their performers, implies Tinctoris, and this implication makes the examples truly invaluable to us.

Now, what is most striking about these mi-against-fa discords is that they all occur in simple counterpoint. This suggests an unexpected solution of

Example 8

our problem: far from being totally unacceptable or acceptable only in diminished counterpoint when used as dissonances, mi-against-fa discords may be tolerated even in simple note-against-note counterpoint. But if the mi-against-fa prohibition is to retain any meaning at all (and it is repeated far too frequently to be entirely meaningless), we must look for the conditions under which such discords may be tolerated, we must examine, that is, how they are used in the examples above.

The conditions which make these intervals tolerable must lie in their context, in the way in which they are followed ('resolved') and preceded ('prepared'). In Faugues, the diminished fifth A-Eb is resolved to the major third

96

Bb-D, that is, the dissonance is resolved to a consonance in such a way that the mi-step goes a diatonic semitone up and the fa-step a diatonic semitone down. In Busnois, E-bb may be seen as resolving either to C-aa or to F-aa: in the upper part, the two semiminims following the dissonant bb are merely an ornamental anticipation of the resolution, and in the lower part, the resolution is delayed by a minim rest and perhaps also the following minim. If we take the resolution to be F-aa, the lesson from Busnois is the same as the one from Faugues, that is, the dissonance must be resolved to a consonance with the mi-step going a semitone up and the fa-step a semitone down. If the resolution is C-aa, the condition can be relaxed to say that in the resolution to a consonance only one of the dissonant steps must be resolved properly (the fa-step by a semitone down or the mi-step by a semitone up). In either case, the resolution may be delayed by notes belonging to the diminished counterpoint and even by rests. Keeping in mind the results obtained thus far, I take it that the resolution of the first diminished fifth E-b in Caron is to F-a (with an intervening minim in a weak metrical position) and the resolution of the second one is to a-a (with an intervening rest in the lower part). Thus, the general rule which can be derived from all four cases is: a mi-against-fa discord will be tolerated even in simple counterpoint, provided it is followed by a consonance with at least one, and preferably both, of the dissonant notes properly resolved (that is, with the mi-step going a diatonic semitone up and/or the fa-step going a diatonic semitone down). The resolution may be delayed by notes belonging to diminished counterpoint or by a rest.

Since in both Faugues and Busnois the offending discords are preceded by the same concords to which they are resolved, we might suspect that also a proper 'preparation' of the discord is required for it to be tolerable, and that the rule governing this preparation mirrors that which governs the resolution. But Caron shows that this is not the case: the second discord is preceded in such a way that neither its fa-step is reached by a semitone going up, nor its mi-step by a semitone going down. Thus, it is likely that a proper 'preparation' is not required for a mi-against-fa discord to be found acceptable, or rather that any consonance would be considered an adequate preparation.

In his examples, Tinctoris quotes only two voices from four-part compositions. An examination of the full four-part texture may be instructive (see Example 9).[13] In each case, the context clarifies why the discords discussed by the theorist could not be corrected by means of additional flats. Each of these discords, however, might conceivably be corrected if the conflicting fa-step was changed into a mi-step (though I am far from recommending this). The fact that they were not meant to be so corrected, clearly implied by Tinctoris, means that they were found tolerable. And the rule I have derived from Tinctoris's examples can be derived equally well from the four-

Example 9

Faugues

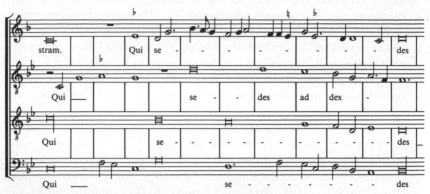

Busnois

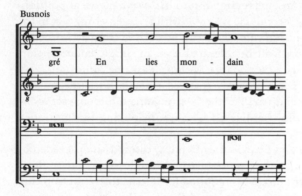

Caron

part excerpts: the discords were tolerated because they were properly resolved. Thus, for instance, the conclusion of the Faugues passage involves a Phrygian cadence between the structurally central cantus and tenor, with the bass and alto playing structurally inessential roles and the bass 'evading' the cadence altogether (to use a Zarlinian expression) by moving from A to B♭ rather than to D or a. It is clear that in this context the conflict between E♭ and A-a is inevitable, unless one chooses as the cadential leading tone c♯ instead of E♭, a most unlikely choice in view of the tenor's key signature and, in any case, a choice which Tinctoris does not even consider. What makes the conflict tolerable is precisely the fact that discords are resolved to concords with the offending fa-step (E♭) going down to a mi-step (D).

The subject is further pursued by Tinctoris in the last chapter of the second book:

Indeed, perfect concords which are made imperfect or superfluous by a chromatic semitone, that is, by alteration, must be avoided, although I am aware that almost all composers use these above all or half or a larger part of the note defining the measure [which in the example below is the semibreve] and immediately preceding a perfection [that is, the completion of a cadence] in a composition of three or many voices, as follows here [see Example 10].[14]

Example 10

Ex. 10 (*cont.*)

The mi-against-fa discords which Tinctoris's contemporaries would find acceptable arise here in the penultimate harmony of a cadential progression in writing for more than two parts. They could not arise in two-part counterpoint in which the penultimate harmony of a cadential progression has to be an imperfect consonance which may proceed to the final perfect consonance by a diatonic semitone in the part containing the leading tone. (In Tinctoris's example, these two-part penultimate harmonies are major sixths resolving to octaves by step: E-c♯ in m. 2 resolving to D-d in m. 3 between the tenor and contratenor; and ♮-g♯ in m. 6 resolving to a-aa in m. 7 between the tenor and superius.) But the discord may be introduced by the third voice against the leading tone. In Tinctoris's two cadences, melodic considerations preclude adjusting this third voice to the leading tone by sharpening it (and, at any rate, Tinctoris makes it clear that, for whatever reasons, his contemporaries would not sharpen the third voice there). The result in the first cadence conforms fully to the rule we have already derived from Tinctoris's preceding chapter: the diminished fifth between the contratenor and superius (c♯-g in m. 2) may be tolerated here since it is followed by a consonance (d-f in m. 3) with the mi-step (c♯) properly resolved a semitone up (to d). Tinctoris's second cadence, however, is troublesome. While outwardly it again fully conforms to our rule, the augmented octave between the contratenor and superius (G-g♯) sounds so awful that I suspect Tinctoris might have overstated the case here. Lest it be thought that my suspicion arises from an anachronistic experience of intervals, we should recall that also in the Middle Ages and the Renaissance the octave was considered the most perfect of intervals and, more to the point perhaps, that we found out in the preceding chapter that the prohibition of a direct melodic imperfect octave was more categorical than that of the tritone and diminished fifth. We should find more evidence than this one example of Tinctoris before we conclude that vertical imperfect octaves were ever acceptable. For now, I am inclined to believe that our rule allowing mi against fa under certain conditions refers to the imperfect fourth and fifth, but not to the imperfect octave.

Several sixteenth-century theorists offer evidence supporting the above interpretation of Tinctoris's examples. Giovanni del Lago, in a letter sent to Piero de Justinis from Venice on June 3, 1538, criticizes the addressee for using the sign of diesis in a passage in one of his motets (see Example 11): [15]

Example 11

Tenor
Bassus
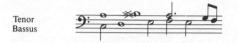

But I believe that you have signed it only in that in such place one sings mi, in order not to make this fifth diminished. I say that it would have been better to have signed in that place the round b than the cross which represents (I speak according to the blind populace) the lying square b. It is proper for the imperfect, or diminished, fifth to go to the third, especially when immediately one part ascends and the other descends. [16]

Evidently Piero marked ♮ in the upper part with ♯ to make sure that no singer would flatten the note on account of the following descent to F, and he did so (as del Lago recognizes) since the use of ♭ instead of ♮ would have produced a diminished fifth with the lower part. Thus Piero noticed the conflict between a melodic and a vertical consideration and decided to make sure that the vertical, rather than the melodic, prohibition was enforced. Del Lago, however, thinks that one does not have to choose between the conflicting requirements here, since the diminished fifth is acceptable, provided it is resolved to the third, especially when the mi-step goes a semitone up and the fa-step a semitone down. A diminished fifth contracting to a third with a diatonic semitone in at least one of the parts was also the most common situation in Tinctoris's examples; it occurred in four out of the six progressions he exemplified, while one more progression involved a diminished fifth resolving to a unison with the fa-step going a semitone down. In addition, del Lago indirectly confirms that a 'preparation' of a diminished fifth does not belong to the requirements, since he talks only about the ways the mi-against-fa discord should be followed, not about how to precede it. Thus, del Lago independently corroborates our interpretation of Tinctoris's examples.

Moreover, there is some evidence that the diminished fifth was allowed also when preceded or followed by the perfect fifth. Several of del Lago's predecessors allowed such progressions in counterpoint. Ramos de Pareia glossed the prohibition of parallel perfect consonances as follows:

To be sure, according to Tristanus de Silva it is not thus prohibited in [the case of] the fifth, since a fifth may be made after a fifth, as long, however, as one would be a diminished fifth, the other a [perfect] fifth, as we find in the song *Sois emprantis* and in other more ancient ones. But this is not allowed in undiminished [note values], well, however, in broken ones, that is, in the diminution of notes. [17]

In other words, Ramos allowed two parallel fifths in smaller note values, provided one of these fifths was diminished. He may have had in mind the beginning of the popular English ballade by Walter Frye, *So ys emprentid*, which appeared in some sources with the Frenchified incipit *Soyez aprentis* (see Example 12).[18] The only parallel fifths in the song occur between the

Example 12

contratenor (c-d) and cantus (g-aa) in m. 3 and again between the contratenor (d-c) and cantus (aa-g) in m. 6. It is most unlikely that Ramos referred to the first of these: the only possibility of having a diminished fifth there would be the addition of the sharp at c in the contratenor in order to make it into a cadential leading tone, but first, a cadence at this point, in the middle of the textual line, is very awkward (and its last harmony would come on a weak part of the breve), and second, even if one wanted to make a cadence there, one would probably produce a secondary leading tone of g♯ and avoid the diminished fifth in any case. The passage in m. 6, on the other hand, may well have been the one Ramos referred to: c in the contratenor may be sharpened to form a cadential leading tone there, while g in the cantus would have to remain unsharpened, since it descends to f. It should be noted that the diminished fifth in the passage is correctly resolved, according to the rule we have derived from Tinctoris. It is, of course, debatable whether all musicians would choose to make a cadence at this point at all; the only absolutely obligatory cadence in the quoted passage comes at the end of the line (mm. 8–9). But a cadence which seems to be suggested by Ramos in m. 7 is at least possible, as we shall see when we discuss cadential uses of *musica ficta* in the next chapter.

In his *Lucidario in musica*, Pietro Aaron refers to Ramos's discussion of the problem and to its exemplification 'in this ancient song called *Soys emprantis*',[19] but does not quote from it. Instead, he quotes approvingly from Philippe Verdelot's *Infirmitatem nostram* (see Example 13).[20] The

Example 13

example reverses the progression discussed above: here the diminished fifth precedes, rather than follows, the perfect one. But also here the resolution of the mi-against-fa discord follows the rule we have derived from Tinctoris. Like Ramos, Aaron stresses that the diminished fifth is allowed in such contexts not 'on undiminished notes, but on diminished parts of the time, as here, that is, on the minim and semiminim',[21] and indeed in both Ramos's and Aaron's examples the discords last a minim. Thus, we should probably amplify our rule as follows: a properly resolved mi-against-fa discord is allowed on a fifth even if this is preceded or followed by a perfect fifth, provided that in such a case this discord lasts no longer than a minim (under the regular mensuration signs).

Another theorist, Franchinus Gaffurius, rejects any exception to the rule prohibiting parallel perfect consonances, but testifies that some musicians thought otherwise:

Yet some have believed that two fifths can be sung in ascending or descending parallel motion, provided that they are altered in quality and size, namely, one perfect and the other diminished by the removal or the lack of a semitone; for example, proceeding directly from A-re and E-la-mi [A and E], or *proslambanomenos* and *hypate meson*, to low b-mi and F-fa-ut [B and F], or *hypate hypaton* and *parhypate meson*.[22]

We have here, once again, a progression exemplified by del Lago, even though, unfortunately, Gaffurius does not bother to tell us how the diminished fifth should be resolved, since – unlike 'some' – he does not think the progression is legitimate.

Some of the musicians who approved of the progression may have belonged to del Lago's immediate circle. In a letter of November 27, 1531, Spataro answered Aaron's inquiry concerning how one might legitimately use a perfect and a diminished fifth one after the other by referring Aaron to his (Spataro's) treatise on counterpoint.[23] Spataro evidently thought that there was a way of using such a progression without error, and – as we already saw – so did Aaron.

Moreover, Aaron discusses in some detail acceptable exceptions to the mi-against-fa prohibition,[24] and he finds the diminished fifth acceptable in the contexts illustrated in Example 14.[25] These are further cases of the diminished fifth contracting by step to a third. Yet another such example was described in Aaron's *Compendiolo* (see Example 15).[26] In writing for three or more voices, one may tolerate in analogous contexts the tritone, 'especially when it will have a third or tenth below, as one sees in the following example [see Example 16]'.[27]

Example 14

Canto

Tenore
Basso

Example 15

Example 16

Canto

Tenore

Basso

Examples of acceptable mi against fa occur also in Adrian Petit Coclico's *Compendium musices*. One should not sing mi against fa on perfect consonances, says Coclico, 'unless the note is part of a scalewise passage'.[28] The examples make his meaning clear. In one, Coclico shows how one may 'make fa against mi, having added a soft b' (see Example 17).[29] In mm. 6–7 one

Example 17

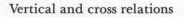

might avoid all mi-against-fa discords by flattening aa and e in the discant, but since the example is to show how one may 'make fa against mi, having added a soft b', it is clear that Coclico does not want any additional flats in those two measures. Both resulting discords are passing notes of semiminim length and neither is correctly resolved by the criteria we have derived from other theorists, in that in both cases the passing mi goes down, not up. Consequently, we must conclude that Coclico's is a new exception to the mi-against-fa prohibition, new in relation to what we have learned from other theorists, even if not new at the time of Coclico's treatise (that is, in 1552), since the theorist claims that the rules of counterpoint among which the exception quoted above was found are 'according to the doctrine of Josquin des Prez'.[30] Three more mi-against-fa discords in the example (♮♮'s in the discant in mm. 1, 9 and 12) are passing semiminims, this time correctly resolved (the dissonant mi proceeding a semitone up). And finally, ♮ in the altus in m. 11 forms a dissonant passing minim against the discant and a dissonant note-against-note with the bass, in both cases correctly resolved. The general exception to the mi-against-fa prohibition we may derive from all this is that a mi against fa is allowed as a passing note of short duration (normally a semiminim in imperfect diminished time), even if this is 'incorrectly' resolved (that is, with mi going down, or fa up).

Another author of the early 1550s to provide us with examples of an acceptable diminished fifth and augmented fourth is Luigi Dentice (see Example 18).[31] Both mi-against-fa discords are allowed here, according to

Example 18

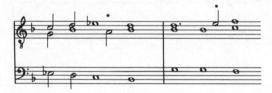

Dentice, because the discordant steps are not attacked simultaneously and because they appear on the upbeat.[32] According to the rule we have derived from Tinctoris, both would be acceptable even without these additional restrictions, that is, even if they were note-against-note dissonances on the downbeat. Dentice's restrictions reflect the growing control over the use of dissonances during the sixteenth century, but – as we shall see shortly – they should not be taken as universally valid in his time.

One of the participants in Dentice's dialogue has this to say on the second example: 'I liked this fourth constituted in this way a lot, but I did not trust myself [sufficiently] to claim that it could stay, until many skillful men had assured me of it.'[33] It is impossible to say whether this reflects a change of taste concerning the use of the secondary leading tone in a cadence. The speaker's hesitation to accept the augmented fourth suggests that he had been accustomed to sharpen the secondary leading tone in cadences. But it may well be that we read too much into his remarks.

We have seen that the mi-against-fa prohibition belongs essentially to the theory of counterpoint, and that most of our information on exceptions to this prohibition comes from counterpoint treatises, from Tinctoris on. It is not surprising, then, to find some important information in the most comprehensive of the sixteenth-century counterpoint treatises, the third part of Gioseffo Zarlino's *Le Istitutioni harmoniche*. Like so many others, Zarlino reminds us that 'the more experienced practical musicians have, in order to avoid these errors, adopted the rule that the syllable mi may never be used against fa in perfect consonances',[34] but he immediately adds: 'However at times the semidiapente is used in counterpoint instead of the diapente, and the tritone in place of the diatessaron, both with good effect.'[35] It is striking that he does not include the imperfect octave among the exceptions. A little later, Zarlino comes to 'the proper manner of doing this [that is, of using the diminished fifth and the tritone]':[36]

We may on occasion write the semidiapente in a single percussion. We may do so when it is immediately succeeded by the ditone [see Example 19]. Here [see Example 20] the parts may be exchanged without disadvantage. This is practiced by the best modern musicians, as it was in the past by some of the older ones. Not only the semidiapente, but also the tritone is sometimes allowed, as we shall discover. We must take care, however, that the semidiapente or tritone be preceded immediately by a perfect or imperfect consonance. The semidiapente is then tempered by the preceding and following consonance in such a way that the effect is no longer poor, but good, as experience has proved.[37]

Example 19

Example 20

This passage is the reason why I have decided not to treat Dentice's additional restrictions on the legitimate use of the diminished fifth and tritone (that they be not attacked simultaneously and that they occur on the upbeat) as universally valid. Zarlino's expertise in counterpoint was incomparably greater than Dentice's, and he clearly allowed the discords even in note-against-note writing and in strong metrical position. Zarlino's restriction on the use of the diminished fifth is that it be resolved to the major third, with the mi-step going a semitone up and the fa-step a semitone down. His rule is more restrictive than the one we have derived from Tinctoris, where any consonance would do as the resolution and where only one of the parts has to proceed by a semitone in the proper direction. It is difficult to decide whether Zarlino reflects a genuine change in the musical practice here, or merely tries to reform and tighten up this practice. I am inclined to think that the latter is the case, since we have seen that as recently as 1545 Aaron quoted approvingly a passage from Verdelot's motet where a resolution of the diminished fifth in which only one part proceeded by a semitone in the proper direction was allowed. But it is certainly true that almost all the examples of legitimate diminished fifths we have been able to find, from Tinctoris on, resolve to thirds (if not necessarily to major ones) and that, consequently, Zarlino is describing the normal, if not necessarily the only possible, practice.

An absolute novelty is Zarlino's observation that the notes of resolution may be exchanged between the two parts. Since, to the best of my knowledge, no earlier theorist mentions such a practice, it is particularly valuable that Zarlino tells us that this was also the practice of some of the musicians of the past. Obviously, only musical sources themselves will allow us to learn how far back this practice extended.

Zarlino seems also to be the first theorist to tell us expressly that a mi-against-fa discord must be preceded immediately by a consonance, but since he does not require anything more specific than that, the restriction is practically superfluous; in the counterpoint of the period, one would not follow a dissonance with a dissonance anyway.

And finally, Zarlino tells us that also the tritone may be used, deferring the discussion of how it is to be handled until later. We shall return to this matter shortly.

We learn more about the allowed use of the diminished fifth in the chapter on the diminished two-part counterpoint: 'Similarly the fourth in syncopation may be succeeded by the semidiapente, which is followed immediately by the major third, provided the semidiapente can be used to good advantage without a false relation between the parts.'[38] There follows an example (see Example 21). This goes beyond what we have learned previously, in that here the diminished fifth is preceded by a dissonance, the suspended fourth, which is correctly resolved, with the diminished fifth intervening between the suspension and resolution. It is striking that also here Zarlino insists that the diminished fifth be resolved to the major third (contracting inwards by semitones in both parts, as the example shows). The clue

Example 21

to this insistence lies in Zarlino's final *caveat*. The theorist wants to avoid cross relations and, indeed, the second most likely resolution of the diminished fifth, the one to the minor instead of the major third, would produce one. Zarlino's insistence that the diminished fifth be *always* (as opposed to *most commonly*) resolved to the major third, the insistence which – as we have seen – restricts the use of mi against fa more than earlier theorists would, results from his distaste for cross relations. Consequently, we must postpone the final decision as to whether Zarlino follows or reforms the common practice here until we have examined the problem of cross relations.

Zarlino returns once more to the subject of acceptable mi-against-fa discords in his comments on Example 22:

Example 22

Cantus

Tenor
Bass

Note that in the first instance there is a tritone. This is bearable because it is followed by a major third that forms a good harmonic relation with the parts containing the tritone. The same goes for the semidiapente followed by a major tenth in the second example. Though the second part of each upbeat is dissonant, it progresses in accordance with the rules and leaves the ear content.[39]

This confirms that for Zarlino allowable mi-against-fa discords (excluding the imperfect octaves, of course) must always be resolved so that the mi-step goes a semitone up and the fa-step a semitone down, that is, the diminished fifth contracting to the major third, and the tritone expanding to the minor sixth, since such resolutions form no non-harmonic cross relations with the discords in question.

And finally, Zarlino offers one more comment on the subject:

At times musicians write a tritone between two parts so that it falls on the second part of a syncopated semibreve written in the bass as in the example [see Example 23]. The notes of the tritone, although heard, are not actually sounded simultaneously,

Example 23

and since the parts are so coordinated as not to depart from the rules, the resulting effect is good.[40]

At first glance, it might appear that Zarlino says nothing new here, but the passage has important implications. It is probably the passage to which the theorist referred above when he said that 'also the tritone is sometimes allowed, as we shall discover'. A fourth over the lowest part is a dissonance, of course, and, consequently, on the strong beat, it may be used only as a suspension. Zarlino's example with tritone suspensions on the strong beat implies a revision of the general rule which allows mi-against-fa discords in simple counterpoint. The use of the tritone above the lowest part is subject to the same rules and restrictions as the use of the perfect fourth above the lowest part.

To the best of my knowledge, Zarlino was the first theorist of counterpoint to treat systematically and in depth the subject of non-harmonic cross relations, that is, the cross relations involving 'an augmented or diminished diapason, or . . . a semidiapente or tritone or similar interval':[41]

To purge our compositions of every error and to assure their correctness, let us avoid this relation [that is, all non-harmonic cross relations]. Especially when we compose for two voices, it is very annoying to sensitive ears, inasmuch as such intervals are not found among the sonorous numbers, and are not sung in any genus despite contrary views of a few. However that may be, they are very difficult to sing and have poor effect. I am appalled at those who have not avoided having these intervals sung in certain parts of their compositions. I cannot imagine any reason for them. Although it is less evil to find this relation between two parts and two melodies than to hear it in one part, it is still bad and the ear is still offended. For a blow inflicted by several, unless it is slighter, is just as offensive as if it came from one. So these intervals, which are not admitted in melodic motion, must also be avoided in the relations between parts . . . It is true, however, that in compositions for many voices it is often impossible to avoid such relations and not to arrive at such an impasse . . . But even when necessity thus presses him, he [the composer] should at least see that these defects occur in diatonic steps and in those which are proper and natural to the mode and not in those which are accidental, that is, those indicated in a composition by the signs ♮, ♯, and ♭. For used in this way they do not have such a poor effect.[42]

I have quoted at such a great length because the passage, when read whole, conveys the impression of the theorist trying to legislate here rather than to record faithfully the contemporary practice. Zarlino tells us to avoid non-harmonic cross relations in writing for two parts, but admits that it is often impossible to avoid them when writing for many voices and, consequently, allows them there, provided they do not involve accidentally inflected steps. The mi against fa on perfect intervals is commonly avoided horizontally and vertically and he can see no reason why it should not be avoided in cross relations as well. But while horizontal non-harmonic relations may be corrected by means of accidentals, as we already know, and so may the vertical ones, as we shall learn shortly, Zarlino nowhere suggests correcting such cross relations by adding inflections. Either he forgot to mention this possibility, or he thought that composers should avoid writing progressions which would have to be corrected. If the latter is the case, only an examination of practical sources could tell us to what extent Zarlino's precepts reflect the practice of his contemporaries. He, at any rate, expressly mentions those who do not avoid cross relations in their works, so we can be sure that the practice was not universal.

Thus, I repeat, Zarlino's discussion gives the impression of an attempt to improve the existing practice, and not simply to describe it. But it is also possible that this attempted reform capitalized on a tendency already present among some mid-sixteenth-century composers. And finally, it is possible, although I have no evidence for this other than that of my ears, that Zarlino made explicit and more systematic an already-existing tendency to avoid the most offensive of the cross relations, that of the imperfect octave. Since in music in which every voice is notated with the same key signature (a practically universal case by Zarlino's time) such a relation can occur only when an internal accidental is introduced, Zarlino's precept to avoid the non-harmonic cross relations involving accidentally inflected steps may perhaps reflect such an effort. To be sure, one can derive from Zarlino's discussion several different lessons, none of them certain. The lesson which I think is most likely to reflect the practice of his contemporaries is, at most, the advice to avoid the imperfect-octave cross relations, but not others.

The subject of cross relations appears also in the context of the discussion of parallel imperfect consonances, since two consecutive major thirds or minor sixths moving by step will produce them. Zarlino advises that one should not write parallel imperfect consonances, but his claim that they are forbidden for the same reason for which parallel perfect consonances are smacks, again, of an attempt to reform rather than describe the practice.[43] Similarly, Nicola Vicentino argued that one should avoid parallel perfect or imperfect consonances of the same size, but conceded that in practice one did use parallel imperfect consonances.[44] Jerome Cardan, in his *De musica* of *ca*. 1546, noted that 'two successive major sixths, minor sixths, major thirds, or minor thirds do not sound well (as Adrian has observed very well) . . . Yet this movement of intervals is allowed by many.'[45] This puts Zarlino's and Vicentino's remarks on the subject in perspective. The two students of Adrian Willaert expressed their teacher's concerns, when arguing against parallel imperfect consonances, but did not follow the common practice. Thus, we may perhaps conclude that within our period the cross relations involving the augmented fourth or diminished fifth began to be a concern for Willaert and his circle, but most likely not yet the general concern.

What is the chronological validity of our findings thus far? We have been trying to find out which vertical and cross relations have to be corrected by means of *musica ficta* steps and we have discovered that, so far as the vertical relations are concerned, from the beginning to the end of our period theorists universally prohibited the same non-harmonic relations which were also prohibited in melodies, that is, the mi against fa on perfect consonances. Just as was the case with melodic intervals, also the prohibition of vertical non-harmonic relations admitted some exceptions. From Tinctoris we have derived the rule according to which a mi-against-fa discord will be tolerated even in simple counterpoint provided it is preceded and followed by a consonance, with at least one, and preferably both, of the dissonant notes properly resolved (that is, with the mi-step going a diatonic semitone up and/or the fa-step going a diatonic semitone down), immediately, or after notes belonging to the diminished counterpoint, or even after a rest. (We have also suggested, though very tentatively and against what was perhaps implied by Tinctoris, that the imperfect octave is to be avoided unconditionally.) This general rule retains its validity through the end of our period, since it is still exemplified in Zarlino. To be sure, Zarlino restricts the use of mi against fa further, by demanding that both dissonant notes must be properly resolved, not just one. This additional restriction follows from Zarlino's wish to avoid the non-harmonic cross relations. Since it is likely that in expressing this wish Zarlino was trying to reform the practice of his contemporaries, his additional restriction was probably also not generally valid and the more liberal rule we have derived from Tinctoris was still followed in the mid sixteenth century.

We can only speculate on whether the rule was valid also before Tinctoris's time. I am inclined to think that it was, for the following reason. The general tendency in the development of counterpoint from 1300 to 1560 was toward an increasing control (through restrictions) on the use of dissonances. Thus I think it to be unlikely that the mi-against-fa prohibition would be followed unconditionally at first and in a liberalized form later. The opposite development (from a more liberal to a stricter rule) would be more probable, but the rule we have derived from Tinctoris could not be liberalized any further without making the mi-against-fa prohibition utterly meaningless. Thus, it is at least possible that something resembling this rule was implicitly followed by musicians from the beginning of the prohibition. And we can be sure that at least a general sense that an augmented and diminished interval could be accepted provided it was properly resolved (in the sense which we gave here to this expression) antedates Tinctoris by more than a century. Johannes Boen, writing in 1357, informs us that a vertical diminished seventh between D♯ and c is allowed when it resolves to a perfect fifth between E and ♮, with D♯-mi going a diatonic semitone up and c-fa a diatonic semitone down.[46]

Further, we have learned from examples which extend from Ramos in 1482 to Aaron in 1545 that a properly handled diminished fifth (that is, one handled according to the rule discussed above) is allowed even if this is preceded or (rarely) followed by a perfect fifth, provided that in such a case the discord lasts no longer than a minim (under the regular mensuration signs). Only an examination of practical sources would tell us how far back beyond Ramos (or Frye) this practice extends. Similarly, when we learn from Zarlino that the diminished fifth may even be preceded by the dissonant suspended fourth, we have no way of knowing how far back this practice extends other than actually examining music. But in both these cases we may guess that it is unlikely that later theorists would be allowing something forbidden earlier. Thus we may justifiably augment our general rule to say that the diminished fifth may be preceded or (rarely) followed by a perfect one, provided the dissonance lasts no longer than a part of the *mensura* or *tactus* (but it is impossible to ascertain on the basis of theoretical sources alone how far back beyond Ramos this last provision extends), and may even be preceded by the dissonant suspended fourth when this is correctly resolved, with the diminished fifth intervening between the suspension and resolution.

We have also learned from Zarlino that the use of the tritone above the lowest part is additionally subject to the same rules and restrictions as the use of the perfect fourth above the lowest part, that is, that on the strong beat it may only be introduced in suspension. Once again, only an examination of practical sources will tell us how far back the validity of this rule extends, but at any rate, the question is of no practical significance to a modern editor or performer. Also the extent of the chronological validity of Zarlino's observation that the notes resolving a mi-against-fa discord may be exchanged between the voices can be ascertained only on the basis of practical sources.

All of the above considerations pertain to the use of mi against fa even in simple counterpoint. In addition, we have learned from Coclico that a mi-against-fa discord is allowed as a passing note of short duration regardless of how this is resolved. Once again, I am inclined to believe that the earlier practice was more lenient rather than stricter and that, consequently, Coclico's observation has a general validity for our whole period. The duration of such passing notes would then be governed by the same rule which regulated the maximum duration of dissonant passing notes in general. In fact, it may be that we should generalize Coclico's observation further and say that in the diminished counterpoint the mi-against-fa discords (most likely excluding the imperfect octave) are treated in the same way in which all other dissonances are.

And finally, we still do not know when precisely musicians began to avoid non-harmonic cross relations, if they ever did. Recent researches based on practical evidence demonstrated widespread tolerance of such cross relations, including the relation of non-harmonic octave, in late fifteenth- and sixteenth-century music.[47] Even Zarlino admitted that not all of his contemporaries avoided them and my guess was that at most only the advice to avoid the imperfect-octave cross relation might have been followed in his time. But even if this guess is correct (and there is practically no evidence for it, other than the evidence of our ears), I do not know how far back the validity of this presumed tendency extended. The wish to avoid the cross relations of augmented fourth and diminished fifth may perhaps have originated with Willaert. In Zarlino's time, it was still not a general concern, but it is possible that the prestige of Zarlino's teaching spread this concern more widely in the later sixteenth century among the followers of what was subsequently to be called the 'first practice'.

Almost all music of our period was notated with no, one, or two flats in the signature, with the same or different signatures in individual voices of the polyphonic whole. When all parts had the same signature, for instance, no flats, the only augmented or diminished vertical intervals which could arise without the use of internal accidentals were the tritone and diminished fifth between B♮ and F. When two parts differed by one flat in their signatures, for instance, one having no flat and the other B♭ in the signature, one more non-harmonic vertical relation arose, that of the imperfect octave between B♮ and B♭, as well as the already-known tritone and diminished fifth involving the new step, that is, between B♭ and E. And when two parts differed by two flats (a somewhat rarer case), one having no flat and the other B♭ and E♭ in the signature, two new non-harmonic relations arose, those of the diminished fourth and augmented fifth between B♮ and E♭, as well as the already-known non-harmonic relations involving the new step, that is, between E♭ and A and between E♭ and E♮. Thus, it should be obvious why the only augmented or diminished vertical intervals regularly discussed by theorists were the imperfect fourth and fifth (and, in particular, the tritone and diminished fifth) and the imperfect octave. These were the only vertical relations which might normally require a correction by means of a *musica ficta* step.

(ii) The method of avoiding mi-against-fa discords

We know now which non-harmonic vertical relations might normally arise and require a correction. How were they corrected? When in the preceding chapter we considered the same non-harmonic relations arising in melody, we saw that the basic choice involved correcting them by means of a flat or sharp. We face the same choice when we consider vertical relations, but since these arise between two different voices, the choice might also conceivably be which of the two voices to correct. We may quickly dispose of the latter possibility. If the musicians of our period were regularly governed by such considerations as, for instance, that one should leave the tenor intact and inflect the other voice, or that one should inflect the note belonging to the higher part, these considerations would have certainly left a trace in music theory. But this is not the case. (A single explicit discussion of the problem I know of will be discussed shortly.)

Correcting a vertical non-harmonic relation must have involved, then, the decision as to whether to use a flat or a sharp. In the preceding chapter, we have seen that the same relations occurring melodically were normally corrected by means of a flat rather than a sharp and I have proposed an explanation as to why this was so. Since the same reasons are valid equally for melodic and for vertical relations, it follows that also the latter should be corrected by flats rather than sharps. And the reasons which I have provided in the preceding chapter apply also to those relations which arise between two parts notated with different key signatures. In addition, note that the 'new' non-harmonic relations which arise between parts with different signatures (that is, the relations which arise in addition to those which we would have if both parts had the same signature as the one with fewer flats has) always involve a step flattened by the signature as one of its terms. Since the flattening of this step is expressly demanded by the signature, it makes more sense, when correcting the relations involving this step, to flatten the other note than to cancel the signature accidental. But even without this additional argument, on the basis of the arguments presented in the last chapter alone, we would have to conclude that all non-harmonic vertical relations which arise normally (that is, without the use of internal accidentals) in polyphony should be corrected by means of flats.

This conclusion is supported to a certain extent by theoretical evidence. There are numerous examples, from the late fifteenth century on, of theorists demonstrating how to correct a mi-against-fa discord and doing so by means of a flat. In his *Liber de natura et proprietate tonorum*, Johannes Tinctoris informs us that one of the reasons why ♭ may be used in the tritus is 'by reason of perfect concords'[48] (that is, to correct mi against fa), the other being 'the need to avoid the tritone',[49] and gives examples of the former, in which the tenor gets the round b, since there is an f against it in the counterpoint.[50] It does not occur to him to point out that one could achieve the same result by sharpening f. And this sense of it being self-evident that one corrects a vertical mi against fa by means of a flat is conveyed by many theorists after Tinctoris as well.[51]

Moreover, some theorists come close to telling us expressly that flat and sharp serve different functions. An early and still very obscure indication of this is perhaps given by Georg Rhau when, having explained what *musica ficta* is and that it has two signs, ♮ which signifies mi, and ♭ which signifies fa, he continues: 'For in fact, fa restores euphony, while mi corrects cacophony. Indeed, they are allowed not only because of the necessity of song, but also because of the agreeableness.'[52] The implication seems to be that fa and mi have two distinct functions, one being used because of necessity (and we already know that *causa necessitatis* means 'in order to avoid mi against fa'), the other because of 'agreeableness' (and Rhau's *propter iucunditatem* may be equivalent to *causa pulchritudinis* of other theorists, the reason to be discussed in the next chapter).

A clearer, but again not entirely unambiguous, indication that the functions of flat and sharp are distinct is provided in an already quoted passage from Giovanni Maria Lanfranco:

Just as the soft b is used in songs of the square b in order to avoid tritones, so the diesis, with which one may also sweeten the harshness of the tritone, is practiced in any order to create sweeter consonances, as are the major sixths going to the octave, or the minor thirds going to the unison, or the major thirds and tenths at the end of cadences, before which one almost always uses this diesis.[53]

One uses flat in order to correct a mi against fa (we may safely generalize Lanfranco's reference to the tritone in this way) and sharp in order to produce a sharpened leading tone in the penultimate harmony of a cadence and a major third in its final harmony. Lanfranco weakens the opposition of the functions when he interjects that sharp may also be used to correct a mi against fa, but the way in which he says this suggests that this is not the sharp's normal function. Since the reasons which explain the use of flats in mi-against-fa contexts pertain only to such contexts which arise naturally and not because of internal accidentals, it may well be that we could justifiably interpret Lanfranco as follows: mi against fa is normally corrected by a flat, but it may be corrected by a sharp if it arises because of an internal accidental. But regardless of whether this interpretation is correct or not,

Lanfranco clearly thinks the functions of the two accidentals are different, even if their opposition is not absolute.

No theoretical evidence presented here to support my claim that mi against fa is normally corrected by means of a flat dates from before the 1470s. Indeed, the evidence from before that time points to a different conclusion: theorists of the fourteenth and earlier fifteenth centuries correct mi against fa by both flats and sharps. In the early fourteenth century, Philippe de Vitry states that 'false music is necessary now and then and also in order that every consonance or melody is perfected in any sign', and shows how one uses the sharp in the discant in order to get a perfect fifth above the tenor's ♮.[54] Petrus frater dictus Palma ociosa shows how the discant has to use a flat or a sharp depending on whether there is B♮ or B♭ in the tenor.[55] Also Philippus de Caserta shows how to produce a perfect fifth above ♮ by means of the sign of ♮,[56] and in the early fifteenth century Ugolino of Orvieto gives examples of intervals perfected by ♮ and by ♭.[57]

We might think that in all of the above cases the sign of mi is introduced in the discant, since the mi-step in the tenor is treated as a given and not to be changed.[58] But another early fifteenth-century theorist, Prosdocimus de Beldemandis, also makes no distinction between the functions of ♭ and ♮:

The sixth and last rule, for understanding the placement of these two signs, round b and square b, in counterpoint, is this: that these signs are to be applied to octaves, fifths, and similar intervals as it is necessary to enlarge or diminish them in order to make them good consonances if they earlier were dissonant, because such intervals ought always to be major or consonant in counterpoint.[59]

Thus, both signs may be used when one avoids mi against fa. And Prosdocimus makes it clear that this is not because we have to treat the tenor as an immutable given in relation to which the discant has to adjust. When, between 1425 and 1428, he revised his counterpoint treatise, he added a lengthy passage at the end of the section dealing with *musica ficta* which is the only explicit discussion of the question whether one inflects the lower or upper voice I have been able to find, and thus is of great interest to us:

And so that you might gain yet more understanding of these two signs, you should know that to vary these intervals with respect to their major and minor inflections you can apply these aforesaid signs to the upper voice as to the lower voice and contrariwise. If the alteration in the upper voice should be made with round b, it would be made in the lower voice with square b, and if the alteration should be made in the upper voice with square b, it would be made in the lower voice with round b. But I advise you to be circumspect in applying these signs, because they should be applied where they sound more agreeable. If they sound better in the tenor, they should be applied in the tenor; if they sound better in the discant, they should be applied in the discant. If they sound equally good in the discant and the tenor, they should be applied in the discant rather than the tenor, lest it be necessary to apply some one of these signs in the contratenor, the triplum, or the quadruplum (if they should be found there), to which none of these signs should be applied. If the appropriate sign sounds equally good, it should be applied to the discant and not the tenor. Knowing where the signs sound better I leave to your ear, because on this, no rule can be given, for the situations are in a certain way infinite.[60]

Prosdocimus advises to inflect either tenor or discant, whichever sounds better (something for which no rule can be given). If both solutions sound equally good, it is better to inflect the discant, because a change in the tenor might produce a clash with another voice written against it, such as the contratenor, triplum or quadruplum.

I know of only one theorist after the middle of the fifteenth century who corrects mi against fa with a sharp as well as with flat. John Hothby, in *La Caliopea legale*, tells us that 'when steps of the first order [which correspond to the white keys of keyboard] do not agree with one another, that is, behave harshly, steps of the second and third order [flat and sharp black-key steps, respectively] intervene in order to remove this harshness and asperity'.[61] On the other hand, in *Spetie tenore del contrapunto prima*, Hothby states that mi against fa on perfect consonances is corrected by means of the round b and does not mention any other possibility.[62]

Note that the last theorist to use both ♭ and ♮ in mi-against-fa contexts is a contemporary of Tinctoris with whom we began to observe the tendency to use only ♭ in such contexts. Thus, all the presented evidence forces us to modify our picture of how one corrected mi against fa and to say that this picture is unconditionally valid not earlier than from the 1470s on. Before that time one probably felt equally free to use sharps for this purpose. It is at least possible, however, that the practical tendency (if not absolute obligation) to use flats rather than sharps in mi-against-fa contexts antedated considerably the period when this tendency came to the surface in theoretical writings. I base this guess on the fact that we have discovered an analogous tendency to correct the melodic mi against fa by means of flats in theory from the beginning of our period, that strong arguments explaining this tendency exist, and that, since the same steps and intervals are involved in the vertical non-harmonic relations as were in the melodic ones, the same arguments will be valid for the vertical mi against fa as well.

(iii) The mi-against-fa discords introduced by internal accidentals and the method of avoiding them

Thus far I have discussed vertical relations arising in music notated without internal accidentals which may have required correction by means of *musica ficta* steps and ways in which such relations were corrected. Since internal accidentals introduced to correct vertical non-harmonic relations would not produce problems we have not discussed already, what remains to be studied is the conflict between vertical and melodic considerations.

What did one do then when a correction of a melodic relation produced an unwanted vertical one, or the reverse? The question is of a considerable practical importance, but - like all the subtler questions of musical practice - it is generally not discussed by theorists. We are fortunate, however, to possess Johannes Tinctoris's discussion of this very problem:

It must not be overlooked, however, that in composed song, so that a fa against a mi may not happen in a perfect concord, occasionally it is necessary to use a tritone. Then, to signify where ♭ normally ought to be sung in order to avoid the tritone, but where mi must be sung, I believe that the sign of hard b, that is, square b, must be prefaced, as is proven here [see Example 24].[63]

Example 24

For melodic reasons, in order to avoid the tritone with the preceding F, one would want to flatten the second ♮ in the counterpoint, but ♭ at this point creates a diminished fifth with E in the tenor. Thus, the example confronts us with these three choices: either correct the melodic relation and produce an incorrect vertical one; or correct the melodic relation and then correct also the resulting non-harmonic vertical relation (by flattening E); or leave the melodic relation uncorrected, so that you do not produce a non-harmonic vertical relation. It is especially noteworthy that in spite of the fact that the second of these choices would allow one to get rid of all non-harmonic relations, both melodic and vertical, Tinctoris explains that the last choice is the correct one. It clearly does not occur to him that the introduction of one accidental might lead to the introduction of another in a kind of a 'chain reaction'. The general lesson we may derive from this is two-fold: first, 'chain reactions' in which the introduction of one accidental necessitates the introduction of another at a place a fourth or fifth apart are not allowed; second, when one must choose between two non-harmonic relations, one melodic and the other vertical, one should correct the latter.

The same is true of music notated with flats in the key signatures:

Further, it must be known that, not only in regular tones and true music but also in irregular tones and fictitious music, we ought to avoid the tritone and to use it by the ways given earlier as in the above quoted examples, as is seen here [see Example 25].[64]

Here, again for melodic reasons one would want to flatten the first a in the counterpoint, but a♭ at this point creates a diminished octave with A in the

Example 25

Contrapunctus as an example of the use of the tritone

Tenor as an example of avoiding the tritone

tenor. It would, again, be possible to avoid also the latter problem by flat-tening the tenor's A in turn. (The resulting melodic indirect tritone between D and A♭ in the tenor would be acceptable, since the A♭ 'resolves' down to Γ with only one note intervening.) But, just as in the previous case, such a 'chain reaction' is not what Tinctoris would consider a proper way of dealing with the problem. Instead, he chooses to live with the melodic tritone in order to preserve the vertical perfect octave.

Tinctoris's discussion is truly invaluable for it provides clear guidelines for dealing with common and puzzling problems of *musica ficta* usage. And we can be sure that in this case Tinctoris is describing the normal practice, rather than advocating his own idiosyncratic ideas, since I have found an independent confirmation of the same practice elsewhere. In a letter of June 3, 1538 addressed to Piero de Justinis, Giovanni del Lago discussed a passage from a motet by Piero (see Example 26).[65] In the example, the alto would

Example 26

normally flatten e in order to correct the melodic tritone. This would produce a diminished octave with the bass which might conceivably be corrected by a flat at E, but E♭ would produce a tritone with the following a, unless this were flattened as well, and so on. Now, del Lago criticizes the passage for reasons which do not have to detain us here, but he fully accepts

Piero's solution of the problem, which is to avoid the 'chain reaction' just described and to opt for the lesser of the two evils, that is, for the toleration of the melodic tritone which enables him to preserve the perfect octave. In short, Piero and del Lago follow in 1538 the usage described by Tinctoris in 1476 and, consequently, we may safely conclude that this was the normal practice, at least in the later part of our period.

The conclusions we have reached thus far have an interesting corollary. If the normal way of correcting melodic and vertical relations was by means of flats, and if 'chain reactions' whereby one flat provoked the next were not practiced, it follows that pieces in which all internal accidentals were introduced in order to avoid melodic and vertical non-harmonic intervals would use at most one more flat than the number of flats in the key signature of the voice with the largest number of flats in the signature. Pieces in which all parts had no flats in the signature would require at most the use of Bb, pieces in which at least one part had a Bb-signature would require at most the use of Bb and Eb, and pieces in which at least one part had a Bb/Eb-signature would require at most the use of Bb, Eb and Ab. Since most of the music of our period used one of these three signatures, it follows that the normal practice discussed thus far would require no more than three flats, Bb, Eb and Ab. I shall return to this point in the next chapter, once we know what was required by contrapuntal progressions.

6 Contrapuntal progressions

(i) Cadences

In the preceding two chapters I have examined, respectively, melodic and vertical relations which have to be corrected by means of feigned steps. In the present chapter I turn to the last type of context which regularly required the use of *musica ficta* steps, namely, to contrapuntal progressions, that is, progressions involving horizontal motion not between individual steps, but between intervals. Once again, our first task will be to identify the progressions which required the use of feigned steps.

The one such progression universally discussed from the beginning through the end of our period was the progression from an imperfect to a perfect consonance. In his *Lucidarium in arte musicae planae* of 1317–18, Marchetto da Padova announced:

Some diaphonies or dissonances are acceptable to the ear and the mind and others are not. The principal ones which are acceptable are the third, the sixth, and the tenth. These, and those similar to them, are acceptable to the ear because, as they approach consonances in contrary motion, they lie in the immediate vicinity of the consonances. When two voices form a dissonance [that is, an imperfect consonance], they must move in contrary motion toward the consonance they seek; and the dissonance must lie as close as possible to the consonance they approach.[1]

The last sentence is crucial here: an imperfect consonance must move to the closest perfect consonance in contrary motion. More specifically, one voice should move by a whole tone and the other by a diatonic semitone (to simplify the discussion, I shall use standard, rather than Marchettan, terms here).[2] It follows that a minor third will contract to a unison, while a major third will expand to a fifth, and a major sixth to an octave, as Marchetto shows in his examples.[3] For obvious reasons, Marchetto does not show how to use the minor sixth: if both voices must move by step, the minor sixth would have to contract to a fourth, which in two-part counterpoint is a dissonance.

In all of the theorist's examples one of the steps in the imperfect consonance is chromatically inflected so that it may proceed to the perfect consonance by a diatonic semitone. Later theorists will say that the feigned step is used in such contexts 'because of beauty' (*causa pulchritudinis*). For instance, Franchinus Gaffurius tells us that 'feigned music was invented for two reasons, first, because of necessity . . . second, because of beauty',[4] the former reason having to do with the prohibition of mi against fa. Gaffurius does not explain what the latter reason is, he merely refers his readers to another part of his treatise, the one in which progressions from imperfect to perfect consonances are one of the matters under discussion.[5] But already Marchetto associates such use of *musica ficta* with the concept of 'beauty':

The 'chromatic' is called the 'color of beauty,' because it is for the sake of the elegance and beauty of the dissonances [that is, imperfect consonances] that the whole tone is divided not only into diatonic and enharmonic genera, but into the chromatic as well – so that the dissonances may lie closer to the [perfect] consonances which follow them. Both voices must move in such a way that there be a progression of a whole tone at a certain interval above or below [the chromatic progression].[6]

Similarly, in his *Pomerium*, Marchetto argues that steps inflected for the purpose discussed here should 'more properly be called "colored" rather than "false" music'[7] and goes on to explain: 'In music colors are sometimes made for the sake of beauty of consonances, just as in grammar rhetorical colors are made for the sake of beauty of sentences.'[8]

Marchetto's rule to the effect that an imperfect consonance must move to a perfect one in contrary motion, with one voice moving a whole tone and the other a semitone, and that one of the steps of the imperfect consonance may have to be inflected for this purpose was repeated by theorists through the end of our period.[9] Some theorists, however, modified the rule. Petrus frater dictus Palma ociosa shows among his examples of imperfect consonances properly proceeding to perfect ones the progressions illustrated in Example 27.[10] Here imperfect intervals move to perfect ones with one voice

Example 27

moving a semitone, but neither the contrary motion nor the requirement that the other voice should move a whole tone is preserved. Thus, the rule is relaxed considerably.

Another modification is implied by an example in Prosdocimus de Beldemandis's *Contrapunctus* (see Example 28).[11] Three progressions in the example follow the strict 'Marchettan' rule: the progression from the second to the third interval (f#-g against a-G), that from the seventh to the eighth (e-d against c#-d) and that from the tenth to the eleventh (f#-g against a-G). Of the remaining progressions, one follows the relaxed rule we know from

Example 28

Upper melody

Lower melody

Petrus: the one from the fifth to the sixth interval (♭♭-aa against d-a). Two remaining progressions from imperfect intervals, the ones from the fourth to the fifth interval (aa-♭♭ against c♯-d) and from the ninth to the tenth (d-f♯ against ♭-a), might appear to be irrelevant since both go to another imperfect interval, but Prosdocimus makes clear that also in such cases one should move by semitones wherever possible (that is, wherever the voice moves by step), inflecting the steps of the first interval if necessary. I have been able to find only one more theorist making this point, Giovanni del Lago, who in 1540 wrote: 'And, therefore, assume as a general rule that each time you go from an imperfect interval ascending to a larger interval, whether perfect or imperfect, if this [first] interval is minor, make it major with the sign of sharpening, which sharpening is shown with this sign: ♯.'[12] Prosdocimus and del Lago appear to be the only theorists ever to consider the progression from an imperfect to an imperfect consonance in this way and, consequently, we may probably safely ignore this aspect of Prosdocimus' discussion. But the rest of the example supports the rule governing the progression from an imperfect to a perfect consonance both in the strict form we know from Marchetto and in the relaxed form of Petrus. (Incidentally, we should probably refrain from deriving any conclusions from the presence of a melodic *direct* tritone, properly 'resolved', in the lower part of Prosdocimus' example, since the example was designed to demonstrate a contrapuntal, and not a melodic, problem.)

Both versions of the rule are present also in the treatise of Ugolino of Orvieto. Thus Ugolino explains how a minor third contracts to a unison and how a major third expands to a fifth with both parts going by step in contrary motion (the strict version of our rule),[13] but he also allows the minor third to go to a fifth with ♭-a moving against G-D (the relaxed version of our rule).[14] Elsewhere, Ugolino shows how to use *musica ficta* steps in progressing from an imperfect to a perfect consonance, in order to diminish the distance between the two (see Examples 29 and 30).[15] In the first example, the first imperfect-to-perfect-consonance progression (f-g against a-G) is not inflected probably by omission, since the identical last one is (f♯-g against a-G). Together with the third one (e♭-d against c-d), they demonstrate the

Example 29

Example 30

strict version of the rule. The second progression (♭♭-aa against d-a), on the other hand, demonstrates the relaxed version of the rule. It is certain that here the flat has not been added for another reason, since Ugolino expressly comments: 'Indeed, the first soft b placed in the first example shows not the perfection of the dissonance [that is, imperfect consonance] but its coloration and with the diminution of its form also its closer and immediate adhesion to the immediate perfection.'[16] In the second example, the first (e♭-d against c-d), third (d-c against ♮-c) and fourth (f♯-g against a-G) imperfect-to-perfect-consonance progressions demonstrate the strict version of the rule, while the second (f-e against d-a) demonstrates again the relaxed version. Toward the end of his treatise, Ugolino gives another example illustrating the same point (see Example 31).[17] Here the first, second, third and fifth

Example 31

progressions follow the strict version of the rule, the fourth and sixth the relaxed version.

Both versions of the rule are also present in the examples discussed by the anonymous author of *Quot sunt concordationes* edited probably in the third quarter of the fifteenth century.[18] We learn there that when a third moves to a fifth or any other perfect consonance with the upper part ascending by step, the third should be made major.[19] Clearly, if the goal is a fifth, the rule in the strict version is followed here, but if the goal is an octave, the rule in the relaxed version is followed. Similarly, when a sixth goes to an octave or any other perfect consonance with the upper part ascending by step, the sixth should be made major.[20] However, if the progressions described above are rewritten so that the upper part descends by step (instead of ascending), then the third and the sixth should be made minor.[21]

Both versions of the rule remained valid through the end of our period. For Gioseffo Zarlino, one reaches an octave from a major sixth, a fifth from a major third, a unison from a minor third, all in contrary motion (that is, following the strict version), but, in addition, the theorist considers other progressions, for instance, an octave reached from a major third, or a fifth reached from a minor third, this time with one voice moving by step and another by leap (that is, following the relaxed version).[22]

We have seen that the strict version of the rule offered no proper way of proceeding from a minor sixth in two-part counterpoint. Now, we find the following rule among those which, according to Ramos de Pareia, govern simple discanting ('organizing' [*organizare*], to be exact) above a given chant: 'The major sixth unites to the octave, while the minor disunites to the fifth. And so the major third divides to the fifth, but the minor one leads to the unison.'[23] Ramos's examples of a minor sixth going to a fifth, ♭-a against D-D or c-c against E-F,[24] show one voice moving a semitone and the other remaining stationary, that is, they follow the relaxed version of the rule. Similarly, one of Gaffurius' rules of counterpoint states that 'when we approach a perfect consonance from an imperfect consonance . . . it is necessary to progress to the perfect interval by contrary motion of the closest imperfect consonance',[25] which is, of course, a progression governed by our rule in the strict version, but also Gaffurius includes a minor sixth going to a fifth in oblique motion as one of such progressions.[26] The implication in both Ramos and Gaffurius seems to be that there is a most proper way of moving from each imperfect consonance, and that for the minor and major thirds as well as the major sixth this is governed by what we have referred to as the rule in its strict version, while for the minor sixth, which could not be followed by step in contrary motion, the oblique motion is allowed.

Evidence for this can be found in the middle of the sixteenth century too.[27] Thus, for instance, Zarlino says:

In addition, imperfect consonances have this feature: their extremities tend in the direction of the nearest perfect consonance rather than toward more distant ones. For everything naturally tends toward attaining perfection in the quickest and best way that it can. Thus the imperfect major intervals desire to expand, and the minor have the opposite tendency. The ditone and the major hexachord tend to expand into a fifth and octave, whereas the semiditone and minor hexachord tend to contract into a unison and a fifth. This is obvious to all experienced musicians of sound judgment, because all these movements involve the interval of the semitone, which, one might say, is truly the salt, the seasoning, and the cause of every good melody and harmony.[28]

Let me summarize the results reached thus far. The progression from an imperfect to a perfect consonance was governed throughout our period by a rule which, in its most general (relaxed) form, stipulated that one part should proceed by a diatonic semitone and that one of the steps forming the imperfect consonance might be inflected if this were necessary to produce the semitone progression. The rule can be found in this most general form in Zarlino:

To make the rule easy to follow, every progression from imperfect to perfect consonance should include in at least one part the step of a large semitone [the diatonic semitone is large in Zarlino's tuning system], expressed or implied. To this purpose the chromatic and enharmonic steps will be found very useful, provided they are written in the manner to be described elsewhere.[29]

Additional criteria were added to the rule (making it stricter) in order to describe the most perfect progressions from imperfect to perfect consonances: the voices should proceed in contrary motion, with one part moving by step and the other by half step. This meant that the most perfect way of proceeding from a minor third was to a unison, from the major third to a fifth, and from the major sixth to an octave. An exception was made for the minor sixth since, according to the strict rule, it would have to be followed by a fourth, an inadmissible interval in two-part simple counterpoint; the most perfect way of proceeding from it was in oblique motion to a fifth.

How strictly was the rule governing progressions from imperfect to perfect consonances observed? On this issue there is some disagreement among theorists. For Gaffurius, the rule is absolutely obligatory only at cadences: 'The seventh rule [of counterpoint] states that when we approach a perfect consonance from an imperfect consonance, as at a final cadence or any other cadence, it is necessary to progress to the perfect interval by contrary motion of the closest imperfect consonance.'[30] Zarlino disagrees:

Nature, which has jurisdiction over everything, has so designed that not only those with musical training but the unschooled and even farmers – who sing after their own fashion, without reasoning about it – are accustomed to progress from major sixth to octave, as if nature had taught them. This is most obvious in the cadences throughout their music, as all musicians can hear. Perhaps it is what persuaded Franchino [Gaffurio] to venture to say that the cadence is the only place where the major sixth must progress to the octave, because there the composition comes to a close. But to me it appears to contradict the remark I quoted from him just above [to the effect that 'it is in the nature of the major sixth to go to the octave and of the minor to go to the fifth'].[31] If we are to obey the natures of these two intervals, I can only conclude that he said it thoughtlessly. Therefore it shall not be lawful to pass from the major sixth to the fifth, nor from the minor sixth to the octave. For neither progression is natural to the consonances involved.[32]

The argument from 'nature' allows us to suspect that Zarlino is writing here in a prescriptive mode, attempting to legislate for the musical practice rather than to describe it. At any rate, even Zarlino allows some exceptions:

So the musician may, when he cannot do otherwise, write a fifth after a major sixth – contrary to the rule given in Chapter 38 – if the sixth is located in the second part of a syncopated semibreve . . . However, we may move from the minor sixth to the octave with a semiminim, since when the fourth semiminim leaves the third in conjunct motion, it may be dissonant.[33]

Another indication that not all musicians considered the imperfect-to-perfect rule to be always obligatory is provided by Luigi Dentice toward the end of a lengthy discussion of various issues pertaining to the rule. One of the interlocutors in Dentice's dialogue explains that one should not flatten *E* in tetrardus and that this consideration overrides the necessity to flatten e in progressions of e-d moving against C-D or against G-G in modes 7 or 8.[34] The speaker follows this example with a general conclusion: 'Whence I hold it fast, and let it be said with the support of Mr Adrian Willaert, Mr Alfonso [della Viola] and others, that the rules of the sixths and thirds, minor and major, are arbitrary and not legal.'[35]

This conclusion is illuminated in an interesting fashion by Ghiselin Danckerts in his critique of the *nuova maniera* perpetrated by *compositori novelli*. Danckerts' main quarrel with these is that they destroy the modes through excessive inflections.[36] Specifically, the theorist says:

Those people want to use too inconsiderately almost always these raisings and lowerings of notes beyond their proper and natural intonations in their compositions (as I have said), binding themselves with certain empty obligations and rules of theirs, prescribing that one should go to a perfect consonance only from the closest imperfect one. This might be believed, if they used it rarely and accidentally. But should this rule be observed ordinarily throughout and always in every place, as the said novel composers do, it would excessively damage the said modes.[37]

In one respect Danckerts is, of course, right. A truly consistent application of the imperfect-to-perfect rule at every opportunity quickly leads to results which are musically absurd, and a somewhat less consistent, but very frequent, application to music which is very chromatic. The latter excited great interest of some *compositori novelli* in the 1550s, but it certainly did not represent the musical norm even then, let alone earlier. These considerations, and the theoretical evidence just presented, indicate that the rule must have been applied selectively.[38] And since the rule prescribes a semitone progression when one goes from an imperfect to a perfect consonance, that is, since it describes a context which, as will be presently seen, is an essential component of a cadence, we have every reason to believe Gaffurius that the rule applies at cadences. In order to be able to apply it, therefore, one must have a clear notion of what constituted a cadence during our period.

Johannes Tinctoris defined cadence as follows: 'Cadence is a small part of any part of a song at the end of which is found either general repose or perfection.'[39] 'Repose' (*quies*) may, but does not have to, signify 'rest', since Tinctoris's technical term for the latter sign is *pausa*.[40] At least some musicians, however, interpreted Tinctoris to mean 'rest' here, as we may ascertain from Dowland's translation of Ornithoparchus: 'Wherfore a *Close* is (as *Tinctor* writes) a little part of a Song, in whose end is found either rest or perfection. Or it is the coniunction of voices (going diversly) in perfect *Concords*.'[41] Returning to Tinctoris's definitions, 'perfection', in turn, 'is a closing of a whole song or of small parts thereof'.[42] Thus Tinctoris's understanding of the term 'cadence' is no different from ours: it is a device signifying closure of the whole musical discourse or of its part. No technical details are given, but 'perfection' undoubtedly calls for a perfect consonance, while 'repose' may involve a following rest, as we already know.

Tinctoris's contemporary, John Hothby, adds a new element to our understanding of cadence:

By 'cadences' one understands all the notes between one line and another. They follow the cadences of the words, of which there are principally three, namely, comma, colon and period . . . As I said, the cadences of a song should be similar to the cadences of the words, so that if the cadence of the words is suspending, that is, the colon, the cadence of the song should be of a long [note value] of the final step [of the mode]. And if the cadence of the words is a smaller punctuation, that is, a grammatic comma, the cadence of the song should be moderate, not too long, and not too close to the final step. But if the cadence of the words is the period, that is, the end of the sentence, the cadence of the song should be on the final step or on the reciting pitch.[43]

In short, musical punctuation is analogous to verbal. There is a hierarchy of cadences, just as there is a hierarchy of textual punctuation marks; both reflect the fact that the desired sense of closure may be greater or lesser. A more complete textual closure may be musically conveyed by a cadence ending on a longer note placed on the final of the mode or on its reciting pitch, while a lesser closure may employ a cadence ending on a shorter note value placed off the final.

Many sixteenth-century theorists confirm this correlation of the textual and musical syntax.[44] Stephano Vanneo, for instance, says: 'On the other hand, the legitimate and proper place of cadences is where the context of the words defines a sentence . . . Indeed, cadence is just as a point, and a certain sign of punctuation, and a repose in a song.'[45] Elsewhere, the theorist provides us with a truly Rabelaisian list of terms synonymous with *cadentia* (*positura, terminatio, conclusio, finis, copulatio, reductio, perfectio, suffragatio, optatio, approbatio, distinctio, terminus finalis, clausula*)[46] and lifts his definition of cadence straight from Tinctoris, but includes the insights we have gleaned from Hothby:

Cadence, therefore, is a small part of any section of a song at the end of which is found either general repose or perfection. Or cadence is a certain close of this same section of song, just as in the context of speech the middle and final signs of punctuation. Experienced musicians are eager for the end of cadences to be made where also ends a part or clause of speech.[47]

Finally, Zarlino stresses that one makes cadence only where the phrase or period of the text ends.[48]

Throughout our period, theorists tell us that the minimum of what is indispensable to create the sense of closure, the cadential effect, is a progression from an imperfect to a perfect consonance. The most fundamental rules of counterpoint prescribe a perfect consonance for the final harmony of a composition, and an imperfect consonance for the penultimate harmony. The anonymous author of the influential *Cum notum sit* of the second quarter of the fourteenth century states:

The eighth conclusion is that in his counterpoint the penultimate [harmony] should always be imperfect and this because of euphony . . . The ninth conclusion is that just as the counterpoint begins with a perfect [consonance], so also should it end. The reason may be that if the song were finished with an imperfect [consonance], the mind would remain in suspense and would neither repose until it heard a perfect sound, nor, consequently, would it be indicated that here is the end of the song.[49]

These fundamental rules remain in force throughout our period.[50]

Clearly, however, not every imperfect-to-perfect progression will produce a cadential effect. What can we learn, then, about the structure of cadences? Ugolino tells us, like so many others, that any song must end on a perfect consonance, and he goes immediately on to show the best ways of approaching perfect consonances from imperfect ones, the ways we have already discussed.[51] The inescapable implication is that everything we have learned about the imperfect-to-perfect progression pertains to cadences. But are we not in a vicious circle here? We have reconstructed a rule which governed progressions from imperfect to perfect consonances and we have concluded that the rule applied only at cadences. We have concluded further that in order to know when to inflect an imperfect consonance one had to be able to recognize a cadence. But now we see that the essential characteristic of a cadence is precisely an imperfect-to-perfect progression governed by our rule. The only way to escape the circle is to find additional criteria which a cadence must fulfil. One of these we have already identified: at least since the late fifteenth century some cadences may reflect various degrees of articulation of the text into clauses, sentences, etc. It may also be that they involve a following rest. Now we shall search for other additional criteria.

One of the basic rules of counterpoint requires that the final harmony be not just any perfect consonance, but the octave or its equivalents. 'The eighth and last rule,' says Gaffurius, 'states that every song should end on a perfect consonance, either on a unison, as has been customary in Venice, or on the octave or fifteenth, as every school of musicians commonly observes for the sake of a perfect harmonic union.'[52] Other sixteenth-century theorists confirm this point.[53] Zarlino says that musicians 'made it a fixed rule that each composition should terminate on the octave or unison and no other interval . . . The rule is well grounded, inasmuch as compositions ending otherwise leave the audience in a state of suspense, awaiting a final perfection.'[54] It appears, then, that at least since the late fifteenth century the octave (or its equivalent) is an indispensable component of the final harmony in a cadence.

We learn more about the structure of cadences from Melchior Schanppecher's text of 1501. He tells us that a cadence consists not of two, but of three harmonies, with the upper part descending and then ascending a step (♪♪♪) and the lower part doing the reverse (♪♪♪), the two parts contracting from an octave to a sixth and then expanding back to the octave. The upper and lower parts may also exchange their characteristic formulas (with the upper part first ascending and then descending a step and the lower part doing the reverse), so that the two parts will expand from a unison to a third and then contract back to the unison.[55]

At about the same time, Johannes Cochlaeus presented examples of cadences, all consisting of three harmonies. The two parts which produce the octave (or unison) cadence behave just as Schanppecher wanted, but, in addition, they may also use the following formulas: the upper part, instead of descending and then ascending by step, may also twice ascend by step (♪♪♪); the lower part, instead of ascending and then descending by step, may also twice descend by step (♪♪♪); also in these cases, the formulas may be exchanged between the upper and lower voices; finally, one of the voices may even remain stationary before it descends a step (♪♪♪); or it may go down a third before descending a step (♪♪♪).[56] In short, one of the parts constituting a cadence will go ♪♪♪ or ♪♪♪, while the other goes ♪♪♪, or ♪♪♪, or ♪♪♪, or ♪♪♪, the two concluding on an octave or its equivalent.

We learn more about cadences from Ornithoparchus, who tells us that 'first, Every *Close* [cadence] consists of three Notes, the last, the last save one, and the last save two'.[57] If we limit our discussion to the pair of voices which end their cadence with a properly reached octave (or its equivalent), the most important of Ornithoparchus' 'rules for Closes' (*clausulis regule*) are: '2 The *Close* of the *Discantus* made with three Notes, shall always have the last upward. 3 The *Close* of the *Tenor*, doth also consist of three Notes, the last always descending.'[58] These formulas may, of course, be exchanged between the tenor and discant, or appear in other voices altogether. The theorist's examples show one of the voices moving ♩♩♩, while the other moves ♩♩♩ or ♩♩♩.[59]

At the same time, Aaron devoted a long discussion to cadences in his *Libri tres de institutione harmonica*. The cadential formula is ♩♩♩, with the other voice going ♩♩♩, or ♩♩♩, or ♩♩♩. (The penultimate imperfect consonance may be preceded by a dissonant suspension).[60] This last point is confirmed in *Toscanello in musica*: 'The dissonance of the seventh may always precede the sixth before the octave, if they [cadences] are not simply composed.'[61] There can be no dissonance in simple note-against-note writing, of course, but Aaron's 'always' suggests that the dissonant suspension before the penultimate imperfect consonance is an obligatory feature of a cadence in diminished counterpoint.

This point is confirmed by Vanneo. The theorist tells us that a cadence in simple counterpoint ends on a perfect consonance reached from the closest imperfect one with both voices going by step in contrary motion.[62] In florid counterpoint, however, the penultima is preceded by a dissonant suspension.[63] Elsewhere, the theorist explains that there are two kinds of cadences, those of simple and of florid counterpoint, the former proceeding note-against-note in equal note values, the latter admitting different note values and even embellishing short notes.[64] His words leave no doubt that a dissonance is required before the penultima: 'It remains for us to teach by examples florid cadences in which composers are accustomed to put by a prescribed rule a dissonance before the penultimate [consonance].'[65] A marginal note highlights the text at this point: 'Florid cadence requires a dissonant antepenultima.'[66] The dissonance is a suspension involving the antepenultima in one voice and the penultima in the other.[67] Another theorist who confirms the necessity of a dissonant suspension resolving to the penultimate consonance is del Lago.[68]

Del Lago discusses also another important feature of cadences:

In your compositions you will always make sure to complete the mensuration unit, whether ternary, binary, or quarternary, with the penultimate note of the cadence. Thus, one should not compute the penultimate note with the following one which concludes the cadence or distinction, since there is the beginning of the mensuration unit there [on the final note of the cadence]. Similarly, one should finish the mensuration unit with the penultimate note of the harmony and not with the last one, because the penultima concludes the preceding mensuration unit. The last note is the end of the song and, therefore, it is not computed with another note.[69]

The 'mensuration unit' (*numero*) is a larger note value containing a number of smaller values prescribed by the mensuration of the piece. Del Lago does not say which note value this is, but clearly, under the normal mensuration signs, it cannot be smaller than a semibreve, since it must contain two, three or four smaller values, and it may well be a still larger value, most likely a breve, perhaps even a long. A study of music by a given composer or even a whole generation of composers would easily tell us what this value was under a given mensuration for the examined repertoire. What is important about the quoted passage from del Lago is that it tells us what we should be looking for when we undertake such a study. What del Lago tells us is, in essence, that the metrical placement of the last note of a cadence matters. The ultima must fall at the beginning of a larger mensural unit, say a breve or whatever we shall discover this unit to be. And this, of course, may be a significant new criterion allowing us to distinguish a truly cadential progression from other imperfect-to-perfect progressions.

At mid sixteenth century, the richest insight into cadences is provided by the two most comprehensive music treatises of the time, those of Nicola Vicentino and Gioseffo Zarlino. Vicentino shows various forms which the cadential formula ♩ ♩ ♩ can take.[70] The formula can be rhythmicized in three ways: as the 'major cadence' (*cadentia maggiore*) (○) ♩♩♩ ; as the 'minor cadence' (*cadentia minore*) (♩) ♩♩♩ ; and as the 'minimal cadence' (*cadentia minima*) (♩) ♩♩♩ . Each of these may be diminished and embellished. The lesson which may be derived from these examples is that, first, the antepenultima is a suspension resolving to the penultima, second, the ultima appears on a strong beat (that is, at the beginning of a mensuration unit), and third, the value of this mensuration unit can be a breve, semibreve, or perhaps even minim. The first two points confirm what we already know, the last one is new. Unfortunately, Vicentino does not supply the examples with time signatures and, consequently, we cannot be sure whether these different cadences can all appear under the same signature or not, just as we cannot be sure what the mensuration units implied by the examples are. These questions, however, can be answered when we study a given repertoire. The value of Vicentino's examples is again that they tell us what sort of questions we should ask when studying music. These questions are: Can different mensuration units be exploited for cadential purposes (that is, can the ultima appear at the beginning of mensuration units of different value) under the same time signature? What are these mensuration units for each time signature?

In Vicentino's examples of cadences, the two voices which end up on an octave use the melodic formulas ♩ ♩ ♩ against ♩ ♩ ♩ , ♩ ♩ ♩ , ♩ ♩ ♩ , ♩ ♩ ♩ , ♩ ♩ ♩ and ♩ ♩ ♩ .[71] If we represent ascending modal degrees with consecutive Arabic numerals beginning with I for the final, we can summarize these formulas as 8–7–8 against 3–2–1, 1–2–1, 4–2–1, 6–5–1,

4-5-1 and 1-5-1, that is, against a voice which in the penultima has either 2 or 5, and which precedes 2 with 1, 3 or 4, and 5 with 1, 4 or 6.

The most comprehensive treatment of cadences is offered by Zarlino in *Le Istitutioni harmoniche*, Part III, Chapter 53.[72] Absolute cadences conclude with a unison or octave. They may be written in simple, note-against-note, consonant counterpoint, or in diminished counterpoint employing a variety of note values and some dissonances. In either case, a cadence consists of at least three harmonies. The final unison must be preceded by a minor third, the final octave by a major sixth. In a diminished cadence, the imperfect consonance is preceded by a dissonant suspension. The melodic formulas involve 8-7-8 (=1-7-1) moving against 1-2-1, 3-2-1, 6-2-1, 5-2-1, 4-2-1, 1-5-1, 3-5-1, 6-5-1 and 4-5-1. Occasionally used is also the formula 6-7-1 against 3-2-1, but these are cadences 'improperly speaking'.[73] All of Zarlino's examples in the chapter involve the common ¢ -time and in most of the cadences the final harmony falls at the beginning of the breve mensuration unit, in some also at the beginning of the semibreve. In Chapter 61, Zarlino gives examples of cadences in writing for more than two parts and, again, all the voice-pairs which end the cadence on the octave behave according to the precepts listed above.[74]

Zarlino devotes also some attention to what he calls 'improper cadences' (*Cadenze impropiamente dette*),[75] that is, 'evaded cadences', as we would call them today. In these, one of the parts has the basic 8-7-8 (=1-7-1) formula and both parts behave normally until the final harmony, at which point the other part goes unexpectedly to a fifth, third, or still other consonance (that is, to a degree other than 1, namely, in Zarlino's examples, to 3, 4 or 6, the only degrees which form a consonance with the 8 of the upper part), thus evading the proper cadential resolution: 'A cadence is evaded,' writes Zarlino '. . . when the voices give the impression of leading to a perfect cadence, and turn instead in a different direction.'[76] The example in the next chapter which is wholly devoted to the subject of evaded cadences seems to indicate that, in addition to the form described above, an evaded cadence may also consist of one of the standard formulas which normally move against 8-7-8 (for instance, 1-2-1), while the formula 8-7-8 is incomplete and resolves to a degree other than 8 (for instance, 8-7-3 against 1-2-1). And, finally, both parts may proceed normally until and including the penultimate harmony, but complete their formulas irregularly on the final harmony (see Example 32).[77] (I have added to the example strokes connecting the notes belonging to the antepenultimate and penultimate harmonies of cadences, arrows below the lower staff of each system marking the ultima of each cadence, and the implied accidentals.) In all cases, the final harmony comes at the beginning of the semibreve or breve mensuration unit (under ¢), and even if both voices interrupt their regular formulas after the penultimate harmony, the intended cadence is easily recognizable by the

Example 32

Ex. 32 *(cont.)*

tell-tale 8-7 progression with 8 as a consonance and then, almost always, as a dissonant suspension resolving to 7. In short, in an evaded cadence, the antepenultimate and penultimate harmonies behave regularly and only the final harmony is irregular because one of the voices or both go in an unexpected direction. Since the penultimate harmony, which contains the leading tone, is regular, we have every reason to assume that it should be inflected, just as it would have been, had the cadence been regular. Such 'evading the cadence' (*fuggir la cadenza*)[78] is used

to make intermediate divisions in the harmony and text, when the words have not reached a final conclusion of their thought . . . They are useful when a composer in the midst of a beautiful passage feels the need for a cadence but cannot write one because the period of the text does not coincide, and it would not be honest to insert one.[79]

Evaded cadences are discussed, if in much less detail, also by other mid-century theorists. Del Lago tells us that 'it is praiseworthy occasionally to pretend that one cadences and then, at the conclusion of this cadence, to take a consonance which is not near to this cadence for it to settle down upon'.[80] Vicentino gives examples of 'cadences which avoid their conclusions' (*cadentie che fuggano la sua conclusione*).[81] These conform fully to del Lago's definition and to Zarlino's more detailed discussion.

In addition, Loys Bourgeois mentions 'interrupted cadences' (*cadences rompues*) which contain only the antepenultimate and penultimate notes of the regular cadential formula (8-7) and states that also in these the leading tone should be sharpened, if this is necessary to produce a semitone between 8 and 7.[82] Also Giovanni Maria Lanfranco exemplifies the interrupted cadential formula 8-7 on various steps with 7 always sharpened.[83] An important feature of an interrupted cadence which seems to have escaped the notice of our theorists but which is obvious to anyone familiar with music of the period is the placement of the 'penultima' (actually the last harmony of the interrupted cadence) in a strong metrical position at the beginning of a mensuration unit. Thus, an interrupted cadence is, of course, not identical with an evaded one, but it is sufficiently similar for us to be able to use Bourgeois' statement as an additional evidence supporting the need to produce a semitonal leading tone also in evaded cadences.

Let me summarize the additional criteria distinguishing a cadence from other imperfect-to-perfect progressions, criteria we have discovered by reading theoretical discussions of cadences:

(1) A cadence signifies a certain degree of closure of the whole musical discourse or of its part.

(2) It is analogous to a punctuation sign marking the articulation of a verbal text into such units as clauses, sentences and paragraphs, and it may reflect such articulation of the text.

(3) It may perhaps involve a following rest.

(4) The octave (or its equivalent) is an indispensable component of the final harmony. In simple counterpoint, a cadence consists of three consecutive harmonies, with the two parts which end on an octave following the characteristic melodic formulas 8-7-8 (=1-7-1) moving against 1-2-1, 3-2-1, 4-2-1, 5-2-1, 6-2-1, 1-5-1, 3-5-1, 4-5-1 or 6-5-1. In other words, the counterpoint against 8-7-8 (or 1-7-1) involves 1 (or 8) as the final step, 2 or 5 as the penultimate step, and any step which produces a consonance against 8 (or 1) as the antepenultimate step. Exceptionally, the 8-7-8 formula may be modified to 6-7-8, with the counterpoint against it involving 2-1 for the penultimate and final steps and, presumably, any consonance against 6 for the antepenultimate one. In diminished counterpoint, the penultimate imperfect consonance is preceded by a dissonant suspension and the cadence may, of course, be further embellished.

(5) The final harmony should fall at the beginning of a larger mensuration unit, which under the 'ordinary measure' (*misura commune*; ¢) of the early sixteenth century seems to have been no smaller than a semibreve. Theorists do not say clearly what was the smallest possible mensuration unit for each of the time signatures used.

(6) A cadence may be 'evaded', in which case the formulas in both structural voices behave normally for the first and second harmonies but go (in just one of the voices, or in both) to unexpected steps for the final harmony. It may also be 'interrupted', in which case the formulas behave normally for the first two harmonies, but are not continued beyond these and, as music of the period reveals, place the last cadential harmony at the beginning of a mensuration unit, that is, in a strong metrical position. In either case, the leading tone is inflected if this is necessary to produce a semitone progression to the final in the corresponding regular cadence.

The first three of the above criteria appear in theory from the late fifteenth century on, the remaining ones from the early sixteenth century on. It will be remembered also that the very idea that the rule governing imperfect-to-perfect progressions should apply only at cadences is explicitly stated only *ca.* 1500, even though some way of limiting the progressions to which the rule applies must have been in operation from the beginning, since the unlimited application of the rule leads to patently unacceptable results. Cadences belong to the most conservative, least changeable features of musical language, and it may well be that our criteria were in operation long before theorists began to discuss them. A full history of the cadence remains to be written. For now, a modern performer or editor will have to study the unmistakable (that is, final) cadences in a given repertoire, see whether our criteria apply and whether additional criteria may be derived from this study, and use the applicable criteria when trying to distinguish cadential from non-cadential imperfect-to-perfect progressions within the repertoire.

We also have to remember that cadences are analogous to, and may reflect, various degrees of punctuation of the text and, consequently, are themselves of various 'strength', 'perfection' or 'finality', from the most regular and perfect cadential progressions ending on long notes in a metrically strong position on the final of the mode, to a variety of evaded and interrupted cadences. This suggests that the borderline between cadential and non-cadential imperfect-to-perfect progressions may be somewhat blurred. A progression may exhibit some, but not all, of the characteristic features of a cadence. While some progressions are certainly cadences and others certainly not, there is a gray area in between in which a decision has to be made (by the composer, performers or editor) as to whether a given progression should be treated as a cadence and properly inflected, or left intact.

The only contrapuntal context other than the imperfect-to-perfect progression which may require the use of accidental inflections is also cadential. From the 1520s on, we learn that, should the final harmony of a cadence contain a third above the final, the third should be major. The earliest remarks to this effect I am aware of appear in Aaron's *Toscanello in musica*. Ending on a minor tenth or third sounds unpleasant, Aaron claims, and one uses the sign of diesis to make these intervals major.[84] Spataro commented on this passage in a letter to Aaron written on May 23, 1524, quibbling in his usual fashion that minor thirds or tenths do not really sound unpleasant, admitting that the major forms of these intervals sound even more pleasant, and concluding that inflecting the third degree in such cases is not a change from the bad to the good, as Aaron would have it, but a change from the good to the better.[85] In the 'Supplement' to the *Toscanello*, Aaron discusses three examples of four-part writing (see Example 33).[86] The

Example 33

first two examples adapt the ones which Spataro sent Aaron in the letter referred to a moment ago, and the point Aaron makes about them was first made by Spataro there.[87] These first two examples in the 'Supplement' have identical cantus parts and in the third example the cantus ends similarly. Only the context of other voices allows the singer to decide whether the last note of the cantus is 1 or 3. In the latter case, and only there, of course, he should sharpen this last note to produce a major third (tenth) above the final.

Similarly, in *Trattato della natura et cognitione di tutti gli tuoni di canto figurato*, Aaron gives polyphonic examples of cadences in modes 1–4, expressly sharpening the third above the final in the final harmony.[88] The practice of sharpening the third in the final harmony was confirmed by Lanfranco,[89] Vanneo,[90] and Vicentino, who stated categorically: 'When one wants to stop some parts near rests or at the end, one makes always the consonance of the major third in this place, even if the composition seeks sadness.'[91] But whether the practice was known before the 1520s and, if so, for how long, must remain a matter of conjecture for now. The question is probably of little importance in any case, since the use of a third above the final in a cadence does not seem to have significantly antedated the theoretical discussions mentioned above.

(ii) The method of correcting cadences

Now that we know which contrapuntal contexts may require the use of feigned steps, we have to find out how these contexts were corrected when two possibilities were open, that is, when it was possible to inflect either the lower or the upper voice, or to use either fa- or mi-sign.

The question clearly arises only in the case of the penultimate cadential harmony which contains both 7 and 2; obviously, it arises neither with the penultimate harmony of 7 and 5, nor with the final harmony containing 3. Moreover, when the penultimate cadential harmony contains 7 and 2, the only other step which may be found in an additional voice is either 4 or 5; all other steps would be dissonant, while the structural harmonies of a cadence have to be all consonant. If this additional step is 5, again the choice does not arise: since 5 has to remain consonant against both 2 and 7 and has to proceed to the final harmony (usually to 1 or 5) by an acceptable melodic interval, it is clearly 7 that will have to go by the semitone to 8. Thus, the only context in which we may be confronted with the question of whether to inflect the lower or the upper part, or whether to use ♭ or ♮, is the penultimate cadential harmony containing only 7 and 2, and optionally 4. Since the only indispensable steps in such a harmony are 7 and 2, it is reasonable to assume that the main decision concerns these two steps. Once this decision has been made, 4 may have to be adjusted accordingly.

We shall begin, then, with the pair of voices containing 7 and 2. We may quickly dispose of the possibility that the choice here was dictated by a preference for inflecting the upper or the lower part. There is no evidence for such a preference and, on the contrary, there is some evidence that a musician was free to inflect either part. Prosdocimus de Beldemandis appears to have been the only theorist to consider this question and I have already quoted (in Chapter 5(ii) above) an extensive passage from his *Contrapunctus* devoted to the problem. The passage may apply equally well to mi-against-fa as to cadential contexts. According to the theorist, either voice may be inflected, depending on which solution sounds better. If both solutions sound equally well, it is better to inflect the discant, because a change in the tenor might produce a clash with another voice written against it, such as the contratenor, triplum or quadruplum. This preference for inflecting the discant where either inflection would be equally sweet may be significant: the discant is much more likely than the tenor to contain the formula 8-7-8, and since we know that the penultimate harmony in a cadence must always contain 7 while the other part has either 2 or 5, it would make sense to think that the discant's 7 is the preferable candidate for inflection, other things being equal.

Prosdocimus was sceptical about the possibility of providing a rule concerning where such inflections fall more sweetly. The task, however, is less daunting than he thought, at least in cadential contexts. The choice as to whether to inflect 7 or 2 in the penultimate harmony of a cadence must have been governed either by the preference to inflect always one of the parts, upper or lower, or by the preference to use the ♭ or ♮ sign. Since we already know that the former preference did not exist, the choice must have been made in terms of whether to use ♭ or ♮. Now, when there are no flats in the key signatures, this choice has to be made only when the cadential 1 is *A*, *D* or *G*, since all other steps of the gamut already have a semitone either below or above. Prosdocimus himself indirectly told us what the choices were when one cadenced on *D* or *G*. In an already-discussed example[92] which preceded the passage in question (see Example 28 on p. 124 above) and which demonstrated how to inflect imperfect consonances in order to make their progressions better, there were three relevant progressions, two consisting of f♯-g moving against a-G, and one of e-d moving against c#-d. Clearly, Prosdocimus' explicit choice when 1 was *D* or *G* was to sharpen 7. This leaves us with only one cadential 1, namely *A*, where the choice of the leading tone is unclear.

For several reasons, I am inclined to think that also in this case the more likely choice would have been to sharpen 7. For one thing, Prosdocimus told us that, other things being equal, we should inflect the discant, and it is this part that is much more likely to contain 7. But there are more important reasons as well. A cadence on *A* represents either an irregularly placed protus or a transposed deuterus. Modal transpositions are indicated by means of signature accidentals. Consequently, an *A*-cadence in a part without a flat in the signature is likely to represent protus, while the same cadence in a part with a one-flat signature is likely to represent deuterus. In the latter case, we do not have to make any choices, since 2 is already flattened by the signature, and the cadence has the same 'Phrygian' form in its transposed version on *A* as in its untransposed version on *E*. But, by the same token, when there is no flat in the signature of the voice containing 2 and the *A*-cadence represents the irregularly placed protus, it makes sense to give it the form which protus-cadences have in their regular location on *D*, that is, to sharpen 7. It would follow that the 'Phrygian' cadence was normally used only when the semitone below 2 occurred naturally under a given key signature and that in cases which offered the choice of either flattening 2 or sharpening 7 the latter solution was preferred. Let us observe that this conclusion is additionally and indirectly supported by the finding that only 7, but not 2, was the absolutely indispensable component of the penultimate harmony of all cadences. Needless to say, the conclusion above assumes an entirely neutral melodic and vertical context for the two voices concerned. In actual music, the context may make the preferred solution impossible. For instance, doubling a step in another voice might well have been an indication that it was not meant to be inflected, since an inflection implied a continuation of the melodic movement (mi going to fa, or fa to mi), while the prohibition of parallel perfect consonances prevented the proper resolution of one of the inflected notes.

Our conclusions thus far are highly speculative, being deduced from few simple assumptions consistent with the theory of the period. There is, however, ample theoretical evidence showing which cadential leading tones were in fact inflected by musicians of our period. I shall examine this evidence now, paying particular attention to the cases we have seen to have been most ambiguous, that is, to the *A*-cadence under no-flat signatures and to its transposed equivalents.

Among Marchetto's examples of progressions from imperfect to perfect consonances may be found those illustrated in Examples 34 and 35.[93] The middle progressions in both examples end on a fifth and may be disregarded

Example 34

Example 35

for the time being. They are, in any case, irrelevant to the present discussion, since they end on $I = C$, that is, on a step which offers no choice as to the leading tone. But the first and third progressions in each example are relevant and suggest that the theorist's choice for *D*-cadences was to sharpen *C* and, what is more important, that his choice for *A*-cadences was also to sharpen 7 rather than flatten 2. (There is no octave-cadence in the second example, of course, but the fifth-cadence is sufficient to tell us that Marchetto wants 7 rather than 2 to be inflected.) Even more revealing is the Fourth Treatise of Marchetto's *Pomerium* which is devoted to the theorist's version of the sharp sign. Marchetto explains there that this sign, rather than the square b or the round b, is used in mensural music in progressions from imperfect to perfect consonances.[94] It will be recalled that Marchetto's sharp differs from the standard mi-sign only in that it divides the whole tone differently, only in the implied tuning. Thus we may infer from his discussion that the sharp, and not the flat, was the normal choice in cadential progressions.

Another early fourteenth-century theorist, Petrus frater dictus Palma ociosa, gives examples of major sixths progressing to octaves on *A*, *D* and *G*, sharpening the 7 in each case.[95] In the later part of the century, an anonymous author tells us that 'a ♮ is always comprehended at the end of any ascent between the next-to-the-last and the final note on the lower one, as is shown here' (see Example 36).[96] The theorist's 'always' suggests again the

Example 36

automatic choice of a sharp rather than a flat for a cadential leading tone and the G♯-a progression in the example is particularly revealing. Also Philippus de Caserta talks about the sign of diesis, and not the flat, as the proper means of inflecting a sixth going to an octave, or a third going to a fifth.[97]

Thus, the fourteenth-century evidence, and in particular that of Marchetto and Petrus, argues in favor of my original conclusion that where a choice of the leading tone had to be made, the sharp, and not the flat, was the preferred solution.

In the early fifteenth century, however, we find an example which may argue in favor of a flat solution for A-cadences. In his *Tractatus musice speculative*, Prosdocimus explains that in the progression of c-d against E-D the minor sixth should be made major and that this is accomplished by means of c♮ in the case of 'ancient' (*antiqui*) and sensible musicians, or by means of c♯ in the case of the 'modern' (*moderni*) followers of Marchetto (the distinction being important to Prosdocimus, but insignificant to us in the present context).[98] In the progression of b-a against G-a, however, both ancients and moderns make the third minor by means of b-fa.[99] This may indicate that, in Prosdocimus' view, the flat 2 was the normal choice for A-cadences. The same two progressions are discussed by Ugolino of Orvieto and by Ramos de Pareia, and they also correct c-d moving against E-D by means of c♯, and b-a moving against G-a by means of ♭.[100] It should be recalled here that Ramos argued against those who made the key between G and a into G♯ instead of a♭ and who claimed that they needed G♯ to correct the progression of G-a against B-A; he preferred this progression to be corrected by means of B♭.[101] The theorist continued his discussion of the problem:

And if someone wished to say that there [at a] the protus was reborn, and the conditions which D had should obtain also at a, and [that] since D was shown to have a whole tone[102] below and above itself, in the same way also a [should have a whole tone below and above], we shall respond by saying that the argument does not succeed, since that [whole tone below and above] has G which assumes for itself complete similarity below and above in the synemmenon tetrachord [that is, a-♭-c-d], but not a which has two whole tones below . . . Therefore, that step [a] is deuterus, authentic as well as plagal, in the conjunct [that is, in the system with the soft b].[103]

The whole passage is of great interest to us, since it shows that musicians of Ramos's time could not agree on which leading tone to use at A-cadences. Ramos himself preferred B♭, but he clearly felt compelled to argue against those who chose G♯. The passage implies that both sides argued in modal terms, Ramos's opponents claiming that A was the final of the protus and, therefore, should take the lower leading tone of the protus, and Ramos himself that it was the final of the deuterus in the system with the soft b (that is, with a one-flat signature) and, therefore, should take the upper leading tone of the deuterus. His argument is less than air-tight, since he does not say explicitly how to interpret an *A*-final when there are no flats in the signature. One gets the impression (by no means certain) that he would consider also the latter case to represent the deuterus, but if this was so, his would be a minority opinion; in the standard view, an *A*-final with no flats in the signature represented the protus.

We may provisionally conclude that during the fifteenth century there was some disagreement as to which leading tone to choose in *A*-cadences when there were no flats in the signature, a disagreement stemming from conflicting modal interpretations of such cadences as representing the protus (in which case one would use *G♯*) or deuterus (in which case one chose *B♭*). Since the interpretation of such cadences as representing the protus was the normal one, it may be that also the use of *G♯* as the leading tone was the more common choice. Theoretical evidence from the time of Ramos on, at any rate, points overwhelmingly in favor of the use of b-mi for cadential leading tones whenever the choice was open.[104]

An anonymous *Quot sunt concordationes*, edited probably in the third quarter of the fifteenth century, states:

Whenever there is la-sol-la in simple song, this sol should be sharpened and sung as fa-mi-fa . . . Whenever there is sol-fa-sol in simple song, this fa should be sharpened and sung as fa-mi-fa . . . Whenever there is re-ut-re in simple song, this ut should be sharpened and sung as fa-mi-fa . . . Note that in counterpoint no other notes are sharpened but these three, namely sol, fa and ut.[105]

The author clearly discusses the cadential melodic formula 8–7–8, placing it on the only three steps of the natural hexachord (*A*, *G* and *D*, respectively) which have a whole tone below and above, so that one must choose the leading tone. In each case, he tells us, the lower neighbor should be sharpened to produce the lower leading tone.

Incidentally, the words of our author might suggest that the cadential formula 8–7–8 with sharp 7 has to be solmizated always fa-mi-fa. This, however, is expressly denied by several theorists throughout our period who tell us that such a formula with 8 on *D*, *G* or *A* may have been also solmizated as if the semitone was not there, that is, re-ut-re, sol-fa-sol and la-sol-la, respectively.[106]

The same information as in *Quot sunt concordationes* is conveyed by Gaffurius in his *Practica musice*:

Very often many sing *sol* as a semitone below *la*, especially in the progression *la sol la*, beginning and ending on *A-la-mi-re*, as in *Salve Regina*. The same happens with *sol* and *fa* in the progression *sol fa sol*, beginning and ending on *G-sol-re-ut*, which Ambrosians are frequently accustomed to sing.[107]

Similarly, Gonzalo Martínez de Bizcargui tells us about the sharpening of the lower-neighbor *C*, *F* and *G* in the formulas re-ut-re, sol-fa-sol, and la-sol-la.[108]

Frequent use of solmization syllables to represent the cadential formula 8-7-8 offers an additional support to my claim that the sharp was the normal choice when one had to inflect cadential leading tones. Before inflecting, the formula is re-ut-re for the protus, and sol-fa-sol for the tetrardus, and only in these does the choice of the leading tone exist. Once we learn that in both these cases the lower neighbor is to be sharpened, we can infer what to do when the cadential formula occurs at A. If there is a flat in the key signature, the formula will be solmized mi-re-mi and the lower neighbor will not be sharpened, just as it is not when this formula occurs at E. But when there are no flats in the key signature, the formula is re-ut-re, and this, we already know, requires the sharpening of the lower neighbor. The result is that while some theorists, such as Gaffurius and Martínez referred to above, tell us expressly what to do with the formula when it occurs at A, others do not bother. Johannes Cochlaeus, for instance, talks only about an implied accidental inflection occurring in the cadences re-ut-re and sol-fa-sol.[109] This is, indeed, the most economical way to discuss the problem, and – as I have just demonstrated – it suffices to clarify it fully.

Simultaneously with Cochlaeus, Arnolt Schlick talks about the black keys below A, G and D as necessary for cadences on these steps.[110] We have already seen that the tuning of the first of these black keys gives him considerable trouble and that he tempers $A\flat$ sufficiently to have a serviceable leading tone for A-cadences. It is significant that he wants to have this leading tone even if it does not sound too well and that it does not occur to him that all A-cadences could use the upper leading tone instead.

Abundant evidence in favor of lower, rather than upper, leading tones continues to appear through the end of our period. Pietro Aaron, in his *Libri tres de institutione harmonica* of 1516, follows a discussion of the 8-7-8 cadential formula at various steps of the gamut[111] with this general observation: 'This, moreover, should be known, that all cadences which are shown to terminate by a whole tone should be sharpened.'[112] Such sharpening in the upper part, however, is not necessary, of course, if the lower part descends to the final by a half step, as happens in cadences on a sung 'through the soft b' (*per b molle*), or in cadences on E.[113] An example of a cadence on a with the lower leading tone expressly sharpened is presented and discussed in Aaron's *Lucidario in musica* of 1545.[114] Aaron criticizes the progression g-g♯-aa moving against c-♮-a as incorrect, because of the chromatic semitone in the upper voice, and recommends that it be corrected by changing the upper voice to aa-g♯-aa, but it does not even occur to him that the chromatic semitone might be avoided also by using ♭ in the lower voice instead of g♯ in the upper one.

Another theorist who expressly prescribes the sharpening of the leading tone even in A-cadences is Guerson:

Moreover, it should be known that every imperfect consonance desiring perfect consonance should be raised in ascent by a semitone . . . You should then sharpen mi from fa and fa from mi situated between two sols, and also ut placed between two res, and also sol located between two las.[115]

In other words, the middle step in the cadential progressions sol-fa-sol, re-ut-re *and* la-sol-la should be sharpened.

Giovanni Maria Lanfranco presents examples of cadential formulas, complete (8-7-8) or interrupted (8-7), with the leading tone (7) always sharpened by the sign of diesis, with 8 on d, g, aa and dd when there is no flat in the signature, and with 8 on d, g, cc and dd when there is one flat (♭ and ♭♭) in the signature.[116] He thus exemplifies all the situations in which 1 has whole tones below and above and shows that in all such situations the sharp leading tone is chosen rather than the flat one. It is interesting to note that Lanfranco allows a certain minimal liberty of choice as to whether to treat a given configuration as a cadence or not, especially when the cadential formula does not contain the characteristic suspension. He follows the examples described above with this remark:

And thus this diesis . . . may be formed in other parts in similar places, as is said. I say 'may be', because it is not always made, even though most often it is. One does not always make it, especially in notes which are not syncopated, as are those in the first parts of the examples above [which contain interrupted formulas 8-7 rhythmicized as ♮♮ , that is, without a suspension, as opposed to the full formulas 8-7-8 rhythmicized as ♮♮♮♮, that is, with a suspension].[117]

Lanfranco's contemporary, Stephano Vanneo, also states that when in the cadential formula ending on an octave both 8 and 1 are approached by whole tones, one uses the sign of diesis to sharpen the leading tone in the upper part.[118] He adds:

Therefore, those desiring to cast away this burden and to leave the wavering cross-road recognize and follow this golden rule and then store it away in the treasury of memory, namely, that every cadence of the soprano [that is, the formula 8-7-8] may be made in five ways. Indeed, the first is re-ut-re, the second mi-re-mi, the third fa-mi-fa, the fourth sol-fa-sol, the fifth and last la-sol-la. Three of these, namely, re-ut-re, sol-fa-sol and la-sol-la, require the assistance of sharpening. However, la-sol-la on both E-la-mi [that is, on E and e] and on both A-la-mi-re under the soft b [that is, on a and aa under the B♭-signature] and on E-la [that is, ee] does not follow this rule, since in these places the tenor gets the cadence of the semitone.[119]

The reference to the 'wavering cross-road' suggests that at least the beginners shared our own uncertainty as to whether to use the sharp or flat for cadential leading tones, but Vanneo's 'golden rule' to use always the sharp agrees fully with what we are learning from other theorists. Vanneo follows the above discussion with an example indicating the necessity of sharpening 7 in the 8-7-8 formula when 8 is on d, g, aa or dd and there is no flat in the key signature, and when 8 is on G, c, d, g, cc or dd and there is one flat in the signature.[120]

Vanneo's 'golden rule' retained validity through the end of our period. Loys Bourgeois expressed it as follows:

Likewise, some complete cadences of the upper voice (which may be encountered in all voices), such as la-sol-la, sol-fa-sol and re-ut-re, or sometimes interrupted ones, such as la-sol, sol-fa and re-ut, should be sung by a semitone. I have said especially 'some cadences', because this should not be done always. Also la-sol-la or mi-re-mi from a-la-mi-re to g-sol-re-ut [that is, a-G or aa-g] sung by the soft b [that is, with B♭ in the signature] and la-sol-la or mi-re-mi from e-la-mi to d-la-sol-re [that is, e-d] should be sung by a whole tone as if this were not a cadence.[121]

Juan Bermudo formulates a similar procedure differently: when a minor sixth expands to an octave, it should be corrected in the upper voice [that is, by means of a sharp], if this is possible; if this is not possible because a mi-against-fa discord would be produced, correct it in the lower part [that is, by means of a flat].[122]

Finally, at the end of our period, Gioseffo Zarlino explains that 'the voice that ascends to the final is intended to have the semitone, unless the other voice descends by the same interval',[123] which may perhaps be taken to say that whenever there is a choice between sharpening 7 or flattening 2, one does the former.

In short, the evidence from the last quarter of the fifteenth century on supports overwhelmingly our original conclusion: if the context leaves the choice of whether to flatten 2 or sharpen 7 open, choose the sharp 7. Additional support for this conclusion is provided by the sixteenth-century evidence, discussed in the preceding chapter, which suggests that the functions of flats and sharps were different, the former correcting mi against fa, the latter serving cadences.

Should we conclude then that the testimony of Prosdocimus, Ugolino and Ramos which indicated that some disagreement existed as to which leading tone to use in *A*-cadences when there were no flats in the key signature applies only to fifteenth-century practice? This may be so, but I am inclined to interpret their testimony differently, especially since practical evidence shows that the sharp and flat solutions were both acceptable also in the sixteenth century.[124] Ramos suggested that the disagreement resulted from conflicting modal interpretations of such *A*-cadences as representing either protus or deuterus. I have claimed, in turn, that normally such cadences were thought to represent protus. This is true, of course, in a piece the tenor of which was conceived in the untransposed protus irregularly placed on a and notated without a key signature. But this does not have to be necessarily true in a piece conceived in another untransposed mode (for instance, in the untransposed protus placed regularly on d) with internal cadences on *A*. In such a piece, the interpretation of these internal *A*-cadences might have depended on the context. An *A*-cadence occurring within a piece representing an untransposed regular protus on d, to continue with our imaginary but very common example, may give just a momentary emphasis to the fifth modal degree within the stable context of the fundamental mode, but it may also signify a temporary shift to the untransposed irregularly placed protus on a. Beginners and hacks would interpret all these cases in a uniform way, but it is likely, I think, that sensitive musicians would apply the flat upper leading tone in the former case (since the flat sixth degree is very common in the protus and, consequently, would not unduly disturb the fundamental mode) and the sharp lower leading tone in the latter (since this would convey the temporary shift to another final much more forcefully).

It may be that the dispute on accidentals which took place in Rome *ca*. 1540 and was described by Ghiselin Danckerts offers a relevant example.[125] The dispute concerned a lamentation by Juan Escribano, the beginning of which Danckerts quotes (see Example 37),[126] a piece which every-

Example 37

body, including the composer, considered to be in the untransposed second mode. The bass wanted to sing his part with a flat at B throughout and put the flat in the signature, while the tenor, with whom the judges agreed, objected that the sign did not belong in the signature. It is not clear whether the tenor objected only to the placement of the flat in the signature, or also to the bass flattening all of his B's, but Danckerts himself thought that the only B♭ in the bass part of his example was the expressly marked one in m. 8. In his illuminating discussion of the dispute, Lewis Lockwood recognized that one of the reasons why the bass wanted flats in his part was to make the sixths before the octaves major.[127] This I think is indeed the most likely reason for the bass's decisions. Because of the vertical mi against fa, he would flatten the last B in his part (m. 8) whether or not the flat was written out. The preceding flat (m. 6) he wanted because the progression of the tenor and bass here has all the features of a cadence. And the first flat (m. 5) was probably added to avoid the use of both B and B♭ in close succession. I take the significance of the dispute for our understanding of how cadential progressions were handled to be twofold. First, we may have here an in-dication that sixteenth-century musicians could disagree on whether to treat a progression like a cadence or not. They would certainly all agree that the quoted passage ends with a strong cadence on the mode's final, a cadence requiring the sharpening of the leading tone in the cantus. But if the bass wanted to treat the progression involving his and the tenor's parts in mm. 5-7 (and presumably the analogous progression of the cantus and alto in mm. 2-4) as a cadence on the fifth degree above the final, Danckerts (and perhaps also some other musicians, though we cannot be sure of that) did not. Good arguments may be imagined on both sides. On the one hand, the progressions have recognizably cadential structure, on the other, they are embedded within a larger phrase the continuity of which might be endan-gered by constant cadencing. The second, and from the standpoint of the problem we are considering presently, more important lesson which can be derived from the dispute is that if musicians wanted to treat the progressions in mm. 2-4 and 5-7 as cadences, they would choose the upper rather than the lower leading tone. The reason is, I think, that the quoted phrase pro-jects and emphasizes from the beginning, both melodically and vertically, the intervallic species of the protus. Thanks to the melodic outline of the bass (and alto), we have no doubt that the cadence in m. 7 (and in m. 4) ends not on the final but on the fourth below it, and we know it even before we hear the confirmation in mm. 8-10. The use of the sharp leading tone would be jarring in this case, since it would give an exaggerated emphasis to this fourth step below the final, and would make it sound like the final in its own right. The use of the flat leading tone, on the other hand, does not con-tradict our hearing of the cadence as ending on the fifth degree of the protus, since the flat sixth degree is so common in this mode.

Moreover, it is imaginable that a certain degree of flexibility as to whether internal *A*-cadences should be treated as representing protus or deuterus existed even in pieces the tenors of which were conceived in the untransposed protus irregularly placed on a and notated without a key signature. The structurally important cadences in such pieces would have to be treated as representing protus, of course, but one cannot exclude the possibility that, for whatever reason, whether for the sake of text expression, or simple variety, the composer might wish to interpret some internal cadences as representing deuterus. In the 'Supplement' to his *Toscanello in musica*, Aaron referred to a case which might be interpreted in this fashion. Among a long list of examples showing composers expressly using the sign of the round b to correct mi-against-fa discords, he included one in which the composer used the sign to make the sixth before an octave major:

For further clearness I want to mention Richafort, who not only considered fifths, octaves, twelfths, and fifteenths, but also the major sixth before the octave, as is shown in his motet, *Miseremini mei*, over the words 'quare me persequemini'. A sixth appears there between contrabass and contralto, to which because it is minor he has applied the sign ♭.[128]

The passage Aaron referred to occurs in an internal duet of a four-part motet with the tenor in untransposed irregular protus (mode 2) on a and with numerous *A*-cadences in which 7 has unmistakably to be raised. In the duet, however, the composer expressly demanded, whether for the sake of expression or variety, flat 2 (see Example 38).[129] Note how this explicit flat at the beginning of the phrase (m. 34, bass) implicitly suggests how the cadence at the phrase's end (mm. 36–7, tenor and bass) should be treated.

It is possible that considerations of this sort led to disagreements noted by some fifteenth-century theorists concerning the proper handling of *A*-cadences. This is, of course, no more than an educated guess, but should this guess prove correct, there would be no strong reason to limit the validity of the testimony of these theorists to the fifteenth century only; theorists who recommend that we sharpen 7 in *A*-cadences would be then seen as telling us simple truth, but not the whole truth. If what we are after is the reconstruction of the practice of the best musicians of the period, my provisional recommendation is to handle *A*-cadences occurring in the untransposed system (as well as their transposed equivalents) flexibly, depending on the context, just as in the imaginary example above. Future studies of accidentals occurring in practical sources will test the validity of this recommendation.

If a third voice in the penultimate cadential harmony contains 4 and the 7 has been sharpened, the question arises whether to sharpen the 4 as well and thus preserve the perfect fourth with the 7, or leave the 4 unsharpened and

Example 38

tolerate the vertical tritone there. In the preceding chapter we have learned that a mi-against-fa discord may be tolerated even in simple counterpoint provided it is preceded and followed by a consonance, with at least one of the dissonant notes properly resolved (that is, with the mi-step going a diatonic semitone up and/or the fa-step going a diatonic semitone down). It follows that the tritone between 4 and 7 would be tolerable. But there is another reason why one might want to sharpen the penultimate 4 if it goes on to the final 5: in the progression of 4–5 moving against 2–1, the vertical third moving to a fifth should be major. We might conclude, therefore, that if the penultimate cadential harmony contains 4 (in addition to the structurally central 7 against 2) which goes on to 5, and if the 7 has been sharpened, the 4 will be sharpened as well, provided the context allows it. It has to be emphasized, however, that the 4 would be sharpened because of the secondary cadential progression of the third going to the fifth, not because it has to be adjusted to the 7.

That in the third-to-fifth progression the third should be major is asserted by theorists from the beginning through the end of our period. Thus we have no purely theoretical evidence which would suggest that at some point the secondary leading tone (the sharp 4) went out of fashion. But practical sources seem to indicate that it did; there seem to be almost no secondary leading tones in sixteenth-century intabulations of vocal models.[130] Observe, moreover, that if a composer, a school, or a generation of composers wanted to avoid the sharpening of the penultimate 4, they would have to indicate this change of taste by regularly resolving the 4 not to 5 but elsewhere (to 3 or 1), or by avoiding the penultimate 4 altogether in favor of 5. Thus, when dealing with a repertoire in which a great many of the cadential 4s do not resolve to 5 but to 3 or 1, or in which a great many cadences for more than two parts use 5 rather than 4, we may be fairly sure that the reason was to avoid the sharpening of the 4. When in such a repertoire the cadential 4 is doubled and one of the 4s goes to 5 while the other resolves elsewhere, it makes sense to assume that also in such cases the 4s were meant to be left unsharpened: the composer is simply using his normal cadence of 7–8 and 4–3 against 2–1, doubles the 4, and, in order to avoid the forbidden parallelism, resolves it to 5. But it is not entirely clear what should be done with the 4 in cadences of 7–8 and 4–5 against 2–1 occurring in a repertoire which normally avoids the sharpening of the 4. One could argue, on the one hand, that here the 'unusual' or 'archaic' double-leading-tone cadence was intended, because otherwise the composer would have used 5 instead of 4, or would have resolved his 4 not to 5 but elsewhere. On the other hand, it is also possible that in the repertoire in question the secondary leading tone went so thoroughly out of fashion that the composer could afford using the penultimate 4 and resolving it to 5 (which produces a more desirable final harmony than either 3 or 1 would) without running the risk that his musicians would sharpen the 4. The problem cannot be resolved on the basis of theoretical evidence alone.

Will cadential accidentals necessitate the use of other additional accidental inflections? Since both cadential inflections, 7-mi and 4-mi, resolve properly a semitone upward to 8-fa and 5-fa, they can create no melodic problems. The only problems they can create are vertical mi against fa on an octave (unison) when 7 or 4 is doubled in another voice, or octave (unison) cross relations. When confronted with such problems, one has the choice of either giving up the regular cadential inflections in favor of the less usual flat solution, or correcting the imperfect octaves by means of additional sharps. Correcting all imperfect octaves produced by the inflected leading tones with additional sharps would not conflict with our earlier discovery of theorists' implicit rejection of flat 'chain reactions' provided we do not allow these additional sharps to create further melodic or harmonic problems, since the rejected 'chain reactions' involved accidentals applied to steps distant by intervals other than the octave. Thus, both choices presented above seem to be plausible. It is possible that Lanfranco had contexts of this sort in mind when, in an already-discussed passage in which he contrasted the use of flats in order to correct mi against fa and of sharps at cadences, he said that sharps may also be used for mi-against-fa discords. If this reading of Lanfranco were correct, this would be an argument in favor of the latter of the two choices presented above, but we have no way of knowing whether it is correct. I have not been able to find an explicit theoretical discussion of such problems, and it is likely that we will have to discover relevant practical evidence in order to be able to solve them. Failing this, we will have to rely on intuitive sense of which solution seems best. I am inclined to believe that doubling of the penultimate 7 or 4 in a cadence (and perhaps even creating an octave cross relation with it) might have been a composer's means of showing that the step should not be sharpened and, in case of the doubled 7, that flat 2 should be used instead. I believe this on the admittedly speculative grounds that a sharpened leading tone suggests a resolution by a half step up but, because of the prohibition of parallel perfect consonances, one of the doubled steps would not get such a resolution.

At the end of the preceding chapter I concluded that the normal practice of our period required no more than three flats (Bb, Eb and Ab). The corollary of what we have learned about the sharpening of cadential leading tones in this chapter is that the normal practice of our period (that is, the practice using one of the common key signatures and employing sharps only for cadential leading tones and for thirds of the final harmonies in cadences) required no more than three or four sharps, three ($C\sharp$, $F\sharp$ and $G\sharp$) for sharpening of the 7, and four (the above plus $D\#$) for sharpening of the 4. Note how well these results agree with the conclusions reached earlier (in Chapter 2(v) above) concerning the most commonly used steps of *musica ficta*.

7 Canon and imitation

In the preceding chapters I have examined melodic, harmonic and contrapuntal contexts which necessitated the use of *musica ficta* steps. The question to be examined in this chapter is whether music of our period employed compositional procedures necessitating the use of such steps.

In addition to the increasingly ubiquitous technique of imitation, early vocal polyphony developed a family of special techniques involving the use of the same *complete* melody more than once in a composition, so that in principle the melody might have been, but in reality did not have to be, notated just once, its repetitions and transformations being directed by a written 'rule' (*canon*). Canon in the broad sense in which the term will be employed here covers the use of the same melody in different voices (this is the narrow, modern sense of the term) as well as successive uses of the same melody in the same voice as an ostinato or in various *cantus firmus* techniques.

Canon and imitation raise two closely related *musica ficta* problems. First, should one aim at preserving exact intervals of the melody at each appearance (whether at the same or at different pitch levels) and, consequently, when forced to introduce an inflection for a harmonic or contrapuntal reason, introduce it always in the non-canonic or non-imitative voice? We have seen in the last two chapters that theorists offered no evidence which would suggest that, when confronted with the need to correct a vertical mi-against-fa discord or a penultimate cadential harmony, musicians worried about which voice to inflect (higher or lower, *cantus firmus* or counterpoint written against it). On the contrary, evidence which we have discussed supports my belief that in such situations the question on musicians' minds was only whether to use a mi- or a fa-step. This fact, coupled with the absence of theoretical injunctions against the use of inflections in canonic or imitative voices, argues in favor of unrestricted use of mi-against-fa and cadential inflections also in such voices. An additional argument in favor of this conclusion is that in a composition in which all the parts are canonic we would have no choice but to inflect a canonic voice occasionally, since we have no reasons to believe that rules governing mi-against-fa contexts and cadences should be suspended in canons. In short, until more evidence is found, it seems reasonable to assume provisionally that, when confronted with a mi-against-fa or cadential situation requiring an accidental inflection, a musician of the period dealt with it in the usual fashion also in canon or imitation.

The second question raised by canon and imitation is whether one should preserve exact intervals of the model melody when reproducing it at a different pitch level. Theoretical evidence relevant to this question is too scarce to allow an entirely certain answer. I can offer only a provisional answer which will have to be tested and refined in the future in confrontation with practical evidence.

The most detailed discussion of various kinds of canon and imitation in our period was provided at its very end by Gioseffo Zarlino in *Le Istitutioni harmoniche*, Part III, Chapters 51-2.[1] Zarlino makes a distinction between *fuga, consequenza* or *reditta* (the three terms are synonymous), on the one hand, and *imitatione*, on the other (discussing them in Chapters 51 and 52, respectively). The distinction is less than precise so far as the general contemporary usage is concerned, since 'musicians sometimes call it [imitation] fugue'.[2] Consequently, the use of specific terms in practical sources can offer no certain indication as to whether 'fugue' or 'imitation' in the precise Zarlinian sense was intended by the composer. Both types can be either 'strict' (*legata*) or 'free' (*sciolta*). In the former case, the entire melody is duplicated (producing canon in the modern sense of the term), in the latter, the model melody is duplicated only up to a point, after which the voices proceed independently (resulting in imitation in the modern sense of the term). Both 'strict fugue' and 'strict imitation' may be notated as one voice only with a 'rule' (*canon*) explaining how to derive another part or parts from it. The difference between 'fugue' and 'imitation' is that in the former the intervals of the model melody have to be reproduced exactly, while in the latter 'the movements of the guide are imitated by the consequent only to the extent of duplicating the steps, without regard for the intervals'.[3] Since both can be reduced in notation to a single voice with a *canon*, it is clear that in both the consequent will reproduce the intervals of the guide, but not with the same exactitude. In 'fugue' the reproduced intervals have to be of exactly the same size (*minor* thirds of the guide, say, being reproduced as *minor* thirds in the consequent), while in 'imitation' the consequent reproduces all the intervals of the guide without paying attention to their exact size (so that *minor* thirds of the guide, say, may be reproduced as either *minor* or *major* in the consequent). Moreover, the interval at which one voice answers the other in a 'fugue' is the unison, fourth, fifth or octave, above or below: 'Imitation, like fugue, may be at the unison, fourth, fifth, octave, or other interval, that is, it may be written also at the second, third, sixth, seventh, and similar intervals.'[4]

Zarlino's distinction between 'fugue' and 'imitation' is directly relevant to our question whether one should preserve exact intervals of the model

melody when reproducing it at a different pitch level. Zarlino's answer is
that one should when one writes a 'fugue', but not when one writes an 'imitation'. When the interval between the first notes of the guide and consequent
is a second, third, sixth or seventh, above or below, we may be sure that an
'imitation' was intended by the composer. But both 'imitation' and 'fugue'
may be at the fourth or fifth, above or below, and Zarlino offers no additional criteria to allow us to recognize the composer's intention in such cases.
My intuitive rule of thumb would be to try to resolve such a canon as if it
were a 'fugue', unless such a resolution leads to difficulties which can be
avoided when the canon is treated as an 'imitation'. My reason for this rule of
thumb is that it is somewhat easier for a singer to resolve a canon as a 'fugue'
(since he can use the solmization syllables of the model, merely transposing
the whole by the prescribed interval) than to resolve it as an 'imitation' (since
in this case he must substitute an imaginary clef for the notated one and use
solmization syllables different from those of the model). Consequently,
performers were likely to try a 'fugal' solution out first, and to resort to an
'imitative' solution only if the 'fugal' one did not work.

In short, the only canons the consequents of which may, but do not absolutely have to, call for accidental inflections in order to preserve the exact
intervals of their guides are those at the unison, fourth, fifth and octave,
above or below.

While Zarlino's discussion concerns canon in the narrow modern sense of
the term, its results may be generalized, I believe, to include canon in the
broad sense in which I use the term here, that is, to include such phenomena
as ostinato and other successive uses of the same melody in the same voice,
because the fundamental principle behind all such phenomena, the use of
the same complete melody more than once in a composition, is the same.
The identity of this fundamental principle is underscored by the fact that all
the compositional techniques belonging to this family could, and often did,
employ the abbreviated notation showing the melody only once and supplying it with a 'rule' according to which the consequent (or consequents) was
(were) to be derived. We cannot, of course, be absolutely sure that this
generalization is legitimate, we can only maintain that it makes sense.[5]

Zarlino's distinction between 'fugue' and 'imitation' applies to both canon
and imitation in the modern sense of these terms. Should we conclude that
performers of Zarlino's time duplicated the intervals of the guide exactly
whenever their consequents entered at the fourth or fifth in a point of imitation? This is the assumption frequently made by Edward E. Lowinsky in his
chromatic interpretations of sixteenth-century music,[6] and, it should be
stressed, thus far it remains no more than an assumption. We cannot
exclude it entirely, but there is not enough evidence to accept it. Unlike in
the case of a canon presented in the abbreviated notation, in an imitation

the composer had the opportunity to indicate his intentions unambiguously, and if he chose to leave the consequent without accidentals, his performers were most likely to conclude that what he wanted was an 'imitation' in the Zarlinian sense, not a 'fugue'.[7] Imitation (in the modern sense) at the unison or octave is another matter, of course. Lewis Lockwood has in fact found evidence in Ghiselin Danckerts' account of the Roman dispute on accidentals suggesting that the preservation of exact sizes of intervals was desirable in imitation at the octave.[8]

No earlier theorist approaches the comprehensiveness of Zarlino's discussion of canon and imitation and, consequently, it is difficult to know with any degree of assurance how long before his time the conclusions I have derived from his discussion were valid. But these conclusions are so simple ('only a canon at the fourth or fifth may call for the use of accidentals in the consequent in order to preserve the exact intervals of the guide') and they agree so well with some other aspects of medieval and renaissance theory (at least since Guido's study of the 'affinities', a study eventually systematized in the gamut's seven hexachords, musicians were aware that the similarity of intervallic patterns around steps distant by the fourth and fifth was much greater than that around steps distant by other intervals; it was, consequently, much more likely that they expected a 'fugal' resolution when the canon was at the fourth or fifth than when it was at another interval) that we may at least use them as a working hypothesis when studying canonic practices in early vocal polyphony.

Zarlino's contemporary, Nicola Vicentino, devoted one chapter of his treatise to the canon.[9] According to Vicentino, 'canons made by the second, third, sixth, seventh and ninth are more modern than the others',[10] that is, those by the unison, fourth, fifth and octave, a remark which could be taken to provide a very indirect support for the validity of Zarlino's distinction between 'strict fugues' and 'strict imitations'. Vicentino remarks further: 'One should observe that when the tenor will make the canon at the fifth with the alto, if the tenor will be by the soft b, the alto will go by the hard b.'[11] Thus, canons at the fifth at least should preserve the intervals of the guide exactly.

We catch a glimpse of the attitudes to our question prior to the 1550s in letters exchanged by Giovanni Spataro of Bologna and Giovanni del Lago of Venice in 1529. Del Lago, in a letter of October 8, argues, not unlike Vicentino above, that in a 'fugue' at the fifth below the lower voice should have a b-signature, supports this claim with references to earlier theorists, and gives as his examples the cantus and tenor of Adrian Willaert's *Ave maris stella* as well as the five-part motet *Plorabant sacerdotes* by Jacquet of Mantua.[12] Spataro, in a letter of November 24, retorts that in 'fugues' one does not always reproduce the intervals of the guide exactly, and refers to Johannes Tinctoris and Bartolomeo Ramos de Pareia in support of his claim.[13] The passages he refers to can be easily identified, [14] but they throw no light on the question which interests us here. All in all, the pre-Zarlinian theory of canon and imitation is too sketchy for our purposes, but at least it does not contradict the conclusions we have derived from Zarlino. [15]

Part III
Written and implied accidental inflections

8 Classes of accidental inflections in early vocal polyphony

In popular, and as should be clear by now not quite correct, musicological usage the term *musica ficta* refers to accidentals implied by the music of the Middle Ages and the Renaissance, but not written down in the sources. Thus far, I have discussed the use of feigned steps without paying much attention to the problem of unwritten but implied accidental inflections. And yet, the fact that not all accidental inflections called for by the music of our period were expressly notated is the main reason why musicologists are interested in problems raised by *musica ficta*, and it is this fact that I would like to discuss now. The two very closely related questions to be considered initially are: Why were some accidental inflections written down and others merely implied? Which kinds of inflections had to be notated and which could be implied?

Theorists of our period discussed the question of implied accidentals infrequently. For most of them the matter was clearly self-evident and there was no problem worth discussing there. In the late fourteenth century, an anonymous author explained the meaning of the b-fa and b-mi signs and added that 'in general, it is not necessary to notate them'.[1] Most theorists of our period who bothered to mention implied accidentals at all limited themselves to similar remarks. In the late fifteenth century, Johannes Legrense wrote concerning the use of ♭ and ♮ in chant:

For our moderns say that we do not sing through the soft b unless it is written and others say that we do it when it is sweeter than the square b, thus imagining to test music like wines. I beg you, my most loved ones, what sort of trifles are these, and what sort of childish and exceedingly insipid opinions? Then should we sing the psalms of introits of the fourth mode, which lie entirely within the tritone, through the square b and render the sweet and more angelic than human melodies of saints harsh and rustic because of our ignorance? If we are not allowed to sing without the sign of boys and uncultivated people, it would not be permitted also to eat without the sign of trumpets and bells. The round b, because of a certain softness of the minor semitone, is indeed sweet, but honey is sweeter, and consumed excessively it gives a belly ache. Therefore, let the signs of the soft b and square b be for boys and those uncultivated people who do not understand the whole tone and semitone. It behoves us, however, to follow reason.[2]

The upshot of this colorful outburst is that, in the author's opinion, the round b must be written down for beginners, but not for experienced musicians. Similarly, in a well-known passage, Johannes Tinctoris says: 'Nor then [when one avoids the melodic tritone] is it necessary that the sign of soft b be added; rather, if it is seen to have been added, it is said to be asinine.'[3] Tinctoris's observation, like the one of Legrense, refers to melodic tritones only and it is not clear whether it can be generalized to embrace also accidentals implied by harmonic and contrapuntal contexts. But John Hothby in *La Caliopea legale* says that 'one should never abandon the first order [that is, "white-key" steps] if the second or third [that is, the flat and sharp "black-key" steps, respectively] are not signed expressly with their letters, or when one sees ♮ and F united and wanting to remain together, which they naturally cannot'.[4] The implication is that the accidentals required by vertical, as well as horizontal, mi against fa need not be expressly notated. From Bartolomeo Ramos de Pareia, in turn, we find out that also cadential sharps do not have to be written down, when he explains that in the progression of c-d against E-D, c should be raised, and adds immediately: 'If this is to be represented, it should be pictured thus: ▭✕▭ .'[5] The implication seems to be that this may, but does not have to be, represented.

Similarly, in the early sixteenth century, Pietro Aaron indicated in his *Libri tres de institutione harmonica* that the sign of diesis is written by the cadential leading tone for the benefit of less experienced musicians,[6] thus implying that more experienced ones could do without it. Aaron had more to say on the subject in *Toscanello in musica*. Talking about the use of the sign of diesis to change an unpleasantly sounding minor third to a smoother-sounding major one (Aaron may well have had the so-called Picardy third in mind here), the theorist added:

Although this sign is little used by learned and experienced singers but given perhaps only for the inexperienced, unintelligent singer, a proper performance would not be given to this position or syllable without it. For since mi-sol is naturally a semiditone, without the sign such a singer will not sing other than what is written unless his ear helps him, as may be seen among some who most certainly do this.[7]

In the 'Supplement' to *Toscanello*, Aaron amplified these remarks considerably.[8] It appears that the common practice allowed the so-called Picardy third to be left unnotated, since only inexperienced musicians needed the sign of diesis in such contexts, but Aaron recommended writing these accidentals down anyway, in order to avoid possible misunderstandings and help an inexperienced singer.[9]

The 'Supplement' to *Toscanello* contains the most extended discussion of the problem of implied accidentals extant. The relevant passages, preceding the one referred to above, are extraordinarily interesting.[10] Aaron testifies that musicians of his time were not in agreement so far as the issue of whether accidental signs should be notated or not was concerned, some musicians claiming that writing accidentals down was required only for beginners' sake. Aaron's own view was that this last opinion was correct only with regard to those flats which corrected melodic tritones and even there he praised composers who notated such flats expressly. Accidentals correcting harmonic mi-against-fa discords should always be written down, he thought, and again praised composers, past and present, who did so. Thus, Aaron's position concerning flats required by melodic tritones and harmonic mi-against-fa discords was the same as his position concerning sharps required by the so-called Picardy thirds. In both cases, the theorist formulated his opinion against those who thought that these accidentals did not have to be notated.

It is noteworthy that Aaron does not have a single example of a leading-tone sharp in the 'Supplement' and altogether only one example of a leading-tone accidental. (Richafort's flat making the sixth before an octave major which was discussed in Chapter 6(ii).) It may be that he thought that leading-tone sharps do not need to be notated, but it is more likely that he simply overlooked them in the 'Supplement'. It would be consistent with his position to recommend that also leading-tone sharps be expressly notated.

Also Spataro attested that not all accidentals required by compositions of his time were written down (and clearly deplored the fact) when, in a letter of January 4, 1529, addressed to Giovanni del Lago, he said in the context in which implied accidentals were discussed:

I say, therefore, that good players of artificial instruments play songs through a certain practice not as they are simply composed and written by the unlearned composers, but play them as they should be signed. Similarly do experienced singers. Often they sing pieces better than they had been composed and signed by the composers.[11]

The passage is interesting in that Spataro includes both singers and instrumentalists among performers who realized accidental inflections implied by composers and thus lends support to those scholars who see in tablatures a valuable type of evidence for the study of implied accidentals.[12]

Still at the end of our period, Nicola Vicentino felt compelled to recommend that composers write all required leading-tone sharps down, thus implying that this was not a common practice.[13] His contemporary, Gioseffo Zarlino, on the other hand, thought it was superfluous for the composer to mark the accidentals implied by the melodic non-harmonic fourths, fifths and octaves, since singers would realize these inflections 'even if the composer has not marked them'.[14] Similarly, it was not necessary, in his opinion, to use an accidental for a cadential leading tone, presumably because performers would recognize the composer's intention anyway.[15]

The theoretical evidence presented above remains so consistent in character and content through the whole period studied here that it allows us to give answers to the questions asked at the beginning of this chapter which will be valid for the whole period. From the beginning to the end of our period we hear that it is not always necessary to write accidentals down.

In particular, flats correcting melodic tritones may be easily left unwritten, but also accidentals required for contrapuntal–cadential reasons need not always be expressly notated, and even those required to correct mi-against-fa discords may sometimes be left out. We learn, further, that without these signs beginners are more likely to go astray than experienced musicians. Toward the end of our period, some theorists increasingly advocate that accidentals be always written down, but they do so against the widespread practice of leaving some accidentals unnotated. The very fact that the accidental signs existed indicates that they had to be used at least occasionally; no theorist advocates that they be always left out in notation. In short, most musicians wrote some accidentals down and left others out, but there was no agreement on exactly how much to notate and how much to leave out.

Why were some accidental inflections notated and others not? Theorists make clear that it was not necessary (but not prohibited, either) to notate those accidentals which were implied by the musical context. This attitude prompts us to pose what I think is the most fundamental question to be asked about the practice of implied accidentals: Do implied accidental inflections in music of our period belong to the domain of musical text which for any given work has to remain invariable from one performance to another if the work is to retain its identity, or do they, rather, belong to the domain of performance which may vary from one realization of the text to another without endangering the identity of the work? It should be noted that the distinction between the domains of musical text and performance proposed here is not identical with the distinction between what must and what does not have to be notated. The idea that not all essential aspects of a musical text must be notated may seem puzzling only on the anachronistic assumption that the function of music notation is to fix completely in a graphic form an ideal musical text existing apart from specific realizations, an attitude for which some evidence may be found in early sixteenth-century German theory, but which certainly did not represent the view of most musicians of our period (and, for that matter, of most musicians until the late eighteenth century).[16] The primary function of music notation of the period was certainly not to fix graphically the complete musical text for the benefit of analysts, but to give adequate instructions for performers. From this standpoint, the pragmatic attitude that what is clearly implied may, but does not have to, be expressly notated was entirely natural. Since the musical training of singers of polyphony in our period was identical with the training of composers, and since composers were very often personally involved in at least the initial realizations of their works, they could afford incomplete notation. In addition, the notation of vocal polyphony of the period shows clear signs of simple economy. Parchment and paper were expensive commodities throughout our period and long thereafter.[17] The very formats in which vocal polyphony of the period was written, the choir-book and the partbook, were considerably more economical, required considerably less writing space, than the score format would. Scribes of linguistic texts could and did save some space by using conventional abbreviations which they knew their readers would be able to spell out. Similarly, music scribes did not need to write down what was clearly implied anyway. There may be an analogy between the use of abbreviations in writing down language and the practice of implying accidentals in writing down music.

It should be stressed that in neither case did the pragmatic attitude expressed in the abbreviated notation imply that the author of the text, whether a linguistic text or a musical one, did not care about the specific way in which his abbreviations were decoded. The practice of implying rather than expressly specifying some accidental inflections in notation should not be construed to mean that such inflections could not belong to the text of the work, the text which maintained its identity in various performances, but belonged instead to the area of performance and, like dynamics, articulation or fingering, could vary rather freely from one realization of the text to the next.

The question whether accidental inflections in music of our period belong to what has been called here the domain of musical text or the domain of performance has been posed with a particular urgency by Carl Dahlhaus's paper of 1969 on 'Tonsystem und Kontrapunkt um 1500'.[18] Dahlhaus's point of departure is the observation that music of the fifteenth and early sixteenth centuries contains passages in which it is impossible to avoid all non-harmonic relations, since correcting a vertical mi-against-fa discord produces a melodic one and the reverse. How were such insoluble contradictions possible and why were they suffered, he asks? To understand this, he suggests, we must observe that the contrapuntal theory of the period formulated its rules using names of abstract interval classes, such as 'perfect' or 'imperfect consonance', rather than names of concrete intervals, such as 'perfect octave' or 'major sixth'. Insoluble conflicts resulting from the requirement to avoid both vertical and horizontal mi-against-fa discords, and mi-against-fa discords themselves, were the consequence of such abstract musical thinking in terms of interval classes rather than specific intervals. Compositions were conceived as if the distinction between, say, the perfect and the diminished fifth did not exist. Dahlhaus's argument rests on the distinction he proposes between the abstract counterpoint conceived in terms of interval classes and the harmonic counterpoint operating with concrete intervals. It is only the former, he claims, that belongs to what I have called here the domain of the invariable musical text preserving the identity of a work through various realizations. The latter belongs to the domain of performance and may vary from one realization to another.[19]

Unfortunately, careful reading of contrapuntal theory from before the

1530s offers no support for Dahlhaus's distinction. It is true, of course, that some rules of counterpoint could be, and often were, most economically expressed in terms of interval classes, while other rules had to be formulated in terms of concrete intervals. There is no evidence, however, that the latter rules were thought to be 'supplementary' to the former. When in the early fifteenth century Prosdocimus de Beldemandis (one of the theorists invoked by Dahlhaus) listed the six rules of counterpoint, he made no indication whatsoever that his fifth rule prohibiting mi against fa was in any way less basic or 'supplementary' to the other five.[20]

Moreover, the lowly serpent of 'concrete counterpoint' creeps close to the very heart of 'abstract counterpoint', one of the fundamental rules of which is, on Dahlhaus's own account, the prohibition of parallel perfect consonances. As I have demonstrated in Chapter 5(i) already late fifteenth-century theorists (Ramos, Gaffurius) testify that this prohibition might have been lifted when one of the two parallel fifths was perfect and the other diminished. Had composers of the period conceived their works in terms of 'abstract counterpoint', this exception to the prohibition of parallel consonances would be incomprehensible; they would have no way of knowing, when writing two parallel fifths, whether these are prohibited or allowed.

But the most fundamental objection to Dahlhaus's theory is that it is internally incoherent. Dahlhaus would have us believe that when a fifteenth-century composer conceived his counterpoint he was indifferent toward the specific sizes of, for instance, vertical fifths he used because he subsumed all such fifths under the interval class of 'perfect consonances'. But the general concept of 'perfect consonance', when applied to the interval of the fifth, sufficed to specify the size of this fifth most precisely; there was only one fifth which belonged to the class of perfect consonances, the one consisting of three diatonic whole tones and one semitone. Dahlhaus's hypothesis would be internally coherent only if fifteenth-century contrapuntal theory operated with interval classes such as the 'fifth' or 'octave', rather than 'perfect consonance'. Indifference toward the lowly empirical realm is, indeed, the obverse side of abstraction.

There is no denying, however, that Dahlhaus, with his customary acuity, identified two problems which have to be addressed and which his unsuccessful attempt to relegate accidental inflections to the domain of performance was meant to resolve. The first, and less important, of these problems is the existence of insoluble conflicts between horizontal and vertical mi-against-fa discords. The problem is not particularly important because such conflicts are much less frequent than is commonly believed. The reason why musicologists have until now been under the impression that such conflicts occur all the time is that they have not been aware of all the exceptions to the prohibitions of horizontal and vertical non-harmonic relations, exceptions the systematic unearthing of which is one of the prin-

cipal results of Chapters 4(i) and 5(i) of the present book. Occasional conflicts do arise, of course (otherwise Tinctoris would not bother to tell us how
to deal with them), but there is no reason to conclude that composers were
indifferent to them. Genuine conflicts might have had a variety of individual causes, ranging from the composer's inability to resolve a technical
problem he had posed for himself without sacrificing some rules (as is the
case in Dahlhaus's own example of an insoluble conflict, from the 'Agnus
Dei' of Nicolaus Gombert's Mass *Media vita* [see Example 39],[21] in which a
vertical mi against fa is tolerated at the beginning of m. 45 because of the
composer's desire to continue the artful six-part sequence) to a simple lack
of skill on the part of the composer or error introduced into the notated text
in the process of transmission.

The second problem addressed by Dahlhaus's hypothesis is more fundamental. The main reason why the idea that implied accidentals belong to
the domain of performance rather than musical text might seem attractive
is that at least some contexts requiring accidentals admit alternative solutions. As we have seen, there are two distinct classes of such contexts. On the
one hand, there are borderline situations in which musicians might hesitate
whether to apply an accidental or not. (If it was felt that the more notes
intervene, the less offensive is the indirect melodic tritone, there would have
to be borderline cases in which it was the performer's decision whether the
tritone is still offensive or not. Similarly, we have seen that progressions
fulfilling some, but not all, criteria one associated with cadence might
sometimes give performers the occasion to decide for themselves whether
they are going to treat a particular progression as a cadence or not. And it
might have been on occasion the singers' decision whether to keep intervals
in a given canon or imitation at the fifth or fourth exact or not.) On the
other hand, there are contexts (such as A-cadences) in which there is no
question that an inflection is required, but the choice of the inflection
(sharp or flat) may be left open. We know, moreover, that singers of our
period could sometimes disagree on how to realize the text; Lewis Lockwood
has discussed in fascinating detail a dispute on accidentals which agitated a
number of Roman musicians around 1540.[22] To be sure, contexts admitting
alternative solutions are much less frequent than those in which there is only
one way of applying an accidental; they exemplify an exception rather than
a rule. But the very possibility of such an exception demands consideration.
While I do not think that we may relegate all accidental inflections to the
domain of performance, the possibility of alternative solutions in some cases
does suggest that the borderline between the domains of musical text and
performance cuts across the area of accidental inflections. Most accidental
inflections in music of our period, whether notated or implied, do belong
unambiguously to the domain of invariable musical text, but some clearly
do not and are a matter of variable performance.

Example 39

Accidentally inflected steps are by no means unique in this respect. Also diatonic steps may find themselves on both sides of the border. While the distinction of 'abstract' and 'concrete' counterpoint cannot be documented, there can be no doubt that musicians of our period thought about pitch organization in terms of the fundamental distinction between simple, note-against-note, consonant counterpoint providing the underlying structure of a composition and diminished counterpoint embellishing this structure with dissonances and introducing rhythmic variety. The distinction is amply documented both in theory and in music itself in which the surface layer of embellishing diminutions can be easily removed to reveal the underlying, note-against-note, consonant structure. It was this fundamental distinction which made improvised ornamentation (for instance, at cadences) possible. But just as we would not conclude from the existence of such variable ornamental notes that all steps which do not form the underlying simple counterpoint belong to the domain of performance, we should not think that simply because some accidental inflections may be optional, all inflections are irrelevant from the standpoint of musical text. There is no justification for Dahlhaus's conclusion that, so far as accidental inflections are concerned, 'it is useless to strive for an "authentic" version'.

On the contrary, for the most part it is proper to think about the problem of implied accidentals in terms of the intended text to be correctly realized by the performers reading a more or less incomplete notation. Better composers and performers of our period shared common stylistic norms concerning correct melodic, harmonic and contrapuntal usage, the norms I have attempted to reconstruct above. A composer, or whoever edited a given version of the musical text, counted on his performers to provide a reading in accordance with these norms. The very fact that the singers involved in the Roman dispute mentioned a moment ago submitted their disagreement to independent musical judges indicates that the proper use of accidental inflections was not a matter of personal preference and subject to arbitrary whim but could be rationally discussed and adjudicated on the basis of commonly shared norms. All the musicians involved clearly assumed that the musical text could not be read in just *any* way, that there was a *correct* reading.

Early sixteenth-century theory, at any rate, shows that it is not anachronistic to think about the problem of implied accidentals in terms of the intended text realized in performance, and I see no compelling reasons to suspect that musicians of the fourteenth and fifteenth centuries thought about these matters differently. Aaron's 'Supplement' to the *Toscanello* would be incomprehensible on the assumption that accidental inflections were not the composer's business. That the theorist thought about the matter in terms of the performers trying to realize the intended text is clear throughout, and in particular in his discussion of the question whether singers can be expected to recognize the composer's intention during the first reading of a piece. Aaron, obediently following Spataro,[23] argued, it will be recalled, against those who believed that experienced musicians could do it. Spataro's and Aaron's texts should give a pause to those who would want to argue that the problem of implied accidentals has nothing to do with the composer's intentions and that the implied inflections were entirely the province of the performer.

I repeat, the function of notation was to give adequate instructions for performers. If the musical context implied the necessity of an accidental inflection, it was redundant and wasteful to write the accidental down. But since not all contexts implied inflections equally clearly (in the choirbook or partbook formats, it was much easier to spot the necessity of the inflection required by a melodic context than that required by a cadential, and especially by a harmonic context), and not all performers were equally experienced, some accidentals could be helpful, even if strictly speaking they were redundant. Consequently, they were written down.

The distinction I have drawn here between the domains of musical text and performance and the understanding of implied accidental inflections as belonging mostly, but not entirely, within the domain of text is directly relevant to our editorial practice. Arthur Mendel, commenting on 'The Purposes and Desirable Characteristics of Text-Critical Editions', argued that since implied accidentals were a matter of performance practice, they should not be included in modern critical editions.[24] It is true, of course, that implied accidental inflections were a matter of performance practice, but it does not follow that they belonged to what I have called here the domain of variable performance as opposed to the domain of invariable text. Once we realize that most of the implied inflections belong to the musical text, and that the modern attitude to notation, unlike the attitude shared by early musicians, requires that the text be fully notated, we must conclude that spelling out the inflections implied in the sources is the inescapable responsibility of the editor.

The accidentals not written but implied by the musical text of the piece clearly belong in the text of the edited work, where they should be distinguished from the written source accidentals. The standard editorial practice of putting such implied accidentals above the staff directly above the note concerned performs this function clearly and economically and I see no reason to revise it. But in addition, the editor should have the means of distinguishing those implied accidentals which he considers absolutely necessary from those he considers optional. For instance, it follows from my discussion of how to recognize a cadence that there will be borderline cases which some performers will want to treat as cadences and others not. Such optional implied accidentals should be clearly distinguished from the necessary implied accidentals, for instance, by means of parentheses. Finally, it may happen that a given context will allow two alternative solutions. An editor may decide, for instance, that a given A-cadence allows either the lower or the upper leading tone. A clear way of indicating such alternative implied accidentals has to be found. One might, for instance, mark the lower leading tone with ♯/♮ above the note and the alternative upper leading tone with ♮/♭ above the note. Parentheses might again be used to indicate the less likely of the alternative solutions, if so desired. Thus, if the editor thought the lower leading tone to be more likely, he might mark 7 with ♯/(♮), placing ♮/(♭) above the 2.

It should be clear why in practice there would be a grey zone of implied inflections within which some musicians would decide to write the necessary accidentals down and others to leave them out. But it is useful to ask whether there existed a class of accidentals which absolutely had to be written, because they were not implied by the musical context at all.

There were two classes of such accidentals. First, a composer could decide to use an internal accidental for reasons other than the melodic, harmonic, cadential and canonic reasons discussed in this book, for reasons which were not conventional. In principle, at least, we cannot exclude the possibility that some of the internal accidentals in the sources belong to this class, even though theorists generally ignore this possibility and for a good reason, since the unconventional cannot be captured in rules.

The second class of accidentals which absolutely had to be written because they were not implied by the musical context comprised signature accidentals. A signature accidental could be implied only in some very special circumstances. One of these circumstances would be the use of the round b in the signature only at E or only at A. A signature flat at E indicates that this E is fa and implies ut at the perfect fourth below, that is, implies $B\flat$ below $E\flat$. Similarly, a signature flat at A indicates that this A is fa and implies ut at the perfect fourth below and sol at the major second above, that is, implies $E\flat$ below and $B\flat$ above $A\flat$. Another special circumstance in which a signature accidental might be implied is a canon. A good example is Dufay's rondeau *Entre vous, gentils amoureux*,[25] in which a canonic rule directs that the tenor be derived from the written-out cantus at a fifth below. The fact that the contratenor, which shares the range with the tenor, has a ♭-signature implies that the tenor should also have a ♭-signature (that is, it implies that Dufay had an exact replication of the cantus' intervals in mind for the tenor), since the resulting combination of signatures is normal for early fifteenth-century pieces in this mode and with these part ranges, while the situation in which only the contratenor would have the ♭-signature would be highly unusual. These, however, are special circumstances. Normally, signature accidentals could not be implied by the context and, consequently, had to be written out.

This conclusion, however, has to be qualified because of the existence of the so-called 'conflicting' or 'partial' signatures in the music of our period. In Chapter 3 I suggested that 'in a piece with different signatures in different voices, the function of the signature in the mode-defining part was to effect a transposition of the mode, while differing signatures in other parts should be considered to "conflict" with that of the mode-defining one mainly in order to ensure perfect fifths against it'. If this way of looking at 'conflicting' signatures is correct, we may have to revise our conclusion. It is certainly valid so far as the key signature of the mode-defining part is concerned, since there was clearly no way of conventionally implying this signature by the context. But is it valid also for 'conflicting' signatures? The answer is, I believe, a qualified 'no'. A 'conflicting' signature could be implied in two ways. First, since a convention governing signatures of voices below and above the mode-defining part in relation to that part's signature did exist, a singer knowing the convention might see, for instance, that his part lies below the mode-defining voice and add a flat to his signature just in case. Second, the same singer might begin to sing his part as notated, notice while singing that he has to flatten many B's because of simultaneous F's in the mode-defining part, and decide to add B♭ in his signature. (This, incidentally, was what the bass did in the Roman dispute on accidentals discussed by Lockwood and summarized in Chapter 6(ii) above, and it is interesting to note that the singer who objected to the bass's action was the one in charge of the mode-defining part, the tenor.) But it should be observed that both ways in which a 'conflicting' signature could be implied differ somewhat from the way in which an internal accidental can be implied. The difference is one of degree. An internal accidental can be implied with much less ambiguity. A 'conflicting' signature can be implied, but almost never unambiguously. Situations in which every B in the bass, for instance, would conflict with F in an upper part are rare. Usually a 'conflicting' signature is implied only to a certain degree. In this area, a singer reading incomplete notation cannot be as sure that he is realizing its intentions correctly as he often can in the area of implied internal accidentals.

We should distinguish several classes of people responsible for the production, transmission and performance of vocal polyphony in our period. On the production side, a given work would have a composer and, if it existed in several distinct versions, each version would have an editor who might, but did not have to, have been the same person as the composer. On the transmission and performance side, there were scribes and printers as well as singers. (The hypothetical figure of the 'editor' is posited here to enable us to identify the function of someone who makes changes in the musical text of the work, but who does not have to be the same person as the work's composer. A scribe, for instance, becomes an 'editor' when he goes beyond merely mechanical copying and makes decisions affecting the musical text.) All of these people may have been responsible in various degrees for accidentals we find in practical sources, and it would be useful for us to be able to distinguish their respective contributions when evaluating source accidentals.

The findings of this chapter suggest that all accidentals found in practical sources of vocal polyphony of our period may be divided into two classes.[26] Some accidentals had to be written down by the composer or by whoever edited a given version of the piece because there was no possibility of implying them. Other accidentals might have been written down by the composer or by the editor of a given version, but they might have been just as well merely implied by the composer or editor and written down by someone else, a scribe or a performer. We may thus distinguish 'unconventional' source accidentals which must be 'authorial' (if it is understood that the term 'author' refers here not only to the composer but also to the editor of a given version) from 'conventional' ones which may be 'non-authorial'. The first group comprises those internal accidentals which are not there to correct conventionally a musical context and the key signatures of the mode-defining voices. The second group contains all internal accidentals conventionally used for reasons discussed in Chapters 4–7 above and 'conflicting' signature accidentals.

I can see at least four areas in which this division of all source accidentals into two classes may prove fruitful. First, the distinction between conventional and unconventional uses of internal accidental inflections which I draw here has implications for future research into the development of tonal language. A study of the use and functions (both structural and expressive) of unconventional internal inflections in compositional practice of the late Middle Ages and the Renaissance would contribute to our understanding of the development of genuine chromaticism. Such genuine chromaticism has to be distinguished from conventional uses of *musica ficta* steps, uses which evidently derived primarily from the wish to preserve diatonic, unaugmented and undiminished, intervals. The practice of conventionally implied inflections is, if anything, opposed to chromaticism and we should stop confusing these two phenomena. It can be suspected that the growth of genuine chromaticism during the sixteenth century was an important factor behind the increasingly frequent calls of theorists to write all accidentals down.

Second, the distinction between the functions of mode-defining and 'conflicting' signatures in pieces with different signatures in different parts opens the way to a more precise understanding of modality in early polyphony.

Third, a study of the functions of 'conventional' source accidentals in a given repertoire would allow us to learn how those situations which we know may have admitted alternative solutions were handled in this particular repertoire. Howard Mayer Brown has demonstrated how much may be learned in this respect from judicious evaluation of lute intabulations of vocal models.[27] We have just as much to learn from accidentals in sources of vocal polyphony. Now that we have identified with the help of theoretical evidence the types of contexts which may have allowed alternative solutions, we should make full use of the evidence of 'conventional' source accidentals to find out how such contexts were in fact handled at any given time and place.

Fourth, the division of all source accidentals into two groups drawn here has interesting implications for textual critics and editors of early vocal polyphony. Before spelling these implications out, however, I must state my general assumptions concerning what it is that editors should be doing. A textual critic and editor should have two goals in mind. First, he should want to reconstruct in modern notation the complete musical text of the work, or the texts of several successive authentic versions of the work, which is, or are, as close as possible to what the composer wanted. Second, the editor should reconstruct (preferably in the critical report) the history of the text independent of the composer's wishes, a history which includes all the distinct inauthentic versions in which the work circulated which can be documented. Current editorial practices which by and large aim at establishing the 'best' authentic text only and neglect the task of reconstructing all the distinct authentic and inauthentic versions of the work are inadequate from the standpoint of a historian whose interest in music includes not only the side of composition but also that of reception.[28] For each version, we should aim to spell out all the alternative realizations implied by the notated text, realizations possible from the standpoint of what we know about contemporary practice, and to evaluate the relative plausibility of alternative readings.[29]

Keeping the above assumptions in mind, let us return now to the implications of the distinction between 'unconventional' (and hence 'authorial') and 'conventional' (and hence possibly 'non-authorial') source accidentals suggested in this book for editing early vocal polyphony. The distinction offers two potential advantages. First, it allows us to distinguish different versions of a given piece. If the sources differ to a significant degree in 'unconventional' accidentals, they must transmit different versions of the work, since differences in 'unconventional' accidentals could not be obliterated in performance. On the other hand, differences between the sources in 'conventional' accidentals, no matter how drastic, do not indicate that the sources transmit different versions of the piece, since such differences could disappear, or at least be vastly reduced, in performance. This suggests, incidentally, that Allan Atlas's ideas concerning 'the methodology of relating sources' could probably be slightly revised so far as source accidentals are concerned.[30] In his work on relations between sources sharing concordances with the Cappella Giulia chansonnier Atlas concluded that source accidentals belong to those 'notational characteristics that do not indicate that the sources that share them are necessarily related, since their nature is such that two or more scribes could very well have happened upon them quite independently of one another'.[31] The conclusion is certainly correct so far as the 'conventional' source accidentals are concerned, but it should probably be revised to exclude the 'unconventional' ones. It is likely that differences among sources in 'unconventional' accidentals constitute 'significant variants', differences 'that could not possibly have been conceived by two musicians or scribes working independently of one another'.[32]

To avoid a possible misunderstanding, it should be stressed here that, since 'authorial' accidentals may stem from either the composer or the 'editor', our classification will not help us to evaluate the relative authenticity of different versions. But it will assist us in distinguishing with precision different versions, and such distinguishing is a necessary precondition for any evaluation of the authenticity of each version (an evaluation in which we shall have to seek assistance from other criteria, such as, for instance, the geographical and chronological proximity of sources transmitting a given version to the composer).

The second advantage of the classification of source accidentals proposed here is that it allows us to distinguish *within each version* of the edited work those accidentals which are 'authorial' from those which are potentially 'non-authorial'. Barring the possibility of a scribal or printing error, 'unconventional' accidentals have behind them the authority of the composer or editor of the given version, authority which 'conventional' accidentals necessarily lack, since we cannot be sure that they were not added by someone else than the composer or editor in the process of transmission. This second advantage becomes, of course, particularly valuable once we have examined the question of the authenticity of the given version and know that it stems directly from the composer.

Thus, the source accidentals belonging to the two groups distinguished above may have different degrees of authority. Those accidentals which must have been written down (whether by the composer or by the editor of a given version) are, of course, most authoritative and belong in the text of the edited work (whether in the text of the authentic version[s] or in the text of the inauthentic one[s]), on the staff. A considerable care should be exercised in the case of the unconventional internal accidentals belonging to this group: someone else than the composer or editor of a given version might have *mistakenly* added an accidental, anticipating, for instance, a vertical mi against fa which is not really there. Mistakes of this sort belong in the critical report, not in the edited text. Clearly, it will be easier to accept unconventional internal accidentals or key signatures of mode-defining voices as not being mistakes when they appear in contexts where there is no possibility that someone might have mistakenly anticipated a problem requiring the accidental, or when they appear in more than one source of the given version of the work.

All other source accidentals (those of the second, 'conventional', group) are relevant to the performing history of the work, but not necessarily to the text intended by the composer or editor of a given version. It is conceivable that some were added in the transmission of the text by a scribe, printer or performer and were not intended by the author (that is, the composer or editor of the given version). But since all accidentals of this group are justi-fied in some degree by the context in which they appear, it will rarely, if ever, be possible to recognize those which were not intended by the author. Those of the accidentals in this group which appear in a source about which we have independent reasons to believe that it is close to the composer or editor in question as well as those appearing in more than one source of the given version will, of course, be more authoritative than the rest. The editor will have to evaluate all accidentals in this group. In the unlikely case that he is able to distinguish the accidentals intended by the author from those added in transmission of the text, he will include only the former in the text of the work on the staff, relegating the latter to the critical report documenting the performing history of the work. But in most cases, all accidentals of this type will have to be included in the text on the staff.

A full-scale demonstration of the advantages offered by our classification of source accidentals for both textual and higher criticism is, of course, beyond the scope of the present work. It might be useful, however, to illus-trate some of the advantages on a sample problem. Example 40 shows

Example 40

Ex. 40 (*cont.*)

tif,   Qui m'a per - cié   le   cuer de   part en
tif,   En ve - ri - te   joy - e de   moy de -
tif,   J'au - ray re - fus con - tre moy, main et

part;
part.
tart.

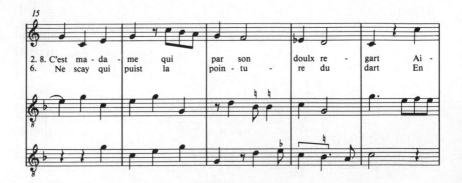

2. 8. C'est ma - da - me qui   par son   doulx re - gart Ai -
6. Ne scay qui puist la poin - tu - re du dart En

178

mab - le me l'a point jus - ques au vif.
moy ga - rir se non le vray mo - tif.

MAIN SOURCE:

O(4) 172, 'Guill(er)mus dufay', white notes.

OTHER SOURCES:

PR III, 197, black notes;
Em 198, 'Duffay', white notes.

MUSIC HITHERTO NOT PUBLISHED.

TEXT:

1. Navré je sui d'un dart penetratif
   Qui m'a percié le cuer de part en part;
2. C'est madame qui par son doulx regart
   Aimable me l'a point jusques au vif.

3. Tout souellement, se confort n'est actif,
   En verite joye de moy depart.
4. Navré je sui d'un dart penetratif
   Qui m'a percié le cuer de part en part.

179

Ex. 40 (*cont.*)

5. Las, que feray, se dangier m'est actif,
   J'auray refus contre moy, main et tart.
6. Ne scay qui puist la pointure du dart
   En moy garir se non le vray motif.

7. Navré je sui d'un dart penetratif
   Qui m'a percié le cuer de part en part;
8. C'est madame qui par son doulx regart
   Aimable me l'a point jusques au vif.

Superius: 1 – text incipit 'Navre je suy', no further text *Em*; 21 – 3 'la' for 'me l'a' *PR*.

Contratenor and *Tenor*: 1 – no text incipit *Em*.

MUSIC:

Superius: 5 – sb g, sb g *Em*; 7 – sb e (b om), mi e, sb f, mi e *Em*; 8 – 2 sb d, sb d *Em*; 9 – 1 not dott sb c, mi c *Em*; 10 – 1 sb c, 2 sb c *Em*; 11 – mi g, mi a, sb c, mi c, mi b *Em*; 12 – 1 b + 2 a no lig *Em*; 13 – imp br e, sb e *Em*; 17 – sb g, sb f, sb f *Em*; 18 – 1 b om *Em*; 21 – 1 a + 2 g no lig *Em*; 25 – 1 b om, 5 sb c *Em*; 26 – sb g, p mi *Em*; 27 – 1 e + 2 d no lig *PR*; 27 – 1 sb e, 2 not dott sb d, mi d, mi c *Em*; 28 – 1 c + 2 b no lig *PR*.

Contratenor ('Contrateneur' *PR*): 3 – 3 'b' *PR*; 3/4 – 3 dott sb e, 1 sb d + 2 not dott sb c lig *PR*, *Em*.

Tenor ('Teneur' *PR*): 4/5/6/7 – no lig *Em*; 5 – imp br g, sb g *Em*; 6 – imp br g, sb g *Em*; 10 – sb c, mi c, sb f, mi d *Em*; 11 – 2 sb c, sb c *Em*; 12 – 1 g + 2 a no lig *Em*; 13 – 1 no sig *Em*; 14 – imp br c, sb c *Em*; 17 – 3 'b' *PR*; 18 – 1 sb c + 2 not dott sb b no lig, mi b, mi a *Em*; 20 – sb a, sb a, sb b *Em*; 22 – 1 e (b om) + 2 d no lig *Em*; 23 – b om *Em*; 25 – 2 '♮' om *PR*; 25 – 1 c + 2 b no lig *Em*; 26 – 1 b om *Em*; 27 – 1 c + 2 g no lig *Em*.

All voices: Six lines *PR*.

NO MENSURATION SIGNS.

Heinrich Besseler's edition of Guillaume Dufay's rondeau *Navré je sui d'un dart penetratif* together with the appropriate section of the critical report, while Figures 5–7 reproduce the three sources of the song in facsimile.[33] A glance at the sources reveals that they differ considerably in 'unconventional' accidentals: *O* and *PR* have one-flat signatures in the tenor and contratenor, signatures lacking in *Em*, and they share 'unconventional' internal e♭s in mm. 18, 22, 25 and 26 as well as aa♭ in m. 23, all of which are lacking in *Em*. All these differences (with the exception of the difference in signatures) are duly noted in the critical report, but, since they are left uninter-

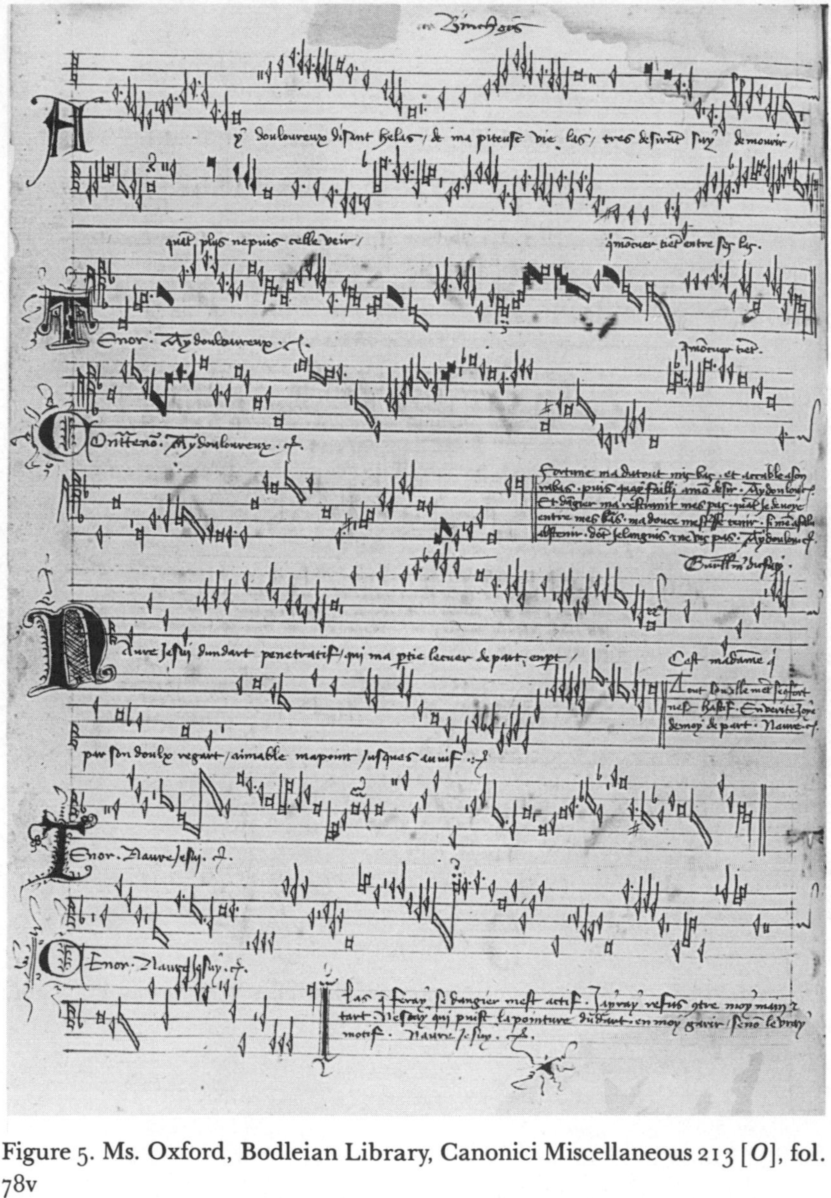

Figure 5. Ms. Oxford, Bodleian Library, Canonici Miscellaneous 213 [*O*], fol. 78v

Figure 6. Ms. Paris, Bibliothèque Nationale, Nouvelles Acquisitions Françaises 6771 [*PR*], fol. 98r

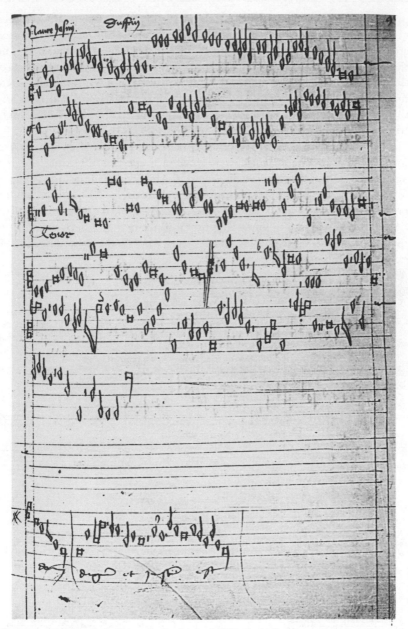

Figure 7. Ms. Munich, Bayerische Staatsbibliothek, Latinus monacensis 14274 (*olim* Mus. 3232a; Cim. 352c) [*Em*], fol. 96r

preted, the knowledge of these differences is of little value to any conceivable user of the edition; a music performer or historian using the edition could not suspect that, so far as accidental inflections are concerned (and they are our sole concern here), the sources transmit two distinct versions of the song, one represented in *O* and *PR*, the other in *Em*. Only our classification of source accidentals into 'conventional' and 'unconventional' ones and the recognition that so many accidentals present in *O* and *PR* but absent from *Em* belong to the latter class allow us to reach this conclusion.

The difference between the two versions is very pronounced. Singers performing from *Em* would not have to make a single flat inflection; the only accidental inflections required by *Em* are the implied leading-tone f♯ and c♯ in m. 4 in the superius and contratenor, respectively. By contrast, singers performing from either *O* or *PR* would, of course, have to execute, in addition to these two leading tones, a number of accidental inflections, most of them written out, some implied. If they sang from *O*, they would most likely execute the inflections indicated in Example 41.[34]

Example 41

part;
part.
tart.

2. 8. C'est ma - da - me qui par son doulx re - gart Ai -
6. Ne scay qui puist la poin - tu - re du dart En

mab - le me l'a point jus - ques au vif.
moy ga - rir se non le vray mo - tif.

Ex. 41 (*cont.*)

With two exceptions, they would make the same inflections if they sang from *PR*. The exceptions are that the contratenor would flatten the e in m. 3 (since the flat is written out in his part) and the tenor would not sharpen the b in m. 25 (since his part lacks the mi-sign there). While we cannot be absolutely sure of this, it is likely that the two accidentals in question should be regarded as being 'unconventional' and that, consequently, the differences between *O* and *PR* would not disappear in performance. If the flat in m. 3 were 'conventional', the convention in question would have to prescribe that upward skips of the major sixth should be made minor. We cannot exclude the possibility that such a convention existed in Dufay's time and the matter should be investigated with the help of manuscript accidentals. The same spot in *Em* seems to offer an intriguing clue in support of the convention's existence: the e is preceded by a flat placed at f, that is, by a cautionary sign of fa ensuring that e will remain mi, will not be flattened. But until the matter of the putative convention has been investigated, we have to assume what is more likely, namely, that the eb in *PR* is 'unconventional'. Similarly, it is possible to see the sign of mi at b in m. 25 as sharpening the cadential leading tone, but in view of its metric placement and its position within the phrase, it is unlikely that any singer would treat this b as a leading tone, if there was no accidental there.

We are confronted, then, with a piece transmitted in two distinct versions, one of which presents two minor variants which, most likely, would not disappear in performance. But the duties of a textual critic do not end with his having sorted out the distinct versions of the edited work. He must also evaluate the versions with respect to authenticity. It is not difficult to evaluate the relative merits and authority of the two versions. *O* was copied *ca.* 1420-36, probably in Venice or its vicinity.[35] Layer III of *PR*, which contains the chanson, was copied *ca.* 1430-40 by a French scribe, probably in

Padua or Venice.[36] The second layer of *Em*, which includes our song, was copied at the turn of the 1430s and in the early 1440s by Hermann Pötzlinger, a priest and bibliophile educated at the University of Vienna between 1436 and 1439.[37] These facts alone suffice to suggest that the *O–PR* version of *Navré je sui* probably represents the composer's intentions, while the musical text transmitted in *Em* is most likely inauthentic. (It should go without saying that it is none the less valuable, since it tells us something about the reception of the work, and its existence should be clearly noted in the report of a critical edition.)

The two variants within the authentic version present us with a more difficult choice. The knowledge of the dates and places of origin of the sources is of no help here, since one could make equally good claims on behalf of both manuscripts for being chronologically and geographically close to the known circumstances of the composer's biography. But a convincing choice can be made, I believe, if we interrupt for a moment the process of searching for the most authentic musical text of Dufay's chanson and attempt an interpretation of the piece. Armed with the results achieved by higher criticism, we will be able to descend back to the level of textual criticism and make the choice between the available variants. The process is going to be circular, of course, but this should not deter us, since the circle is of the benign, hermeneutic kind, not a vicious one. The process simply reflects the well-known hermeneutic fact that we often must already partially understand a text before we can fully have it, since, in the process of interpretation, detail and totality are related in a circular fashion; to understand the whole, one has to understand the parts, but to understand the parts, one must have some idea of the meaning of the whole.

Let us consider the *O–PR* version of the rondeau for a moment without the two troublesome accidentals. The music of the refrain divides, like its text, into two halves of fourteen and fifteen measures, respectively, each consisting of two texted phrases and an untexted melisma. The correspondence of the two halves is audibly underscored by their similar beginnings. They both begin with a motif constructed of the notes of the triad above the final of the mode, c-e-g, and they both present this motif in three-part imitation. These two features (triadic motif and three-part imitation) are bound to attract attention, since they are still relatively uncommon at the time. But the two halves of the music not only correspond, but also oppose one another: the initial motif of the second half (g-c-e-g) inverts the direction of intervals of the initial motif of the first half (c-g-e-c). Once we become aware of this opposition, we notice that the two halves differ also in the versions of the third step above the final they employ: the first half uses e-mi (and ee-mi) throughout, while the second starts with e-mi, then mixes e-mi with e-fa in mm. 17–26, and finally returns to using e-mi (and ee-mi) only in the last measures. It is likely, then, that the structural function of e-fa in the rondeau is to emphasize the contrast between the two halves of the refrain.[38]

It is, further, likely that the contrast is rhetorically motivated, that is, that e-fa has not only a structural, but also a rhetorical role in the song.[39] In the first half of the refrain, the lyrical subject describes the sorry state in which an essential component of his anatomy finds itself: 'I am rent by a penetrating dart which has pierced my heart through and through.' Such mishaps are most likely to occur during a battle and Dufay's musical–rhetorical topic is the appropriately martial triadic trumpet fanfare of the opening motif. But in the second half of the refrain the motif is inverted as we are transferred from the battle field or jousting court to the court of love and learn who the knight responsible for the subject's wounded heart is: 'It is my lady who, with her soft, kind glance, has stabbed it to the quick.' The 'dart penetratif' of the first half has now been identified as the lady's 'doulx regart', and it is this 'soft' weapon that Dufay accompanies with the first 'soft' e (e flattened by the sign of the 'soft b' [*b molle*]) of the song. (Incidentally, in view of the rhetorically motivated e-mi/e-fa contrast between the two halves of the music, it is certainly significant that the *Em* version, which does not preserve this contrast, is textless.)

Once this interpretation is accepted, it follows that the e♭ in the contratenor in m. 3 demanded by *PR* cannot correspond to Dufay's wishes. On the contrary, the 'hard' version of e (e-mi which could be marked by the sign of the 'hard b' [♮ *durum*]) is an appropriate accompaniment of the 'penetratif' weapon at this point, before we have learned that the weapon is in fact 'doulx'. (Similarly, ee-mi in the superius in m. 7 is proper for 'percié' ['pierced'] in the first half of the refrain and e-fa in the tenor in m. 22 is proper for the corresponding 'point' ['stabbed'] in the second half.) Consequently, we have to conclude that *O* transmits a reading of the rondeau closest to Dufay's intentions and that the *PR* variants are inauthentic and should be relegated to the critical report.

In short, what the example illustrates, I hope, is that the classification of source accidentals proposed in this chapter has a potential for becoming a useful tool of both textual critics concerned with editing early vocal polyphony and critical historians interested in structural and expressive functions of what I have called here, in distinction to conventionally used *musica ficta*, 'genuine chromaticism'.

Notes

1 Within the hand

1 'Dabit . . . operam ut . . . Musicalem manum sive scalam perdiscat . . . et mox claves istas cognoscat, postea sensim incipiat solmisando ad Choralem seu Gregorianum cantum se exercere, et voces Musicas suo ordine, et phtongis pronunciare. Quibus octo tonorum cognitionem subjungat . . . Deinde cognoscet signa, quantitatem, et valores eorum, mox notarum figuras, ligaturas, punctos, pausas postea prolationes: maiorem, et minorem, Augmentationem, diminutionem, imperfectionem, alterationem, syncopationem, una cum tactibus, et proportionibus quibusdam usitatis . . . Incipiat tandem non solum recte, sed etiam ornate canere, et artificiose, suaviter, et colorate pronunciare, recte intonare, et quamlibet syllabam suo in loco, suis sub notis collocare . . . Ubi quis illa quae supra commemoravi, probe addidicit, poterit is contrapunctum, et compositionem quoque addiscere.' *Compendium musices* (Nuremberg: Ioannes Montanus and Ulricus Neuber, 1552), sigs. Bijr-Biijr, trans. Albert Seay, Colorado College Music Press Translations 5 (Colorado Springs: The Colorado College Music Press, 1973), pp. 6f.
2 Tinctoris, *Opera theoretica*, ed. A. Seay, Corpus Scriptorum de Musica 22, vol. I (n.p.: American Institute of Musicology, 1975), pp. 31-57. For a chronology of Tinctoris's treatises, see Rudolf Schäfke, *Geschichte der Musikästhetik in Umrissen*, 2nd edn (Tutzing: Hans Schneider, 1964), pp. 236ff., n. 1.
3 *Terminorum musicae diffinitorium* ([Treviso: Gerardo de Lisa, *ca.* 1473]).
4 'And this teaching hand is called by another name, "gamut", from that letter Γ which is called gamma by the Greeks, not without cause, for a naming is made from a most appropriate element; but that which comes first is seen to be more appropriate. Therefore, since gamma, that is, G, comes first in the hand, from this it is correctly named gamut.' ('Atquae manus haec doctrinalis alio nomine Gamma dicitur ab ista littera Γ quae apud Graecos gamma vocatur, nec sine causa namque a digniori fit denominatio, sed quod praecedit dignius esse videtur. Ergo quom in manu gamma, id est G, praecedat, ab eo manus gamma recte nominatur.') Tinctoris, *Expositio manus*, p. 32, trans. Albert Seay, 'The Expositio manus of Johannes Tinctoris', *Journal of Music Theory*, IX (1965), 201.
5 'A place is the site of the steps.' ('Locus est vocum situs.') Tinctoris, *Expositio manus*, p. 32.
6 'A letter is the sign of the place of the line or space.' ('Clavis est signum loci lineae vel spatii.') *Ibid.*, p. 37. For an excellent discussion of the term, see Fritz Reckow, 'Clavis' in H. H. Eggebrecht, ed., *Handwörterbuch der musikalischen Terminologie* (Wiesbaden: Fritz Steiner, 1971).
7 Unlike most theorists, Tinctoris additionally distinguishes the 'lowest' (*gravissima*) letter from the low ones and uses capital letters for both the low and the high letters, lower-case letters for the highest ones.

189

8 The way Tinctoris introduces the syllables shows clearly that their function was to define intervals: 'There are, moreover, six universal syllables, namely, ut, re, mi, fa, sol, la, which we may define one by one as follows: Ut is the first syllable, distant from the second by a whole tone', etc. ('Sex autem sunt voces universales, scilicet ut, re, mi, fa, sol, la, quasquidem per ordinem sic diffinire possumus. Ut est prima vox tono distans a secunda.') Tinctoris, *Expositio manus*, p. 41.

9 'A mutation is the change of one syllable into another.' ('Mutatio est unius vocis in aliam variatio.') *Ibid.*, p. 48, trans. Seay, 'The Expositio manus of Johannes Tinctoris', p. 218. And, furthermore, 'a mutation has necessarily to be made through two syllables coming together in a unison' ('mutatio habet fieri necessario per duas voces unisono convenientes'). *Ibid.*, p. 52, trans. Seay, 'The Expositio manus of Johannes Tinctoris', p. 223. A change made through two syllables present in a single place but differing in pitch was called by Marchetto da Padova (and some later Italian theorists familiar with him) a 'permutation' (*permutatio*): 'Permutation is a change in the name of a solmization syllable or note when the pitch changes although the note lies in the same position on the staff' ('Permutatio est variatio nominis vocis seu notae in eodem spatio seu linea in diverso sono'). Marchetto da Padova, *Lucidarium in arte musicae planae* in J. W. Herlinger, *The Lucidarium of Marchetto of Padua. A Critical Edition, Translation and Commentary*, Ph.D. diss., The University of Chicago, 1978, p. 430. See also, for example, Franchinus Gaffurius, *Practica musice* (Milan: Ioannes Petrus de Lomatio, 1496), Bk I, Ch. 4; Pietro Aaron, *Libri tres de institutione harmonica* (Bologna: Benedetto di Ettore, 1516), fol. 10v; the letter of Giovanni del Lago to Giovanni da Legge, Venice, May 13, 1523 in Ms. Vatican, lat. 5318, fol. 62v; Giovanni Maria Lanfranco, *Scintille di musica* (Brescia: Lodovico Britannico, 1533), p. 12. For an unsympathetic view of the term from across the Alps, see Heinrich Glarean, *Isagoge in musicen* (Basle: Joannes Frobenius, 1516), Ch. 3.

10 For representative examples from the beginning and end of our period, see Jacques de Liège, *Speculum musicae*, ed. R. Bragard, Corpus Scriptorum de Musica 3, vol. VI (n.p.: American Institute of Musicology, 1973), p. 138 and Heinrich Glarean, *Dodecachordon* (Basle: Heinrich Petri, 1547), p. 13.

11 See, for example, Andreas Ornithoparchus, *Musice active micrologus* (Leipzig: Valentin Schumann, 1517), sig. Br and Hermann Finck, *Practica musica* (Wittenberg: Haeredes Georgii Rhau, 1556), Bk I, Ch. 1. Reckow, 'Clavis', pp. 3–8, demonstrated that throughout our period the term *clavis* was used for a key of a keyboard as well as for a step, a letter or a combination of a letter and syllable(s) designating a step, a clef, or an accidental. From the mid-fifteenth century on, theorists started to differentiate between *claves signatae* or *signandae* (letters actually used in notational practice, that is, clefs and accidentals) and *claves non signatae* or *non signandae* (other letters), distinguishing additionally accidentals as *claves minus signandae, minus praecipue*, or *minus principales*.

12 Guido of Arezzo, *Prologus in antiphonarium*, ed. J. Smits van Waesberghe, Divitiae Musicae Artis A.III (Buren: Frits Knuf, 1975). I follow the chronology of Guido's treatises presented by Claude V. Palisca in *Hucbald, Guido and John on Music*, ed. Palisca (New Haven: Yale University Press, 1978), pp. 50f. For a study of Guido's notation, see Joseph Smits van Waesberghe, 'The Musical Notation of Guido of Arezzo', *Musica Disciplina*, V (1951), 15–53.

13 H. Schmid, ed., *Musica et Scolica enchiriadis*, Veröffentlichungen der Musikhistorischen Kommission 3 (Munich: Verlag der Bayerischen Akademie der Wissenschaften, 1981). See also Nancy Phillips' review of the edition in *Journal*

of the American Musicological Society, XXXVI (1983), 128-42. The much-discussed question of the provenance, date and authorship of this treatise has been recently summarized in Lawrence Gushee, 'Musica enchiriadis' in S. Sadie, ed., *The New Grove Dictionary of Music and Musicians,* vol. XII (London: Macmillan, 1980), pp. 800ff. There can be little doubt that Guido was familiar with the treatise. See Michel Huglo, 'L'auteur du "Dialogue sur la musique" attribué à Odon', *Revue de musicologie,* LV (1969), 119-71.

14 On the author and date of the *Dialogus,* see Huglo, 'L'auteur du "Dialogue sur la musique"'. The text of the treatise is in M. Gerbert, ed., *Scriptores ecclesiastici de musica sacra potissimum,* vol. I (St Blasien: Typis San Blasianis, 1784), pp. 251-64; partial translation in Oliver Strunk, *Source Readings in Music History* (New York: Norton, 1950), pp. 103-16. Guido's relation to Pseudo-Odo is discussed in Hans Oesch, *Guido von Arezzo. Biographisches und Theoretisches unter besonderer Berücksichtigung der sogenannten odonischen Traktate,* Publikationen der Schweizerischen Musikforschenden Gesellschaft II/4 (Berne: Paul Haupt, 1954), pp. 71-100 and in Lawrence A. Gushee, 'Questions of Genre in Medieval Treatises on Music' in W. Arlt, E. Lichtenhahn and H. Oesch, eds., *Gattungen der Musik in Einzeldarstellungen. Gedenkschrift Leo Schrade,* vol. I (Berne and Munich: Francke Verlag, 1973), pp. 404-10.

15 'The Hand and the Art of Memory', *Musica Disciplina,* XXXV (1981), 87-120.

16 It is present in the writings of Elias Salomon (*Scientia artis musicae* in Gerbert, *Scriptores,* vol. III, pp. 16-64; written in 1274), Jerome of Moravia (*Tractatus de musica,* ed. S. M. Cserba, Freiburger Studien zur Musikwissenschaft 2 [Regensburg: Friedrich Pustet, 1935], pp. 46-55; written between 1272 and 1304) and Engelbert of Admont (*De musica* in Gerbert, *Scriptores,* vol. II, pp. 287-369; written between 1276 and 1325).

17 Guido of Arezzo, *Micrologus,* ed. J. Smits van Waesberghe, Corpus Scriptorum de Musica 4 (n.p.: American Institute of Musicology, 1955), pp. 117-21.

18 *Ibid.,* pp. 124f.

19 Pseudo-Odo affirms the heptatonic and diatonic structure of the gamut when he explains that the reason 'why the same letters are used both in the first and in the second part' (that is, octave) is that 'both parts so agree with each other that whatever letters form a tone, semitone, diatessaron, diapente, or diapason in the first part will likewise be found to do so in the second part' ('cur eaedem litterae in prima et secunda parte fiant . . . adeo inter se utraque pars concordat, ut quaecumque litterae in prima parte tonum vel semitonium, vel diatessaron vel diapente vel diapason faciunt, similiter et in secunda parte facere comprobentur'; Pseudo-Odo, *Dialogus* in Gerbert, *Scriptores,* Vol. I, pp. 254f, trans. Strunk, *Source Readings,* p. 108) and that the round b and the square b are two different forms of a single letter since they represent two different versions of a single step and, moreover, 'both are not regularly found in the same melody' ('utraque in eodem cantu regulariter non invenietur'; Pseudo-Odo, *Dialogus,* p. 253, trans. Strunk, *Source Readings,* p. 106), that is, they are not only different but also alternative versions.

20 'Hermann's Major Sixth', *Journal of the American Musicological Society,* XXV (1972), 19-37. For an earlier attempt, see Walter Wiora, 'Zum Problem des Ursprungs der mittelalterlichen Solmisation', *Die Musikforschung,* IX (1956), 262-74.

21 'Hermann's Major Sixth', p. 36.

22 'A property is a certain individual quality of the deduced syllables. There are, moreover, three properties, namely, [those of] the hard b, nature, and soft b.

The hard b is the first property, through which ut is sung in every place whose letter is *G*, and from it are deduced successively the other five syllables. It is called hard b because through it mi is sung in the place whose letter is the square b, which mi is hard, that is, harsh, in respect to the fa sung occasionally in the same place through the soft b. The nature is the second property, through which ut is sung in every place whose letter is *C*, and from it are deduced successively the other five syllables. It has been called nature because all the steps of this property remain regularly fixed and stable after the fashion of natural things . . . The soft b is the third property, through which ut is sung in every place whose letter is *F*, and from it are deduced successively the other five syllables. It is called soft b since through it fa is sung in the place whose letter is the round b, which fa is soft, that is, sweet, in respect to the mi sung occasionally in the same place through the hard b . . . A deduction is the ordered succession of the syllables from one place to another through one of the properties. And since there are three properties, as we have stated previously, namely, the hard b whose fundamental letter is *G*, the nature whose fundamental letter is *C*, and the soft b whose fundamental letter is *F*, and in our hand there are three *G*'s, namely, Γ . . . G and g, two *C*'s on which ut is found, namely, C and c, and two *F*'s, namely, F and f, if three and twice two make seven, it must be that in this hand of ours there are seven deductions, namely, three of the hard b, two of nature, and two of the soft b.' ('Proprietas est vocum deducendarum quaedam singularis qualitas. Tres autem sunt proprietates, scilicet ♮ durum, natura et b molle. ♮ durum est prima proprietas per quam in omni loco cuius clavis est G ut canitur, et ex eo aliae quinque voces per ordinem deducuntur. Et dicitur ♮ durum quoniam mi per eam in loco cuius clavis est ♮ quadrum canitur, quod-quidem mi durum, id est asperum, est respectu fa in ipso interdum loco per b molle canendi. Natura est secunda proprietas per quam in omni loco cuius clavis est C ut canitur, et ex eo aliae quinque voces per ordinem deducuntur. Dictaque natura est eo quod omnes ipsius proprietatis voces regulariter fixae manent et stabiles instar naturalium . . . b molle est tertia proprietas per quam in omni loco cuius clavis est F ut canitur, et ex eo aliae quinque voces per ordi-nem deducuntur. Et dicitur b molle quia per eam fa in loco cuius clavis est b rotundum canitur, quodquidem fa molle, id est dulce, est respectu mi in ipso interdum loco per ♮ durum canendi . . . Deductio est vocum de uno loco ad alium per aliquam proprietatum ordinata ductio. Et quom tres, ut praemisi-mus, sint proprietates, scilicet ♮ durum, cuius clavis fundamentalis est G, natura cuius clavis fundamentalis est C, et b molle, cuius clavis fundamentalis est F; et in manu nostra tria sint G, videlicet Γ . . . G de G sol re ut gravi, et G de G sol re ut acuto; duo C in quibus habetur ut, scilicet C de C fa ut et C de C sol fa ut; et duo F, videlicet F de F fa ut gravi, et F de F fa ut acuto. Si tria et bis duo septem efficiant ut in ipsa manu nostra sint septem deductiones necesse est, scilicet tres ♮ durales, duae naturales et due b mollares.') Tinctoris, *Expositio manus*, pp. 44f.

23 'Similitudo nisi in diapason perfecta non est.' *Micrologus*, p. 132, trans. Warren Babb in *Hucbald, Guido and John on Music*, p. 65.
24 In Gerbert, *Scriptores*, vol. II, pp. 43–50.
25 See Carl-Allan Moberg, 'Die Musik in Guido von Arezzos Solmisationshymne', *Archiv für Musikwissenschaft*, XVI (1959), 187–206.
26 See Joseph Smits van Waesberghe, *Musikerziehung. Lehre und Theorie der Musik im Mittelalter*, Musikgeschichte in Bildern III/3 (Leipzig: VEB Deutscher Verlag für Musik, 1969), pp. 116f.

27 'Solmization is the pronouncing of the syllables by their names in. singing.'
('Solfisatio est canendo vocum per sua nomina expressio.') Tinctoris, *Expositio
manus*, p. 52. For other forms of the term used during the Middle Ages and the
Renaissance, see Georg Lange, 'Zur Geschichte der Solmisation', *Sammelbände
der Internationalen Musikgesellschaft*, I (1899–1900), pp. 541f.

28 The distinction is discussed (whether under these or still other terms), for
instance, in Adam von Fulda, *Musica* in Gerbert, *Scriptores*, vol. III, p. 346;
Nicolaus Wollick, *Opus aureum*, ed. K. W. Niemöller, Beiträge zur Rheinischen
Musikgeschichte 11 (Cologne and Krefeld: Staufen-Verlag, 1955), pp. 37f;
Johannes Cochlaeus, *Tetrachordum musices* (Nuremberg: Johannes Weyssen-
burger, 1511), Bk II, Ch. 9; Stefan Monetarius, *Epithoma utriusque musices
practice* (Cracow: Florian Ungler, 1515), Ch. 8; Georg Rhau, *Enchiridion
utriusque musicae practicae* (Wittenberg: Rhau, 1538), sigs. Ciir-Cvr; the letter
of Giovanni Spataro to Giovanni del Lago, Bologna, November 24, 1529 in
Ms. Vatican, lat. 5318, fol. 149v; the letter of Spataro to Pietro Aaron, Bologna,
October 30, 1533, *ibid.*, fol. 126v; Lanfranco, *Scintille di musica*, p. 17;
Stephano Vanneo, *Recanetum de musica aurea* (Rome: Valerius Doricus, 1533),
fols. 16v-17r; Finck *Practica musica*, Bk I, Ch. 8.

29 See, for example, Bartolomeo Ramos de Pareia, *Musica practica*, ed. Johannes
Wolf, Publikationen der Internationalen Musikgesellschaft 2 (Leipzig: Breit-
kopf und Härtel, 1901), pp. 37f and Nicolaus Wollick, *Enchiridion musices*
(Paris: Francoys Regnault, 1512), sig. ciiir.

30 'Tribus insuper modis voces quas notulae declarant pronuntiari solent. Primo
modo solfizando idest syllabas ac nomina vocum exprimendo . . . Quem quidem pronuntiationis modum tanquam legem initiandis pueris praeponendam
tradunt. Secundo modo: sonos ac voces tantum emittendo omnissis penitus
litteris ac syllabis et dictionibus: quod exercitatus cantor facile prosequitur . . .
Tertio modo: quascumque dictiones ut antiphonas et responsoria: et ipsarum
verba cantilenarum notulis ipsis subscripta pronunciando: Ad quem tanquam
ad finem ellecti modulaminis clerici deducuntur.' *Practica musice*, Bk I, Ch. 3,
trans. Clement A. Miller, Musicological Studies and Documents 20 (n.p.:
American Institute of Musicology, 1968), pp. 30f. See also Cochlaeus, *Tetrachordum musicès*, Bk II, Ch. 6; Lanfranco, *Scintille di musica*, p. 16; Vanneo,
Recanetum de musica aurea, fols. 12r-12v.

31 See *Micrologus*, p. 117 and *Epistola*, p. 46.

32 See Ramos de Pareia, *Musica practica*, pp. 11, 19–22, 27, 44–7; Johannes Octobi,
Excitatio quaedam musicae artis per refutationem in *Tres tractatuli contra
Bartholomeum Ramum*, ed. A. Seay, Corpus Scriptorum de Musica 10 (n.p.:
American Institute of Musicology, 1964), pp. 45f; *idem, Epistola, ibid.*, p. 83;
Nicolaus Burtius, *Florum libellus*, ed. G. Massera, Historiae Musicae Cultores
28 (Florence: Leo S. Olschki, 1975), pp. 53–6, 80. For this and subsequent
attempts to extend the hexachord to an octave, see Lange, 'Zur Geschichte der
Solmisation', pp. 573–90.

33 'Indice manus dextrae loca in ipsa manu sinistra aptius indicantur, licet nonnulli loca pollicis sinistrae manus indice eiusdem et loca caeterorum digitorum
pollice similiter eiusdem aptissime indicent. Quo fit ut unica manu, scilicet
sinistra, in traditione huiusmodi doctrinae utantur.' *Expositio manus*, p. 32,
trans. Seay, 'The Expositio manus of Johannes Tinctoris', pp. 200f. Similar
explanations may be found, for example, in Prosdocimus de Beldemandis,
Tractatus plane musice, Ms. Lucca, Biblioteca Governativa, 359, fol. 58r and
Domingo Marcos Durán, *Comento sobre Lux bella* (Salamanca: [Juan de
Porras], 1498), p. 64.

2 Beyond the hand

1 'Quando facimus de semitonio tonum, vel e converso.' *Ars nova*, ed. G. Reaney, A. Gilles and J. Maillard, Corpus Scriptorum de Musica 8 (n.p.: American Institute of Musicology, 1964), p. 22. The treatise has been convincingly dated by Ulrich Michels in Jehan de Murs, *Notitia artis musice*, ed. Michels, Corpus Scriptorum de Musica 17 (n.p.: American Institute of Musicology, 1972), pp. 9f.

2 'Falsa musica est quae non potest inveniri in Gamma manus.' *Compendium de discantu mensurabili* in Johannes Wolf, 'Ein Beitrag zur Diskantlehre des 14. Jahrhunderts', *Sammelbände der Internationalen Musikgesellschaft*, XV (1913–14), 513.

3 *Parvus tractatulus de modo dividendi monacordum*, Ms. Lucca, Biblioteca Governativa, 359, fols. 72r–78r; a 1413 version of this treatise is in E. de Coussemaker, ed., *Scriptorum de musica medii aevi nova series a gerbertina altera*, vol. III (Paris: A. Durand, 1869), pp. 248–58.

4 'La Musica plana & mensurale se divide in vera, la qual domandar si puo reale, e fitta . . . La Musica fitta, non e altro che la transpositione delle note, dalla propria sede.' *Fior angelico di musica* (Venice: Agostino Bindoni, 1547), Bk I, Ch. 11. Here, and in much else, Angelo echoes Stephano Vanneo, *Recanetum de musica aurea* (Rome: Valerius Doricus, 1533), fol. 7r.

5 'Ficta musica est vocum fictio sive vocum positio in aliquo loco manus musicalis ubi nullo modo reperiuntur, sicut ponere mi ubi non est mi, et fa ubi non est fa, et sic de aliis vocibus.' *Contrapunctus*, ed. and trans. J. Herlinger, Greek and Latin Music Theory 1 (Lincoln and London: University of Nebraska Press, 1984), pp. 70f. A similar definition may be found in Prosdocimus, *Parvus tractatulus*, Ms. Lucca, Biblioteca Governativa, 359, fol. 73v, or E. de Coussemaker, ed., *Scriptorum*, vol. III, p. 251.

6 'Musica ficta est alicuius vocis in loco ubi per se non est . . . positio.' *Declaratio musicae disciplinae*, ed. A. Seay, Corpus Scriptorum de Musica 7, vol. II (n.p.: American Institute of Musicology, 1960), p. 45.

7 '. . . voces, debitos suos locos non sortiuntur, veluti cum Ut in E, Re in F, Mi in G &c. aut secus, canitur'. *Musica* (Nuremberg: Iohan. Petreius, 1549), sig. b4v, trans. Albert Seay, Translations 6 (Colorado Springs: The Colorado College Music Press, 1975), p. 14. For other examples of this understanding of *musica ficta*, see Nicolaus Burtius, *Florum libellus*, ed. G. Massera, Historiae Musicae Cultores 28 (Florence: Leo S. Olschki, 1975), p. 123; Adam von Fulda, *Musica* in M. Gerbert, ed., *Scriptores ecclesiastici de musica sacra potissimum*, vol. III (St Blasien: Typis San Blasianis, 1784), p. 333; Stefan Monetarius, *Epithoma utriusque musices practice* (Cracow: Florian Ungler, 1515), Ch. 12; Heinrich Faber, *Ad musicam practicam introductio, non modo praecepta, sed exempla quoque ad usum puerorum accommodata, quàm brevissime continens* (Nuremberg: Ioannes Montanus and Ulricus Neuber, 1550), Ch. 3; Gregor Faber, *Musices practicae erotematum libri II* (Basle: Heinrich Petri, 1553), pp. 63f; Hermann Finck, *Practica musica* (Wittenberg: Haeredes Georgii Rhau, 1556), Bk I, Chs. 3 and 8.

8 'Vocatur autem irregularis mutatio "falsa mutatio" propterea quia vox mutatur in vocem quae sibi non vere, sed false coniungitur; vocatur etiam falsa musica, quia vadit contra regularem vocum in gammate dispositionem. Ex his patet quod descendens a *mi* de b *fa* ♮ *mi* per tonum et semitonium, falsam committit musicam quia oportet tunc ut, cum *mi* in unisono iungatur, *sol* mutetur . . . dicendo *mi sol fa mi*.' *Speculum musicae*, ed. R. Bragard, Corpus Scriptorum de Musica 3, vol. VI (n.p.: American Institute of Musicology, 1973), p. 185.

9 *Ars nova*, ed. G. Reaney, A. Gilles and J. Maillard, p. 17.

10 *Musica practica*, ed. Johannes Wolf, Publikationen der Internationalen Musik-gesellschaft 2 (Leipzig: Breitkopf und Härtel, 1901), p. 12.

11 *Musica* in M. Gerbert, ed., *Scriptores*, vol. III, p. 350.

12 *Enchiridion utriusque musicae practicae* (Wittenberg: Georg Rhau, 1538), Ch. 1.

13 *Fior angelico di musica*, Bk I, Ch. 22.

14 *Lux bella*, 2nd edn (Salamanca: [Juan de Porras?], 1509); *Comento sobre Lux bella* (Salamanca: [Juan de Porras], 1498), sig. ev.

15 *Comento sobre Lux bella*, sig. ev.

16 *Recanetum de musica aurea*, fols. 10r-11v.

17 *Fior angelico di musica*, Bk I, Chs. 17-18.

18 'Quandocumque aliqua vox assumitur in scala vel extra. si huiusmodi in eius octava correspondentiam habuerit est vox vera. si vero non iam dicetur ficta.' *Enchiridion musices* (Paris: Francoys Regnault, 1512), sig. biiir.

19 'At si vox huiusmodi, habuerit in octava correspondentiam. est vox vera: ut si la canatur in Dsolre: sol in Cfaut: & fa in ♮mi. quia in earum octavis expresse reperiuntur huiusmodi voces, non igitur sunt fictae Quandoquidem octavae eiusdem sunt naturae, atque de eis idem est iudicium.' *Tetrachordum musices* (Nuremberg: Fridericus Peypus, 1514), sigs. Cr-Cv, trans. Clement A. Miller, Musicological Studies and Documents 23 (n.p.: American Institute of Musicology, 1970), p. 46. The translation has been slightly changed.

20 *Recanetum de musica aurea*, fols. 11r-11v.

21 'Ultimam coeli metam, pro meo iudicio in E la terminari credentes.' *Ibid.*, fol. 11v. The function of the sign of the round b before ff was first elucidated on the basis of Vanneo's statement in Edward E. Lowinsky, 'The Function of Conflicting Signatures in Early Polyphonic Music', *The Musical Quarterly*, XXXI (1945), 254ff.

22 *Fior angelico di musica*, Bk I, Ch. 18.

23 In addition to the theorists already quoted, see, for example, Monetarius, *Epithoma utriusque musices practice*, Ch. 12; Heinrich Glarean, *Isagoge in musicen* (Basle: Joannes Frobenius, 1516), sig. B2v; *idem*, *Dodecachordon* (Basle: Heinrich Petri, 1547), p. 5; Rhau, *Enchiridion utriusque musicae practicae*, Chs. 3, 4 and 7; Heinrich Faber, *Ad musicam practicam introductio*, Ch. 3; Gregor Faber, *Musices practicae erotematum*, p. 64; Finck, *Practica musica*, Bk I, Ch. 3.

24 'Re fictum in Gamma ut'. *Liber de arte contrapuncti* in *Opera theoretica*, ed. A. Seay, Corpus Scriptorum de Musica 22, vol. II (n.p.: American Institute of Musicology, 1975), p. 98; 'se' is a misprint.

25 Ms. Florence, Biblioteca Riccardiana, 734, fols. 4v-5r. For the date of the treatise, see Suzanne Clercx-Lejeune, 'Ciconia' in S. Sadie, ed., *The New Grove Dictionary of Music and Musicians*, vol. IV (London: Macmillan, 1980), p. 391.

26 'Ficta musica est cantus praeter regularem manus traditionem aeditus.' *Terminorum musicae diffinitorium* ([Treviso: Gerardo de Lisa, 1475]).

27 'Est autem musica ficta . . . cantus preter regularem schalarum exigentiam editus.' *Musice active micrologus* (Leipzig: Valentin Schumann, 1517), Bk I, Ch. 10 trans. as *Micrologus* (London: Thomas Adams, 1609), p. 24.

28 'Non tamen est falsa musica sed inusitata.' *Ars nova*, ed. G. Reaney, A. Gilles and J. Maillard, p. 22.

29 *Regule contrapuncti* in Nigel Wilkins, 'Some Notes on Philipoctus de Caserta (*c.* 1360?-*c.* 1435)', *Nottingham Mediaeval Studies*, VIII (1964), 98.

30 'Ideo salva reverentia aliorum dicimus quod magis deberet et proprius nominari musica colorata quam falsa, per quod falsitatis nomen attribuimus eidem.' *Pomerium*, ed. G. Vecchi, Corpus Scriptorum de Musica 6 (n.p.: American Institute of Musicology, 1961), p. 70.

31 See, for example, Guillaume Guerson, *Utilissime musicales regule necessitate plani cantus simplicis contrapuncti: rerum factarum tonorum usualium: nec non artis accentuandi tam speculative quam practice: accriori lima mundate* (Paris: François Regnault, 1526), Bk II, Pt I; Vanneo, *Recanetum de musica aurea*, fol. 43r.

32 See my 'The Hand and the Art of Memory', *Musica Disciplina*, XXXV (1981), 87–120.

33 F. Alberto Gallo, 'Beziehungen zwischen grammatischer, rhetorischer und musikalischer Terminologie im Mittelalter', D. Heartz and B. Wade, eds., *International Musicological Society. Report of the Twelfth Congress Berkeley 1977* (Kassel: Bärenreiter, 1981), p. 789.

34 'Falsa musica dicitur esse quando locatur b molle vel ♮ quadrum in loco non usitato. Sunt enim duo signa falsae musicae, scilicet, b molle, et ♮ quadratum. Ubi ponitur b rotundum dicitur fa; ubi vero ♮ quadrum dicitur mi.' Anonymus II, *Tractatus de discantu*, ed. and trans. Albert Seay, Critical Texts with Translations 1 (Colorado Springs: The Colorado College Music Press, 1978), pp. 32f.

35 See, for example, Philippe de Vitry, *Ars nova*, ed. G. Reaney, A. Gilles, and J. Maillard, p. 22; Ugolino of Orvieto, *Declaratio musicae disciplinae*, ed. A. Seay, vol. II, pp. 46 and 50f; Nicolaus Burtius, *Florum libellus*, ed. G. Massera, p. 123; Franchinus Gaffurius, *Extractus parvus musice*, ed. F. A. Gallo, Antiquae Musicae Italicae Scriptores 4 (Bologna: Forni, 1969), p. 128; Guillaume Guerson, *Utilissime musicales regule*, Bk II, Pt I.

36 *Declaratio musicae disciplinae*, vol. II, p. 45, ex. 121.

37 *Lucidarium in arte musicae planae* in Jan W. Herlinger, *The Lucidarium of Marchetto of Padua. A Critical Edition, Translation and Commentary*, Ph.D. diss., The University of Chicago, 1978, pp. 430–40.

38 *Ars nova*, ed. G. Reaney, A. Gilles and J. Maillard, pp. 22f.

39 'Preterea notandum est in generali, quod falsa musica dicitur proprie, quando locabitur b molle vel ♮ quadratum in locis non usitatis. Et ubi ponitur b, in eodem loco et sub eadem voce deprimitur semitonium ultra cantum consuetum. Et ubi ponitur ♮, in eodem loco et sub eadem voce sustinetur semitonium ultra cantum consuetum in locis non usitatis.' *Compendium de discantu mensurabili* in J. Wolf, 'Ein Beitrag zur Diskantlehre des 14. Jahrhunderts', 515.

40 'b-fa littera signum est depressionis note sequentis in eadem clave et ♮-mi nota elevationis . . . quantum b-fa deprimit, tantum ♮-mi acuit, quia utraque per semitonium maius precise.' *Musica* in Wolf Frobenius, *Johannes Boens Musica und seine Konsonanzlehre*, Freiburger Schriften zur Musikwissenschaft 2 (Stuttgart: Musikwissenschaftliche Verlags-Gesellschaft mbH, 1971), p. 54. *Cf.* also Boen, *Ars (musicae)*, ed. F. A. Gallo, Corpus Scriptorum de Musica 19 (n.p.: American Institute of Musicology, 1972), p. 35.

41 See, for example, *The Berkeley Manuscript. University of California Music Library, MS. 744 (olim Phillipps 4450)*, ed. O. B. Ellsworth, Greek and Latin Music Theory 2 (Lincoln and London: University of Nebraska Press, 1984), pp. 52f; Prosdocimus de Beldemandis, *Contrapunctus*, ed. and trans. J. Herlinger, p. 76; Bartolomeo Ramos de Pareia, *Musica practica*, ed. J. Wolf, p. 29; Pietro Aaron, *Lucidario in musica* (Venice: Girolamo Scotto, 1545), fols. 38r–38v; Giovanni del Lago, letter to Giovanni Spataro, Venice, August 15, 1533,

Ms. Vatican, lat. 5318, fols. 47v–48r; Stephano Vanneo, *Recanetum de musica aurea*, fol. 43r; Giovanni Maria Lanfranco, *Scintille di musica* (Brescia: Lodovico Britannico, 1533), p. 125.

42 Ms. Vatican, lat. 5318, fol. 234r. The mistaken date in the manuscript (1537) was corrected in Knud Jeppesen, 'Eine musiktheoretische Korrespondenz des früheren Cinquecento', *Acta Musicologica*, VIII (1941), 19 and 25. See also Spataro, letter to Aaron, Bologna, June 30, 1533, Ms. Vatican, lat. 5318, fol. 250v.

43 'Et quantum una littera notam extorquet et distemperat, tantum sequens littera temperat et retorquet et per consequens reducit ad suam propriam mansionem.' *Musica* in W. Frobenius, *Johannes Boens Musica*, p. 55.

44 *L'antica musica ridotta alla moderna prattica* (Rome: Antonio Barré, 1555), fols. 46v–47r.

45 'Quando aliquod horum duorum signorum ponitur . . . semper poni debet immediate ante notam que in voce . . . varianda est . . . sive ipsa sit in linea sive in spacio, cum quodlibet tale signum non deserviat nisi note ipsum immediate sequenti, nisi b rotundum in principio alicuius cantus pro clavi poneretur, quoniam tunc ipsum b totum cantum denominat cantari debere per b rotundum sive molle.' Prosdocimus, *Contrapunctus*, ed. and trans. J. Herlinger, pp. 78f.

46 'Si in exordio linearum ponatur, totus cantus per b molle cantabitur. Si vero in quavis alia parte positum sit, quam diu deductio cui praeponetur durabit, tam diu cantus b mollaris erit.' *Liber de natura et proprietate tonorum* in *Opera theoretica*, ed. A. Seay, Corpus Scriptorum de Musica 22, vol. I, (n.p.: American Institute of Musicology, 1975), p. 74.

47 See Ramos de Pareia, *Musica practica*, ed. J. Wolf, p. 39; Giovanni del Lago, letter to Giovanni Spataro, Venice, October 8, 1529, Ms. Vatican, lat. 5318, fol. 14r; Lanfranco, *Scintille di musica*, p. 18; Martin Agricola, *Rudimenta musices* (Wittenberg: Georg Rhau, 1539), Ch. 2; Sebald Heyden, *De arte canendi, ac vero signorum in cantibus usu* (Nuremberg: Ioh. Petreius, 1540), pp. 23f.

48 'Ipsius autem maioris semitonii signum secundum antiquos est ♮ quadrum, secundum modernos est ♯.' Ugolino of Orvieto, *Declaratio musicae disciplinae*, ed. A. Seay, vol. III, p. 243.

49 Ramos de Pareia, *Musica practica*, ed. J. Wolf, p. 29.

50 'Opusculum' in Giuseppe Massera, *La 'mano musicale perfetta' di Francesco de Brugis dalle prefazioni ai corali di L. A. Giunta, Venezia, 1499-1504*, Historiae Musicae Cultores 18 (Florence: Leo S. Olschki, 1963), p. 88.

51 Letter to Piero de Justinis, Venice, June 3, 1538, Ms. Vatican, lat. 5318, fol. 102v.

52 In addition to the theorists already mentioned, see, for example, Heinrich Faber, *Ad musicam practicam introductio*, Pt I, Chs. 1 and 3; Philibert Jambe de Fer, *Epitome musical des tons, sons et accordz, es voix humaines, fleustes d'Alleman, fleustes à neuf trous, violes, & violons* (Lyon: Michel du Bois, 1556), p. 20; Ghiselin Danckerts, *Trattato sopra una differentia musicale*, Ms. Rome, Biblioteca Vallicelliana, R.56, fols. 386v–387v.

53 3rd edn (Venice: Marchio Sessa, 1539), 'Aggiunta', sig. Iv.

54 (Venice: Girolamo Scotto, 1545), Bk I, Oppenione 10 and fols. 3v–4r.

55 *Ibid.*

56 Letter from Bologna, November 27, 1531, Ms. Vatican, lat. 5318, fols. 228v–229r.

57 *Ibid.*

58 Ed. E. de Coussemaker, *Histoire de l'harmonie au moyen âge* (Paris: Librairie Archéologique de Victor Didron, 1852), pp. 297ff.

59 *Ibid.*, p. 303.
60 *Le Istitutioni harmoniche* (Venice, 1558), pp. 170f.
61 'I Moderni quando vogliono porre alle volte la chorda Paramese in luogo della Tritesynemennon, pongono la cifera ♯ in luogo del ♮; ancora che tal cosa si faccia contra ogni dovere: conciosiache si doverebbe usare la propia cifera della cosa, che vogliono intendere, et non un'altro segno forestiero: quantunque questo importi poco.' *Ibid.*, p. 170, trans. Guy A. Marco and Claude V. Palisca in *Zarlino, The Art of Counterpoint* (New Haven: Yale University Press, 1968), p. 49.
62 Bourgeois, *Le droict chemin de musique* (Geneva: [Jean Gérard], 1550), Ch. 2; Coclico, *Compendium musices* (Nuremberg: Ioannes Montanus and Ulricus Neuber, 1552), sig. Cv and *passim*; Boen, *Musica* in W. Frobenius, *Johannes Boens Musica*, p. 51.
63 Various aspects of Marchetto's division of the whole tone, the invention of the diesis sign, and the historical influence of these developments have been discussed in Marie Louise Martinez, *Die Musik des frühen Trecento*, Münchner Veröffentlichungen zur Musikgeschichte 9 (Tutzing: Schneider, 1963), pp. 55–70; Martinez-Göllner, 'Marchettus of Padua and Chromaticism', F. A. Gallo, ed., *L'Ars nova italiana del trecento. Secondo convegno internazionale 17–22 luglio 1969* (Certaldo: Edizioni Centro di Studi sull'Ars Nova Italiana del Trecento, 1970), pp. 187–202; Jan W. Herlinger, 'Fractional Divisions of the Whole Tone', *Music Theory Spectrum*, III (1981), 74–83; Herlinger, 'Marchetto's Division of the Whole Tone', *Journal of the American Musicological Society*, XXXIV (1981), 193–216; Giuseppe Massera, 'Suggestioni Teoretiche nel *Lucidarium* di Marchetto da Padova: dai "Generi" alla "Musica Colorata"', M. D. Grace, ed., *A Festschrift for Albert Seay* (Colorado Springs: The Colorado College Music Press, 1982), pp. 1–20.
64 In J. W. Herlinger, *The Lucidarium of Marchetto of Padua*, pp. 231–68; for the dating of the treatise, see p. 13.
65 *Ibid.*, pp. 430–42 and musical examples *passim*. See also Marchetto, *Pomerium*, ed. G. Vecchi, Corpus Scriptorum de Musica 6 (n.p.: American Institute of Musicology, 1961), pp. 68–74.
66 *Pomerium*, ed. G. Vecchi, p. 73. The treatise has been dated in Herlinger, *The Lucidarium of Marchetto of Padua*, p. 14.
67 *Pomerium*, ed. G. Vecchi, p. 70.
68 J. W. Herlinger, *The Lucidarium of Marchetto of Padua*, pp. 440ff. See also Marchetto, *Pomerium*, ed. G. Vecchi, pp. 68–74.
69 Prosdocimus de Beldemandis, *Tractatus plane musice*, Ms. Lucca, Biblioteca Governativa, 359, fol. 52v.
70 Ed. in D. Raffaello Baralli and Luigi Torri, 'Il "Trattato" di Prosdocimo de' Beldomandi contro Il "Lucidario" di Marchetto da Padova', *Rivista musicale italiana*, XX (1913), 731–62.
71 *Ibid.*, p. 731.
72 *Ibid.*, pp. 732–49.
73 'Diesis secundum aliquos idem est quod semitonium minus, secundum alios ipsius semitonii minoris dimidium. Nonnulli vero diesim esse volunt quintam partem toni, alii tertiam quartam et octavam.' Tinctoris, *Diffinitorium musice*, Ms. Brussels, Bibliothèque Royale, II.4147, fol. 119v. This occurs in a late fifteenth-century manuscript version of the dictionary, but the printed version (*Terminorum musicae diffinitorium* [Treviso: Gerardo de Lisa, 1475]) has this, purely Marchettan, definition: 'Diesis is one part of a whole tone divided into five [parts].' ('Diesis est una pars toni in quinque divisi.')

74 *Opera theoretica*, ed. A. Seay, vol. II, p. 91.
75 'Caeterorum minimum, constans secundum aliquos quinta parte toni'. *Ibid.*, p. 92, trans. Albert Seay in *Tinctoris, The Art of Counterpoint*, Musicological Studies and Documents 5 (n.p.: American Institute of Musicology, 1961), p. 87.
76 *Liber de arte contrapuncti*, ed. A. Seay, p. 104.
77 Ed. F. A. Gallo, Antiquae Musicae Italicae Scriptores 4 (Bologna: Forni, 1969), pp. 70ff; for the dating of the treatise, see p. 7.
78 (Turin: Augustinus di Vicomercato, 1520), sig. Av.
79 'Valde aperta et pulchra'. *Brevis collectio artis musicae . . . quae dicitur 'Venturina'*, Ms. Bologna, Civico Museo Bibliografico Musicale, 105 (A57), fols. 29r-30r.
80 'Benche alcuni lo dividano in cinque Diesi'. *Lucidario*, fol. 2v.
81 *L'antica musica ridotta alla moderna prattica*, fols. 11r-11v, 14v-15r, 17v-20r.
82 The two versions may be compared in Prosdocimus, *Contrapunctus*, ed. and trans. J. Herlinger; for Herlinger's comments on the Marchettan traces in one of the sources of the first version, see pp. 20 and 55. For the dates of both versions, see F. Alberto Gallo, 'La tradizione dei trattati musicali di Prosdocimo de Beldemandis', *Quadrivium*, VI (1964), 57-84.
83 Prosdocimus, *Contrapunctus*, ed. and trans. J. Herlinger, pp. 54-7.
84 'Ista fuit una de principalioribus falsitatibus quas dictus Marchetus per totam ytaliam seminavit. et est in praesenti haec falsitas apud cantores in tanto valore quod qui eam habet Sollemnissimus inter cantores reputatur.' D. R. Baralli and L. Torri, 'Il "Trattato" di Prosdocimo de' Beldomandi', p. 752.
85 *Ritus canendi vetustissimus et novus* in E. de Coussemaker, ed., *Scriptorum*, vol. IV, (Paris: A. Durand, 1876), pp. 328f.
86 *Musica practica*, ed. J. Wolf, pp. 41f.
87 *Tractatus quarundam regularum artis musicae*, Ms. Florence, Biblioteca Nazionale Centrale, Palat. 472, fol. 9v.
88 In Hothby, *Tres tractatuli contra Bartholomeum Ramum*, ed. A. Seay, Corpus Scriptorum de Musica 10 (n.p.: American Institute of Musicology, 1964), pp. 17-57. The passage in question is on pp. 51-5.
89 *Ibid.*, pp. 79-92.
90 *Ibid.*, pp. 84f and 91.
91 *Ibid.*, p. 87.
92 *Ibid.*, pp. 87f.
93 *Ibid.*, p. 90.
94 'A pluribus . . . semitonium diatonicum appellatur.' *Terminorum musicae diffinitorium*, sig. biiiir.
95 'Ab aliis semitonium Enarmonicum appellatur.' *Ibid.*
96 'Est & aliud semitonium quod Cromaticum dicitur.' *Ibid.*
97 *Brevis collectio*, fols. 30v-31r.
98 ([Brescia]: Angelo Britannico, 1497), Ch. 12.
99 See Ake Davidsson, *Bibliographie der musiktheoretischen Drucke des 16. Jahrhunderts* (Baden-Baden: Heitz, 1962), pp. 17f.
100 Ed. A. Seay, Critical Texts 2 (Colorado Springs: The Colorado College Music Press, 1977), p. 14.
101 'Secondo Bonaventura, & tutti li musici noi havemo in la mano tre specie di Semitoni, cioè Semitono Enharmonico, Semitono Diatonico, & Semitono Cromatico, over cosi Semitono minore, Semitono maggiore, & Semitono eccellente.' Pietro Cinciarino, *Introduttorio abbreviato di musica piana, o vero canto fermo* (Venice: Domenico de' Farri, 1555), fols. 8v-9r.

102 '. . . (secondo alcuni dotti Musici) . . . Diatonico'. *Fior angelico di musica*, Bk I, Ch. 35, sig. Iiir.

103 For a relatively early instance, see Philippus de Caserta, *Regule contrapuncti* in Nigel Wilkins, 'Some Notes on Philipoctus de Caserta', 97.

104 Letter to Piero de Justinis, Venice, June 3, 1538, Ms. Vatican, lat. 5318, fol. 102v.

105 'Patet ergo ex hiis que dicta sunt de istis signis manifeste error modernorum qui loco ♮ quadri ponunt talem crucem, ♯, sive talem, 𝕏, secundum moderniores, et denominant hec sua signa hoc nomine, dyesis, vel falsa musica, doctrinam malam Marcheti paduani supradicti in sequendo. Fuit ergo predictus Marchetus principium huius erroris.' *Contrapunctus*, ed. and trans. J. Herlinger, pp. 86–9.

106 'Moderni tamen hoc non inteligentes Sed ad libitum et absque ratione operantes loco ♮. quadri ponunt talem crucem. ♯ et aliqui moderniores tale signum 𝕏. etiam ad libitum et absque ratione operantes. et horum plurimi et maxime ytalici falsam Doctrinam Marcheti Paduanj insequentes et multi etiam alij nominant hec duo signa hoc nomine Diesis ignorantes quid apud musicos hoc nomen Diesis importet. Nam diesis apud musicos est medietas Semitonij minoris . . . Dicitque ulterius major pars horum modernorum et maxime ytalicorum ex falsa doctrina suj marcheti Paduanj quod pro tanto signa vocantur hoc nomine diesis. quoniam per illa signa in ascensu fit additio unius Diesis quae Diesis apud suum Marchetum et suos sequaces est .5.a pars toni. et in descensu fit subtractio ipsius Diesis.' D. R. Baralli and L. Torri, 'Il "Trattato" di Prosdocimo de' Beldemandi', pp. 750 (with the form of the diesis sign corrected from Ms. Lucca, Biblioteca Governativa, 359, fol. 87v). Further below, Prosdocimus concluded: 'Briefly, therefore, wherever you will find the above-said Marchetus or any follower of his saying something about those semitones and dieses of his, do not listen to him because they know of this as much as oxen.' ('Breviter ergo ubicunque invenies Marchetum supradictum vel aliquem suum sequacem aliquid loqui de istis suis Semitonijs et de istis suis Diesibus non auscultes ipsum quoniam isti tantum de hoc sciverunt quantum boves.') *Ibid.*, p. 759.

107 *Libellus monochordi* in E. de Coussemaker, *Scriptorum*, vol. III, p. 254.

108 *Parvus tractatulus de modo dividendi monacordum*, Ms. Lucca, Biblioteca Governativa, 359, fols. 72r–78r.

109 'Crux scribi deberet potius sub forma talis ♮ quadri quam cruce tali ♯.' *Libellus monochordi* in E. de Coussemaker, *Scriptorum*, vol. III, p. 258.

110 'Sunt . . . plerique clavem hanc figurantes taliter ♯.' *Expositio manus* in *Opera theoretica*, ed. A. Seay, vol. I, p. 40, trans. A. Seay, 'The Expositio manus of Johannes Tinctoris', *Journal of Music Theory*, IX (1965), 207.

111 'Hoc enim signum est semitonii cromatici proprium.' *Ibid.*

112 'Sunt & qui appositione huius signi ♮ notulam cui apponitur deprimi volunt minimo dieseos intervallo. quod Enarmonici generis est. Est enim Diesis dimidium semitonij minoris intervallum duobus sonis circumscriptum.' (Milan: Ioannes Petrus de Lomatio, 1496), sig. eeiijr, trans. Clement A. Miller, Musicological Studies and Documents 20 (n.p.: American Institute of Musicology, 1968), p. 146.

113 'Questo signo ♯ predicto: e stato chiamato dal mio preceptore signo de b quadro tantum: et da frate Zoanne othobi, e stato chiamato signo de b quadro jacente: et questo .♮. da lui e stato chiamato signo de b quadro recto: li quali nomi son piu rectamente considerati: che non e chiamando questo signo ♯ diesis: perche el nome e consequente al suo effecto: . . . pertanto opperando questo signo

effectivamente come fa el b quadrato recto predicto dico, che tale signo sera piu rectamente chiamato b quadro, che diesis. perche dicendo diesis lo effecto et el nome non hano inseme corespondentia. Ma si bene, essendo chiamato b quadro.' Letter to Pietro Aaron, Bologna, May 23, 1524, Ms. Vatican, lat. 5318, fols. 21 1r–21 1v.

114 *Trattato sopra una differentia musicale*, fols. 386v–387r.

115 *Recanetum de musica aurea*, fols. 20v–21r.

116 *Ibid.*, fol. 90r.

117 *Fior angelico di musica*, Bk I, Ch. 35.

118 *Trattato sopra una differentia musicale*, fol. 399f.

119 *Le Istitutioni harmoniche*, p. 281.

120 'Impossibile est duo maiora semitonia supra seinvicem collocare.' W. Frobenius, *Johannes Boens Musica*, p. 59.

121 'Ubi media et finalis sunt totaliter equales, cum illa secunda littera b-fa non potest plus notam sequentem extra naturam suam extorquere quam per semitonium maius per primam suppositionem; . . . frustra igitur ponitur secunda littera b-fa.' *Ibid.*

122 *Ibid.*, pp. 55–8.

123 'Non liceat poni ♮-mi litteram in clave ♮-mi nec in e-la-mi aut in octavis . . . ad istas, nisi in casu, quo b-fa littera in eisdem clavibus precessisset, quod tunc liceret, ut effectus littere b-fa precedentis per litteram ♮-mi extingueretur . . . non liceat poni b-fa litteram in c-fa-ut vel in f-fa-ut nec in duplis ad istas . . . nec liceat in a-la-mi-re poni litteram ♮-mi.' *Ibid.*, p. 62.

124 'Modernus usus dictas litteras in clavibus extra naturam monocordi manualis admittit.' *Ibid.*, p. 63.

125 *Ibid.*, pp. 63f.

126 The revised version is in Ms. Lucca, Biblioteca Governativa, 359, fols. 72r–78r. The original version appeared under the title *Libellus monocordi* in E. de Coussemaker, ed., *Scriptorum*, vol. III, pp. 248–58.

127 'Ficta musica inter duas litteras immediatas tonum resonantes reponi habet, ut ibidem semitonium habeatur.' Ms. Lucca, Biblioteca Governativa, 359, fol. 73v.

128 'Iste due ficte musice . . . rarissime in cantu aliquo occurant.' *Ibid.*, fol. 77v.

129 The monochord is reproduced in M. Gerbert, ed., *Scriptores*, vol. III, title page, and in Oswald Koller, 'Aus dem Archive des Benedictinerstiftes St Paul im Lavantthal in Kärnten', *Monatshefte für Musikgeschichte*, XXII (1890), 40. It is discussed in Joseph S. Levitan, 'Adrian Willaert's Famous Duo *Quidnam ebrietas*. A Composition which Closes Apparently with the Interval of a Seventh', *Tijdschrift van de Vereniging voor Nederlandse Muziekgeschiedenis*, XV (1939), 227ff.

130 A few mistakes are corrected convincingly in J. S. Levitan, 'Adrian Willaert's Famous Duo', 227ff.

131 Ed. A. Seay, Corpus Scriptorum de Musica 7, vol. III (n.p.: American Institute of Musicology, 1962), pp. 227–53. On Ugolino's gamut, see also Andrew Hughes, 'Ugolino: The Monochord and *Musica Ficta*', *Musica Disciplina*, XXIII (1969), 21–39.

132 *Declaratio musicae disciplinae*, ed. A. Seay, vol. III, pp. 249–51.

133 *Ibid.*, pp. 244ff.

134 *De musica*, ed. G. Massera, Historiae Musicae Cultores 14 (Florence: Leo S. Olschki, 1961), pp. 125–40.

135 *Ibid.*, p. 140.

136 Giuseppe Massera, 'Il *"de Musica"* di Giorgio Anselmi parmense dal mano-

scritto H 233 Inf. della Biblioteca Ambrosiana di Milano' in Anselmi, *De musica*, ed. G. Massera, pp. 23ff.

137 2nd edn (Milan: Ioannes Petrus de Lomatio, 1492), Bk V, Ch. 5.

138 *Compositio clavicordiorum secundum librum Baudeceti*, Ms. Paris, Bibliothèque Nationale, lat. 7295, fol. 128v. Facsimile in G. Le Cerf and E.-R. Labande, eds., *Les traités d'Henri-Arnaut de Zwolle et de divers anonymes (Ms. B. N. latin 7295)* (Paris: Auguste Picard, 1932), Plate VII. Transcribed and translated into French, *ibid.*, pp. 11f.

139 'Fictas autem seu coloratas contrapuncti species . . . in monochordo chordulis ipsis singulos tonos dividentibus considerantur.' *Practica musice*, sig. eeijv, trans. C. A. Miller, p. 145.

140 'In Diatonico autem Guidonis introductorio musica ficta unico toni monstratur intervallo: ubi videlicet b mollis exachordum quartam disponit chordam fa quae toniaeam scindit distantiam inter Alamire & ♮ mi.' *Ibid.*

141 John Hothby, *La Caliopea legale* in E. de Coussemaker, ed., *Histoire de l'harmonie au moyen âge*, pp. 297ff.

142 *Ibid.*, pp. 300ff.

143 *Musica practica*, ed. J. Wolf, p. 30.

144 (Venice: Bernardino de Vitali, 1525), Chs. 26-45.

145 Compare the 1517 formulation of Andreas Ornithoparchus: 'The feigned music feigns in each key every syllable.' ('Musica ficta fingit in quacunque clave quamcunque vocem.') *Musice active micrologus*, Bk I, Ch. 10. John Dowland's translation of 1609 (p. 25) is somewhat misleading: 'Musicke may Fict in any Voyce and *Key*.'

146 The significance of the correspondence for the evolution of Aaron's thinking about the gamut was recognized in Edward E. Lowinsky, 'Matthaeus Greiter's *Fortuna*: An Experiment in Chromaticism and in Musical Iconography', *The Musical Quarterly*, XLIII (1957), 72. See also Lowinsky, 'Echoes of Adrian Willaert's Chromatic "Duo" in Sixteenth- and Seventeenth-Century Compositions' in H. S. Powers, ed., *Studies in Music History. Essays for Oliver Strunk* (Princeton: Princeton University Press, 1968), pp. 208f, n. 40. For an earlier discussion of the subject, see Ed Peter Bergquist, Jr., *The Theoretical Writings of Pietro Aaron*, Ph.D. diss., Columbia University, 1964, pp. 426-54. For a chronology of Spataro's relations with Aaron, see *ibid.*, pp. 40-4.

147 Ms. Vatican, lat. 5318, fol. 139v.

148 *Ibid.*, fol. 144r.

149 *Ibid.*, fol. 219v.

150 *Ibid.*, fol. 216r.

151 (Venice: Girolamo Scotto, 1545), fols. 38r-38v. Bergquist, *The Theoretical Writings of Pietro Aaron*, p. 458, points out that Chapters 11-12 of *Lucidario* 'reproduce the *Trattato* Supplement almost word for word'.

152 (Milan: Io. Antonio da Castelliono, n.d.), Ch. 59.

153 'Sono gia passati molti giorni che hebi una de vostra excellentia con laquale era uno doctissimo, subtile, et degno tractatetto novamente impresso, elquale allegantemente et con optime et vere demonstratione demonstrava come in ciascuna de le positione de la mano de Guido ciascuno de li sei nomi officiali se possono trovare . . . Bartolomeo solo atese et hebe respecto a producere tante positione de la mano de Guido signate quanto era delusono circa la divisione de li toni in dui semitonij del monochordo et organo al suo tempo usitati, et . . . vostra excellentia ha considerato piu alto et subtilemente, perche haveti havuto respecto che ciascuno spatio de tono de li predicti instrumenti resti diviso in

modo che in grave et in acuto appara el mazore et el minore semitonio con la differentia del coma la quale cade intra loro . . . de nulla˙vostra excellentia haveva pretento l'ordine de la mera verita demonstrata da frate Zoanne Othobi, ma . . . asai meglio et piu plenamente havevi scripto de lui.' Ms. Vatican, lat. 5318, fols. 224r–224v. For the date of the letter, see Bergquist, *The Theoretical Writings of Pietro Aaron*, p. 443, n. 57.

154 'Come da Frate Giovanni Ottobi è stato dimostrato in la sua Calliopea. la quale verita Frate Pietro mio honorato da vostra Eccellènza è stata tacito approbata in quello vostro trattato dove insegnate de trovare li sej nomj officialj in ciaschuna positione della mano de Guido Monacho.' Ms. Vatican, lat. 5318, fol. 121r.

155 '. . . (ridendo) dicevano che veramente credevano che in me era tornato el senso puerile, perche mai non troverno che io dicesse che el mio preceptore fusse inferiore ad alcuno altro musico, excepto che al presente'. *Ibid.*, fol. 224v.

156 The piece was published and discussed in Giovanni Maria Artusi, *L'Artusi, overo delle imperfettioni della moderna musica* (Venice: Giacomo Vincenti, 1600), fols. 20v–25v. For modern discussions, see J. S. Levitan, 'Adrian Willaert's Famous Duo', pp. 166–233; Edward E. Lowinsky, 'Adrian Willaert's Chromatic "Duo" Re-Examined', *Tijdschrift van de Vereniging voor Nederlandse Muziekgeschiedenis*, XVIII (1956), 1–36; Lowinsky, 'Echoes of Adrian Willaert's Chromatic "Duo"', pp. 183–238. Relevant to the question of the dating of the piece are the discoveries concerning Willaert's early career in Lewis Lockwood, 'Josquin at Ferrara: New Documents and Letters' in E. E. Lowinsky, ed., *Josquin des Prez. Proceedings of the International Josquin Festival-Conference . . . New York City*, 21–25 June 1971 (London: Oxford University Press, 1976), pp. 118ff.

157 Artusi, *L'Artusi, overo delle imperfettioni della moderna musica*, fols. 22r–24r. Another, very similar, discussion is contained in Spataro's letter of November 10, 1524 to Marc'Antonio Cavazzoni, Ms. Vatican, lat. 5318, fols. 213r–214v.

158 'Dalli Musici è stato solo ordinato dui segni, per li quali li soni naturalmente considerati si possono removere dal loco proprio; liquali segni sono questi .S. ♯, b, il primo .S. ♯ remove el sono naturale per semitonio maggiore in acuto: el secondo .S. b opera per contrario; S. che remove el sono dal loco naturale per Semitonio maggiore in grave.' Artusi, *L'Artusi, overo delle imperfettioni della moderna musica*, fol. 23v.

159 'Due volte el suo effetto'. *Ibid.*

160 For an example of 'possibly the only notation of B♭♭ in a sixteenth-century score', see Lowinsky, 'Matthaeus Greiter's *Fortuna*', p. 504. Also this example, however, differs somewhat from the modern double flat in that the double flattening of B is indicated by a single flat at B and a single flat at F a fourth below.

161 Artusi, *L'Artusi, overo delle imperfettioni della moderna musica*, fols. 22v–23r.

162 Ms. Paris, Bibliothèque Nationale, it. 1110, fols. 45r–46r.

163 Lowinsky, 'Willaert's Chromatic "Duo" Re-Examined', p. 6, n. 10.

164 Del Lago, letter to Spataro(?), May 25, 1533, Ms. Vatican, lat. 5318, fols. 165r–166r and Spataro, letter to Aaron, August 20, 1533, *ibid.*, fol. 234v. For the date of the latter document, see Knud Jeppesen, 'Eine musiktheoretische Korrespondenz des früheren Cinquecento', *Acta Musicologica*, VIII (1941), 19 and 25.

165 Ms. Vatican, lat. 5318, fols. 47r–53v.

166 *Ibid.*, fols. 116r–129v.

167 *Ibid.*, fols. 118v–119v, 124r–125v, 127r.

168 *Ibid.*, fols. 125r–125v.

169 *Ibid.*, fols. 117r–118v, 125v–126r, 127r.

170 *Ibid.*, fols. 102r–103r.

171 Fols. 37r–39r. See also Bergquist, *The Theoretical Writings of Pietro Aaron*, pp. 454–8 and Lowinsky, 'Echoes of Adrian Willaert's Chromatic "Duo"', p. 210, n. 47.

172 'Volendo tu adunque immaginarti il segno di, b, in C, grave . . . a te potrebbe intervenire forse quello, che altrui è intervenuto, iquali hanno creduto, che quando il Musico, over Compositore ne suoi processi musicali adduce la figura del, b, molle, o del Diesi, che quella nota dal proprio suo luogo non si rimova, ma sti permanente & che tali segni siano quasi di soverchio. Pero per isganarti di questo errore saperai, che tal sillaba, o nota, fa, posta in C, col detto segno, b, è indi rimossa, & piu non è la dove prima si ritrovava, ma sotto di, b, mi grave, per un spatio del Coma.' Aaron, *Lucidario*, fol. 37r.

173 *Ibid.*, fols. 37r–38v. See also Aaron, *Compendiolo*, Ch. 59.

174 (Wittenberg: Georg Rhau, 1539), Ch. 2.

175 The two unmistakably experimental pieces of the first half of the sixteenth century have been explored in particular in Lowinsky, 'Willaert's Chromatic "Duo" Re-Examined' and 'Matthaeus Greiter's *Fortuna*'. For other, more debatable, candidates to the experimental status, see Lowinsky, 'Music in Titian's *Bacchanal of the Andrians*: Origin and History of the *Canon per Tonos*' in D. Rosand, ed., *Titian: His World and His Legacy* (New York: Columbia University Press, 1982), pp. 191–282; Howard Mayer Brown, 'Introduction', *A Florentine Chansonnier from the Time of Lorenzo the Magnificent. Florence, Biblioteca Nazionale Centrale MS Banco Rari 229*, Monuments of Renaissance Music 7, vol. I (Chicago and London: The University of Chicago Press, 1983), pp. 16–22.

176 Margaret Bent, 'Diatonic *Ficta*', *Early Music History*, IV (1984), 1–48. I would like to thank Professor Bent for kindly sending me the proofs of her paper prior to publication and for an extremely stimulating correspondence on the subject.

177 *Ibid.*, p. 1.

178 *Ibid.*, pp. 21ff and 34f.

179 *Ibid.*, pp. 40–4.

180 *Ibid.*, pp. 45ff.

181 Lowinsky, *Secret Chromatic Art in the Netherlands Motet* (New York: Columbia University Press, 1946).

182 Bent, 'Diatonic *Ficta*', p. 16.

183 *Ibid.*, pp. 34–41.

184 The same confusion accounts for the following: 'We name those differences [e.g. between F and F♯, or B and B♭] in relation to letter-norms, F♯ as a modified F, B♭ as a modified B; late-medieval nomenclature, however, could express such differences neither for the monochord . . . nor on the scale, where the letter B served the whole area between A and C.' *Ibid.*, p. 8. In fact, we shall see that late medieval nomenclature expresses such differences just as well as ours as soon as we realize that 'F' is not a full name of a step, while 'F-fa' is. Just as our F♯ is a 'black-key' modification of the 'white-key' norm, F, so their F-mi is a *musica ficta* modification of the *musica vera* norm, F-fa (or F-ut).

185 *Ibid.*, pp. 16–20.

186 'Diversi musici diversum posuerunt numerum coniunctarum; nam alii 7, alii vero 8, alii vero plures dixerunt esse coniunctas.' *The Berkeley Manuscript*, ed. and trans. O. B. Ellsworth, pp. 52f.

187 *Ibid.*, pp. 52–67.

188 'In omnibus [clavibus], in quibus fa localiter non ponitur, potest poni B. molle; similiter in omnibus clavibus, in quibus fa localiter ponitur, potest poni ♮. durum.' M. Gerbert, ed., *Scriptores*, vol. III, p. 333.

189 *[Libellus] Ex Codice Vaticano Lat. 5129*, ed. A. Seay, Corpus Scriptorum de Musica 9 (n.p.: American Institute of Musicology, 1964), pp. 46f. For the date and origin of the treatise, see Albert Seay, 'Introduction', *ibid.*, p. 11.

190 *Tractatus de musica plana et mensurabili* in E. de Coussemaker, ed., *Scriptorum*, vol. III, pp. 426–9.

191 Ed. J. Wolf, Publikationen der Internationalen Musikgesellschaft 2 (Leipzig: Breitkopf und Härtel, 1901).

192 'Sed alibi non solum in paramese signant istis signis tonos aut semitonia cantores. Dicunt namque: ubicunque *fa* sine *mi* reperitur, ibi *mi* faciendum est, sicut in b *fa* ♮ *mi*. Idem quoque, ubi *mi* sine *fa*, quod appellant multi fictam musicam.' *Ibid.*, p. 29.

193 'Locabitur igitur istud b molle in quinque locis secundum eos, scilicet in b *mi* et in *e la-mi*, in *a la-mi-re* primo, in *e la-mi* acuto et in *a la-mi-re* secundo . . . sed istud ♮ vel istud ♯ in *c fa-ut*, in *f fa-ut*, in *c sol-fa-ut*, in *f fa-ut* acuto et in *c sol-fa*.' *Ibid.*

194 *Ibid.*, pp. 29f.

195 'Et alii minus periti'. *Ibid.*, p. 40.

196 'Quemadmodum in b *fa* ♮ *mi* ambo signa possunt locari, ita et in aliis locis, ubi nec *fa* nec *mi*.' *Ibid.*

197 'Quod ita fieri possit, minime negandum est; at quod debeat, concedendum non arbitror . . . Si per iam dicta tonus in duo semitonia manet divisus, frustra fiunt reliqua supervacanea, quoniam ad hoc istud permittitur . . . ut tonum et semitonium a qualibet voce possimus habere.' *Ibid.*

198 'Quidam . . . practicorum minus bene praevidentes'. *Ibid.*, p. 101.

199 *Ibid.*, pp. 101f.

200 *Ibid.*, p. 102.

201 *Ibid.*, pp. 30f.

202 *Ibid.*, p. 35.

203 'Ideoque post coniunctarum additionem manus perfecta dicitur, quoniam tota per semitonia recte divisa est.' *Ibid.*, p. 31. In a letter of April 20, 1984, Professor Howard Mayer Brown has kindly (and convincingly) pointed out to me that a gamut combining the regular hand with a transposition of the hand a whole tone down and up has been described more than a hundred years earlier in O. B. Ellsworth, ed., *The Berkeley Manuscript*, pp. 52–67. The author of this treatise makes also a half-hearted attempt to transpose the hand a diatonic semitone up, including in this transposition only the natural and hard, but not soft, hexachords.

204 Ms. Bologna, Civico Museo Bibliografico Musicale, 105 (A57), fols. 1r–41r.

205 *Ibid.*, fols. 35r–36r.

206 Modern edition in G. Massera, *La 'mano musicale perfetta' di Francesco de Brugis*, pp. 73–96.

207 'Non solum cantoribus verumetiam organistis citharedisque ac ceteris'. *Ibid.*, p. 75.

208 *Ibid.*, pp. 75ff.

209 *Ibid.*, Table III after p. 56.

210 *Ibid.*, p. 79.

211 *Ibid.*, pp. 79f.

212 *Ibid.*, pp. 80f.

213 'Qua divisione omne perfectum musicale instrumentum divisum esse debet.' *Ibid.*, p. 80.

214 Letter to Pietro Aaron, Bologna, October 24, 1531, Ms. Vatican, lat. 5318, fol. 224r.

215 'Quellj versi, li quali dice che sono stati assignati dalli Antichj li quali demos-
    trano, che in A et in ♮ et in E naturalj . . . se debba segnare questo segno b. Et
    che questo ♯ solemente debba segnarse in C et in F naturalj.' Ms. Vatican, lat.
    5318, fol. 127v. *Cf.* also *ibid.*, fol. 123v.

216 'Le congiunte familiare, cio è quelle che sono usate nel canto figurato.' *Ibid.*,
    fol. 107r.

217 *Ibid.*, fols. 107r-107v.

218 'Le coniuncte certamente sono due, cioe una de b rotondo, la quale se signa con
    questo signo b in ciascuno loco dove naturalemente se trova mi, et laltra
    sechiama coniuncta de b quadrato, la quale se signa con questo signo ♯ in cias-
    cuno loco dove naturalemente cade fa . . . come dal mio preceptore e stato
    scripto et e affirmato da ciascuno docto.' *Ibid.*, fols. 139v-140r.

219 *Ibid.*, fols. 49v-50r.

220 Fols. 4r-5v.

221 Fols. 43r-44r.

222 (Basle: [M. Furter], 1511), sigs. Fiiiv-Gv.

223 Pt II, Ch. 6. According to Klaus Wolfgang Niemöller, 'Wollick, Nicolaus' in
    S. Sadie, ed., *The New Grove Dictionary*, vol. XX, p. 512, the first edition
    appeared in 1509.

224 Bk I, Ch. 10.

225 'In cantu ficto praecipue debet observari fa in a & E, & mi in F & c.' Ch. 3.

226 'Duo sunt eius signa, b rotundum in locis ♮ duralibus, & ♮ quadratum in locis
    bmollaribus, quorum illud b fa: hoc verò ♮ mi designat.' Sigs. Biijr-Biijv.

227 *Musica practica*, ed. J. Wolf, p. 101.

228 Speyer: Peter Drach.

229 'Fa in alamire post soll oder gis'. *Spiegel der Orgelmacher und Organisten*,
    fol. 16.

230 'Fa in elami post re oder dis, wie du es nennest'. *Ibid.*

231 *Ibid.*, fols. 16-17. See also Mark Lindley, 'Early Sixteenth-Century Keyboard
    Temperaments', *Musica Disciplina*, XXVIII (1974), 129-51.

232 'Dovon han ich vil red gehabt, und mir zu underweysung gefragt die höchsten
    und berümpsten musicos speculativos und practicos so bey unsern zeitten
    meiner achtung gewesst und noch sein, und jr vil meiner meynung funden.'
    Spiegel der Orgelmacher und Organisten, fol. 17. It is at least possible that long
    before Schlick organ makers pragmatically tempered 'black-key' steps so as to
    make them serviceable as both fas and mis. An anonymous *Ars et modus pul-
    sandi organa* which, according to R. Casimiri, dates from the fourteenth cen-
    tury, describes an instrument the keyboard of which encompasses three octaves
    and a whole tone, with B♭ in every octave, and with 'black-key' steps between C
    and D, D and E, F and G and G and A everywhere above the lowest octave.
    (R. Casimiri, 'Un trattatello per organisti di *anonimo* del sec. XIV', *Note
    d'archivio per la storia musicale*, XIX (1942), 99-101.) The author claims that
    on this instrument one can have the fa-mi-re-ut tetrachord with fa placed on B♮,
    B♭, A, A♭, G, G♭, E, E♭, D and D♭, and this suggests that his five 'black-key' steps
    are serviceable as both flats and sharps.

233 Ed. A. Seay, Critical Texts 9 (Colorado Springs: The Colorado College Music
    Press, 1979), pp. 14f.

234 *Ibid.*, p. 24.

235 Ossuna: Juan de Leon.

236 *Ibid.*, fol. 24v.

237 *Ibid.*, fol. 26r.

238 The text was not revised after the second edition brought out by Bernardino and Matheo de Vitali of Venice in 1529.

239 Venice: Girolamo Scotto.

240 *Ibid.*, fols. 35v-36r. *Cf.* also fols. 2v and 4r.

241 *Ibid.*, fol. 36v.

242 Pp. 119-23.

243 Pp. 138f.

244 London, British Library, Ms. Add. 28550, fols. 43-4, ed. W. Apel, *Keyboard Music of the Fourteenth and Fifteenth Centuries*, Corpus of Early Keyboard Music I (n.p.: American Institute of Musicology, 1963), pp. 1-9; Faenza, Biblioteca Comunale, Ms. 117, ed. D. Plamenac, *Keyboard Music of the Late Middle Ages in Codex Faenza 117*, Corpus Mensurabilis Musicae 57 (n.p.: American Institute of Musicology, 1972).

245 For split black keys on Italian instruments, see John Barnes, 'The Specious Uniformity of Italian Harpsichords' in E. M. Ripin, ed., *Keyboard Instruments. Studies in Keyboard Organology* (Edinburgh: Edinburgh University Press, 1971), pp. 1-10. For experimental keyboards, see my *Theories of Chromatic and Enharmonic Music in Late 16th-Century Italy*, Studies in Musicology 10 (Ann Arbor: UMI Research Press, 1980), pp. 7-25 and 44-56.

246 Franchinus Gaffurius, *De harmonia musicorum instrumentorum* (Milan: Gotardus Pontanus, 1518), fols. 15v-18v. The same gamut reappears in Gaffurius, *Apologia adversum Ioannem Spatarium & complices musicos Bononienses*, sig. Aiiiv.

247 Aaron, *Toscanello in musica*, Bk II, Ch. 40.

248 'Piu tosto vogliono acommodare il C fa ut de la terza minore, che il ♮ mi de la maggiore: perche ♮ mi da essi poco è operato.' *Ibid.*, trans. P. Bergquist, p. 5.

249 Ms. Vatican, lat. 5318, fol. 244v.

250 *Compendiolo di molti dubbi, segreti et sentenze intorno al canto fermo, et figurato* (Milan: Io. Antonio da Castelliono, n.d.).

251 'Come si vede in alcuni Istromenti nella Italia'. *Ibid.*, Ch. 75.

252 Ms. Venice, Biblioteca Nazionale di S. Marco, lat. VIII.85 (=3579), fols. 84v-88v.

3 Signatures

1 'Talis tonus a parte compositionis dicetur proprius, eo quod ex speciebus suis propriis sit formatus, sed dicetur improprius a parte locationis, quia in loco alio quam in proprio collocatur.' Jan W. Herlinger, *The Lucidarium of Marchetto of Padua. A Critical Edition, Translation and Commentary*, Ph.D. diss., The University of Chicago, 1978, p. 622.

2 *Opera theoretica*, ed. A. Seay, Corpus Scriptorum de Musica 22, vol. I (n.p.: American Institute of Musicology, 1975), pp. 97f.

3 'Ipsi tamen toni in omnibus locis aliis regularibus aut per veram aut per fictam musicam correspondentibus sive intra manum sive extra finire possunt, et tunc irregulares appellati sunt.' *Ibid.*, p. 98, trans. Albert Seay, Translations 2, rev. edn (Colorado Springs: The Colorado College Music Press, 1976), p. 41.

4 *Opera theoretica*, ed. A. Seay, vol. I, pp. 98-103.

5 The only exception to this last 'rule', in Example 67, 'the third example of the seventh mode' ('exemplum tertium septimi'), appears to be a mistake: the signature there does not require ♭, but it does require E♭ below Γ.

6 *Opera theoretica*, ed. A. Seay, vol. I, pp. 73f.

7 'Plura denique alia irregularia loca intra manum et extra sunt, in quibus ob
convenientiam quam habent ad regularia nostri octo toni finire possunt.' *Ibid.*,
p. 102, trans. A. Seay, Translations 2, p. 46.

8 See, for example, in addition to the texts mentioned below, Pietro Aaron, *Trat-
tato della natura et cognitione di tutti gli tuoni di canto figurato non da altrui
piu scritti* (Venice: Bernardino de Vitali, 1525), Chs. 4-7; Martin Agricola,
Musica choralis deudsch (Wittenberg: Georg Rhau, 1533), Ch. 9; Stephano
Vanneo, *Recanetum de musica aurea* (Rome: Valerius Doricus, 1533), fol. 92r;
Heinrich Glarean, *Dodecachordon* (Basle: Heinrich Petri, 1547), pp. 31 and
101f; Nicola Vicentino, *L'antica musica ridotta alla moderna prattica* (Rome:
Antonio Barré, 1555), fols. 46r-50v.

9 'Prima. Solfizans cantum aliquem, pre omnibus tonum respiciat, necesse est.
Toni enim cognitio, est schale: sub qua cantus decurrit, inventio. Secunda.
Omnes toni decurrunt sub schala ♮ durali, preter quintum et sextum. Tertia.
Cantum sub schala ♮ durali decurrere, est nihil aliud, quam in bfa♮mi mi
canere, Sub schala autem b molli, fa . . . Quinta. Omni solfizanti videre erit
necessarium, an cantus regularis existat, nec ne. Cantus enim transpositio,
mutationis schale plerumque est occasio. Sexta. Omnis cantus in finalibus ter-
minatus, est regularis et non transpositus.' Andreas Ornithoparchus, *Musice
active micrologus*, Bk I, Ch. 5, trans. John Dowland (London: Thomas Adams,
1609), p. 15.

10 See, for example, Sebastian z Felsztyna, *Opusculum musice compilatum . . . pro
institutione adolescentum in cantu simplici seu gregoriano* (Cracow: Jan Haller,
1517), sig. Diiir; Agricola, *Musica choralis deudsch*, Ch. 9; Glarean, *Dodecachordon*, p. 31.

11 'Nullus modus simpliciter et ex natura sua bfa habet quia nulla figura diapason
(quod est proprium systema modi) bfa habet. Accidit vero omni modo secundum quid ut ita loquar et cum additamento aliquo pacto posse habere bfa
praecipue sexto.' Johannes Aventinus, *Musicae rudimenta, Augsburg, 1516*,
ed. and trans. T. H. Keahey, Musical Theorists in Translation 10 (Brooklyn:
Institute of Mediaeval Music, 1971), p. 27.

12 Aaron, *Trattato della natura et cognitione di tutti gli tuoni*, Ch. 6.

13 'Unde quidam *katholikōs* canonem prodiderunt. Omnem modum posse in
quinta supra finalem clavem, aliam habere confinalem, quam finalem appellant. Verum illud prorsus in nullo modo verum est, ubique enim diatessaron
repugnat. Atqui hic erat verus canon, ac magis ponendus. In quarta quaque
clave per diatessaron cuiusvis modi cantum supra finalem finiri posse, siquidem
fa in b clave fuerit.' Glarean, *Dodecachordon*, p. 31, trans. Clement A. Miller,
Musicological Studies and Documents 6 (n.p.: American Institute of Musicology, 1965), p. 70.

14 Juan Bermudo, *El arte Tripharia* (Ossuna: Juan de Leon, 1550), fols. 25v-26r.

15 *Ibid.*, fol. 26r.

16 Heinrich Faber, *Ad musicam practicam introductio* (Nuremberg: Ioannes
Montanus and Ulricus Neuber, 1550), Pt I, Ch. 4.

17 Gioseffo Zarlino, *Le Istitutioni harmoniche* (Venice, 1558), p. 319.

18 *Ibid.*, p. 286.

19 Ghiselin Danckerts, *Trattato sopra una differentia musicale*, Ms. Rome, Biblioteca Vallicelliana, R.56, fols. 405r-407v. The dispute has been thoroughly
examined in Lewis Lockwood, 'A Dispute on Accidentals in Sixteenth-Century
Rome', *Analecta Musicologica*, II (1965), 24-40.

20 Heinrich Glarean, *Isagoge in musicen* (Basle: Joannes Frobenius, 1516), Ch. 10.

21 Glarean, *Dodecachordon*, p. 31. See also pp. 101f.

22 *Isagoge in musicen*, Ch. 10; *Dodecachordon*, p. 31.
23 Ornithoparchus, *Musice active micrologus*, Bk I, Ch. 11.
24 'Trasportatione nel canto Fermo non si fa per altro: se non per schivare le voci fitte: Et nel Figurato, per havere piu spatio di consonanze: o pur per arbitrio del Componente.' Giovanni Maria Lanfranco, *Scintille di musica* (Brescia: Lodovico Britannico, 1533), p. 108, trans. Barbara Lee, *Giovanni Maria Lanfranco's 'Scintille di Musica' and Its Relation to 16th-Century Music Theory*, Ph.D. diss., Cornell University, 1961, p. 206.
25 Zarlino, *Le Istitutioni harmoniche*, p. 319.
26 'Ideo musicorum sollertia duas schalas: sub quibus omnis cantus regulatur, atque decurrit: excogitavit. Et primam quidem a ♮ duro, ♮ duralem. Secundam vero a b molli, b mollem nominari precepit . . . Est itaque Schala in genere, nihil aliud, nisi cognitio mi et fa, in b fa ♮ mi, et octavis eius . . . Schala ♮ duralis est vocum musicalium progressio, scandens ex a in ♮ duriter, id est per vocem mi . . . Schala vero b mollis est vocum musicalium progressio, scandens ex a in b molliter, id est per vocem fa.' Ornithoparchus, *Musice active micrologus*, sigs. Biiir-Biiiv, trans. Dowland, p. 14.
27 Ornithoparchus, *Musice active micrologus*, sig. Biiiv.
28 *Ibid.*, Bk I, Ch. 10.
29 'Scale' is used, for example, in Nicolaus Wollick, *Opus aureum* in K. W. Niemöller, ed., *Die Musica gregoriana des Nicolaus Wollick. Opus aureum, Köln 1501, pars I/II*, Beiträge zur Rheinischen Musikgeschichte 11 (Cologne and Krefeld: Staufen-Verlag, 1955), pp. 15 and 35; Wollick, *Enchiridion musices* (Paris: Francoys Regnault, 1512), Pt II, Ch. 5. 'Hand' is used, for example, in Lanfranco, *Scintille di musica*, pp. 12, 26, 30. 'Song' is used, for example, in Sebald Heyden, *De arte canendi, ac vero signorum in cantibus usu* (Nuremberg: Ioh. Petreius, 1540), pp. 19f; H. Faber, *Ad musican practicam introductio*, Pt I, Ch. 4; Zarlino, *Le Istitutioni harmoniche*, p. 170.
30 The feigned scale with three flats may be seen, for example, in Wolfgang Khainer, *Musica choralis* in Renate Federhofer-Königs, 'Wolfgang Khainer und seine "Musica choralis"', *Kirchenmusikalisches Jahrbuch*, XLIII (1959), 44; Wollick, *Opus aureum*, ed. K. W. Niemöller, p. 35; Wollick, *Enchiridion musices*, Pt II, Ch. 5. The feigned scale with two flats may be seen, for example, in Lanfranco, *Scintille di musica*, p. 30.
31 Carl Dahlhaus, 'Zur Akzidentiensetzung in den Motetten Josquins des Prez' in R. Baum and W. Rehm, eds., *Musik und Verlag. Karl Vötterle zum 65. Geburtstag am 12. April 1968* (Kassel: Bärenreiter, 1968), pp. 207ff; Margaret Bent, 'Musica Recta and Musica Ficta', *Musica Disciplina*, XXVI (1972), 73–100; Andrew Hughes, *Manuscript Accidentals: Ficta in Focus 1350-1450*, Musicological Studies and Documents 27 (n.p.: American Institute of Musicology, 1972).
32 M. Bent, 'Musica Recta and Musica Ficta', p. 99. For the discussion referred to, see Ugolino of Orvieto, *Declaratio musicae disciplinae*, ed. A. Seay, Corpus Scriptorum de Musica 7, vol. II (n.p.: American Institute of Musicology, 1960), pp. 48ff.
33 For a more complex interpretation of Ugolino's hands, see Hughes, *Manuscript Accidentals*, pp. 38f.
34 'Ideo duplicem manum invenimus, ubi omnes rectae musicae atque fictae voces ordinatae ponuntur . . . Aliam fictae musicae manum atque rectae invenimus a Γ inferius per diapente distantem, et in C incipientem a prima parum excepta gravitate distantem.' Ugolino of Orvieto, *Declaratio musicae disciplinae*, ed. A. Seay, vol. II, pp. 48, 50.
35 O. B. Ellsworth, ed. and trans., *The Berkeley Manuscript. University of Cali-*

fornia Music Library, MA. 744 (olim Phillipps 4450), Greek and Latin Music Theory 2 (Lincoln and London: University of Nebraska Press, 1984), pp. 50–67. See also Ch. 2, n. 203 above.

36 Tinctoris, *Liber de natura et proprietate tonorum* in *Opera theoretica*, ed. Seay, vol. I, pp. 75f.

37 'Re fictum in Gamma ut'. Tinctoris, *Liber de arte contrapuncti* in *Opera theoretica*, ed. A. Seay, vol. II, p. 98; 'se' is a misprint.

38 The most substantial explanations of the phenomenon appeared in Edward E. Lowinsky, 'The Function of Conflicting Signatures in Early Polyphonic Music', *The Musical Quarterly*, XXXI (1945), 227–60; Richard H. Hoppin, 'Partial Signatures and Musica Ficta in Some Early 15th-Century Sources', *Journal of the American Musicological Society*, VI (1953), 197–215; Lowinsky, 'Conflicting Views on Conflicting Signatures', *ibid.*, VII (1954), 181–204; Hoppin 'Conflicting Signatures Reviewed', *ibid.*, IX (1956), 97–117.

39 R. H. Hoppin, 'Partial Signatures and Musica Ficta', p. 203. See also Hans Heinrich Eggebrecht, 'Machauts Motette Nr. 9', *Archiv für Musikwissenschaft*, XXV (1968), 189, n. 17 and Gilbert Reaney, 'Transposition and "Key" Signatures in Late Medieval Music', *Musica Disciplina*, XXXIII (1979), 31f.

40 R. H. Hoppin, 'Conflicting Signatures Reviewed', p. 108.

41 E. E. Lowinsky, 'The Function of Conflicting Signatures in Early Polyphonic Music', p. 234.

42 R. H. Hoppin, 'Conflicting Signatures Reviewed', p. 98.

43 John Hothby, *Spetie tenore del contrapunto prima* in Hothby, *De arte contrapuncti*, ed. G. Reaney, Corpus Scriptorum de Musica 26 (n.p.: American Institute of Musicology, 1977), p. 86.

44 'Nel secondo contrapunto non bisognia porre alcuno b molle, perche non ocorre alcuna quinta o vero 8 ove sia mi contra fa o fa contra mi. Ma nel primo contrapunto basso v'è posto piu volte b molle per regolare tal contrapunto, accio che non si senta o fa contra mi o mi contra fa.' *Ibid.*

45 'Si oppone anchora a la inadvertenza di alcuni compositori, liquali senza altra consideratione in una parte sola del suo concento, adducono in luce la figura del b molle, massimamente ne la parte grave, dico che tal licenza e denegata & non concessa, ne manco in consideratione e al vero musico. Onde volendo ristringersi al suo concetto & male pensamento, non altrimenti credono essere scusati sol per il procedere molte volte, a la chorda del ♮ mi grave, ilquale risponde un diapente con il tenore imperfetto, laqual consideratione e frustratoria & vana, perche ne risulta & nasce dui inconvenienti, il primo e, che ciascheduna spetie vien permutata & variata dal suo naturale, come sara da Γ ut, a D sol re, & quello che dittono si mostra, in terza minore o semidittono si truova, come discorrendo dal D sol re al ♮ mi si vede, & similmente da ♮ mi al Γ ut lequali risoneranno re la, la fa, & fa re, & prima erono, ut sol, sol mi, & mi ut, spetie contrarie a tutte le altre occorrenti nel soprano, tenore, & controalto, & questo e usitato piu da loro ne gli canti del settimo overo ottavo tuono. Per tanto il secondo inconveniente sara, che le ottave & quinte decime non corrisponderanno insieme giuste, si che a te e dibisogno prima considerare di conseguire lo effetto con i processi simili & spetie, & pur volendo passare con la intentione tua per il detto ♮ mi, segna anchora a tutte le altri parti la figura b, & senza errore alcuno ogni processo & consonanze, si troveranno concorde & sonore insieme, dove priemieramente alcuni discordanvano.' Pietro Aaron, *Toscanello in musica* (Venice: Marchio Sessa, 1539), sig. Iiir, trans. Peter Bergquist, Translations 4, vol. III (Colorado Springs: The Colorado College Music Press, 1970), pp. 23f.

The significance of this passage for the problem of 'conflicting' signatures was pointed out in E. E. Lowinsky, 'The Function of Conflicting Signatures', pp. 258f.

46 'Alcuni altri appariranno col sopra detto segno nel contro basso, et alcuni altri nel tenore, Dico che simile ordine non e concesso ne conveniente a un concento o canto eccettuando quando sara considerato et con artificio messo, come lo excellente Iosquino nel patrem della messa. De virgine maria ha osservato, et similmente el divino Alexandro in molti suoi canti.' Pietro Aaron, *Trattato della natura et cognitione di tutti gli tuoni*, Ch. III, sig. br.

47 Josquin des Prez, *Werken*, ed. A. Smijers, Missen III/16 (Amsterdam: G. Alsbach and Co., 1952), pp. 139–50. The editor indicated the implied inflections internally.

48 Harold S. Powers, 'Mode' in S. Sadie, ed., *The New Grove Dictionary of Music and Musicians*, XII (London: Macmillan, 1980), 400. See also Bernhard Meier, 'Die Handschrift Porto 714 als Quelle zur Tonartenlehre des 15. Jahrhunderts', *Musica Disciplina*, VII (1953), 175–97.

4 Horizontal relations

1 'De ista ergo ficta musica notande sunt hee regule, quarum prima est hec, quod ficta musica nunquam ponenda est nisi loco neccessitatis, eo quod in arte nichil est ponendum, et maxime fictio, sine neccessitate.' Prosdocimus de Beldemandis, *Contrapunctus*, ed. and trans. J. Herlinger, Greek and Latin Music Theory 1 (Lincoln: University of Nebraska Press, 1984), pp. 70–3.

2 'Musica ficta nisi necessitate cogente penitus non utamur.' Ugolino of Orvieto, *Declaratio musicae disciplinae*, ed. A. Seay, Corpus Scriptorum de Musica 7, vol. II (n.p.: American Institute of Musicology, 1960), p. 45.

3 'Considerantes antiqui musici diezeugmenon tetrachordum in eius disiunctione a mese cantibus multa offendicula praetendere propter inconsonantiam ipsius tritoni inter .♮. et .F. ut tritus authenticus et plagalis, idest quintus et sextus tonus, supra suam propriam vocem finalem, quae est .F., per diatessaron posset procedere, tetrachordum synemmenon ceteris addiderunt tetrachordis, idest cantum per .b. molle.' Jacques de Liège, *Speculum musicae*, ed. R. Bragard, Corpus Scriptorum de Musica 3, vol. VI (n.p.: American Institute of Musicology, 1973), p. 59. For the date of the treatise, see Ulrich Michels, *Die Musiktraktate des Johannes de Muris*, Beihefte zum Archiv für Musikwissenschaft 8 (Wiesbaden: Franz Steiner, 1970), pp. 50–5.

4 Jacques de Liège, *Speculum musicae*, ed. R. Bragard, pp. 138f.

5 E. de Coussemaker, ed., *Scriptorum de musica medii aevi nova series a gerbertina altera*, vol. IV (Paris: A. Durand, 1876), pp. 200–98.

6 'Igitur secundum expertos hujus scientiae, cum quis in gravibus litteris per naturam modulari inceperit et mutationem in G gravem aut in A acutam faciat, si in c acutam vel in d aut in e acutas ascenderit priusquam in F gravem descendat, per ♮ quadratam cantari debet. Et ista regula per omnes modos habet intelligi tam in gravibus quam in acutis litteris . . . Praeterea si in loco supradicto mutatio fiat et descensio fit in F gravem, antequam ascendatur ad c acutam vel d aut e acutas post mutationem, per b molle in b acuto cantari oportet . . . Exceptis deutero et tetrardo et ejus plagali, in quibus b molle non intrabit. Et sicut dictum est de gravibus, ita intelligendum est de acutis et superacutis.' *Ibid.*, pp. 247f.

7 'Deuteri autem cantus minime b molle recipit. Plaga vero deuteri interdum b

molle possidet, nam cum ascensus fuerit a litteris gravibus ut praedicitur in protho, per b molle modulari oportet. Aut cum descensus fuerit ab acutis litteris ad a acutam vel ad G gravem, et ab eis litteris ascensus ad b acutam, et ab illa descensio fuerit in F gravem, antequam ascendatur in b acutam, per b molle in b acuta cantari debet.' *Ibid.*, p. 248.

8 'Nota quod quandocumque ab vel de sub F-fa-ut ascenditur usque ad b-fa-♮-mi mediate vel immediate, et iterum descenditur usque ad F-fa-ut priusquam ascendatur ad C-sol-fa-ut, debet cantari fa in b-fa-♮-mi per b, nisi cantus finiat in G basso.' *The Berkeley Manuscript. University of California Music Library, MS. 744 (olim Phillipps 4450)*, ed. and trans. O. B. Ellsworth, Greek and Latin Music Theory 2 (Lincoln and London: University of Nebraska Press, 1984), pp. 44f.

9 See, in addition to those mentioned below, Ugolino of Orvieto, *Declaratio musicae disciplinae*, ed. A. Seay, vol. I, pp. 45f, 56f; Johannes Legrense, *Ritus canendi vetustissimus et novus*, ed. Coussemaker, *Scriptorum*, vol. IV, pp. 360f, 371f; Franchinus Gaffurius, *Extractus parvus musice*, ed. F. A. Gallo, Antiquae Musicae Italicae Scriptores 4 (Bologna: Forni, 1969), pp. 82f; John Hothby, *La Caliopea legale* in E. de Coussemaker, ed., *Histoire de l'harmonie au moyen âge* (Paris: Librairie Archéologique de Victor Didron, 1852), pp. 341, 347; *idem, Tractatus quarundam regularum artis musicae*, Ms. Florence, Biblioteca Nazionale Centrale, Palat. 472, fol. 13v; Bartolomeo Ramos de Pareia, *Musica practica*, ed. Johannes Wolf, Publikationen der Internationalen Musikgesellschaft 2 (Leipzig: Breitkopf und Härtel, 1901), pp. 50f; Bonaventura da Brescia, *Brevis collectio artis musicae . . . quae dicitur 'Venturina'*, Ms. Bologna, Civico Museo Bibliografico Musicale, 105 (A57), fol. 18v; *idem, Breviloquium musicale* ([Brescia]: Angelo Britannico, 1497), Chs. 16, 36; Anonymus, *Quaestiones et solutiones*, ed. A. Seay, Critical Texts 2 (Colorado Springs: The Colorado College Music Press, 1977), pp. 3, 16, 28; Andreas Ornithoparchus, *Musice active micrologus* (Leipzig: Valentin Schumann, 1517), Bk I, Chs. 5 and 10; Sebastian z Felsztyna, *Opusculum musice compilatum . . . pro institutione adolescentum in cantu simplici seu gregoriano* (Cracow: Jan Haller, 1517), sig. Diiiv; Pietro Aaron, *Libri tres de institutione harmonica* (Bologna: Benedetto di Ettore, 1516), fols. 12r-12v; Martin Agricola, *Musica choralis deudsch* (Wittenberg: Georg Rhau, 1533), Ch. 8; Stephano Vanneo, *Recanetum de musica aurea* (Rome: Valerius Doricus, 1533), fol. 15r; Giovanni del Lago, *Breve introduttione di musica misurata* (Venice: Brandino e Ottaviano Scotto, 1540), p. 40; Angelo da Picitono, *Fior angelico di musica* (Venice: Agostino Bindoni, 1547), Chs. 28-9; Heinrich Glarean, *Dodecachordon* (Basle: Heinrich Petri, 1547), pp. 19, 22; Juan Bermudo, *El arte Tripharia* (Ossuna: Juan de Leon, 1550), fol. 1 iv.

10 Johannes Tinctoris, *Opera theoretica*, ed. A. Seay, Corpus Scriptorum de Musica 22, vol. I (n.p.: American Insitute of Musicology, 1975), pp. 73f.

11 'Notandum autem quod non solum in hiis duobus tonis tritonus est evitandus, sed etiam in omnibus aliis. Unde regula haec generaliter traditur, quod in quolibet tono si post ascensum ad b fa ♮ mi acutum citius in F fa ut gravem descendatur quam ad C sol fa ut ascendatur, indistincte per b molle canetur.' *Ibid.*, vol. I, p. 74, trans. Albert Seay, Translations 2, rev. edn (Colorado Springs: The Colorado College Music Press, 1976), p. 11. (Translation slightly amended.)

12 *Ibid.*, vol. I, p. 75, ex. 18. See also Ch. 16 (*ibid.*, vol. I, p. 80), where an example described as representing mode 8 gets ♭ in order to avoid the tritone.

13 'Quamvis humana vox tritono mediato possibiliter utatur eam tamen immediate uti, aut est difficile aut impossibile.' *Ibid.*, vol. I, p. 76, trans. A. Seay, p. 14.

14 *Ibid.*, vol. I, p. 76, ex. 21.

15 'Tritonus immediatus semper causat disiunctas, ut si ab *f* fiat saltus usque *c sol-fa-ut* transiens ♮ unica notula, tunc dicitur in *f fa* et in b *fa* ♮ *mi mi* et sequitur *c fa* et tunc disiuncta dicitur, quoniam illud *mi* non sequitur nec dependet ab illo *fa* graviori.' Ramos de Pareia, *Musica Practica*, ed. J. Wolf, p. 37.

16 Nicolaus Burtius, *Florum libellus*, ed. G. Massera, Historiae Musicae Cultores 28 (Florence: Leo S. Olschki, 1975), p. 90.

17 'Sed si post tertium tonum semitonus minor sequatur, tritonus cantari potest cum non sit simplex.' Franciscus de Brugis, 'Opusculum' in G. Massera, *La 'mano musicale perfetta' di Francesco de Brugis dalle prefazioni ai corali di L. A. Giunta, Venezia, 1499–1504*, Historiae Musicae Cultores 18 (Florence: Leo S. Olschki, 1963), p. 82.

18 'Ma el tritono immediato, over incomposito da se per la sua durezza è incantabile cioe cantar non si puote . . . ma el tritono mediato, over composito alcuna volta è cantabile.' Ms. Vatican, lat. 5318, fol. 80v. See also Del Lago, letter to Piero de Justinis, Venice, June 3, 1538, *ibid.*, fols. 102r–102v.

19 Franciscus de Brugis, 'Opusculum' in G. Massera, *La 'mano musicale perfetta' di Francesco de Brugis*, pp. 87f.

20 *Ibid.*, p. 88.

21 Gonzalo Martínez de Bizcargui, *Arte de canto llano et de contrapunto et canto de órgano con proporciones et modos*, ed. A. Seay, Critical Texts 9 (Colorado Springs: The Colorado College Music Press, 1979), pp. 17f.

22 *Ibid.*, p. 19.

23 *Ibid.*, pp. 19f.

24 'Sempre questi tre tuoni continuati l'uno dapoi l'altro, debbono essere mollificati & temperati, pur che non tochino la quinta chorda.' Pietro Aaron, *Toscanello in musica* (Venice: Marchio Sessa, 1539), 'Aggiunta', trans. Peter Bergquist, Translations 4, vol. III (Colorado Springs: The Colorado College Music Press, 1970), p. 14.

25 *Ibid.* See also Aaron, *Lucidario in musica* (Venice: Girolamo Scotto, 1545), Bk I, Oppenione X.

26 Aaron, *Toscanello in musica*, 'Aggiunta'.

27 Aaron, *Lucidario in musica*, Bk I, Oppenione VIII.

28 *Ibid.*, Bk I, Oppenione X.

29 *Ibid.*, fol. 13v.

30 Nicola Vicentino, *L'antica musica ridotta alla moderna prattica* (Rome: Antonio Barré, 1555), fol. 23v.

31 'Si detto Tritono si canta composto, perche non si può cantare incomposto esser-citandolo?' *Ibid.*, fol. 23v.

32 'Ma quelli del Tritono, della Semidiapente, & altri simili non si debbeno usare; si come hanno usato alcuni Moderni, volendo cio attribuire al procedere delle modulationi Chromatiche.' Gioseffo Zarlino, *Le Istitutioni harmoniche* (Venice, 1558), p. 203, trans. G. A. Marco and C. V. Palisca (New Haven: Yale University Press, 1968), p. 110.

33 Prosdocimus de Beldemandis, *Tractatus plane musice*, Ms. Lucca, Biblioteca Governativa, 359, fol. 57r.

34 'Item propter similes causas fuit necessarium mutare la repertum in a acuto in mi, si ascendere volebamus ab F gravi ad B acutum sine tritono.' *Ibid.*

35 *Ibid.*, fol. 57v.

36 Johannes Cochlaeus, *Tetrachordum musices* (Nuremberg: Fridericus Peypus, 1514), sigs. Fr-Fv.
37 *Ibid.*, sig. Fv.
38 'In canticis primi & secundi toni ultra la ad proximam vocem tantum procedendo, sempre fa canitur, si cantus mox relabitur ad Ffaut. Si vero talis per tertiam sive quartam supra alamire elevatur, tunc mi in bfa♮mi modulandum est.' Georg Rhau, *Enchiridion utriusque musicae practicae* (Wittenberg: Georg Rhau, 1538), sig. Ciiijv.
39 'Ubi vero una tamen supra La erit notula, cognomine Fa nuncupabitur.' Vanneo, *Recanetum de musica aurea*, fol. 16r.
40 'Si vocem La, notula quaepiam excesserit, uno tantum intervallo, ea canatur per Fa, sine mutatione, maxime in cantu primi & secundi tonorum.' Nikolaus Listenius, *Musica* (Nuremberg: Iohan. Petreius, 1549), Ch. 5.
41 Loys Bourgeois, *Le droict chemin de musique* (Geneva: [Jean Gérard], 1550), Ch. 2.
42 Heinrich Faber, *Ad musicam practicam introductio* (Nuremberg: Ioannes Montanus and Ulricus Neuber, 1550), Ch. 4.
43 Adrian Petit Coclico, *Compendium musices* (Nuremberg: Ioannes Montanus and Ulricus Neuber, 1552), sig. Dr.
44 Hermann Finck, *Practica musica* (Wittenberg: Haeredes Georgii Rhau, 1556), Bk I, [Ch. 8].
45 Agricola, *Musica choralis deudsch*, Ch. 4.
46 Angelo da Picitono, *Fior angelico di musica*, Ch. 28.
47 'Certo in me partorisce non poca maraviglia, quando considero la trascuraggine di molti, & molti, i quali volendo dar precetti nella frequentata Musica, avolgono in mille errori gli ingegni di coloro che nulla sanno, percioche inconsideratamente danno per ferma regola, che quella nota, overo sillaba, che sara sopra la nota chiamata la, sempre sara pronontiata fa, per la qual vana oppenione inducono il nuovo discepolo a una falsa intelligenza . . . Non sara di necessita in tai discorsi considerare il piu soave, ne il piu duro, eccetto se non vi nascesse la spetie Tritonale, nel qual caso saresti costretto pronontiare la voce fa, sopra la sillaba la . . . perche nel canto piano non se canta per b molle altrimenti, se non per addolcire il Tritono.' Aaron, *Lucidario in musica*, Bk I, Oppenione VIII.
48 'La nota sopra la voce la, non sempre dee essere appellata, & pronontiata fa.' *Ibid.*, fol. 4r.
49 Valuable warnings against the application of the rule to pre-sixteenth-century music have been issued in Margaret Bent, 'Musica Recta and Musica Ficta', *Musica Disciplina*, XXVI (1972), 92 and Andrew Hughes, *Manuscript Accidentals: Ficta in Focus 1350–1450*, Musicological Studies and Documents 27 (n.p.: American Institute of Musicology, 1972), pp. 63f, n. 18.
50 Hothby, *La Caliopea legale*, pp. 341 and 347.
51 See, for example, in addition to the theorists discussed below, Burtius, *Florum libellus*, p. 95; Nicolaus Wollick, *Opus aureum*, ed. K. W. Niemöller, *Die Musica gregoriana des Nicolaus Wollick. Opus aureum, Köln 1501, pars I/II*, Beiträge zur Rheinischen Musikgeschichte 11 (Cologne and Krefeld: Staufen-Verlag, 1955), p. 46; Ornithoparchus, *Musice active micrologus*, Bk I, Chs. 7 and 10; Sebastian z Felsztyna, *Opusculum musice compilatum*, sig. Diiiv; Agricola, *Musica choralis deudsch*, Ch. 8; Del Lago, *Breve introduttione di musica misurata*, p. 40; Angelo da Picitono, *Fior angelico di musica*, Ch. 29; Bermudo, *El arte Tripharia*, fol. 1 iv; Finck, *Practica musica*, Bk I, Ch. 4; Zarlino, *Le Istitutioni harmoniche*, pp. 203 and 287.

52 'Est tamen alia quantitas, quae quasi nihil differt in sono, in quam diapason
dividi potest, utputa tritonus et diapente imperfecta, quae vocatur semidiapente, ut *b f* et *f* ♮, quoniam tanta distantia est inter *b f*, quanta inter *f* ♮ nec
differt practicorum differentia, secus tamen theoricorum, qui differentiam
semitonii speculantur. In sono tamen non minus discors est quam ipse tritonus
immediate considerata . . . Notanter tamen diximus immediate, quoniam, si
per voces intermedias procedatur, tam in ascensu quam in descensu suavis est et
lasciva ut *f e d c b* et e contra *b c d e f*. Non tamen debet cantus quiescere in *f*,
quando ascendit, sed converti ad *e*. Sic et in descensu converti debet ad *c*.'
Ramos de Pareia, *Musica practica*, p. 50.

53 'Potrà similmente usare alle volte: ma non spesso, una modulatione di una
Semidiapente, quando tornarà commodo nello accommodar la modulatione
alle parole, & procederà per le chorde diatoniche naturali del Modo, sopra
ilquale è fondata la cantilena . . . Ma quando vi entrasse alcuna delle chorde
chromatiche (quantunque si ponesse per lo acquisto di alcuna consonanza) non
si debbe usare: Conciosia che tali chorde non furono ritrovate a destruttione
delle buone harmonie, & delli buoni costumi musicali: ma si bene alla loro cos-
truttione, & al loro bene essere.' Zarlino, *Le Istitutioni harmoniche*, p. 236,
trans. G. A. Marco and C. V. Palisca, pp. 173f.

54 Giovanni Maria Lanfranco, *Scintille di musica* (Brescia: Lodovico Britannico,
1533), p. 17.

55 'In cantu non admittitur uno saltu, sed continuato vel descensu vel ascensu.'
Glarean, *Dodecachordon*, p. 20, trans. Clement A. Miller, Musicological
Studies and Documents 6 (n.p.: American Institute of Musicology 1965), p. 60.

56 'Quae uno saltu prope in nullo sint usu'. *Ibid.*, p. 22, trans. C. A. Miller, p. 61.

57 For the tritone, see Jacques de Liège, *Speculum musicae*, ed. R. Bragard,
vol. VI, pp. 59 and 138; *The Berkeley Manuscript*, ed. and trans. O. B. Ellsworth, pp. 44f; Pseudo-Tunstede, *Quatuor principalia musicae* in E. de Coussemaker, ed., *Scriptorum*, vol. IV, pp. 215, 247ff; Ugolino of Orvieto, *Declaratio
musicae disciplinae*, ed. A. Seay, vol. I, pp. 18 and 26; Johannes Legrense, *Ritus
canendi vetustissimus et novus* in E. de Coussemaker, ed., *Scriptorum*, vol. IV,
p. 360; Johannes Tinctoris, *Liber de natura et proprietate tonorum* in *Opera
theoretica*, ed. A. Seay, vol. I (n.p.: American Institute of Musicology, 1975),
pp. 73–6 and 80; Nicolaus Burtius, *Florum libellus*, ed. G. Massera, pp. 90 and
95; Franchinus Gaffurius, *Extractus parvus musice*, ed. F. A. Gallo, p. 82;
Bonaventura da Brescia, *Brevis collectio artis musicae . . . quae dicitur 'Venturina'*, Ms. Bologna, Civico Museo Bibliografico Musicale, 105 (A57), fol. 18v;
Anonymus, *Quaestiones et solutiones*, ed. A. Seay, pp. 3 and 28; Franciscus de
Brugis, 'Opusculum' in G. Massera, *La 'mano musicale perfetta' di Francesco de
Brugis*, pp. 87f; Giovanni Spataro, *Bartolomei Rami pareie honesta defensio in
Nicolai Burtii parmensis opusculum* (Bologna: Plato de Benedecti, 1491), fols.
25v–26r; Pietro Aaron, *Libri tres de institutione harmonica*, fols. 12r–12v; *idem*,
Toscanello in musica, 'Aggiunta'; *idem*, *Lucidario in musica*, Bk I, Oppenioni
VIII and X; fols. 13r–13v; Stephano Vanneo, *Recanetum de musica aurea*, fols.
15r, 24v; Angelo da Picitono, *Fior angelico di musica*, Chs. 28–9; Juan Bermudo,
El arte Tripharia, fol. 13r; Ghiselin Danckerts, *Trattato sopra una differentia
musicale*, Ms. Rome, Biblioteca Vallicelliana, R.56, fol. 407r; Pietro Cinciarino, *Introduttorio abbreviato di musica piana, o vero canto fermo* (Venice:
Domenico de' Farri, 1555), fol. 9r. For the diminished fifth, see Burtius, *Florum
libellus*, ed. G. Massera, pp. 91 and 123; Cinciarino, *Introdultorio abbreviato di
musica piana*, fol. 9r. For non-harmonic relations corrected by flats in trans-

posed systems, see Tinctoris, *Liber de natura et proprietate tonorum*, ed. Seay, pp. 75f and ex. 20; Bonaventura da Brescia, *Breviloquium musicale*, Ch. 16; Anonymus, *Quaestiones et solutiones*, ed. A. Seay, p. 16; Franciscus de Brugis, 'Opusculum' in G. Massera, *La 'mano musicale perfetta' di Francesco de Brugis*, pp. 87f; Gonzalo Martínez de Bizcargui, *Arte de canto llano*, ed. A. Seay, pp. 16-24; Sebastian z Felsztyna, *Opusculum musice compilatum*, sig. Diiiv; Angelo da Picitono, *Fior angelico di musica*, Ch. 29.

58 Franchinus Gaffurius, *Theorica musice* (Milan: Ioannes Petrus de Lomatio, 1492), Bk V, Ch. 5.

59 'Ubi autem & quoties evenerit seccandus tonus ad delibandam asperitatem tritoni nullo unquam pacto maius semitonium minori praeponere licebit.' *Ibid.*

60 John Hothby, *La Caliopea legale* in E. de Coussemaker, ed., *Histoire de l'harmonie au moyen âge*, pp. 342f, n. 1.

61 Bonaventura da Brescia, *Breviloquium musicale*, Ch. 17. Bonaventura's text is closely imitated in the anonymous *Quaestiones et solutiones*, ed. A. Seay, p. 17.

62 'Si come il, b, molle nelle Cantilene del, ♮, quadro si usa per fuggir i Tritoni, cosi il Diesis, col qual medesimamente la durezza del Tritono si puo addolcire: si prattica in ciascun ordine, per formar piu soavi Consonanze.' Giovanni Maria Lanfranco, *Scintille di musica*, p. 126, (my italics).

63 Jacques de Liège, *Speculum musicae*, ed. R. Bragard vol. VI, pp. 59f and 138f. Various, or all, elements of this doctrine can be found, for example, in Marchetto da Padova, *Lucidarium in arte musicae planae* in Jan W. Herlinger, *The Lucidarium of Marchetto of Padua. A Critical Edition, Translation and Commentary*, Ph.D. diss., The University of Chicago, 1978, pp. 580-6, 628, 634, 640ff, 650-4, 668, 674, 688, 706; Pseudo-Tunstede, *Quatuor principalia musicae* in Coussemaker, *Scriptorum*, vol. IV, pp. 247ff; Ugolino of Orvieto, *Declaratio musicae disciplinae*, ed. Seay, vol. I, pp. 159-65; John Hothby, *Tractatus quarundam regularum artis musicae*, Ms. Florence, Biblioteca Nazionale Centrale, Palat. 472, fol. 13v; Gaffurius, *Extractus parvus musice*, pp. 104f; Burtius, *Florum libellus*, ed. G. Massera, p. 91; Adam von Fulda, *Musica* in M. Gerbert, ed., *Scriptores ecclesiastici de musica sacra potissimum*, vol. III (St Blasien: Typis San Blasianis, 1784), p. 357; Martínez de Bizcargui, *Arte de canto llano*, ed. A. Seay, p. 18; Nicolaus Wollick, *Enchiridion musices* (Paris: Francoys Regnault, 1512), Pt II, Ch. 5; Martin Agricola, *Musica choralis deudsch*, Ch. 9; *idem*, *Rudimenta musices* (Wittenberg: Georg Rhau, 1539), Ch. 2; Johannes Aventinus, *Musicae rudimenta, Augsburg, 1516*, ed. and trans. T. H. Keahey, Musical Theorists in Translation 10 (Brooklyn: Institute of Mediaeval Music, 1971), p. 27; Andreas Ornithoparchus, *Musice active micrologus*, Bk I, Chs. 5 and 11; Sebastian z Felsztyna, *Opusculum musice compilatum*, sig. Diiir; Pietro Aaron, *Trattato della natura et cognitione di tutti gli tuoni di canto figurato non da altrui piu scritti* (Venice: Bernardino de Vitali, 1525), Ch. 6; *idem*, *Lucidario in musica*, Bk I, Oppenione X; Vanneo, *Recanetum de musica aurea*, fol. 15r; Angelo da Picitono, *Fior angelico di musica*, Chs. 28, 52-3; Heinrich Glarean, *Dodecachordon*, pp. 31, 72, 92f, 129ff; Bermudo, *El arte Tripharia*, fol. 13r; Nicola Vicentino, *L'antica musica ridotta alla moderna prattica*, fol. 56v.

64 Margaret Bent, 'Musica Recta and Musica Ficta', 73-100; Andrew Hughes, *Manuscript Accidentals*, pp. 18, 48 and *passim*.

65 Bent, 'Musica Recta and Musica Ficta', p. 83.

66 'Ficta musica nunquam ponenda est nisi loco neccessitatis.' Prosdocimus de Beldemandis, *Contrapunctus*, ed. and trans. J. Herlinger, pp. 72f. See Bent,

'Musica Recta and Musica Ficta', pp. 83f; Hughes, *Manuscript Accidentals*, p. 18.

67 'Secunda regula est hec, quod ficta musica inventa est solum propter consonantiam aliquam colorandam, que consonantia aliter colorari non posset quam per fictam musicam.' Prosdocimus, *Contrapunctus*, ed. and trans. J. Herlinger, pp. 72f.

68 *Ibid.*, pp. 94f. I quote and discuss the passage in Chapter 5(ii) below.

69 'Denique sciendum quod non solum in tonis regularibus et vera musica secundum exempla praemissa tritonum praedictis modis fugere ac eo uti debemus, verum etiam in irregularibus tonis et musica ficta.' Tinctoris, *Liber de natura et proprietate tonorum*, ed. A. Seay, pp. 75f, trans. A. Seay, Translations 2, rev. edn (Colorado Springs: The Colorado College Music Press, 1976), p. 13.

70 Bonaventura da Brescia, *Breviloquium musicale*, Ch. 16. The passage is reproduced in the anonymous *Quaestiones et solutiones*, ed. A. Seay, p. 16.

71 See, for example, Nicolaus Wollick, *Opus aureum* in K. W. Niemöller, ed., *Die Musica gregoriana des Nicolaus Wollick*, p. 46; Andreas Ornithoparchus, *Musice active micrologus*, Bk I, Chs. 7 and 10; Sebastian z Felsztyna, *Opusculum musice compilatum*, sig. Diiiv; Martin Agricola, *Musica choralis doudsch*, Ch. 8; Giovanni del Lago, *Breve introduttione di musica misurata*, p. 40; Pietro Aaron, *Lucidario in musica*, fol. 30r; Angelo da Picitono, *Fior angelico di musica*, Ch. 29; Hermann Finck, *Practica musica*, Bk I, Ch. 4; Gioseffo Zarlino, *Le Istitutioni harmoniche*, pp. 236f.

72 See, for example, Jacques de Liège, *Speculum musicae*, ed. R. Bragard, p. 60; Pseudo-Tunstede, *Quatuor principalia musicae* in E. de Coussemaker, ed., *Scriptorum*, vol. IV, p. 215; Bartolomeo Ramos de Pareia, *Musica practica*, ed. J. Wolf, pp. 66 and 99f; Franchinus Gaffurius, *Extractus parvus musice*, ed. F. A. Gallo, 1969), p. 78; *idem*, *Theorica musice*, Bk V, Ch. 5; Franciscus de Brugis, 'Opusculum' in G. Massera, *La 'mano musicale perfetta' di Francesco de Brugis*, pp. 74 and 78; Ornithoparchus, *Musice active micrologus*, Bk I, Ch. 6.

73 'Uno saltu prope in nullo sint usu . . . prorsus evitanda'. Heinrich Glarean, *Dodecachordon*, p. 22, trans. A. Miller, p. 61.

74 'Quem quidem transitum quoniam difficilis & admodum dissonus est: omni solertia devitandum musicorum scola precepit: . . . Dissonum huiusmodi permutationis transitum . . . urgente notularum dispositione fieri necesse est.' Gaffurius, *Practica musice*, Bk I, Ch. 4, trans. C. A. Miller, p. 40.

75 'Per se non si prononza, benche alcuni habbiano tal falso parere.' Aaron, *Lucidario in musica*, fol. 30v.

76 'Habbiamo piu volte considerato una non buona oppenione di alcuni compositori, i quali ne lor concenti figurano in una riga, o Spatio due Brevi, o Semibrevi, delle quali l'una sara sospesa, overo sostentata, & l'altra naturalmente procedera, Et questo intenderai in tutte le corde, o positioni, dove il segno del b giacente havra signoria, come nel, C, nel F, & nel G, et come la figura chiaramente dimostra.' *Ibid.*, fol. 8v.

77 *Ibid.*, fol. 9r.

78 Ramos de Pareia, *Musica practica*, ed. J. Wolf, p. 66.

79 'Propter aliquam dissonantiam colorandam supple tertiam, sextam, sive decimam tendendo ad aliquam consonantiam'. Marchetto da Padova, *Lucidarium in arte musicae planae* in J. W. Herlinger, *The Lucidarium of Marchetto of Padua*, p. 245.

80 *Ibid.*, pp. 245–9.

81 *Ibid.*, pp. 249–57.

82 'Permutatio est variatio nominis vocis seu notae in eodem spatio seu linea in diverso sono. Fit enim permutatio ubi tonus dividitur propter consonantiam in diatonicum et enharmonicum aut in chromaticum et diesim vel e converso, ut hic.' *Ibid.*, pp. 430-3.

83 John Hothby, *Tractatus quarundam regularum artis musicae*, Ms. Florence, Biblioteca Nazionale Centrale, Palat. 472, fol. 10r. The same information, though framed in Marchettan terms, is conveyed in Gaffurius, *Extractus parvus musicae*, ed. F. A. Gallo, p. 70.

84 'Questo Semituono, ancorache non si adoperi nelle modulationi del genere Diatonico; si ritrova tuttavia esser stato usato alcune fiate da i Compositori nelle lor cantilene.' Zarlino, *Le Istitutioni harmoniche*, p. 170, trans. G. A. Marco and C. V. Palisca, p. 48.

85 'Se el ♮. del primo no fusse troppo apresso ad A del secondo. perche allora discordarebbe .♮. ad A. et cosi per il contrario. Et di questo essere piu presso o. si o non. lo audito sara iudice. Ma piu apresso non possono essere che intra loro cada una sola voce.' Hothby, *Tractatus quarundam regularum artis musicae*, Ms. Florence, Biblioteca Nazionale Centrale, Palat. 472, fol. 13v.

86 See, for example, Georg Rhau, *Enchiridion utriusque musicae practicae*, sig. Dv.

87 Domingo Marcos Durán, *Lux bella* (Sevilla, 1492), [p. 6]; *idem*, *Comento sobre Lux bella* (Salamanca: [Juan de Porras,] 1498), [p. 59.]

88 'Dico che a forza tu sei astretto eleggere fra dui mali il manco incommodo, de liquali sara il dire del proprio mi di detto b ♮ acuto, quantunque sia manco errore a commettere un diapente imperfetto, che non e a commettere un tritono.' Pietro Aaron, *Toscanello in musica*, 'Aggiunta', trans. P. Bergquist, p. 15.

89 'Dicendo fa nel ♮ mi acuto, con ilqual fa, non mai rettamente discendera al vero suono di quella voce mi.' *Ibid.*, trans. P. Bergquist, p. 14.

90 See Edward E. Lowinsky, *Secret Chromatic Art in the Netherlands Motet* (New York: Columbia University Press, 1946). For critical reactions, see the reviews of the book by W. Apel, *The Musical Quarterly*, XXXII (1946), 471-6; M. van Crevel, *Tijdschrift van de Vereniging voor Nederlandse Muziekgeschiedenis*, XVI (1946), 253-304; A. Einstein, *Notes*, III (1946), 283f; L. Schrade, *Journal of Renaissance and Baroque Music*, I (1946), 159-67; J. A. Westrup, *Music and Letters*, XXVII (1946), 268; C. van den Borren, *Revue belge de musicologie*, II (1948), 38-43; F. Lesure, *Revue musicale*, CCXXI (1953), 7f. See also Ludwig Finscher, 'Zu den Schriften Edward E. Lowinskys', *Die Musikforschung*, XV (1962), 54-77; Willem Elders, *Studien zur Symbolik in der Musik der alten Niederländer* (Bilthoven: A. B. Creyghton, 1968), pp. 165-91; E. E. Lowinsky, '*Secret Chromatic Art* Re-Examined' in B. S. Brook, E. O. D. Downes and S. Van Solkema, eds., *Perspectives in Musicology. The Inaugural Lectures of the Ph.D. Program in Music at the City University of New York* (New York: Norton, 1972), pp. 91-135.

91 For illuminating discussions of such experiments, see especially Edward E. Lowinsky, 'Adrian Willaert's Chromatic "Duo" Re-Examined', *Tijdschrift van de Vereniging voor Nederlandse Muziekgeschiedenis*, XVIII (1956), 1-36 and *idem*, 'Matthaeus Greiter's *Fortuna*: An Experiment in Chromaticism and in Musical Iconography', *The Musical Quarterly*, XLII (1956), 500-19; XLIII (1957), 68-85.

92 Lowinsky, *Secret Chromatic Art*, ex. 56 and pp. 84ff.

93 Lowinsky, 'Matthaeus Greiter's *Fortuna*', ex. 7 and pp. 78ff.

94 Lowinsky, *Secret Chromatic Art*, p. 84.
95 Lowinsky, 'Matthaeus Greiter's *Fortuna*', pp. 79f.
96 Aaron, *Lucidario in musica*, Bk I, Oppenione X.
97 Franchinus Gaffurius, *Theorica musice*, Bk V, Ch. 5; Stephano Vanneo, *Recanetum de musica aurea*, fol. 91r; Aaron, *Lucidario in musica*, fol. 30v.
98 'Per quartam, quintam, simul octavam, fuge saltum/ Ad mi manantem de fa, nec non viceversa/ Si talis quando saltus tibi veneri ipsum/ De mi duc ad mi, de fa salubrium ad fa.' Rhau, *Enchiridion utriusque musicae practicae*, sig. Dv. See also Sebastian z Felsztyna, *Opusculum musice compilatum*, sig. Diiiv.
99 'Il :mi: contra il :fa: ne in quarta ne in quinta: & manco in ottava non ha sonorita alcuna: ne processo naturale.' Giovanni Maria Lanfranco, *Scintille di musica*, p. 17, trans. Barbara Lee, *Giovanni Maria Lanfranco's 'Scintille di musica' and its Relation to 16th-Century Music Theory*, Ph.D. diss., Cornell University, 1961, p. 90. See also Glarean, *Dodecachordon*, p. 21.

5 Vertical and cross relations

1 Philippe de Vitry, *Ars nova*, ed. G. Reaney, A. Gilles and J. Maillard, Corpus Scriptorum de Musica 8 (n.p.: American Institute of Musicology, 1964), p. 22.
2 Petrus frater dictus Palma ociosa, *Compendium de discantu mensurabili* in Johannes Wolf, 'Ein Beitrag zur Diskantlehre des 14. Jahrhunderts', *Sammelbände der Internationalen Musikgesellschaft*, XV (1913–14), 514.
3 *Ibid.*, p. 515.
4 *Ibid.*, p. 516.
5 See, for example, Gioseffo Zarlino, *Le Istitutioni harmoniche* (Venice, 1558), pp. 169ff.
6 'Nequaquam de prodictis consonancijs possumus facere *mi* contra *fa*, nec *fa* contra *mi*.' Philippus de Caserta, *Regule contrapuncti* in Nigel Wilkins, 'Some Notes on Philipoctus de Caserta (*c.* 1360?–*c.* 1435)', *Nottingham Mediaeval Studies*, VIII (1964), 96.
7 *Ibid.*, p. 99.
8 'In combinationibus perfecte consonantibus nunquam ponere debemus mi contra fa, nec e contra, quoniam statim ipsas vocum combinationes perfecte consonantes minores vel maximas constitueremus, que discordantes sunt.' Prosdocimus de Beldemandis, *Contrapunctus*, ed. and trans. J. Herlinger, Greek and Latin Music Theory I (Lincoln and London: University of Nebraska Press, 1984), pp. 62–5.
9 'Sexta et ultima regula pro noticia collocationis horum duorum signorum in contrapuncto, scilicet b rotundi et ♮ quadri, est hec, quod octavis, quintis, et sibi similibus ponenda sunt hec signa secundum quod oportet addere vel diminuere ad ipsas reducendum ad bonas consonantias, si prius forent dissonantes, eo quod tales combinationes in contrapuncto semper maiores sive consonantes esse debent.' *Ibid.*, pp. 78–81.
10 See, for example, Ugolino of Orvieto, *Declaratio musicae disciplinae*, ed. A. Seay, Corpus Scriptorum de Musica 7, vol. II (n.p.: American Institute of Musicology, 1960), pp. 31, 44–7; Anonymus XI, *Tractatus de musica plana et mensurabili* in E. de Coussemaker, ed., *Scriptorum de musica medii aevi nova series a gerbertina altera*, vol. III (Paris: A. Durand, 1869), p. 463; Anonymus II, *Tractatus de discantu*, ed. A. Seay, Critical Texts with Translation I (Colorado Springs: The Colorado College Music Press, 1978), pp. 28, 32; Anonymus, *Quot sunt concordationes* in Coussemaker, *Scriptorum*, vol. III,

pp. 71f; Anonymus, *Regole di far contrapuncto di nota per nota*, Ms. London, British Museûm, Add. 36986, fol. 27v; Anonymus, *Regule contrapuncti secundum usum Regni Siciliae* in Paolo Nalli, '*Regulae contrapuncti secundum usum Regni Siciliae* tratte da un codice siciliano del Sec. XV', *Archivio storico per la Sicilia Orientale*, 2nd series, IX (1933), 287; Anonymus, *Tractatus de musica figurata et de contrapuncto* in Coussemaker, *Scriptorum*, vol. IV, p. 446; Johannes Tinctoris, *Liber de natura et proprietate tonorum* in *Opera theoretica*, ed. A. Seay, Corpus Scriptorum de Musica 22, vol. I (n.p.: American Institute of Musicology, 1975), pp. 73ff, 81; Bartolomeo Ramos de Pareia, *Musica practica*, ed. J. Wolf, Publikationen der Internationalen Musikgesellschaft 2 (Leipzig: Breitkopf und Härtel, 1901), p. 74; Nicolaus Burtius, *Florum libellus*, ed. G. Massera, Historiae Musicae Cultores 28 (Florence: Leo S. Olschki, 1975), p. 122; John Hothby, *Regule dil contrapuncto* in *Hothby, De arte contrapuncti*, ed. G. Reaney, Corpus Scriptorum de Musica 26 (n.p.: American Institute of Musicology, 1977), p. 74; *idem, Regulae supra contrapunctum, ibid.*, p. 101; *idem, Spetie tenore del contrapunto prima, ibid.*, p. 85; Guillelmus Monachus, *De preceptis artis musicae*, ed. A. Seay, Corpus Scriptorum de Musica 11 (n.p.: American Institute of Musicology, 1965), p. 35; Franchinus Gaffurius, *Extractus parvus musice*, ed. F. A. Gallo, Antiquae Musicae Italicae Scriptores 4 (Bologna: Forni, 1969), pp. 119, 128; Guillaume Guerson, *Utilissime musicales regule* (Paris: François Regnault, 1526), sig. Ciiv; Andreas Ornithoparchus, *Musice active micrologus* (Leipzig: Valentin Schumann, 1517), Bk I, Ch. 10 and Bk IV, Ch. 4; Giovanni del Lago, *Breve introduttione di musica misurata* (Venice: Brandino e Ottaviano Scotto, 1540), p. 35; Pietro Aaron, *Libri tres de institutione harmonica* (Bologna: Benedetto di Ettore, 1516), fol. 41r; Stephano Vanneo, *Recanetum de musica aurea* (Rome: Valerius Doricus, 1533), fols. 15r, 74v.

11 'Quod discordantiae quas falsas concordantias vocant omnino sunt evitandae.' Johannes Tinctoris, *Liber de arte contrapuncti* in *Opera theoretica*, vol. II, p. 143, trans. Albert Seay, Musicological Studies and Documents 5 (n.p.: American Institute of Musicology, 1961), p. 130.

12 'Porro quaecumque superius de praemissu ac ordinatione discordantiarum conscripsimus, non de discordantiis quas falsas concordantias alii nuncupant, intelligenda esse quisquis claro pollet ingenio facillime comprehendit. Quippe et falsum unisonum et falsum diapente et falsum diapason et quamlibet aliam falsam concordantiam per defectum aut superabundantiam semitonii maioris effectam evitare debemus. Id enim est quod in primis a magistris scholaribus praecipitur, ne mi contra fa in concordantiis perfectis admittant. Verumtamen saepissime apud infinitos compositores etiam celeberrimos oppositum comperi, ut apud Faugues in *Missa Le serviteur*, apud Busnois in carmine *Je ne demande* et apud Caron etiam in uno carmine quod dicitur *Hellas*, sicut hic patet.' *Ibid.*, pp. 143f, trans. A. Seay, p. 130.

13 Guillaume Faugues, 'Qui tollis' of *Missa Le serviteur, Collected Works*, ed. G. C. Schuetze, Jr (Brooklyn: Institute of Mediaeval Music, 1960), pp. 17f, mm. 71-82; Antoine Busnois, *Je ne demande*, Ottaviano dei Petrucci, publ., *Harmonice musices Odhecaton A*, ed. H. Hewitt (Cambridge: Mediaeval Academy of America, 1942), p. 311, mm. 19-23; Philippe Caron, *Hélas! que pourra devenir!*, *Les Oeuvres complètes*, ed. J. Thomson, vol. II (Brooklyn: The Institute of Mediaeval Music, n.d.), p. 177.

14 'Concordantiae vero perfectae quae per semitonium chromaticum, hoc est per sustentionem aut imperfectae aut superfluae efficientur etiam sunt evitandae,

licet et his uti supra totam aut dimidiam aut maiorem partem notae mensuram dirigentis, et perfectionem immediate praecedentis omnes fere compositores in compositione trium aut plurium partium, ut in sequentibus exemplis patet expertus sum.' Tinctoris, *Liber de arte contrapuncti* in *Opera theoretica*, vol. II, pp. 144f, trans. A. Seay, Musicological Studies and Documents 5, p. 131.

15 Ms. Vatican, lat. 5318, fols. 102v–103r.

16 'Ma credo che che vostra Reverentia la ha signata solamente accioche in tale loco si dica mi, per non fare quella quinta diminuta. dico che saria stato meglio havere segnato il b rotondo in quel luoco che la croce la qual representa (dico secondo il volgo cieco) il b quadro giacente. il proprio de la quinta imperfetta, over diminuta è andare alla terza, massime quando immediate una parte ascende, et l'altra descende.' *Ibid.*, fol. 103r.

17 'Tristanus vero de Silva in quinta, ut ait, non prohibetur taliter, quoniam potest fieri quinta post quintam, dum tamen una sit semidiapente, alia vero diapente, sicut reperimus in cantilena *Sois emprantis* et in aliis antiquioribus. Sed hoc non est concedendum in integris, bene tamen in fractis, idest in diminutione notularum.' Ramos de Pareia, *Musica practica*, ed. J. Wolf, p. 65.

18 Walter Frye, *Collected Works*, ed. S. W. Kenney, Corpus Mensurabilis Musicae 19 (n.p.: American Institute of Musicology, 1960), pp. 5f. The two passages have been identified in Gustave Reese, *Music in the Renaissance*, rev. edn (New York: Norton, 1959), p. 93, n. 302.

19 'Quello antico canto chiamato Soys emprantis.' Pietro Aaron, *Lucidario in musica* (Venice: Girolamo Scotto, 1545), fol. 7v.

20 *Ibid.*

21 'Nelle note intere, ma nelle parti minute del tempo, come [q]ui, cioè di Minima, & di Semiminima.' *Ibid.*

22 'Nonnulli tamen sunt arbitrati duas quintas simul ascendentes vel descendentes pronuntiari posse: modo diversis protensae sint quantitatibus & intervallis: una scilicet perfecta: altera subtractione vel defectu semitonij diminuta: puta procedendo ab Are ad Elami: sive a proslambanomene ad hypatenmeson: Inde subsequenter & immediate ascendendo a ♮mi gravi ad Ffaut: sive ab hypate-hypaton: ad parhypatenmeson.' Franchinus Gaffurius, *Practica musice* (Milan: Ioannes Petrus de Lomatio, 1496), sig. ddiv, trans. Clement A. Miller, Musicological Studies and Documents 20 (n.p.: American Institute of Musicology, 1968), p. 125 (translation slightly amended).

23 Ms. Vatican, lat. 5318, fol. 228r.

24 Aaron, *Lucidario in musica*, fols. 6v–7v.

25 *Ibid.*, fol. 7r.

26 Pietro Aaron, *Compendiolo di molti dubbi, segreti et sentenze intorno al canto fermo, et figurato* (Milan: Io. Antonio da Castelliono, n.d. [after 1545]), Ch. 68.

27 'Massimamente quando havra la terza, overo la decima nella parte grave, come seguitando si vede'. Aaron, *Lucidario in musica*, fol. 14r.

28 'Nisi nota fuerit ligata'. Adrian Petit Coclico, *Compendium musices* (Nuremberg: Ioannes Montanus and Ulricus Neuber, 1552), sig. [Iivv], trans. Albert Seay, Translations 5 (Colorado Springs: The Colorado College Music Press, 1973), p. 22.

29 'Facere fa contra mi, apposito b molli'. *Ibid.*, sigs. [Livv]-Mr, trans. A. Seay, p. 25 and ex. 63.

30 'Secundum doctrinam Iosquini de Pratis'. *Ibid.*, sig. [Iivr], trans. A. Seay, p. 21.

31 Luigi Dentice, *Duo dialoghi della musica* (Rome: Vincenzo Lucrino, 1553), fol. [39r].

32 *Ibid.*, fols. [39r–39v].

33 'Questa quarta constituita a questo modo mi piaceva molto, ma non m'ho fidato di me medesimo a tenere ch'ella potesse stare, infino a tanto che molti valenti huomini me n'hanno fatto certo.' *Ibid.*, fol. [39v].

34 'I Musici prattici più periti diedero una Regola, per schivar questi errori, Che non si dovesse mai porre la voce del Mi contra quella del Fa, nelle consonanze perfette.' Zarlino, *Le Istitutioni harmoniche*, p. 169, trans. Guy A. Marco and Claude V. Palisca (New Haven: Yale University Press, 1968), p. 47 (translation slightly amended).

35 'Si debbe però avertire, che alle volte si pone la Semidiapente ne i Contrapunti in luogo della Diapente; similmente il Tritono in luogo della Diatessaron, che fanno buoni effetti.' *Ibid.*, pp. 169f, trans. G. A. Marco and C. V. Palisca, p. 47.

36 'In qual maniera si habbiano a porre'. *Ibid.*, p. 170, trans. G. A. Marco and C. V. Palisca, p. 47.

37 'Potremo usare alle volte la Semidiapente in una istessa percussione; & ciò faremo, quando immediatamente da esse verremo al Ditono; come nello essempio vedemo: Percioche le parti si possono mutar tra loro senza alcun discommodo; come nello essempio di sotto si vede. Et questo si osserva da i migliori Musici moderni, come è stato etiandio osservato per il passato da alcuni delli più antichi. Ne solamente sarà lecito usare la Semidiapente: ma il Tritono anco alle volte, si come vederemo al suo luogo. Si debbe però avertire, che quelle parti, che haveranno la Semidiapente, overo il Tritono, debbino havere primieramente avanti la Diapente senza alcun mezo, una consonanza, sia poi perfetta, overo imperfetta, che questo non fa cosa alcuna: percioche dalla consonanza precedente, & dalla seguente, la detta Semidiapente viene a temperarsi di maniera, che non fa tristo effetto, anzi buono; come si prova con la esperienza.' *Ibid.*, pp. 180f, trans. G. A. Marco and C. V. Palisca, pp. 67f.

38 'Usaremo etiandio la Quarta sincopata, dopo laquale segua senza alcun mezo la Semidiapente, & dopo questa immediatamente succeda la Terza maggiore: Percioche la Semidiapente è posta in tal maniera, che fà buono effetto: essendo che tra le parti non si ode alcuna trista relatione.' *Ibid.*, pp. 197f, trans. G. A. Marco and C. V. Palisca, pp. 97f.

39 'Ma si debbe avertire, che in uno essempio, cioè nel primo si contiene il Tritono, & nel secondo la Semidiapente; liquali tanto più sono sopportabili, quanto che dopo sè hanno l'uno la Terza, & l'altro la Decima maggiori, che fanno relatione harmonica con le voci, che contengono il Tritono, over la Semidiapente. Et se bene gli intervalli, che sono nelle seconde figure delli mostrati essempi, sono veramente dissonanti; tuttavia sono in tal maniera collocati, che per il loro procedere, secondo l'ordine mostrato nelle Regole, se ne passano di maniera, che l'udito se ne contenta.' *Ibid.*, p. 248, trans. G. A. Marco and C. V. Palisca, p. 197 (translation and example slightly amended).

40 'Pongono i Prattici alle volte il Tritono tra due parti, ilquale casca sopra la seconda parte di alcuna semibreve sincopata, posta nel grave in cotal maniera; Ilquale si ode nella relatione delle parti: ma non è percossa l'una delle parti acute con la parte grave da tale intervallo. Et perche le parti procedeno in cotal modo, & sono concatenate tra loro di maniera, che senza partirsi dalla osservanza delle regole date, fanno buono effetto.' *Ibid.*, pp. 248f, trans. G. A. Marco and C. V. Palisca, pp. 197f.

41 'Una Diapason superflua, o . . . una Semidiapason; overamente . . . una Semidiapente, o . . . un Tritono, o altre simili.' *Ibid.*, p. 179, trans. G. A. Marco and C. V. Palisca, p. 65.

42 'Onde accioche le nostre compositioni siano pugate da ogni errore, & accioche siano corrette, cercaremo di fuggire tale relatione; massimamente quando componeremo a due voci: percioche genera alle purgate orecchie alquanto di fastidio: conciosia che simili intervalli non si ritrovano esser collocati tra i numeri sonori, et non si cantano in alcuno genere, sia qual si voglia; ancora che alcuni habbiano havuto contraria opinione: ma sia come si voglia, sono molto difficili da cantrare, et fanno tristo effetto. Et molto mi meraviglio di costoro, che non si habbiano punto schivato, di far cantare in alcuna delle parti delle lor cantilene alcuno di questi intervalli; ne mi sò imaginare, per qual regione l'habbiano fatto. Et anchorache sia minor male, il ritrovarlo per relatione tra due parti, & tra due modulationi, che udirlo nella modulatione di alcuna parte; tuttavia quel male istesso, che si ode in una parte, si ritrova diviso tra due, et è quella istessa offesa dell'udito: Percioche nulla, o poco rileva l'essere offeso di uno istesso colpo più da uno, che da molti, quando il male non è minore. Questi intervalli adunque, che nel modulare non si ammettono, si debbeno schivare di porli nelle cantilene di maniera, che si odino per relationi tra le parti; . . . E ben vero, che nelle compositioni di più voci molte volte è impossibile di poterli schivare, & di non incorrere in simili intrichi: . . . Ma quando la necessità ne astringesse, dovemo almeno haver riguardo, che tale diffetto si commetta nelle chorde diatoniche, & in quelle, che sono propie & naturali del Modo, & non tra quelle, che sono accidentali, cioè tra quelle, che nel mezo delle cantilene si segnano con questi segni ♮, ♯, & b: percioche allora non generano tanto tristo effetto.' *Ibid.*, pp. 179f, trans. G. A. Marco and C. V. Palisca, pp. 65ff.

43 *Ibid.*, pp. 177f.

44 Nicola Vicentino, *L'antica musica ridotta alla moderna prattica* (Rome: Antonio Barrè, 1555), fol. 34v. See also *ibid.*, fols. 36v, 83v.

45 'Eadem ratione nec bene sonare, si vel duae sextae maiores aut duae minores aut duae eadem ratione tertiae maiores aut minores, quod observavit optimè Adrianus, iunctae erant . . . admittitur tamen à plerisque hoc.' Hieronymus Cardanus, *De musica* in *Opera*, vol. X (Lyons: Ioannes Antonius Huguetan and Marcus Ravaud, 1663), p. 106, trans. Clement A. Miller, Musicological Studies and Documents 32 (n.p.: American Institute of Musicology, 1973), p. 42.

46 Johannes Boen, *Musica* in Wolf Frobenius, *Johannes Boens Musica und seine Konsonanzlehre*, Freiburger Schriften zur Musikwissenschaft 2 (Stuttgart: Musikwissenschaftliche Verlags-Gesellschaft mbH, 1971), p. 68.

47 James Haar, 'False Relations and Chromaticism in Sixteenth-Century Music', *Journal of the American Musicological Society*, XXX (1977), 391-418. See also Jaap van Benthem, 'Fortuna in Focus: Concerning "Conflicting" Progressions in Josquin's *Fortuna dun gran tempo*', *Tijdschrift van de Vereniging voor Nederlandse Muziekgeschiedenis*, XXX (1980), 1-50; Thomas Noblitt, 'Chromatic Cross-Relations and Editorial *Musica Ficta* in Masses of Obrecht', *ibid.*, XXXII (1982), 30-44; Robert Toft, 'Pitch Content and Modal Procedure in Josquin's *Absalon, fili mi*', *ibid.*, XXXIII (1983), 3-27.

48 'Ratione concordantiarum perfectarum'. Johannes Tinctoris, *Liber de natura et proprietate tonorum* in *Opera theoretica*, ed. A. Seay, vol. I, p. 73, trans. Albert Seay, Translations 2, rev. edn (Colorado Springs: Colorado College Music Press, 1976), p. 10.

49 'Ratione tritoni evitandi'. *Ibid.*

50 *Ibid.*, pp. 73f; see also p. 81.

51 See, for example, in addition to those mentioned below, Nicolaus Burtius, *Florum libellus*, ed. G. Massera, p. 122; Anonymus, *Regole di far contrapunto*

di nota per nota, Ms. London, British Library, Add. 36986, fols. 27v-28v; Giovanni Spataro, *Bartolomei Rami pareie honesta defensio in Nicolai Burtii parmensis opusculum* (Bologna: Plato de Benedecti, 1491), fols. 26r, 36v; Giovanni del Lago, letter to Piero de Justinis, Venice, June 3, 1538, Ms. Vatican, lat. 5318, fols. 103r-103v; Ghiselin Danckerts, *Trattato sopra una differentia musicale*, Ms. Rome, Biblioteca Vallicelliana, R.56, fol. 407r.

52 'Quippe fa *euphoniam*, mi vero *kakophatom* sanat. Admittuntur autem coniunctae, cum propter cantus necessitatem, tum iucunditatem.' Georg Rhau, *Enchiridion utriusque musicae practicae* (Wittenberg: Georg Rhau, 1538), sig. [Dviiiv].

53 'Si come il, b, molle nelle Cantilene del, ♮, quadro si usa per fuggir i Tritoni, cosi il Diesis, col qual medesimamente la durezza del Tritono si puo addolcire: si prattica in ciascun ordine, per formar piu soavi Consonanze: come sono le seste maggiori, andando allottava, o le Terze minori, andando allo Unisono, o le Terze: & Decime maggiori nel fine delle cadenze, inanzi alle quali quasi per lo continuo esso Diesis si fa.' Giovanni Maria Lanfranco, *Scintille di musica* (Brescia: Lodovico Britannico, 1533), p. 126.

54 'Falsa musica est necessaria quandoque, et etiam ut omnis consonantia seu melodia in quolibet signo periciatur.' Philippe de Vitry, *Ars nova*, ed. G. Reaney, A. Gilles and J. Maillard, p. 22.

55 Petrus frater dictus Palma ociosa, *Compendium de discantu mensurabili* in J. Wolf, 'Ein Beitrag zur Diskantlehre des 14. Jahrhunderts', 514ff.

56 Philippus de Caserta, *Regule contrapuncti* in N. Wilkins, 'Some Notes on Philipoctus de Caserta', 98.

57 Ugolino of Orvieto, *Declaratio musicae disciplinae*, ed. A. Seay, vol. II, pp. 45f.

58 This is the conclusion derived from Ugolino's evidence in Margaret Bent, 'Musica Recta and Musica Ficta', *Musica Disciplina*, XXVI (1972), 76.

59 'Sexta et ultima regula pro noticia collocationis horum duorum signorum in contrapuncto, scilicet b rotundi et ♮ quadri, est hec, quod octavis, quintis, et sibi similibus ponenda sunt hec signa secundum quod oportet addere vel diminuere ad ipsas reducendum ad bonas consonantias, si prius forent dissonantes, eo quod tales combinationes in contrapuncto semper maiores sive consonantes esse debent.' Prosdocimus de Beldemandis, *Contrapunctus*, ed. and trans. J. Herlinger, pp. 78-81.

60 'Et ut adhuc maiorem noticiam de istis signis accipias, scire debes quod in huiusmodi combinationibus vocum variationibus quantum ad sui maioritatem vel minoritatem potes ponere signa supradicta, ita ad cantum superiorem sicut ad cantum inferiorem et e contra, unde si variatio aliqua in cantu superiori fiat per b rotundum, in cantu inferiori fiet per ♮ quadrum, et si in cantu superiori fiat variatio per ♮ quadrum in cantu inferiori fiet per b rotundum. Sed consulo tibi ut sis cautus in ponendo hec signa, quoniam ubi dulcius cadunt, ibi poni debent, unde si dulcius cadunt in tenore, ponantur in tenore, et si dulcius in discantu, ponantur in discantu. Si vero eque dulciter in discantu et tenore, potius ponantur in discantu quam in tenore, ne propter hoc oporteat etiam te ponere aliquod horum signorum ad contratenorum vel triplum vel quadruplum, si ibi reperiantur, ad que nichil horum signorum poneretur. Si signum opportunum sonans eque dulciter, ad discantum ponatur et non ad tenorem. Scire autem ubi hec signa dulcius cadunt auri tue dimitto, quia de hoc regula dari non potest, cum hec loca quodammodo infinita sint.' *Ibid.*, pp. 94f.

61 'Quando le voci del primo ordine intra se non convengano, cio è duramente si portano, si interpongono le voci del secondo e del terzo per rimovere quella

durezza e asperità.' John Hothby, *La Caliopea legale* in E. de Coussemaker, ed., *Histoire de l'harmonie au moyen âge* (Paris: Librairie Archéologique de Victor Didron, 1852), pp. 319f. See also Hothby, *Tractatus de arte contrapuncti* in *De arte contrapuncti*, ed. G. Reaney, p. 28.

62 John Hothby, *Spetie tenore del contrapunto prima* in *De arte contrapuncti*, ed. G. Reaney, pp. 85ff.

63 'Non tamen ignorandum est quod in cantu composito ne fa contra mi in concordantia perfecta fiat, interdum tritono uti necessarium sit, et tunc ad significandum ubi fa evitandi tritoni gratia cantari deberet ibi mi esse canendum, ♮ duri signum, hoc est ♮ quadrum, ipsi mi censeo praeponendum, ut hic probatur.'

Johannes Tinctoris, *Liber de natura et proprietate tonorum* in *Opera theoretica*, ed. A. Seay, vol. I, p. 75, trans. A. Seay, Translations 2, rev. edn, p. 13.

64 'Denique sciendum quod non solum in tonis regularibus et vera musica secundum exempla praemissa tritonum praedictis modis fugere ac eo uti debemus, verum etiam in irregularibus tonis et musica ficta, ut hic patet.'

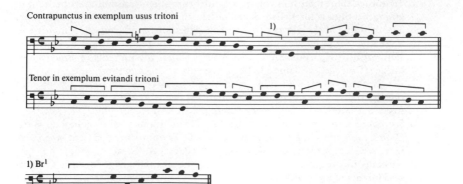

Ibid., pp. 75f, trans. A. Seay, Translations 2, rev. edn, p. 13.

65 Ms. Vatican, lat. 5318, fols. 102r–102v. The example is on fol. 102v.

6 Contrapuntal progressions

1 'Harum autem diaphoniarum seu dissonantiarum aliae compatiuntur secundum auditum et rationem et aliae non. Quae vero compatiuntur sunt tres principaliter, scilicet tertia, sexta, decima. Hae autem dissonantiae et his similes

ideo compatiuntur ab auditu, quia sunt magis propinquae consonantiis, cum moventur sursum et deorsum. Oportet enim quod quando duae voces sunt in dissonantia quae compatitur ab auditu quod ipsarum quaelibet requirens consonantiam moveatur ita videlicet, ut si una in sursum tendit, reliqua in deorsum, semper distando per minorem distantiam a consonantia ad quam tendunt.' Marchetto da Padova, *Lucidarium in arte musicae planae* in Jan W. Herlinger, *The Lucidarium of Marchetto of Padua. A Critical Edition, Translation and Commentary*, Ph.D. diss., The University of Chicago, 1978, pp. 335ff.

2 *Ibid.*, p. 347. See also *ibid.*, pp. 239, 245ff, 257ff, 261ff; and Marchetto da Padova, *Pomerium*, ed. G. Vecchi, Corpus Scriptorum de Musica 6 (n.p.: American Institute of Musicology, 1961), pp. 69f.

3 Marchetto, *Lucidarium* in Herlinger, *The Lucidarium of Marchetto of Padua*, pp. 247, 259, 263, 353.

4 'Inventa autem fuit musica ficta duabus de causis, primo propter necessitatem . . ., secundo propter pulcritudinem.' Franchinus Gaffurius, *Extractus parvus musice*, ed. F. A. Gallo, Antiquae Musicae Italicae Scriptores 4 (Bologna: Forni, 1969), p. 128.

5 See *ibid.*, p. 75.

6 'Inde chromaticum color pulchritudinis appellatur, quia propter decorem pulchritudinemque dissonantiarum dividitur tonus ultra divisionem diatonici et enharmonici generis, ut a consonantia quae sequitur dissonantias per minorem distantiam per motum utriusque distetur, ita videlicet quod in tali distantia supra vel infra unius toni prolatio semper exstet.' Marchetto, *Lucidarium* in Herlinger, *The Lucidarium of Marchetto of Padua*, p. 261.

7 'Proprius nominari musica colorata quam falsa'. Marchetto, *Pomerium*, ed. Vecchi, p. 70.

8 'In musica fiunt interdum colores ad pulchritudinem consonantiarum, sicut in gramatica fiunt colores rhetorici ad pulchritudinem sententiarum.' *Ibid.*, p. 71. The meaning of the distinction between inflections used *causa necessitatis* and those used *causa pulchritudinis* was clearly recognized in Edward E. Lowinsky, 'Foreword' to H. Colin Slim, ed., *Musica nova*, Monuments of Renaissance Music I (Chicago and London: The University of Chicago Press, 1964), pp. VIII–IX: 'Necessity deals with rules pertaining to perfect consonances, beauty with rules pertaining to imperfect consonances.' See also Margaret Bent, 'Musica Recta and Musica Ficta', *Musica Disciplina*, XXVI (1972), 78f.

9 See, for example, in addition to the theorists mentioned below, Jehan de Murs, *Quilibet affectans* in E. de Coussemaker, ed., *Scriptorum de musica medii aevi nova series a gerbertina altera*, vol. III (Paris: A. Durand, 1869), pp. 59f; Nicolaus Burtius, *Florum libellus*, ed. G. Massera, Historiae Musicae Cultores 28 (Florence: Leo S. Olschki, 1975), pp. 118f; Pietro Aaron, *Toscanello in musica* (Venice: Marchio Sessa, 1539), Bk II, Ch. 14; Giovanni Maria Lanfranco, *Scintille di musica* (Brescia: Lodovico Britannico, 1533), p. 116.

10 Petrus frater dictus Palma ociosa, *Compendium de discantu mensurabili* in Johannes Wolf, 'Ein Beitrag zur Diskantlehre des 14. Jahrhunderts', *Sammelbände der Internationalen Musikgesellschaft*, XV (1913–14), 513f.

11 The theorist's revealing comments deserve a full quotation: 'And if you wish to know the difference – when they [that is, the imperfect consonances] should be major and when minor – you should consider the location to which you must move immediately after leaving the imperfect consonance; then you must see whether the location you leave is more distant from that location which you intend immediately to reach, making the imperfect consonance major or

making it minor: for you should always choose that form, whether major or minor, that is less distant from that location which you intend immediately to reach, and you should, by means of the signs posited above [that is, ♭ or ♮], make a major interval minor or, contrariwise, a minor one major as appropriate. There is no other reason for this than a sweeter-sounding harmony. Why the sweeter-sounding harmony results from this can be ascribed to the sufficiently persuasive reason that the property of the imperfect or less perfect thing is to seek the perfect or to become more perfect, which it cannot do except through approximating itself to the perfect. This is because the closer the imperfect consonance approaches the other consonance it intends immediately to reach, the more perfect it becomes, and the sweeter the resulting harmony. And so that what has already been said above about the placement of these two signs may be better understood, I present this example [see Example 28 on p. 124]. If you carefully consider the signs placed in this example, you will see that the first square ♮ placed in the upper melody makes that minor sixth major, because in its major inflection it is less distant from the location it intends immediately to reach – the major octave immediately following – than in its minor inflection. The soft or round b found in the upper melody makes that major sixth minor, because in its minor inflection it is less distant from the location it intends to reach – the major octave immediately following – than in its major inflection. Similarly, the first square ♮ in the lower melody is placed there for the same reason. This sixth in its minor inflection is less distant from the location it intends to reach immediately – the other sixth immediately following – than in its major inflection. The second square ♮ found in the upper melody is placed there for the same reason as the first in that upper melody; the second square ♮ placed in the lower melody makes that major third minor, because in its minor inflection it is less distant from the location it intends to reach immediately – the unison immediately following – than in its major inflection. Anyone of sound intellect who is knowledgeable in this art to some degree will be able to understand all these things by considering them closely. The round b placed in the lower melody indicates that the entire melody should be sung with soft or round b; it is placed there as a signature.' ('Et si hanc diversitatem scire cupis, quando, scilicet, ipse debent esse maiores et quando minores, considerare debes locum ad quem immediate accedere debes post tuum recessum a tali consonantia imperfecta, et tunc videre debes an locus a quo recedis magis distet a loco ad quem immediate accedere intendis, faciendo talem consonantiam imperfectam maiorem an in faciendo ipsam minorem, quoniam illam semper sumere debes que minus distat a loco ad quem immediate accedere intendis, sive illa sit maior sive minor, et debes tunc facere ipsam per signa superius posita, de maiori minorem vel e contra, scilicet de minori maiorem, secundum quod oportet, cuius ratio non est alia quam dulcior armonia. Sed quare hec dulcior armonia ex hoc proveniat potest talis assignari ratio satis persuasiva, quoniam si de ratione imperfecti vel minus perfecti sit sui appetere perfectionem vel perfectius effici, quod aliter esse non potest quam per approximationem sui ad rem perfectam. Hinc est quod quanto consonantia imperfecta magis appropinquat alteri consonantie ad quam immediate accedere intendit, tanto perfectior efficitur, et inde dulcior armonia causatur. Et ut melius hec iam supradicta de collocatione horum duorum signorum intelligantur, pono hoc exemplum: Unde si hec signa in hoc exemplo posita bene consideras, primum ♮ quadrum in cantu superiori positum facit illam sextam minorem esse maiorem, eo quod in sua maioritate minus distat a loco ad quem immediate accedere intendit, scilicet ab octava maiori

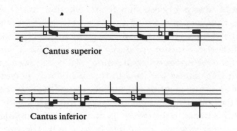

Cantus superior

Cantus inferior

immediate sequenti, quam in sua minoritate; b vero molle sive rotundum in cantu superiori repertum facit illam sextam maiorem esse minorem, eo quod in sua minoritate minus distat a loco ad quem accedere intendit, scilicet ab octava maiori immediate sequenti, quam in sua maioritate; et per simile ponitur primum ♮ quadrum in cantu inferiori et propter eandem causam, quoniam talis sexta in sua minoritate minus distat a loco ad quem immediate accedere intendit, scilicet ab alia sexta immediate sequenti, quam in sua maioritate; ♮ vero quadrum secundum in cantu superiori repertum positum est propter eandem causam propter quam positum est et primum ipsius cantus superioris; sed ♮ quadrum secundum in cantu inferiori positum facit illam terciam maiorem esse minorem, eo quod in sua minoritate minus distat a loco ad quem immediate accedere intendit, scilicet ab unisono immediate sequenti, quam in sua maioritate, que omnia comprehendere poterit quilibet boni ingenii in hac arte aliquantulum intelligens ad supradicta subtiliter inspiciendo; b vero rotundum in cantu inferiori positum totum cantum denominat per b molle sive rotundum cantari debere et pro clavi ibi ponitur.') Prosdocimus de Beldemandis, *Contrapunctus*, ed. and trans. J. Herlinger, Greek and Latin Music Theory 1 (Lincoln and London: University of Nebraska Press, 1984), pp. 80-7, © University of Nebraska Press.

12 'Et perho assumate una regola generale che ogni volta, che voi anderete ad una specie imperfetta, & poi vorrete ascendere ad una maggiore specie d'essa, cosi perfetta, come imperfetta, se quella specie e minore, fatela maggiore con il segno de la sustentatione, la quale sustentatione si dimostra con questo segno .♯.' Giovanni del Lago, *Breve introduttione di musica misurata* (Venice: Brandino e Ottaviano Scotto, 1540), p. 37.

13 Ugolino of Orvieto, *Declaratio musicae disciplinae*, ed. A. Seay, Corpus Scriptorum de Musica 7, vol. II (n.p.: American Institute of Musicology, 1960), pp. 12f.

14 *Ibid.*, vol. II, p. 13 and ex. 3.

15 *Ibid.*, vol. II, p. 47, exx. 128-9.

16 'Primum vero B molle in exemplo primo locatum non dissonantiae perfectionem sed colorationem eius atque cum suae formae diminutione etiam eius immediatae perfectioni propinquiorem et immediatam adhaesionem ostendit.' *Ibid.*, vol. II, p. 48.

17 *Ibid.*, vol. III, p. 248, ex. M-8.

18 Anonymus, *Quot sunt concordationes* in Coussemaker, *Scriptorum*, vol. III, pp. 70-4. For the date of the treatise, see Klaus-Jürgen Sachs, *Der Contrapunctus im 14. und 15. Jahrhundert. Untersuchungen zum Terminus, zur Lehre und zu den Quellen*, Beihefte zum Archiv für Musikwissenschaft 13 (Wiesbaden: Franz Steiner, 1974), p. 180.

19 Anonymus, *Quot sunt concordationes* in Coussemaker, *Scriptorum*, vol. III, p. 72.
20 *Ibid.*
21 *Ibid.*, pp. 72f.
22 Gioseffo Zarlino, *Le Istitutioni harmoniche* (Venice: 1558), p. 188.
23 'Sexta maior coniungit ad octavam, minor vero disiungit ad quintam. Sic et tertia maior ad quintam disgregat, minor autem ad unisonum adducit.' Bartolomeo Ramos de Pareia, *Musica practica*, ed. Johannes Wolf, Publikationen der Internationalen Musikgesellschaft 2 (Leipzig: Breitkopf und Härtel, 1901), p. 65.
24 *Ibid.*, pp. 66f.
25 'Quando ex concordantia imperfecta perfectam petimus concordantiam . . . ad propinquiorem perfectam diversis utriusque partis motibus acquirendam concurrere necessum est.' Franchinus Gaffurius, *Practica musice* (Milan: Ioannes Petrus de Lomatio, 1496), sig. ddiiv, trans. Clement A. Miller, Musicological Studies and Documents 20 (n.p.: American Institute of Musicology, 1968), p. 128.
26 *Ibid.*, sigs. ddiiv-ddiiir. It should be noted, however, that the whole passage seems to contain a contradiction. Gaffurius does state expressly that the sixth preceding an octave should be major and the one preceding a fifth should be minor, but he also exemplifies the rule by, for instance, a *minor* third expanding to a fifth and a *minor* sixth expanding to an octave. (I am indebted to Professor Anthony Newcomb for drawing my attention to this ambiguity.) This seeming contradiction may probably be explained by the fact that, as will be shown below, for Gaffurius the rule of the semitone progression is absolutely obligatory only at cadences.
27 See, for example, in addition to those mentioned below, Juan Bermudo, *El arte Tripharia* (Ossuna: Juan de Leon, 1550), fols. 34r-36r.
28 'Hanno oltra di questo le Consonanze imperfette tal natura, che i loro estremi con più commodo, & miglior modo si estendeno verso quella parte, che è più vicina alla sua perfettione, che verso quella, che le è più lontana: percioche ogni cosa naturalmente desidera di farsi perfetta, con quel modo più breve, & migliore, che puote. Onde le imperfette maggiori desiderano di farse maggiori; & le minori hanno natura contraria: conciosia che il Ditono, et lo Essachordo maggiore desiderano di farsi maggiori, venedo l'uno alla Quinta, & l'altro alla Ottava; & il Semiditono, & lo Essachordo minore amano di farsi minori, venedo l'uno verso l'Unisono, & l'altro verso la Quinta: come è manifesto a tutti quelli, che nelle cose della Musica sono periti, & hanno il loro giuditio sano: perciocheè tutti li movimenti, che fanno le parti, vengono a farsi col movimento di alcuno intervallo, nel quale si contiene il Semituono, che è veramente il Sale (dirò cosi) il condimento, & la cagione di ogni buona Modulatione, & ogni buona Harmonia.' Zarlino, *Le Istitutioni harmoniche*, pp. 156f, trans. Guy A. Marco and Claude V. Palisca (New Haven: Yale University Press, 1968), p. 23. See also Zarlino, *Le Istitutioni harmoniche*, pp. 188ff.
29 'Onde bisogna avertire, accioche con facilità si osservi questa Regola, che qualunque volta si vorrà procedere dalla consonanza Imperfetta alla Perfetta; di fare, che almeno una delle parti si muova con alcuno movimento, nel quale sia il Semituono maggiore, tacito, overo espresso. Et per conseguire tal cosa gioverà molto l'uso delle chorde Chromatiche, & delle Enharmoniche, adoperandole nel modo, che altrove son per dimostrare.' *Ibid.*, p. 190, trans. Marco and Palisca, p. 83.

30 'Septima regula est quod quando ex concordantia imperfecta perfectam petimus concordantiam tanquam cantilenae terminationem: vel alicuius partis eius
harmonicae: ad propinquiorem perfectam diversis utriusque partis motibus
acquirendam concurrere necessum est.' Gaffurius, *Practica musice*, sig. ddiiv,
trans. Miller, p. 128.

31 'Il propio della Sesta maggiore sia, di venire alla Ottava; & il propio della
Minore sia, di avicinarsi alla Quinta.' Zarlino, *Le Istitutioni harmoniche*,
pp. 189f, trans. Marco and Palisca, p. 82.

32 'La onde la Natura, laquale hà iurisditione in ogni cosa, hà fatto, che non pur
quelli, che sono periti nella Musica, ma gli Idioti, & li Contadini ancora, i quali
cantano a loro modo, senza alcuna ragione, usano di andare dalla Sesta maggiore alla Ottava, come sono insegnati naturalmente; ilche si ode maggior-
mente nelle Cadenze, che in ogn'altra parte delle lor Canzoni; come è manifesto
a ciascuno perito nella Musica. Et forse, che il detto Franchino da questo prese
ardir di dire, che lo andare dalla Sesta maggiore alla Ottava, si dovea osservare
solamente nelle Cadenze: perciocche in esse si fanno le terminationi delle cantilene: ma al mio giuditio parmi (come si può comprendere) dalle sue parole
poste di sopra, che ciò non sia detto con ragione, se vorremo attendere alla
Natura dell'una, & dell'altra. Non sarà adunque lecito volendo osservare cotal
Regola, di passare dalla Sesta maggiore alla Quinta, ne anco dalla minore alla
Ottava; senza depravatione della natura delle predette consonanze.' *Ibid.*,
p. 190, trans. Marco and Palisca, p. 83.

33 'Potrà adunque il Musico, quando gli verrà commodo; & non potrà fare
altramente, per qualche accidente, por la Quinta dopo la Sesta maggiore,
contra la Regola data di sopra nel Cap. 38. quando la Sesta sarà posta nella
seconda parte della Semibreve sincopata . . . Potrà etiandio dalla Sesta minore
andare alla Ottava con una figura di Semiminima; perche la Quarta Semiminima, che si parte dalla Terza co'l movimento congiunto, si può sempre
pigliar per non buona.' *Ibid.*, pp. 235f, trans. Marco and Palisca, pp. 172f.

34 Luigi Dentice, *Duo dialoghi della musica* (Rome: Vincenzo Lucrino, 1553),
[fols. 37r-37v].

35 'La onde io hò per fermo, & sia detto con sopportatione di M. Adriano Villart,
di M. Alfonso, & deglialtri, che le regole delle seste & terze minori & maggiori,
siano arbitrarie & non legali.' *Ibid.*, [fol. 37v].

36 Ghiselin Danckerts, *Trattato sopra una differentia musicale*, Ms. Rome, Biblioteca Vallicelliana, R.56, fols. 407v-410r.

37 'Costoro troppo inconsideratamente vogliono quasi sempre usare questi
alzamenti et abbassamenti delle note, fuora delle lor proprie è naturali
intonationi nelle compositioni loro (come ho detto) legandosi con certe vane
obligationi è leggi loro, di non volere andare alla consonantia perfetta, se non
con la imperfetta piu propinqua, il che si potrebbe supportare quando l'usas-
sero rare volte. et accidentalmente; ma osservandosi questa legge ordinari-
amente per tutto, et in ogni luogo sempre [(] come fanno li detti Compositori
Novelli) verrebbe in troppo pregiuditio delli tuoni predetti.' *Ibid.*, fol. 408r.

38 Also Klaus-Jürgen Sachs concluded, on the basis of theoretical evidence from
the fourteenth and fifteenth centuries, that the teaching concerning the half-
step progression from an imperfect consonance was ambiguous and that in
practice the rule must have been followed much less consistently than some
orthodox texts suggested. Klaus-Jürgen Sachs, "Die Contrapunctus-Lehre im 14.
und 15. Jahrhundert', F. Zaminer, ed., *Die mittelalterliche Lehre von der Mehrstimmigkeit*, Geschichte der Musiktheorie 5 (Darmstadt: Wissenschaftliche
Buchgesellschaft, 1984), pp. 199-208.

39 'Clausula est cuiuslibet partis cantus particula. in fine cuius vel quies generalis vel perfectio reperitur.' Johannes Tinctoris, *Terminorum musicae diffinitorium* ([Treviso: Gerardo de Lisa, 1475]), sig. aiiiir. For terminological aspects of cadence, see Siegfried Schmalzriedt with Elke Mahlert and Bernd Sunten, 'Clausula' and 'Kadenz' in H. H. Eggebrecht, *Handwörterbuch der musikalischen Terminologie* (Wiesbaden: Fritz Steiner, 1974).

40 Tinctoris, *Terminorum musicae diffinitorium*, sig. biir.

41 'Est igitur clausula (ut Tinctor scribit) Cantilene particula, in cuius fine vel quies vel perfectio reperitur. Vel est vocum diversimode gradiencium in consonantijs perfectis coniunctio.' Andreas Ornithoparchus, *Musice active micrologus* (Leipzig: Valentin Schumann, 1517), Bk IV, Ch. 5, trans. John Dowland (London: Thomas Adams, 1609), p. 84.

42 'Perfectio est totius cantus aut particularum ipsius conclusio.' Johannes Tinctoris, *Diffinitorium musice*, Ms. Brussels, Bibliothèque Royale, II.4147, fol. 122r.

43 'Per le clausule sintende tutte le note intra luna righa et laltra. Et seguitano le clausule delle parole. che principalmente sono. 3. Cioe. Coma. Colon. et periodus: . . . Et come decto: le clausule della cantilena deno essere simile: alle clausule delle parole: per tal modo che se la clausula delle parole e suspensiva Cioe. Colon: la clausula della cantilena de essere da longa dalla voce finale. Et se la clausula delle parole e una subdistinctione. Cioe una Coma gramatica: la clausula del canto de essere mediocre: non troppo da longa: ne troppo apresso alla voce finale. Ma se la clausula delle parole e parieto (.l. periodus). Cioe fine della sententia: La clausula del canto de essere nella voce finale. overo nel tenore.' John Hothby, *Tractatus quarundam regularum artis musicae*, Ms. Florence, Biblioteca Nazionale Centrale, Palat. 472, fols. 12r-12v.

44 See, for example, in addition to those discussed below, Giovanni del Lago, *Breve introduttione di musica misurata*, p. 40; Angelo da Picitono, *Fior angelico di musica* (Venice: Agostino Bindoni, 1547), Bk II, Ch. 39.

45 'Legitimus autem peculiarisque Cadentiarum locus est, ubi verborum contextus definit sententia . . . Est enim cadentia veluti punctum, & distinctio quaedam & quies in Concentu.' Stephano Vanneo, *Recanetum de musica aurea* (Rome: Valerius Doricus, 1533), fol. 93v.

46 *Ibid.*, fol. 86r.

47 'Cadentia igitur est, cuiuslibet partis cantus particula, in fine cuius, vel quies generalis, vel perfectio reperitur. Vel Cadentia est quaedam ipsius Cantilenae partis terminatio, perinde atque in orationis contextu Media distinctio, atque Distinctio finalis. Studentque periti Musici, ut Cadentiarum Meta fiat, ubi & orationis pars, seu membrum terminat.' *Ibid.*, fols. 85v-86r.

48 'A cadence is a certain simultaneous progression of all the voices in a composition accompanying a repose in the harmony or the completion of a meaningful segment of the text upon which the composition is based. We might also say that it is a sort of termination of part of the harmonic flow at a mid point or at the end, or a separation of the main portions of the text. The cadence is very necessary in harmonic writing, since it is needed for marking off sections of the music, as well as of the text. But it should not be used unless the end of a clause or period of the prose or verse has been reached, that is, only at the end of a section or part of a section. The cadence has a value in music equivalent to the period in prose and could well be called the period of musical composition. It is found also at resting points in the harmony, that is, where a section of the harmony terminates, in the same way that we pause in a speech, both at intermediate points and at the end.' ('La Cadenza adunque è un certo atto, che fanno

le parti della cantilena cantando insieme, la qual dinota, o quiete generale dell-
'harmonia, o la perfettione del senso delle parole, sopra le quali la cantilena è
composta. Overamente potemo dire, che ella sia una certa terminatione di una
parte di tutto'l concento, & quasi mezana, o vogliamo dire finale terminatione,
o distintione del contesto della Oratione. Et benche la Cadenza sia molto necessaria nelle harmonie: percioche quando non l'hanno, mancano di un grande
ornamento necessario, si per la distintione delle sue parti, come anco di quella
della Oratione; non è però da usarla, se non quando si ariva alla Clausula, overo
al Periodo contenuto nella Prosa, o nel Verso; cioè in quella parte, che termina
il Membro di essa, overo una delle sue parti. Onde la Cadenza è di tanto valore
nella Musica, quanto il Punto nella Oratione; & si può veramente chiamare
Punto della Cantilena. È ben vero, che si pone anco dove si riposa, cioè dove si
trova la terminatione di una parte dell'harmonia, nel modo che si fermiamo
etiandio nel contesto della Oratione, quando si trova non solamente la distintione mezana, ma ancora la finale.') Zarlino, *Le Istitutioni harmoniche*, p. 221,
trans. Marco and Palisca, pp. 141f. See also Zarlino, *Le Istitutioni harmoniche*,
pp. 193 and 320.

49 'Octava conclusio est quod in suo contrapuncto penultima semper debet esse
imperfecta et hoc ratione euphonie . . . Nona conclusio est quod sicut contrapunctus incipit per perfectam, sic etiam debet finire. Ratio potest esse, quia,
si fineretur cantus per imperfectam, tunc remaneret animus suspensus, nec
adhuc quiesceret cum non audiret perfectum sonum, nec per consequens
indicatur ibi finem esse cantus.' Anonymus, *Cum notum sit* in Coussemaker,
Scriptorum, vol. III, p. 62.

50 See, for example, John Hothby, *Regule dil contrapuncto* in *De arte contrapuncti*, ed. G. Reaney, Corpus Scriptorum de Musica 26 (n.p.: American
Institute of Musicology, 1977), p. 75; Burtius, *Florum libellus*, ed. Massera,
p. 119; Guillelmus Monachus, *De preceptis artis musicae*, ed. A. Seay, Corpus
Scriptorum de Musica 11 (n.p.: American Institute of Musicology, 1965), p. 34;
del Lago, *Breve introduttione di musica misurata*, p. 33; Heinrich Glarean,
Dodecachordon (Basle: Heinrich Petri, 1547), p. 26.

51 Ugolino of Orvieto, *Declaratio musicae disciplinae*, ed. Seay, vol. II, pp. 12–15.

52 'Octava & ultima Regula est quod omnis Cantilena debet finiri & terminari in
concordantia perfecta videlicet aut in unisono ut Venetis mos fuit. aut in octava
aut in quintadecima: quod omnis musicorum scola frequentius observat gratia
harmonicae mediocritatis perficiendae.' Gaffurius, *Practica musice*, sig. ddiijr,
trans. Miller, p. 129.

53 See, for example, Vanneo, *Recanetum de musica aurea*, fol. 86r.

54 'Volsero che tal Regola fusse fatale; et che si dovesse finire le cantilene nella
Ottava, overamente nell'Unisono; & per alcun modo non si facesse al contrario:
. . . Questa Regola veramente fù molto bene istituita: conciosia che se cantilene
finissero altramente, le orecchie de gli ascoltanti starebbeno sospese, et desider-
arebbeno la loro perfettione.' Zarlino, *Le Istitutioni harmoniche*, p. 191, trans.
Marco and Palisca, p. 84.

55 K. W. Niemöller, ed., *Die Musica figurativa des Melchior Schanppecher. Opus
aureum, Köln 1501, pars III/IV*, Beiträge zur Rheinischen Musikgeschichte 50
(Cologne: Arno Volk, 1961), pp. 26f. Schanppecher's pupil, Nicolaus Wollick,
reproduced these ideas in his *Enchiridion musices* (Paris: Francoys Regnault,
1512), Pt VI, Ch. 6.

56 Johannes Cochlaeus, *Tetrachordum musices* (Nuremberg: Fridericus Peypus,
1514), sigs. [Eviv]-Fr.

57 'Prima, Omnis clausula tribus constat notis, ultima, penultima, et antepenultima.' Ornithoparchus, *Musice active micrologus*, Bk IV, Ch. 5, trans. Dowland, p. 84.

58 'Secunda, clausula discantus tribus notis conflata, ultimam semper habebit sursum. Tertia, Clausula tenoris tribus etiam constat notis ultima semper descendente.' *Ibid.*

59 *Ibid.*, Bk IV, Ch. 4.

60 Pietro Aaron, *Libri tres de institutione harmonica* (Bologna: Benedetto di Ettore, 1516), fols. 49r–49v.

61 '& sempre mai si oppone la settima dissonanza nanzi la sesta precedente l'ottava, pur che non siano semplicemente composte.' Aaron, *Toscanello in musica*, Bk II, Ch. 18, trans. Peter Bergquist, Translations 4, vol. II (Colorado Springs: The Colorado College Music Press, 1970), p. 31.

62 Vanneo, *Recanetum de musica aurea*, fol. 75v.

63 *Ibid.*, fol. 77r.

64 *Ibid.*, fol. 86r.

65 'Reliquum est ut floridas exemplis doceamus cadentias, in quibus Compositores ex statuto praecepto dissonantiam consueverunt ponere ante penultimam.' *Ibid.*, fol. 86v.

66 'Cadentia florida antepenultimam dissonam requirit.' *Ibid.*

67 *Ibid.*, fols. 87r–87v.

68 'When you want to go to a perfect cadence, the [ante]penultima should always be a suspended dissonance with the penultima, which should be an imperfect interval . . . So that, desiring to come to the cadence of the octave, make the antepenultima into a suspended seventh and the penultima into a sixth.' ('Et quando voi vorrete andare alla cadentia perfetta sempre la [ante]penultima de essere dissonantia in sincopa con la penultima la quale de essere specie imperfetta . . . Si che volendo pervenire a la cadentia de la ottava, fate che l'antepenultima sia settima sincopa, & la penultima sesta.') Del Lago, *Breve introduttione di musica misurata*, p. 37.

69 'Osserverete questo nelle vostre compositioni sempre compire il numero ternario, o binario, overo quaternario nella penultima nota della cadentia, cioe non si debbe computare la penultima nota con la sequente, la quale include la cadentia, overo distintione, perche la e principio di numero, similmente si debbe finire il numero nella penultima nota del concento, & non nel l'ultima, perche la penultima include il numero precedente. & l'ultima nota e fine del canto, & perho non si computa con altra nota.' *Ibid.*, pp. 39f.

70 Nicola Vicentino, *L'antica musica ridotta alla moderna prattica* (Rome: Antonio Barré, 1555), fol. 51v.

71 *Ibid.*, fols. 52r, 53r, 55r–58v.

72 Zarlino, *Le Istitutioni harmoniche*, pp. 221–5.

73 'impropiamente'. *Ibid.*, p. 222, trans. Marco and Palisca, p. 145.

74 Zarlino, *Le Istitutioni harmoniche*, pp. 250f.

75 *Ibid.*, p. 224.

76 ''l Fuggir la Cadenza sia . . . un certo atto, il qual fanno le parti, accennando di voler fare una terminatione perfetta, secondo l'uno de i modi mostrati di sopra, & si rivolgono altrove.' *Ibid.*, p. 226, trans. Marco and Palisca, p. 151.

77 *Ibid.*, p. 226, trans. Marco and Palisca, pp. 152f.

78 *Ibid.*, p. 225, trans. Marco and Palisca, pp. 151.

79 'Quando si vorrà fare alcuna distintione mezana dell'harmonia, & delle parole insieme, le quali non habbiano finita perfettamente la loro sentenza . . . concio-

sia che alle volte accasca al Compositore, che venendoli alle mani un bel passaggio, nel quale si accommodarebbe ottimamente la Cadenza, & non havendo fatto fine al Periodo nelle parole; non essendo honesto, che habbiano a finire in essa.' *Ibid*.

80 'Alcuna volta fingere di far cadentia, & poi nella conclusione di essa cadentia pigliare una consonantia non propinqua ad essa cadentia per accommodarsi e cosa laudabile.' Del Lago, *Breve introduttione di musica misurata*, p. 39.

81 Vicentino, *L'antica musica ridotta alla moderna prattica*, fols. 53v, 54v.

82 Loys Bourgeois, *Le droict chemin de musique* (Geneva: [Jean Gérard], 1550), Ch. 2.

83 Lanfranco, *Scintille di musica*, p. 127.

84 Aaron, *Toscanello in musica*, Bk II, Ch. 20.

85 Giovanni Spataro, letter to Pietro Aaron, Bologna, May 23, 1524, Ms. Vatican, lat. 5318, fol. 21 iv.

86 Aaron, *Toscanello in musica*, sigs. Iv-Iiir, trans. Bergquist, vol. III, p. 22.

87 Ms. Vatican, lat. 5318, fols. 21 iv-212r.

88 Pietro Aaron, *Trattato della natura et cognitione di tutti gli tuoni di canto figurato non da altrui piu scritti* (Venice: Bernardino de Vitali, 1525), Chs. 4-5.

89 Lanfranco, *Scintille di musica*, p. 126.

90 Vanneo, *Recanetum de musica aurea*, fol. 88v, last example.

91 '& come si vorrà fermar qualche parti, appresso le pause, ò ne gli fini si farà che sempre la consonanza, della Terza maggiore, sarà nel sopradetto luogo, anchora che la compositione ricerchi mestitia.' Vicentino, *L'antica musica ridotta alla moderna prattica*, fol. 82r.

92 See Ch. 6.1, ex. 28 above.

93 Marchetto da Padova, *Lucidarium in arte musicae planae* in Herlinger, *The Lucidarium of Marchetto of Padua*, pp. 263 and 353.

94 Marchetto da Padova, *Pomerium*, ed. Vecchi, pp. 69f.

95 Petrus frater dictus Palma ociosa, *Compendium de discantu mensurabili* in Wolf, 'Ein Beitrag zur Diskantlehre des 14. Jahrhunderts', 515.

96 'In fine cuiuscumque ascensus inter penultimam et ultimam semper sub intelligitur ♮, ut hic patet.' *The Berkeley Manuscript*, ed. and trans. O. B. Ellsworth, Greek and Latin Music Theory 2 (Lincoln and London: University of Nebraska Press, 1984), pp. 242f.

97 Philippus de Caserta, *Regule contrapuncti* in Nigel Wilkins, 'Some Notes on Philipoctus de Caserta (*c.* 1360?-*c.* 1435)', *Nottingham Mediaeval Studies*, VIII (1964), 97.

98 Prosdocimus de Beldemandis, *Tractatus musice speculative contra Marchetum de Padua* in D. Raffaello Baralli and Luigi Torri, 'Il "Trattato" di Prosdocimo de' Beldomandi contro Il "Lucidario" di Marchetto da Padova', *Rivista musicale italiana*, XX (1913), 750.

99 *Ibid.*, pp. 751f.

100 Ugolino of Orvieto, *Declaratio musicae disciplinae*, ed. Seay, vol. II, pp. 51f; Bartolomeo Ramos de Pareia, *Musica practica*, ed. Wolf, pp. 66f.

101 Ramos de Pareia, *Musica practica*, ed. Wolf, p. 101.

102 The text edited by Wolf has 'semitone' here.

103 'Et si quis vellet dicere, quod ibi renascitur protus et condiciones, quas habuit *d*, debet et *h* obtinere et cum *d* semitonium sub se et supra se habere monstratum sit, eodem modo et *h*, respondebimus dicentes argumentum non procedere, quoniam illud habuit *g*, quae totalem similitudinem sub et supra in synemmenon tetrachordo vendicat sibi, non tamen *h*, quia sub se duos tonos habet . . .

Igitur illa chorda in coniuncto deuterus est tam autenticus quam plagalis.'
Ramos de Pareia, *Musica practica*, ed. Wolf, p. 101.

104 An argument in favor of the flat leading tone for *A*-cadences made on the basis
of the Bent-Hughes theory of *recta* preference discussed in Chapter 4(ii) above
to the effect that ♭ and ♭♭, being steps of *musica vera*, might have been preferable to *G♯* of *musica ficta*, ignores the fact that the great majority of theorists
from the early fourteenth to the late sixteenth century who exemplified the
treatment of such cadences used the sharp leading tone.

105 'Quandocumque in simplici cantu est *la sol la*, hoc *sol* debet sustineri et cantari
sicut *fa mi fa* . . . Quandocumque habetur in simplici cantu *sol fa sol*, hoc *fa*
sustineri debet et cantari sicut *fa mi fa* . . . Quandocumque habetur in simplici
cantu *re ut re*, hoc *ut* sustineri debet et cantari sicut *fa mi fa*. Et est notandum
quod in contrapunctu nulle alie note sustinentur, nisi iste tres, scilicet: *sol fa* et
ut.' Anonymus, *Quot sunt concordationes* in Coussemaker, *Scriptorum*, vol. III,
p. 73.

106 Pseudo-Tunstede, *Quatuor principalia musicae* in Coussemaker, *Scriptorum*,
vol. IV, p. 250; Ramos de Pareia, *Musica practica*, ed. Wolf, pp. 43f; Franchinus Gaffurius, *Practica musice*, sig. eeiijr; Gonzalo Martínez de Bizcargui,
Arte de canto llano, ed. A. Seay, Critical Texts 9 (Colorado Springs: The
Colorado College Music Press, 1979), p. 25. Pseudo-Tunstede is quoted and discussed in Margaret Bent, 'Musica Recta and Musica Ficta', 89f.

107 'Persaepe etiam plerique pronuntiant sol sub la semitonij intervallo: quum
potissime proceditur his notulis la sol la incipiendo in Alamire rursusque in
ipsam terminando. ut Salve Regina. Atque item inrer sol & fa incipiendo &
terminando in Gsolreut hoc transitu sol fa sol: quod Ambrosiani plerumque
modulari solent.' Gaffurius, *Practica musice*, sig. eeiijr, trans. Miller, p. 146.
Carl Dahlhaus's ingenious interpretation of the first sentence quoted above ('Zu
Costeleys chromatischer Chanson', *Die Musikforschung*, XVI [1963], 261f, n. 38)
is immediately falsified by the second quoted sentence, as well as by the material
referred to in the preceding note. *Cf.* also Dahlhaus, 'Zur Akzidentiensetzung in
den Motetten Josquins des Prez' in R. Baum and W. Rehm, eds., *Musik und
Verlag. Karl Vötterle zum 65. Geburtstag am 12. April 1968* (Kassel: Bärenreiter,
1968), p. 209, n. 7.

108 Martínez de Bizcargui, *Arte de canto llano*, ed. Seay, p. 25.

109 Johannes Cochlaeus, *Tetrachordum musices*, sig. Cv.

110 Arnolt Schlick, *Spiegel der Orgelmacher und Organisten* (Speyer: Peter Drach,
1511), Ch. 8.

111 Pietro Aaron, *Libri tres de institutione harmonica*, fol. 50r.

112 'Sciendum autem illud est, cadentias omneis, quae terminatae per tonos mon-
strantur, debere suspendi.' *Ibid.*, fol. 50v.

113 *Ibid.* But note that earlier on the same page Aaron lists even the mi-re-mi
formula among those that are sharpened. (I am grateful to Professor Anthony
Newcomb for drawing my attention to this fact.)

114 Pietro Aaron, *Lucidario in musica* (Venice: Girolamo Scotto, 1545), fols. 8v–9r.

115 'Item notandum est quod omnis consonantia imperfecta cupiens consonantiam
perfectam, ascendendo debet elevari a semitonio . . . Tunc etiam sustinere
debes mi de fa: et fa de mi situatum inter duo sol. Et etiam ut positum inter duo
re, ac etiam sol locatum inter duo la.' Guillaume Guerson, *Utilissime musicales
regule* (Paris: François Regnault, 1526), sig. Ciir.

116 Giovanni Maria Lanfranco, *Scintille di musica*, p. 127.

117 'Et cosi nelle altre parti in luoghi simili: come e detto, esso Diesis . . . si puo for-

mare. Et dico: si puo: perche (anchora che per lo piu si faccia) non sempre si fa: Et tanto piu nelle note: che sincopate non sono: non sempre si usa di fare: come sono quelle delle prime parti de i sopraposti essempi.' *Ibid.*

118 Stephano Vanneo, *Recanetum de musica aurea*, fol. 90r.

119 'Isti ergo cupientes hoc oneris abiicere, & ab ancipiti discedere trivio, Aureum hoc praeceptum suscipiant atque sequantur, ac Denique memoriae Thesauro recondant. Omnem scilicet Suprani cadentiam, quinque posse fieri modis. Primo quidem sic Re ut re, Secundo Mi re mi, Tertio Fa mi fa, Quarto Sol fa sol, Quinto & ultimo La sol la, ex quibus tres videlicet, Re ut re, Sol fa sol, & La sol la, Sustentationis indigent adminiculo. La sol la tamen in utroque E la mi, & utroque A la mi re sub b molli, & E la, hanc non sequitur regulam. Nam in huiusmodi locis Tenor Semitonii sortitur cadentiam.' *Ibid.*, fols. 90r–90v.

120 *Ibid.*, fol. 90v.

121 'Semblablement plusieurs cadences de dessus entiers (qui se peuvent rencontrer en toutes parties) comme, la, sol, la, sol, fa, sol. & re, ut, re: ou aucunesfois rompues, comme la, sol: sol, fa: & re, ut: doivent estre entonnées en demiton. I'ay dy notamment plusieurs cadences, car cela ne se doibt pas tousiours faire. Pareillement la, sol, la: ou mi, re, mi: de a, mi, la, re, en g, re, sol, ut, chantant par b mol, & la, sol, la: ou mi, re, mi de e, mi, la, en d la, re, sol, doivent estre entonnées de ton en ton, comme si ce n'estoit point cadence.' Loys Bourgeois, *Le droict chemin de musique*, Ch. 2.

122 Juan Bermudo, *El arte Tripharia*, fol. 35v.

123 'In quella parte, che tra la penultima figura, & la ultima si trova il movimento, che ascende, sempre si intende essere collocato il Semituono; pur che l'altra parte non discenda per simile intervallo.' Gioseffo Zarlino, *Le Istitutioni harmoniche*, p. 222, trans. Marco and Palisca, pp. 144f.

124 See especially Howard Mayer Brown, 'Accidentals and Ornamentation in Sixteenth-Century Intabulations of Josquin's Motets', E. E. Lowinsky, ed., *Josquin des Prez* (London: Oxford University Press, 1976), pp. 475–522.

125 Lewis Lockwood, 'A Dispute on Accidentals in Sixteenth-Century Rome', *Analecta Musicologica*, II (1965), 24–40.

126 *Ibid.*, p. 32. All accidentals above notes are mine.

127 *Ibid.*, p. 39.

128 'Ma per piu chiarezza ti voglio addure, Richafort ilquale non tanto considera a le quinte, ottave, duodecime & quintedecime, quanto anchora a osservare la sesta maggiore nanzi la ottava, come dimostra il suo motetto, Miseremini mei, sopra le parole, quare me persequimini, laquale sesta appare nel controbasso con il controalto, & perche era minore, ha voluto segnare la figura ♭.' Aaron, *Toscanello in musica*, sig. Ir, trans. Bergquist, vol. III, p. 18.

129 Quoted from a modern edition of the motet in A. Smijers, ed., *Treize livres de motets parus chez Pierre Attaingnant en 1534 et 1535*, vol. I (Paris: Editions de l'Oiseau Lyre, 1934), p. 178, with the clefs of the alto and tenor corrected and the accidental in m. 36 added. The motet appears in the sources with conflicting attributions.

130 Private communication from Professor Howard M. Brown.

7 Canon and imitation

1 Gioseffo Zarlino, *Le Istitutioni harmoniche* (Venice, 1558), pp. 212–20.

2 'E da i Prattici etiandio chiamata Fuga.' *Ibid.*, p. 217, trans. Guy A. Marco and Claude V. Palisca (New Haven: Yale University Press, 1968), p. 135.

3 'Il Consequente imitando li movimenti della Guida, procede solamente per quelli istessi gradi, senza havere altra consideratione de gli intervalli.' *Ibid.* The distinction and its implications for the problems which interest us here have been studied and convincingly elucidated in James Haar, 'Zarlino's Definition of Fugue and Imitation', *Journal of the American Musicological Society*, XXIV (1971), 226-54.

4 'La onde; si come la Fuga si può fare all'Unisono, alla Quarta, alla Quinta, alla Ottava, overo ad altri intervalli; cosi la Imitatione si può accommodare ad ogni intervallo dall'Unisono, & dalli nominati in fuori. Per il che, si potrà porre alla Seconda, alla Terza, alla Sesta, alla Settima, & ad altri intervalli simili.' *Ibid.*, p. 217, trans. Marco and Palisca, p. 135.

5 *Cf.* Marcus van Crevel, 'Verwante Sequensmodulaties bij Obrecht, Josquin en Coclico', *Tijdschrift van de Vereniging voor Nederlandse Muziekgeschiedenis*, XVI (1942), 107-24.

6 See, in particular, Edward E. Lowinsky, 'The Goddess Fortuna in Music, with a Special Study of Josquin's *Fortuna d'un gran tempo*', *The Musical Quarterly*, XXIX (1943), 45-77; *idem*, *Secret Chromatic Art in the Netherlands Motet* (New York: Columbia University Press, 1946); *idem*, 'Introduction' to H. Hewitt, ed., *Ottaviano Petrucci, Canti B*, Monuments of Renaissance Music 2 (Chicago and London: The University of Chicago Press, 1967), pp. v-xvi.

7 *Cf.* Carl Dahlhaus, 'Zur Akzidentiensetzung in den Motetten Josquins des Prez' in R. Baum and W. Rehm, eds., *Musik und Verlag. Karl Vötterle zum 65. Geburtstag am 12. April 1968* (Kassel: Bärenreiter, 1968), p. 213.

8 Lewis Lockwood, 'A Dispute on Accidentals in Sixteenth-Century Rome', *Analecta Musicologica*, II (1965), 38f.

9 Nicola Vicentino, *L'antica musica ridotta alla moderna prattica* (Rome: Antonio Barré, 1555), Bk IV, Ch. 33, fols. 89r-90v.

10 'I canoni fatti alla seconda, alla terza, alla sesta, & settima, & alla nona sono piu moderni de gl'altri.' *Ibid.*, fol. 89v.

11 'Et si dè avvertire che quando il Tenore farà il Canon con il Contr'alto in quinta, che s'il Tenore sarà per b. molle, il Contr'alto verrà per ♮. incitato.' *Ibid.*

12 Ms. Vatican, lat. 5318, fols. 15r-15v.

13 *Ibid.*, fol. 149r.

14 Johannes Tinctoris, *Terminorum musicae diffinitorium* ([Treviso: Gerardo de Lisa, 1475]), 'Fuga'; Bartolomeo Ramos de Pareia, *Musica practica*, ed. Johannes Wolf, Publikationen der Internationalen Musikgesellschaft 2 (Leipzig: Breitkopf und Härtel, 1901), p. 68.

15 Haar ('Zarlino's Definition of Fugue and Imitation', pp. 232ff) demonstrates the similarity between Zarlino's and Aaron's view of fugue and imitation.

8 Classes of accidental inflections in early vocal polyphony

1 'Virtualiter licet semper non signentur.' *The Berkeley Manuscript*, ed. and trans. O. B. Ellsworth, Greek and Latin Music Theory 2 (Lincoln and London: University of Nebraska Press, 1984), pp. 44f.

2 'Dicunt namque nostri moderni non cantemus per *b* molle, nisi sit signatum et alii dicunt tunco cantemus, cum dulce sit magis quam ♮ quadrum, sic musicam ut vina probare putantes. Quae quaeso frivola sunt haec carissimi, quaeque pueriles ac insipidae nimis opiniones. Ergone psalmos introituum de quarto tono canere debemus per ♮ quadrum, qui toti jacent in tritono, dulcesque sanctorum et angelicas magisquam humanas modulationes ob nostram ignoran-

tiam duras atque rusticanas reddere? Si nobis non licet absque signo puerorum ac rudium bene canere, non liceat etiam absque signo tubarum aut campanarum manducare. Dulce quidem est *b* rotundum, ob quandam minoris semitonii molliciem, sed dulcius est mel, quod nimie sumptum facit dolere ventrem. Sint ergo signa *b* mollis et ♮ quadri pro pueris et qui non intelligunt tonum ac semitonium rudibus, nos vero sectari decet rationem.' Johannes Legrense, *Ritus canendi vetustissimus et novus* in E. de Coussemaker, ed., *Scriptorum de musica medii aevi nova series a gerbertina altera*, vol. IV (Paris: A. Durand, 1876), pp. 360f.

3 'Neque tunc b mollis signum apponi est necessarium, immo si appositum videatur, asinimum esse dicitur.' Johannes Tinctoris, *Liber de natura et proprietate tonorum* in *Opera theoretica*, ed. A. Seay, Corpus Scriptorum de Musica 22, vol. I (n.p.: American Institute of Musicology, 1975), p. 74, trans. Albert Seay, Translations 2, rev. edn (Colorado Springs: The Colorado College Music Press, 1976), p. 12.

4 'Mai si debbe abandonare il primo ordine, si expresse il secondo ordine overo il terzo non siano signati per le loro clave, overo che se videssi ♮ et F uniti che volessino stare insieme, che naturalmente non possono,' John Hothby, *La Caliopea legale* in E. de Coussemaker, ed., *Histoire de l'harmonie au moyen âge* (Paris: Librairie Archéologique de Victor Didron, 1852), p. 309.

5 'Quod si depingatur, debet sic figurari ▭▬◼▭.' Bartolomeo Ramos de Pareia, *Musica practica*, ed. Johannes Wolf, Publikationen der Internationalen Musikgesellschaft 2 (Leipzig: Breitkopf und Härtel, 1901), p. 66. Similar expressions occur several times in similar contexts on the next page of the treatise.

6 Pietro Aaron, *Libri tres de institutione harmonica* (Bologna: Benedetto di Ettore, 1516), fol. 50v.

7 'Benche tal segno appresso gli dotti & pratichi cantori manco e di bisogno, ma sol si pone perche forse il mal pratico & non intelligente cantore, non darebbe pronuntia perfetta a tal positione over syllaba, perche essendo naturalmente dal mi & sol un semidittono, senza quel segno esso cantore non canterebbe altro che il suo proprio, se gia l'orecchio non gli dessi aiuto, come si vede in alcuni che questo molto bene fanno.' Pietro Aaron, *Toscanello in musica* (Venice: Marchio Sessa, 1539), Bk II, Ch. 20, trans. Peter Bergquist, Translations 4, vol. II (Colorado Springs: The Colorado College Music Press, 1970), pp. 33f.

8 'Since I have shown enough above about the sign of *b molle*, it seems appropriate to reconsider some matters about the sign ♯. Although I spoke of it somewhat in Book II, Chapter 20 above, the discussion in this Supplement will be more ample for the aid of those who are interested in more. Since I sought brevity and ease in our *Toscanello*, in that chapter I was accommodating to the common taste, but now that real understanding is to be sought, you will see why I said what I did in that chapter . . . The obligation or necessity then devolves on the composer to remove all danger and cause of the singer falling into error. The composer should show that sign, because of the various intentions and manners occurring in our free counterpoint as shown in the above Book II, Chapter 20, and as is shown in the present example [see Example 33 on p. 139 above]. In this example [(a)] the composer does not intend that the last breve, or the last interval, should be raised or diminished, because there is no sign showing any such raising, as is understood in the figure. If it were raised, the last interval would be an imperfect octave with the bass and no unison with the alto. But when such raising is intended, it should be shown, as in the following example [(b)]. Here the intent was to change the first harmony, although the progression is the same

as in the first. Thus he needs to show the singer his second meaning with the sign, so that one will not think that he means what he did in the first example, as happens if one finds the following example [(c)]. But note now that I should not be accused of being contrary to myself, considering that I said in the above mentioned Chapter 20 that the sign diesis is not needed by the learned and experienced singers, since they will easily recognize with their intellect and excellent ear definite progressions where the raised note should properly be used or not used, as the composer intends. They would be so familiar with noticing this through continuous practice of music that they would take the attitude that it does little harm when the sign is not found. This attitude and practice cannot help, let alone give notice to the inexperienced and unintelligent singer, so for this reason it is necessary that the composer signify when and where the sign is necessary.' ('Havendo di sopra a sufficienza dimostrato circa il segno del b molle, & venendo al proposito retrattare qualche particula de la figura apparente ♯ dato che innanzi al vigesimo capitolo del secondo libro ne sia alquanto parlato, nondimeno piu diffusamente ne la presente agiunta a coloro che piu di questo si dilettono, si esponera. Havendo io ricercato brevita, facilita nel sopradetto Toscanello nostro, mi sono piu tosto in tal capitolo acommodato secondo il vulgo, che altrimenti. Ma hora perche piu si ricerca la vera intelligenza, ti advertisco, quando da me e stato detto queste parole, nel sopradetto capitolo . . . Quale obbligo, o necessita sia al compositore attribuita, per rimuovere ogni pericolo & causa del cantore ne la quale potessi incorrere, el ditto compositore e òbbligato a dover segnare tal figura, per gli varii intenti & modi occorrenti al libero nostro contrapunto, come appare nel sopradetto capitolo vigesimo nominato, del secondo libro, & si come appare ne la presente dimostratione [see Example 33(a) on p. 139 above]. Ne la quale lo intento del compositore non ha considerato che quella ultima breve, o veramente intervallo ultimo, habbia a essere sospeso, overo disminuito, perche non appare segno dimostrante alcuna sospensione, come e compreso per la figura, ma volendo sospendere detto intervallo ultimo, sarebbe ottave imperfetta col basso, & non unisono col controalto. Ma quando sara proposto a tal sospenso, lo segnera come seguitando si vede [see Example 33(b)]. Et perche lo intento suo e stato di rimuovere la prima harmonia, benche sia simile processo con il primo, a lui e stato dibisogno con il segno presente advertire el cantore de la seconda sua consideratione, acio non pensassi al primo modo da lui dimostrato, come acadera se tal discorso troverrai [see Example 33(c)]. Ma hora attendi di non mi appropriare di contrario alcuno di me stesso, considerando che da me e stato concluso rationabilmente al nominato sopradetto .xx. capitolo, che la figura diesis, non si ricerca appresso gli dotti & pratichi cantori, imperoche il dotto & pratico cantore, facilissimamente cognoscera con l'intelletto & ottimo suo orecchio, un certo procedere a dovere cadere propriamente a quella nota sospesa, o non sospesa esaminata per il compositore, laqual notitia sara a lui tanto familiare per essere stato continuo ne lo esercitio cantabile, che habbia preso tal habito che poco gli nocera, non ritrovando il segno di sopra allegato, ilquale habito & continuo esercitio non potra aiutare ne manco dar notitia al mal pratico & non intelligente cantore, de laqual cosa e necessario al compositore per questa cagione segnarlo al tempo & luogo dove necessario sara.') *Ibid.*, sigs. Iv–Iiir, trans. Bergquist, vol. III, pp. 21ff.

9 This revision of Aaron's earlier views in the 1529 'Supplement' to the second edition of *Toscanello* was provoked by Giovanni Spataro's letter of May 23, 1524, addressed to our author, in which Spataro criticized the theorist's discussion of

the sign of diesis in the first edition of 1523 for his claim that experienced singers
did not need the sign to be expressly written down. Ms. Vatican, lat. 5318,
fols. 211v–212r. Aaron's dependence on Spataro's letter has been pointed out in
Lewis Lockwood, 'A Sample Problem of *Musica Ficta*: Willaert's *Pater Noster*' in
H. Powers, ed., *Studies in Music History. Essays for Oliver Strunk* (Princeton:
Princeton University Press, 1968), pp. 165ff.

10 'Doubts and disputations are circulating among some lovers of music about the
signs of *b molle* and *diesis*, whether the composers are constrained by necessity
to show them in their compositions, or whether the singer should be held to
understand and recognize the hidden secret of all the places where these figures
or signs are needed . . . Although some say that the signs of *b molle* and *b duro*
or *b rotundus* and *quadratus* are signs pertaining to new scholars which have no
reason, one answers that this usage is intended solely for the mitigation and
temperament of the tritone. Even if *b molle* is not shown, with every learned and
unlearned musician, it is understood that this harshness is never to be tolerated
. . . Many composers have observed this rule. Although they understood the rule
themselves, they considered the carelessness of the singer, which arises easily. For
this reason they have brought into light and shown openly the sign ♭ . . . [There
follow examples from works by Jean Mouton, Josquin des Prez, Antoine de
Févin, Carpentras and Jean L'Héritier.] It will now be considered whether the
singer should or indeed can recognize at once the intent and secret of a composer, when singing a song he has not seen before. The answer is no, although
among those who celebrate music there are some who think the contrary. They
give the reason that every composer considers that his songs are to be understood
by the learned and experienced, by a quick and perceptive ear, especially when
imperfect fifths, octaves, twelfths, and fifteenths occur. I say that only God is
master of such things, and such silent intelligence belongs to Him only and not
to a mortal man. For it would be impossible for any learned and practiced man
to be able to sense instantly an imperfect fifth, octave, twelfth or fifteenth
without first committing the error of a little dissonance. It is true that it would
be sensed more quickly by one than another, but there is not a man who would
not be caught. For this reason I say that those who do not indicate the sign of
b molle where it might naturally appear to be otherwise, commit no little error,
because *propositum in mente retentum, nihil operatur* [an intention retained in
the mind accomplishes nothing]. Some worthy composers have shown this in
their songs . . . [There follow examples from works by Josquin, Mouton, Févin,
Constanzo Festa, Antoine de Longueval, Philippe Verdelot, Pierre de la Rue
and L'Héritier.] Since all these are moderns, you may not have unshakeable faith
in them, but I have considered these things carefully, and I wish to show you for
your greater clearness and satisfaction some other pertinent examples from our
ancients, such as Orto, Alexander Agricola, Pierre de la Rue, Japart, Compère,
Isaac, and Obrecht . . . [Examples follow.] Just as God has taught us and
painted before our eyes the way of salvation and also that of damnation,
through which we distinguish the good from the bad, since otherwise without
this we might easily be able to fall into doing evil always, or doing good, or sometimes into good and other into evil; since life then is both good and bad, it was
necessary for Him to ordain His precepts and the ways through which we may
distinguish the right way to live from its contrary. Further, in travelling one sees
places where there are various signs, because there are several roads one might
take. By means of these signs those who do not know the country may correctly
choose the right road. If there were no sign, they doubtless might choose the

wrong road, at the end of which might rise a river by which they might easily become stranded in trying to cross it; or avoiding this misfortune, they at least would have to turn back. Thus the musician or composer is obliged to show his intention so that the singer will not stumble into something the composer did not intend. I conclude then, as I have said, that the sign is as useful to the learned as to the untaught, and I say that the singer is not obliged at first trial to sing the notes in the places where that sign might appear, if it is not there. They might err, since it might or might not be intended. Thus it should appear in any necessary place, and when it is not needed, it should not be shown. And this is to be understood also in songs that are not being sung for the first time.' ('Si muove fra alcuni de la musica desiderosi, dubii & disputationi circa la figura del b molle & diesis, utrum se de necessita gli Compositori sono constretti a segnare ne gli canti da loro composti, dette figure, cioe b molle & diesis, o veramente se il cantore e tenuto a dovere intendere, & cognoscere lo incognito secreto di tutti gli luoghi dove tal figure o segni bisogneranno . . . Benche alcuni altri dicono che el segno del b molle & ♮ duro, overamente b rotondo, & quadro, sono segni appartenenti a nuovi scholari, liquali non hanno ragione alcuna. Si risponde che tal modo solo si intende a la mitigatione & temperamento del tritono, alquale benche non sia apparente el b molle, appresso ogni dotto & non dotto, per ordinaria & spetial regola da gli musichi constituita, sara inteso sempre non esser tal durezza tollerata . . . & questo hanno osservato molti compositori liquali benche tal segno da loro sia stato inteso, nondimeno hanno advertito a la inadvertenza del cantore, laquale facilmente nascerebbe. Onde per tal cagione hanno in luce messo, & in apparenza dimostrato la presente figura ♭ . . . Hora si risponde se il cantore e ubligato o veramente puo cantando uno canto non da lui piu visto cognoscere, o intendere l'intento & secreto del compositore da lui pensato al primo moto, si conclude che no, se bene fussi quello che celebro la musica benche alcuni il contrario pensono, allegando la ragione dicono. Che ogni compositore fanno giuditio che gli loro canti habbino a essere intesi da gli dotti, & buoni pratichi, per uno audito presto & repentino, massimamente quando occorrerano quinte, ottave, duodecime & quinte decime imperfette. Dico che a questo solo ne e maestro Iddio, & tale intelligenza muta, sola appartiene a lui, & non a huomo mortale, perche sara impossibile a ogni dotto & pratico poter sentire in uno subito una quinta, ottava, duodecima, o quintadecima imperfetta, che non commetta primamente lo errore di qualche poco di dissonanza, vero e, che piu presto sara sentito da uno che da l'altro, pur nondimeno non sara huomo che in questo non incappi. De laqual cosa dico, che coloro liquali non segnerano il segno del b molle dove naturalmente altro si vede, commetteranno non poco errore, perche. Propositum in mente retentum, nihil operatur. Si come hanno dimostrato alcuni degni compositori, ne gli suoi canti . . . de liquali per esser moderni, forse non presterai a loro indubitata fede, ma io che questo infra di me ho considerato, voglio per piu chiarezza, & satisfatione tua, adducere alcuni altri al proposito nostro antichi, come Orto, Alessandro agricola, Pierazzon de larue, Iapart, Compere, Isach, & Obreth . . . Ma si come Iddio a noi ha insegnato, & dipinto dinanzi a gli occhi nostri la via de la salvatione, & anchora de la damnatione, per laquale cognoscemo il bene dal male, che forse senza questa facilmente havessimo potuto incorrere semper al male operare, o al bene, overamente alcuna volta al bene & quando al male. Essendo adunque la via buona & cattiva, a lui e stato necessario ordnare gli suoi precetti, & modi per liquali habbiamo a cognoscere il ben vivere, da quello che e contrario. Et piu si vede in alcuni viaggi dove si truovono varii segnali, &

questo per essergli piu strade da potere caminare, onde acio che quegli che non sanno per quel paese andare, possino rettamente pigliare il buon camino dove non essendo segno alcuno, senza dubbio potrebbono pigliare la cativa via, al fin de la quale nascerebbe un fiume dove bisognando passarlo, facilmente si potrebbono arenare, o per il manco male tornare indietro. Per tanto il Musico overo Compositore e ubbligato segnare lo intento suo, acio che il cantore non incorra in quello che dal detto compositore non fu mai pensato. Concludo adunque come ho detto che tal segno e cosi conveniente a gli dotti, come a gli indotti, & dico che il cantore non e tenuto nel primo moto, cantare le note ne gli luoghi dove tal segno puo accadere, se tal segno non appare, perche potrebbe errare, impero che puo stare, & non puo stare. Per tanto debbe apparere al tempo opportuno, & quando non bisogna, non si debbe in luce adducere, Et questo si intende ne gli concenti non provisti, cioe non prima cantati, overamente considerati.') Aaron, *Toscanello in musica*, 'Aggiunta', trans. Bergquist, vol. III, pp. 12-20.

11 'Dico adonca che li boni pulsatori de li instrumenti facti per arte per certa sua practica sonano li canti non come simplicemente sono composti et scripti da li indocti compositori ma li sonano come debeno esser signati: et similemente fano li periti cantori: molte volte cantano li concenti meglio che non sono stati compositi: et signati da li compositori.' Ms. Vatican, lat. 5318, fol. 144v.

12 See especially Howard Mayer Brown, 'Accidentals and Ornamentation in Sixteenth-Century Intabulations of Josquin's Motets', E. E. Lowinsky, ed., *Josquin des Prez* (London: Oxford University Press, 1976), pp. 475-522.

13 Nicola Vicentino, *L'antica musica ridotta alla moderna prattica* (Rome: Antonio Barré, 1555), fol. 53r.

14 'Ancora che non sia stata segnata dal Compositore'. Gioseffo Zarlino, *Le Istitutioni harmoniche* (Venice, 1558), p. 237, trans. Guy A. Marco and Claude V. Palisca (New Haven: Yale University Press, 1968), p. 174.

15 *Ibid.*, p. 222.

16 See interesting remarks on this matter in Carl Dahlhaus, *Esthetics of Music* (Cambridge: Cambridge University Press, 1982), pp. 10f.

17 Philip Gaskell estimates that printing paper (a cheaper material than either parchment or vellum) accounted for about 75 per cent of the total direct cost of book production in the sixteenth century. *A New Introduction to Bibliography* (New York and Oxford: Oxford University Press, 1972), p. 177.

18 Carl Dahlhaus, 'Tonsystem und Kontrapunkt um 1500', *Jahrbuch des Staatlichen Instituts für Musikforschung Preussischer Kulturbesitz*, (1969), 7-18. See also Dahlhaus, 'Relationes harmonicae', *Archiv für Musikwissenschaft*, XXXII (1975), 208-27.

19 'The object of theory is primarily the abstract counterpoint which reckons not with definite intervals but with interval classes. Only supplementary rules transform it into the concrete or harmonic counterpoint from which theorists expect that it will remain within the borders of the system of *relationes harmonicae*. The rules governing dissonances and the prohibition of parallel perfect consonances refer to the abstract counterpoint which may be represented graphically by a notation without accidentals and clefs, while the prohibition of mi against fa relates to the harmonic counterpoint . . . Indeed, one composed as if they [*falsae concordantiae*] did not exist; as if each fifth or octave which one notated were representable as perfect fifth or octave. And in places in which a collision was unavoidable . . . the inflected note which conflicted with an uninflected one was experienced literally as an accident, as a coincidence which did

not touch the heart of the matter, the abstractly conceived counterpoint. Indifference toward the lowly empirical realm, toward the difficulties arising in the realization of a composition, is the obverse side of abstraction . . . The decision between the *subsemitonium* cadence and the Phrygian cadence [on *A*] belongs not to the composition, but to the "exterior" of the work, the layer which may change from one performance to another without distorting thereby the musical text or falsifying the intention of the composer. The setting of accidentals was gradually consolidated into an aspect of composition first in the second third of the sixteenth century. Leaving aside a few written-out accidentals, around 1500 it was still the preserve of reproduction, so that it is useless to strive for an "authentic" version.' ('Gegenstand der Theorie ist primär der abstrakte Kontrapunkt, der nicht mit bestimmten Intervallen, sondern mit Intervallklassen rechnet; erst durch Zusatzbestimmungen wird er zum konkreten oder harmonischen Kontrapunkt, von dem die Theoretiker erwarten, dass er sich in den Grenzen des Systems der relationes harmonicae halte. Auf den abstrakten Kontrapunkt, der durch eine Notation ohne Vorzeichen und Schlüssel graphisch dargestellt werden kann, sind die Dissonanzregeln und das Parallelenverbot, auf den harmonischen Kontrapunkt die Warnungen, Mi gegen Fa zu setzen, bezogen . . . Allerdings wurde so komponiert, als gäbe es sie nicht: als sei jede Quinte oder Oktave, die man notierte, als reine Quinte oder Oktave darstellbar. Und dort, wo eine Kollision unvermeidbar war, . . . wurde der alterierte Ton, der mit einem nicht alterierten zusammenstiess, als Akzidens im Wortsinn: als Zufall empfunden, der das Wesen der Sache, den abstrakt gedachten Kontrapunkt, nicht berührte. Gleichgültigkeit gegenüber der niederen Empirie – gegenüber Schwierigkeiten bei der Realisierung des Tonsatzes – ist die Reversseite der Abstraktion . . . Die Entscheidung zwischen der Subsemitonium-Klausel und der phrygischen Kadenz gehört nicht zur Komposition, sondern zur "Aussenschicht" des Werkes, die von einer Aufführung zur anderen wechseln kann, ohne dass dadurch der musikalische Text verzerrt oder die Intention des Komponisten verfehlt würde. Erst im zweiten Drittel des 16. Jahrhunderts verfestigte sich die Akzidentiensetzung allmählich zu einem Teil der Komposition. Um 1500 war sie noch – von wenigen ausgeschriebenen Vorzeichen abgesehen – der Reproduktion vorbehalten, so dass die Bemühung um eine "authentische" Fassung vergeblich ist.') *Ibid.*, pp. 12ff.

20 Prosdocimus de Beldemandis, *Contrapunctus*, ed. and trans. J. Herlinger, Greek and Latin Music Theory 1 (Lincoln and London: University of Nebraska Press, 1984), pp. 58–69.

21 Nicolaus Gombert, *Opera omnia*, ed. J. Schmidt-Görg, Corpus Mensurabilis Musicae 6, vol. II (Rome: American Institute of Musicology, 1954), pp. 29f.

22 Lewis Lockwood, 'A Dispute on Accidentals in Sixteenth-Century Rome', *Analecta Musicologica*, II (1965), 24–40.

23 See n. 9 above.

24 Arthur Mendel, 'The Purposes and Desirable Characteristics of Text-Critical Editions', E. Olleson, ed., *Modern Musical Scholarship* (Stocksfield: Oriel Press, 1980), pp. 14–27.

25 Guillaume Dufay, *Opera omnia*, ed. H. Besseler, Corpus Mensurabilis Musicae 1, vol. VI (n.p.: American Institute of Musicology, 1964), p. 49. The editor missed the implied signature in this case.

26 The classification proposed here spells out and develops the implications of a similar classification proposed in Lockwood, 'A Sample Problem of *Musica Ficta*', p. 176.

27 Brown, 'Accidentals and Ornamentation', *passim*.
28 *Cf*. interesting remarks on this subject in Carl Dahlhaus, *Foundations of Music History* (Cambridge: Cambridge University Press, 1983), pp. 164f.
29 The question of the basic assumptions which should govern editors of early polyphony in matters concerning implied accidentals has been posed in a particularly acute form in Lockwood, 'A Sample Problem of *Musica Ficta*', pp. 163 and 168f. I am in fundamental agreement with Lockwood's proposal that, for any given piece, we should search for 'a set of more or less probable alternative hypotheses as to its pitch-content' and try to 'evaluate these as having greater or lesser plausibility'. In the remaining portion of this chapter, I attempt to show precisely how this can be done.
30 Allan Atlas, *The Cappella Giulia Chansonnier (Rome, Biblioteca Apostolica Vaticana, C.G. XIII. 27)*, Musicological Studies 27, vol. I (Brooklyn: Institute of Mediaeval Music, 1975), pp. 39–48.
31 *Ibid.*, p. 46. See also Howard Mayer Brown, 'Introduction', *A Florentine Chansonnier from the Time of Lorenzo the Magnificent. Florence, Biblioteca Nazionale Centrale MS Banco Rari 229*, Monuments of Renaissance Music 7, vol. I (Chicago and London: The University of Chicago Press, 1983), pp. 150–67.
32 Atlas, *The Cappella Giulia Chansonnier*, p. 43.
33 Guillaume Dufay, *Opera omnia*, ed. Besseler, vol. VI, pp. 55f and XLII. *O* stands for Ms. Oxford, Bodleian Library, Canonici Miscellaneous 213; the rondeau appears on fol. 78v. *PR* stands for Ms. Paris, Bibliothèque Nationale, Nouvelles Acquisitions Françaises 6771 ('Reina Codex'); the rondeau appears on fol. 98r. *Em* stands for Ms. Munich, Bayerische Staatsbibliothek, Latinus monacensis 14274 (*olim* Mus. 3232a; Cim. 352c; 'St Emmeram Codex'); the rondeau appears on fol. 96r.
34 A careful reader of this book will have no difficulty in understanding the reasons for the differences between Besseler's interpretation of *O* (Example 40) and mine (Example 41). I see no justification for the inflections suggested by Besseler in mm. 3 (superius), 8 (contratenor), 10 (here the bb-mi 'resolves' after two intervening notes to cc-fa), 17, 20 and 26 (contratenor). Besseler's eebs in mm. 7–8 (superius) result from a misreading of the source's *extra manum* ffb.
35 The University of Illinois Musicological Archives for Renaissance Manuscript Studies, comp., *Census-Catalogue of Manuscript Sources of Polyphonic Music 1400–1550*, Renaissance Manuscript Studies 1, vol. II (n.p.: American Institute of Musicology, 1982), pp. 275f.
36 *Ibid.*, vol. III (1984), pp. 33f.
37 Ian Rumbold, 'The Compilation and Ownership of the "St Emmeram" Codex (Munich, Bayerische Staatsbibliothek, Clm 14274)', *Early Music History*, II (1982), 161–235.
38 *Cf*. David Fallows' remarks on the song in *Dufay* (London: J. M. Dent and Sons Ltd, 1982), p. 100: 'This song shows a third characteristic that seems to have fascinated Dufay particularly from about 1430: the alternation of major and minor triads, particularly when based on C. This matter has been discussed by Besseler who called it *Terzfreiheit* – mobility of the third. In *Navré je sui* the interlocking of the voices at the outset asserts the C major triad as strongly as possible so that the appearance of the Eb in bar 3 and particularly in bar 7 makes its point almost too clearly. This mobility of the third in the triad on C will continue to appear in Dufay's works, to find its apotheosis in his last Mass, the *Ave regina celorum* (iii/10).' Besseler's and Fallows' observations provide a useful context for my discussion of the song, even though it should be clear by now that

if my interpretation of the rondeau is correct, the contrasting e♭ makes its appearance only in the second half of the refrain.

39 I would like to thank my colleague, William P. Mahrt, for an illuminating discussion of rhetorical aspects of the rondeau. For a recent paper on Dufay's relation to the rhetorical tradition, see Willem Elders, 'Guillaume Dufay as Musical Orator', *Tijdschrift van de Vereniging voor Nederlandse Muziekgeschiedenis*, XXXI (1981), 1-15. More immediately relevant to my interpretation of the song, however, is the persuasive view of the relation of poetry and music in Dufay's rondeaux presented in Don Michael Randel, 'Dufay the Reader', *Studies in the History of Music*, I (1983), 38-78, in particular, Randel's observation that 'settings of rondeaux are to be understood first and foremost as settings of their refrains' (*ibid.*, p. 71) and his conclusion that 'Dufay knew how to use declamation, imitation, melodic motion, register, harmonic rhythm, and even chromaticism in the reading of his texts' (*ibid.*, p. 78).

Bibliography

I Sources

Aaron, Pietro. *Libri tres de institutione harmonica.* Bologna: Benedetto di Ettore, 1516
— . *Toscanello in musica,* 3rd edn. Venice: Marchio Sessa, 1539
— . *Trattato della natura et cognitione di tutti gli tuoni di canto figurato non da altrui piu scritti.* Venice: Bernardino de Vitali, 1525
— . *Lucidario in musica di alcune oppenioni antiche, et moderne con le loro oppositioni, & resolutioni, con molti altri secreti appresso, & questioni da altrui anchora non dichiarati.* Venice: Girolamo Scotto, 1545
— . *Compendiolo di molti dubbi, segreti et sentenze intorno al canto fermo, et figurato.* Milan: Io. Antonio da Castelliono, n.d. [after 1545]
— . Letters in Ms. Vatican, lat. 5318
Adam von Fulda. *Musica* in M. Gerbert, ed., *Scriptores ecclesiastici de musica sacra potissimum,* vol. III. St Blasien: Typis San Blasianis, 1784, pp. 329-81
Agricola, Martin. *Musica choralis deudsch,* 3rd edn. Wittenberg: Georg Rhau, 1533
— . *Musica instrumentalis deudsch,* 3rd edn. Wittenberg: Georg Rhau, 1532
— . *Rudimenta musices.* Wittenberg: Georg Rhau, 1539
Angelo da Picitono. *Fior angelico di musica.* Venice: Agostino Bindoni, 1547
Anonymus. *Ars et modus pulsandi organa secundum modum novissimum inventum per magistros musicos modernos* in R. Casimiri, 'Un trattatello per organisti di anonimo del sec. XIV', *Note d'Archivio per la Storia Musicale,* XIX (1942), 99-101
Anonymus. *Concioscia cossa che el contrapuncto abbia duoe consonancie* in A. Seay, ed., *Quatuor tractatuli italici de contrapuncto,* Critical Texts 3. Colorado Springs: The Colorado College Music Press, 1977
Anonymus. *Cum notum sit* in E. de Coussemaker, ed., *Scriptorum de musica medii aevi nova series a gerbertina altera,* vol. III. Paris: A. Durand, 1869, pp. 60-8
Anonymus. *Introductorium musicae* in Hugo Riemann, 'Anonymi Introductorium Musicae (c. 1500). Nach dem Unicum der Leipziger Universitätsbibliothek', *Monatshefte für Musikgeschichte,* XXIX (1897), 147-54, 157-64; XXX (1898), 1-8, 11-19
Anonymus. *[Libellus] Ex Codice Vaticano Lat. 5129,* ed. A. Seay, Corpus Scriptorum de Musica 9. N.p.: American Institute of Musicology, 1964
Anonymus. *Musica enchiriadis* in Gerbert, *Scriptores,* vol. I, pp. 152-73
Anonymus. *Musica et Scolica enchiriadis,* H. Schmid, ed., Veröffentlichungen der Musikhistorischen Kommission 3. Munich: Verlag der Bayerischen Akademie der Wissenschaften, 1981
Anonymus. *Musice compilatio* in F. A. Gallo, ed., *Mensurabilis musicae tractatuli,* Antiquae Musicae Italicae Scriptores 1, vol. I. Bologna: Calderini, 1966, pp. 61-75

246

Anonymus. *Quaestiones et solutiones*, ed. A. Seay, Critical Texts 2. Colorado Springs: The Colorado College Music Press, 1977

Anonymus. *Quot sunt concordationes* in Coussemaker, *Scriptorum*, vol. III, pp. 70-4

Anonymus. *Regole di far contrapunto di nota per nota*. Ms. London, British Library, Add. 36986, fols. 26r-30r

Anonymus. *Regule contrapuncti secundum usum Regni Siciliae* in Paolo Nalli, '*Regulae contrapuncti secundum usum Regni Siciliae* tratte da un codice siciliano del Sec. XV', *Archivio storico per la Sicilia Orientale*, 2nd series, IX (1933), 277-92

Anonymus. *Tertius liber musicae*. Ms. Venice, Biblioteca Nazionale di S. Marco, lat. VIII.85 (=3579), fols. 84v-88v

Anonymus. *Tractatus de contrapuncto* in O. B. Ellsworth, ed. and trans., *The Berkeley Manuscript. University of California Music Library, MS. 744 (olim Phillipps 4450)*, Greek and Latin Music Theory 2. Lincoln and London: University of Nebraska Press, 1984

Anonymus. *Tractatus de musica figurata et de contrapuncto* in Coussemaker, *Scriptorum*, vol. IV, pp. 434-69

Anonymus. II. *Tractatus de discantu*, ed. and trans. A. Seay, Critical Texts with Translations 1. Colorado Springs: The Colorado College Music Press, 1978

Anonymus. XI. *Tractatus de musica plana et mensurabili* in Coussemaker, *Scriptorum*, vol. III, pp. 416-75

Anselmi, Giorgio. *De musica*, ed. G. Massera, Historiae Musicae Cultores 14. Florence: Leo S. Olschki, 1961

Antonius de Leno. *Regulae de contrapuncto*, ed. A. Seay, Critical Texts 1. Colorado Springs: The Colorado College Music Press, 1977

Arnaut de Zwolle, Henri. [Treatises] in G. Le Cerf and E.-R. Labande, eds., *Les traités d'Henri-Arnaut de Zwolle et de divers anonymes (Ms. B. N. latin 7295)*. Paris: Auguste Picard, 1932

Artusi, Giovanni Maria. *L'Artusi, overo delle imperfettioni della moderna musica*. Venice: Giacomo Vincenti, 1600

Aventinus, Johannes. *Musicae rudimenta, Augsburg, 1516*, ed. and trans. T. H. Keahey, Musical Theorists in Translation 10. Brooklyn: Institute of Mediaeval Music, 1971

Bermudo, Juan. *El arte Tripharia*. Ossuna: Juan de Leon, 1550

—. *Declaración de instrumentos musicales*. Ossuna: Juan de Leon, 1555

Boen, Johannes. *Ars (musicae)*, ed. F. A. Gallo, Corpus Scriptorum de Musica 19. N.p.: American Institute of Musicology, 1972

—. *Musica* in Wolf Frobenius, *Johannes Boens Musica und seine Konsonanzlehre*, Freiburger Schriften zur Musikwissenschaft 2. Stuttgart: Musikwissenschaftliche Verlags-Gesellschaft mbH, 1971, pp. 31-105

Bonaventura da Brescia. *Brevis collectio artis musicae . . . quae dicitur 'Venturina'.* Ms. Bologna, Civico Museo Bibliografico Musicale, 105 (A57), fols. 1r-41r

—. *Breviloquium musicale*. [Brescia]: Angelo Britannico, 1497

Bourgeois, Loys. *Le droict chemin de musique*. Geneva: [Jean Gérard], 1550

Burtius, Nicolaus. *Florum libellus*, ed. G. Massera, Historiae Musicae Cultores 28. Florence: Leo S. Olschki, 1975

Cardan, Jerome. *De musica* in *Opera*, vol. X. Lyons: Ioannes Antonius Huguetan and Marcus Antonius Ravaud, 1663, pp. 105-16

Ciconia, Johannes. *Nova musica*. Ms. Florence, Biblioteca Riccardiana, 734, fols.

1r–57r
—. *De tribus generibus melorum*. *Ibid.*, fols. 57r–61v
Cinciarino, Pietro. *Introduttorio abbreviato di musica piana, o vero canto fermo.* Venice: Domenico de' Farri, 1555
Cochlaeus, Johannes. *Tetrachordum musices.* Nuremberg: Fridericus Peypus, 1514
Coclico, Adrianus Petit. *Compendium musices.* Nuremberg: Ioannes Montanus and Ulricus Neuber, 1552
Conrad von Zabern. *Novellus musicae artis tractatus* in K. W. Gümpel, ed., *Die Musiktraktate Conrads von Zabern.* Mainz: Akademie der Wissenschaften und der Literatur, 1956
—. *Opusculum de monochordo. Ibid.*
—. *De modo bene cantandi choralem cantum. Ibid.*
Danckerts, Ghiselin. *Trattato sopra una differentia musicale.* Ms. Rome, Biblioteca Vallicelliana, R.56
Del Lago, Giovanni. *Breve introduttione di musica misurata.* Venice: Brandino e Ottaviano Scotto, 1540
—. Letters in Ms. Vatican, lat. 5318
Dentice, Luigi. *Duo dialoghi della musica*, 2nd edn. Rome: Vincenzo Lucrino, 1553
Durán, Domingo Marcos. *Lux bella*, 2nd edn. Salamanca: [Juan de Porras?], 1509
—. *Comento sobre Lux bella.* Salamanca: [Juan de Porras], 1498
—. *Sumula de canto de órgano.* Salamanca: [Juan de Porras?, *ca.* 1507]
Eger von Kalkar, Heinrich. *Cantuagium*, ed. H. Hüschen, Beiträge zur Rheinischen Musikgeschichte 2. Cologne and Krefeld: Staufen-Verlag, 1952
Elias Salomo. *Scientia artis musicae* in Gerbert, *Scriptores*, vol. III, pp. 16–64
Engelbert of Admont. *De musica* in Gerbert, *Scriptores*, vol. II, pp. 287–369
Espinosa, Juan de. *Tractado de principios de musica practica et theorica sin dexar ninguna cosa atras.* Toledo: Guillem de Brocar, 1520
Faber, Gregor. *Musices practicae erotematum libri II.* Basle: Heinrich Petri, 1553
Faber, Heinrich. *Ad musicam practicam introductio, non modo praecepta, sed exempla quoque ad usum puerorum accommodata, quàm brevissime continens.* Nuremberg: Ioannes Montanus and Ulricus Neuber, 1550
Finck, Hermann, *Practica musica.* Wittenberg: Haeredes Georgii Rhau, 1556
Finé, Oronce. *Epithoma musice instrumentalis ad omnimodam hemispherii seu luthine et theoricam et practicam.* Paris: Pierre Attaingnant, 1530
Foliani, Lodovico. *Musica theorica.* Venice: Io. Antonius and Fratres de Sabbio, 1529
Franciscus de Brugis. 'Opusculum' in G. Massera, *La 'mano musicale perfetta' di Francesco de Brugis dalle prefazioni ai corali di L. A. Giunta, Venezia, 1499–1504*, Historiae Musicae Cultores 18. Florence: Leo S. Olschki, 1963, pp. 73–96
Frosch, Johannes. *Rerum musicarum opusculum rarum ac insigne*, 2nd edn. Strasbourg: Petrus Schoeffer and Mathias Apiarius, 1535
Gaffurius, Franchinus. *Extractus parvus musice*, ed. F. A. Gallo, Antiquae Musicae Italicae Scriptores 4. Bologna: Forni, 1969
—. *Theorica musice.* Milan: Ioannes Petrus de Lomatio, 1492
—. *Practica musice.* Milan: Ioannes Petrus de Lomatio, 1496
—. *De harmonia musicorum instrumentorum.* Milan: Gotardus Pontanus, 1518
—. *Angelicum ad divinum opus musicae.* Milan: Gothardus Pontanus, 1508
—. *Apologia adversum Ioannem Spatarium & complices musicos Bononienses.* Turin: Augustinus di Vicomercato, 1520
—. *Epistula prima in solutiones obiectorum Ioannis Vaginarii Bononiensis.* [Milan, 1521]

Bibliography

—. *Epistula secunda apologetica in solutiones obiectorum Ioannis Vaginarii Bononiensis ad Antonium de Albertis Florentinum iuvenem studiosissimum.* [Milan, 1521]

Galliculus, Johannes. *Isagoge de compositione cantus.* Leipzig: Valentin Schumann, 1520

Ganassi dal Fontego, Sylvestro di. *Opera intitulata Fontagara.* Venice: l'autore, 1535

—. *Regola rubertina. Regola che insegna sonar de viola d'archo tastada.* Venice: l'autore, 1542

—. *Lettione seconda pur della prattica di sonare il violone d'arco da tasti.* Venice: l'autore, 1543

Glarean, Heinrich. *Isagoge in musicen.* Basle: Joannes Frobenius, 1516

—. *Dodecachordon.* Basle: Heinrich Petri, 1547

Guerson, Guillaume. *Utilissime musicales regule necessitate plani cantus simplicis contrapuncti: rerum factarum tonorum usualium: nec non artis accentuandi tam speculative quam practice: accriori lima mundate.* Paris: François Regnault, 1526

Guido frater. *Ars musice mensurate,* ed. F. A. Gallo, Antiquae Musicae Italicae Scriptores 1. Bologna: Forni, 1966

Guido of Arezzo. *Prologus in antiphonarium,* ed. J. Smits van Waesberghe, Divitiae Musicae Artis A.III. Buren: Frits Knuf, 1975

—. *Micrologus,* ed. J. Smits van Waesberghe, Corpus Scriptorum de Musica 4. N.p.: American Institute of Musicology, 1955

—. *Epistola de ignoto cantu* in Gerbert, *Scriptores,* vol. II, pp. 43–50

Guillelmus Monachus. *De preceptis artis musicae,* ed. A. Seay, Corpus Scriptorum de Musica 11. N.p.: American Institute of Musicology, 1965

Guilliaud, Maximilian. *Rudiments de musique pratique.* Paris: Du Chemin, 1554

Heyden, Sebald. *De arte canendi, ac vero signorum in cantibus usu.* Nuremberg: Ioh. Petreius, 1540

Horner, Thomas. *De ratione componendi cantus* in Heinrich Hüschen, 'Thomas Horner und seine Kompositionslehre "De ratione componendi cantus", Königsberg 1546'. *Musik des Ostens,* IV (1967), 150–69

Hothby, John. *La Caliopea legale* in E. de Coussemaker, ed., *Histoire de l'harmonie au moyen âge.* Paris: Librairie Archéologique de Victor Didron, 1852, pp. 297–349

—. *Tractatus quarundam regularum artis musicae.* Ms. Florence, Biblioteca Nazionale Centrale, Palat. 472, fols. 9r–15r

—. *Ars plane musice.* Ms. Florence, Biblioteca Nazionale Centrale, Magliabecchiana XIX, 36, fols. 78v–81v

—. *Regulae de monocordo manuali.* Ms. Faenza, Biblioteca Comunale, 117, fol. 62r

—. *Tractatus de arte contrapuncti* in Hothby, *De arte contrapuncti,* ed. G. Reaney, Corpus Scriptorum de Musica 26. N.p.: American Institute of Musicology, 1977, pp. 25–49

—. *Regule contrapuncti, ibid.,* pp. 63–9

—. *Regule dil contrapuncto, ibid.,* pp. 74–8

—. *Regulae supra contrapunctum, ibid.,* pp. 101–3

—. *Spetie tenore del contrapunto prima. Ibid.,* pp. 81–94

—. *Excitatio quaedam musicae artis per refutationem* in Hothby, *Tres tractatuli contra Bartholomeum Ramum,* ed. A. Seay, Corpus Scriptorum de Musica 10. N.p.: American Institute of Musicology, 1964, pp. 17–57

—. *Epistola. Ibid.,* pp. 79–92

Jacques de Liège. *Speculum musicae*, ed. R. Bragard, Corpus Scriptorum de Musica 3, 7 vols. N.p.: American Institute of Musicology, 1955-73

Jambe de Fer, Philibert. *Epitome musical des tons, sons et accordz, es voix humaines, fleustes d'Alleman, fleustes à neuf trous, violes, & violons*. Lyon: Michel du Bois, 1556

Jehan de Murs. *Notitia artis musicae*, ed. U. Michels, Corpus Scriptorum de Musica 17. N.p.: American Institute of Musicology, 1972, pp. 11-110

—. *Musica speculativa* in Gerbert, *Scriptores*, vol. III, pp. 249-83

—. *Quilibet affectans* in Coussemaker, *Scriptorum*, vol. III, pp. 59f

Jerome of Moravia. *Tractatus de musica*, ed. S. M. Cserba, Freiburger Studien zur Musikwissenschaft 2. Regensburg: Friedrich Pustet, 1935

Johannes Afflighemensis. *De musica cum tonario*, ed. J. Smits van Waesberghe, Corpus Scriptorum de Musica 1. N.p.: American Institute of Musicology, 1950

Khainer, Wolfgang. *Musica choralis* in Renate Federhofer-Königs, 'Wolfgang Khainer und seine "Musica choralis"'. *Kirchenmusikalisches Jahrbuch*, XLIII (1959), 32-48

Lanfranco, Giovanni Maria. *Scintille di musica*. Brescia: Lodovico Britannico, 1533

Legrense, Johannes. *Ritus canendi vetustissimus et novus* in Coussemaker, *Scriptorum*, vol. IV, pp. 298-396

Listenius, Nikolaus. *Musica*. Nuremberg: Johan. Petreius, 1549

Lusitano, Vicente. *Introdutione facilissima et novissima di canto fermo, figurato, contraponto semplice, et in concerto*. Rome: Antonio Blado, 1553

Marchetto da Padova. *Lucidarium in arte musicae planae* in Jan W. Herlinger, *The Lucidarium of Marchetto of Padua. A Critical Edition, Translation and Commentary*, 2 vols. Ph.D. diss., The University of Chicago, 1978, pp. 135-758

—. *Pomerium*, ed. G. Vecchi, Corpus Scriptorum de Musica 6. N.p.: American Institute of Musicology, 1961

Martínez de Bizcargui, Gonzalo. *Arte de canto llano et de contrapunto et canto de órgano con proporciones et modos*, ed. A. Seay, Critical Texts 9. Colorado Springs: The Colorado College Music Press, 1979

Monetarius, Stefan. *Epithoma utriusque musices practice*. Cracow: Florian Ungler, 1515

Ornithoparchus, Andreas. *Musice active micrologus*. Leipzig: Valentin Schumann, 1517

—. *Micrologus*, trans. John Dowland. London: Thomas Adams, 1609

Paulo da Firenze. *Ars ad adiscendum contrapunctum* in Pier Paolo Scattolin, 'I trattati teorici di Jacopo da Bologna e Paolo da Firenze'. *Quadrivium*, XV/1 (1974), 63-79

Petrus frater dictus Palma ociosa. *Compendium de discantu mensurabili* in Johannes Wolf, 'Ein Beitrag zur Diskantlehre des 14. Jahrhunderts'. *Sammelbände der Internationalen Musikgesellschaft*, XV (1913-14), 504-34

Philippus de Caserta. *Regule contrapuncti* in Nigel Wilkins, 'Some Notes on Philipoctus de Caserta (c. 1360?-c. 1435)'. *Nottingham Mediaeval Studies*, VIII (1964), 82-99

Prosdocimus de Beldemandis. *Tractatus plane musice*. Ms. Lucca, Biblioteca Governativa, 359, fols. 49r-71r

—. *Contrapunctus*, ed. and trans. J. Herlinger, Greek and Latin Music Theory 1. Lincoln and London: University of Nebraska Press, 1984

—. *Parvus tractatulus de modo dividendi monacordum*. Ms. Lucca, Biblioteca Governativa, 359, fols. 72r-78r

—. *Tractatus musice speculative contra Marchetum de Padua* in D. Raffaello

Bibliography

Baralli and Luigi Torri, 'Il "Trattato" di Prosdocimo de' Beldomandi contro Il "Lucidario" di Marchetto da Padova', *Rivista musicale italiana*, XX (1913), 731-62

Pseudo-Odo. *Dialogus* in Gerbert, *Scriptores*, vol. I, pp. 251-64

Pseudo-Tunstede, Simon. *Quatuor principalia musicae* in Coussemaker, *Scriptorum*, vol. IV, pp. 200-98

Ramos de Pareia, Bartolomeo. *Musica practica*, ed. Johannes Wolf, Publikationen der Internationalen Musikgesellschaft 2. Leipzig: Breitkopf und Härtel, 1901

Rhau, Georg. *Enchiridion utriusque musicae practicae*, 9th edn. Wittenberg: Georg Rhau, 1538

Schanppecher, Melchior. *Opus aureum* in K. W. Niemöller, ed., *Die Musica figurativa des Melchior Schanppecher. Opus aureum, Köln 1501, pars III/IV*, Beiträge zur Rheinischen Musikgeschichte 50. Cologne: Arno Volk, 1961

Schlick, Arnolt. *Spiegel der Orgelmacher und Organisten*. Speyer: Peter Drach, 1511

Sebastian z Felsztyna. *Opusculum musice compilatum . . . pro institutione adolescentum in cantu simplici seu gregoriano*. Cracow: Jan Haller, 1517

Spataro, Giovanni. *Bartolomei Rami pareie honesta defensio in Nicolai Burtii parmensis opusculum*. Bologna: Plato de Benedecti, 1491

—. *Dilucide, et probatissime demonstratione contra certe frivole et vane excusatione, da Franchino Gafurio (maestro de li errori) in luce aducte*. Bologna: Hieronymus de Benedictis, 1521

—. Letters in Ms. Vatican, lat. 5318

Theodonus de Caprio. *Regule contrapuncti* in Raffaele Casimiri, 'Theodono de Caprio non Teodorico de Campo teorico musicale italiano del sec. XV'. *Note d'archivio per la storia musicale*, XIX (1942), 94-8

Tinctoris, Johannes. *Expositio manus* in Tinctoris, *Opera theoretica*, ed. A. Seay, Corpus Scriptorum de Musica 22, vol. I. N.p.: American Institute of Musicology, 1975, pp. 31-57

—. *Liber de natura et proprietate tonorum, ibid.*, vol. I, pp. 65-104

—. *Liber de arte contrapuncti, ibid.*, vol. II, pp. 11-157

—. *Terminorum musicae diffinitorium*. [Treviso: Gerardo de Lisa, 1475]

—. *Diffinitorium musicae*. Ms. Brussels, Bibliothèque Royale, II.4147, fols. 117r-124v

Ugolino of Orvieto. *Declaratio musicae disciplinae*, ed. A. Seay, Corpus Scriptorum de Musica 7, 3 vols. N.p.: American Institute of Musicology, 1959-62

Vanneo, Stephano. *Recanetum de musica aurea*. Rome: Valerius Doricus, 1533

Vicentino, Nicola. *L'antica musica ridotta alla moderna prattica*. Rome: Antonio Barré, 1555

Virdung, Sebastian. *Musica getutscht*. Basle: [M. Furter], 1511

Vitry, Philippe de. *Ars nova*, ed. G. Reaney, A. Gilles and J. Maillard, Corpus Scriptorum de Musica 8. N.p.: American Institute of Musicology, 1964

Wollick, Nicolaus. *Opus aureum*, in K. W. Niemöller, ed., *Die Musica gregoriana des Nicolaus Wollick. Opus aureum, Köln 1501, pars I/II*, Beiträge zur Rheinischen Musikgeschichte 11. Cologne and Krefeld: Staufen-Verlag, 1955

—. *Enchiridion musices*. Paris: Francoys Regnault, 1512

Zarlino, Gioseffo. *Le Istitutioni harmoniche*. Venice, 1558

II Literature

Adkins, Cecil Dale. *The Theory and Practice of the Monochord*. Ph.D. diss., State University of Iowa, 1963

—. 'The Technique of the Monochord'. *Acta Musicologica*, XXXIX (1967), 34-43

Albrecht, Christoph. 'Zur Akzidentienfrage im 16. Jahrhundert'. *Musik und Kirche*, L (1980), 125–30

Allaire, Gaston G. *The Theory of Hexachords, Solmization and the Modal System: A Practical Application*, Musicological Studies and Documents 24. N.p.: American Institute of Musicology, 1972

—. 'Les énigmes de l'Antefana et du double hoquet de Machault: une tentative de solution'. *Revue de musicologie*, LXVI (1980), 27–56

Apel, Willi. *Accidentien und Tonalität in den Musikdenkmälern des 15. und 16. Jahrhunderts*, 2nd edn. Baden-Baden: Verlag Valentin Koerner, 1972

—. 'Accidentals and the Modes in 15th- and 16th-Century Sources'. *Bulletin of the American Musicological Society*, II (1937), 6–7

—. 'The Partial Signatures in the Sources up to 1450'. *Acta Musicologica*, X (1938), 1–13; XI (1939), 40–2

—. *The Notation of Polyphonic Music 900–1600*, 5th edn. Cambridge: The Medieval Academy of America, 1953

—. 'Musica ficta'. *Harvard Dictionary of Music*, 2nd edn. Cambridge: Harvard University Press, 1969, pp. 549ff

—. '*Punto intenso contra remisso*' in T. Noblitt, ed., *Music East and West. Essays in Honor of Walter Kaufmann*. New York: Pendragon Press, 1981, pp. 175–82

Appel, Margarete. *Terminologie in den mittelalterlichen Musiktraktaten; ein Beitrag zur musikalischen Elementarlehre des Mittelalters*. Bottrop i. w.: Wilh. Postberg, 1935

Atlas, Allan. *The Cappella Giulia Chansonnier (Rome, Biblioteca Apostolica Vaticana, C.G. XIII. 27)*, 2 vols., Musicological Studies 27. Brooklyn: Institute of Mediaeval Music, 1975

Balmer, Lucie. *Tonsystem und Kirchentöne bei Johannes Tinctoris*. Berner Veröffentlichungen zur Musikforschung 2. Berne: P. Haupt, 1935

Barbour, J. Murray. *Tuning and Temperament: An Historical Survey*, 2nd edn. East Lansing, Michigan: State College Press, 1953

Barnes, John. 'The Specious Uniformity of Italian Harpsichords' in E. M. Ripin, ed., *Keyboard Instruments. Studies in Keyboard Organology*. Edinburgh: Edinburgh University Press, 1971, pp. 1–10

Bent, Margaret. 'Musica Recta and Musica Ficta'. *Musica Disciplina*, XXVI (1972), 73–100

—. '*Resfacta* and *Cantare Super Librum*'. *Journal of the American Musicological Society*, XXXVI (1983), 371–91

—. 'Diatonic *Ficta*'. *Early Music History*, IV (1984), 1–48

—. Lockwood, Lewis, Donington, Robert, and Boorman, Stanley. 'Musica ficta'. *The New Grove Dictionary of Music and Musicians*, XII (1980), 802–11

Benthem, Jaap van. 'Fortuna in Focus: Concerning "Conflicting" Progressions in Josquin's *Fortuna dun gran tempo*'.*Tijdschrift van de Vereniging voor Nederlandse Muziekgeschiedenis*, XXX (1980), 1–50

Berger, Karol. *Theories of Chromatic and Enharmonic Music in Late 16th-Century Italy*, Studies in Musicology 10. Ann Arbor: UMI Research Press, 1980

—. 'The Hand and the Art of Memory'. *Musica Disciplina*, XXXV (1981), 87–120

—. '*Musica Ficta*: Implied Accidental Inflections in Early Vocal Polyphony', to appear in H. M. Brown and S. Sadie, eds., *Handbook of Performance Practice*, The Grove-Norton Music Handbook Series. New York: Norton

Bergquist, Jr, Ed Peter. *The Theoretical Writings of Pietro Aaron*. Ph.D. diss., Columbia University, 1964

—. 'Mode and Polyphony around 1500: Theory and Practice'. *The Music Forum*, I (1967), 99–161

Bibliography

Bernet Kempers, Karel Ph. 'Accidenties' in J. Robijns, ed., *Renaissance-Muziek 1400-1500. Donum natalicium René Bernard Lenaerts*. Leuven: Kotholieke Universiteit, Seminarie voor Muziekwetenschap, 1969, pp. 51-9

Bernoulli, E. 'Hinweis auf gewisse Alterationszeichen in Drucken des 16. Jahrhunderts'. *Internationale Musikgesellschaft, III. Kongress, Wien 25. bis 29. Mai 1909*. Vienna and Leipzig: Artaria and Breitkopf und Härtel, 1909, pp. 126-7

Bielitz, Mathias. *Musik und Grammatik: Studien zur mittelalterlichen Musiktheorie*. Beiträge zur Musikforschung 4. Salzburg: Katzbichler, 1977

Blackburn, Bonnie J. 'Josquin's Chansons: Ignored and Lost Sources'. *Journal of the American Musicological Society*, XXIX (1976), 30-76

Borren, Charles van den. 'Y avait-il une pratique musicale ésotérique au temps de Roland de Lassus?' *Revue belge de musicologie*, II (1948), 38-43

Bray, Roger. 'The Interpretation of Musica Ficta in English Music c. 1490-c. 1580'. *Proceedings of the Royal Musical Association*, XCVII (1970-1), 29-45

—. 'Sixteenth-Century *Musica Ficta*: the Importance of the Scribe'. *Journal of the Plainsong and Mediaeval Music Society*, I (1978), 57-80

Bridgman, Nanie. 'De l'attribution à Tinctoris des exemples musicaux du *Liber de arte contrapuncti*' in M. D. Grace, ed., *A Festschrift for Albert Seay*. Colorado Springs: The Colorado College Music Press, 1982, pp. 33-43

Brown, Howard Mayer. 'Accidentals and Ornamentation in Sixteenth-Century Intabulations of Josquin's Motets' in E. E. Lowinsky, ed., *Josquin des Prez*. London: Oxford University Press, 1976, pp. 475-522

—. 'Introduction', *A Florentine Chansonnier from the Time of Lorenzo the Magnificent. Florence, Biblioteca Nazionale Centrale MS Banco Rari 229*, Monuments of Renaissance Music 7, vol. I. Chicago and London: The University of Chicago Press, 1983

Bukofzer, Manfred. *Geschichte des englischen Diskants und des Fauxbourdons nach den theoretischen Quellen*. Strasbourg: Heitz and Co., 1936

Caldwell, John. *Editing Early Music*. Oxford: Oxford University Press, 1985

—. 'Musica Ficta'. *Early Music*, XIII (1985), 407-8

Chilesotti, Oscar. 'Le alterazioni cromatiche nel secolo XVIo'. *Internationale Musikgesellschaft, III. Kongress, Wien, 25. bis 29. Mai 1909*. Vienna and Leipzig: Artaria and Breitkopf und Härtel, 1909, pp. 128-35

Clercx, Suzanne. 'Les accidents sous-entendus et la transcription en notation moderne'. *Les Colloques de Wégimont*, II (1955), 167-95

—. 'Johannes Ciconia théoricien'. *Annales musicologiques*, III (1955), 39-75

—. *Johannes Ciconia. Un musicien liégeois et son temps (vers 1335-1411)*. Brussels: Académie Royale de Belgique, 1960

Crawford, David. 'Performance and the Laborde Chansonnier: Authenticity of Multiplicities: Musica Ficta'. *College Music Symposium*, X (1970), 107-11

Crevel, Marcus van. *Adrianus Petit Coclico: Leben und Beziehungen eines nach Deutschland emigrierten Josquinschülers*. The Hague: M. Nijhoff, 1940

—. 'Verwante Sequensmodulaties bij Obrecht, Josquin en Coclico'. *Tijdschrift van de Vereniging voor Nederlandse Muziekgeschiedenis*, XVI (1941), 107-24

—. 'Secret Chromatic Art in the Netherlands Motet?' *Tijdschrift van de Vereniging voor Nederlandse Muziekgeschiedenis*, XVI (1946), 253-304

Crocker, Richard. 'Discant, Counterpoint, and Harmony'. *Journal of the American Musicological Society*, XV (1962), 1-21

—. 'A New Source for Medieval Music Theory'. *Acta Musicologica*, XXXIX (1967), 161-71

—. 'Hermann's Major Sixth'. *Journal of the American Musicological Society*, XXV (1972), 19-37

253

Bibliography

Cumming, Julie E. 'The Goddess Fortuna Revisited'. *Current Musicology*, XXX (1980), 7-23

D'Accone, Frank A. 'Matteo Rampolini and His Petrarchan Canzoni Cycles'. *Musica Disciplina*, XXVII (1973), 65-106

Dahlhaus, Carl. 'Die Termini Dur und Moll'. *Archiv für Musikwissenschaft*, XII (1955), 280-96

—. 'Ockeghems "Fuga trium vocum"'. *Die Musikforschung*, XIII (1960), 307-10

—. 'Zu Costeleys chromatischer Chanson'. *Die Musikforschung*, XVI (1963), 253-65

—. 'Zu einer Chanson von Binchois'. *Die Musikforschung*, XVII (1964), 398-9

—. 'Zur chromatischen Technik Carlo Gesualdos'. *Analecta Musicologica*, IV (1967), 77-96

—. 'Zur Akzidentiensetzung in den Motetten Josquins des Prez'. R. Baum and W. Rehm, eds., *Musik und Verlag. Karl Vötterle zum 65. Geburtstag am 12. April 1968.* Kassel: Bärenreiter, 1968, pp. 206-19

—. 'Tonsystem und Kontrapunkt um 1500'. *Jahrbuch des Staatlichen Instituts für Musikforschung Preussischer Kulturbesitz*, (1969), 7-18

—. 'Relationes harmonicae'. *Archiv für Musikwissenschaft*, XXXII (1975), 208-27

—. '"Reine" oder "adäquate" Stimmung?' *Archiv für Musikwissenschaft*, XXXIX (1982), 1-18

Dèzes, Karl. *Prinzipielle Fragen auf dem Gebiet der fingierten Musik*. Ph.D. diss., Humboldt Universität, Berlin, 1922

Doe, Paul. 'Another View of Musica Ficta in Tudor Music'. *Proceedings of the Royal Musical Association*, XCVIII (1971-2), 113-22

Duchez, Marie-Elisabeth. 'La représentation spatio-verticale du caractère musical grave-aigu et l'élaboration de la notion de hauteur de son dans la conscience musicale occidentale'. *Acta Musicologica*, LI (1979), 54-73

Dyer, Joseph. 'A Thirteenth-Century Choirmaster: The *Scientia Artis Musicae* of Elias Salomon'. *The Musical Quarterly*, LXVI (1980), 83-111

Eggebrecht, Hans Heinrich. 'Machauts Motette Nr. 9'. *Archiv für Musikwissenschaft*, XIX-XX (1962-3), 281-93; XXV (1968), 173-95

—. *Studien zur musikalischen Terminologie*, 2nd edn. Mainz: Verlag der Akademie der Wissenschaften und der Literatur, 1968

Elders, Willem. *Studien zur Symbolik in der Musik der alten Niederländer*. Bilthoven: A. B. Creyghton, 1968

—. 'Report of the First Josquin Meeting, Utrecht 1973'. *Tijdschrift van de Vereniging voor Nederlandse Muziekgeschiedenis*, XXIV (1974), 20-82

—. 'Guillaume Dufay as Musical Orator'. *Tijdschrift van de Vereniging voor Nederlandse Muziekgeschiedenis*, XXXI (1981), 1-15

Ellsworth, Oliver. 'The Origin of the Coniuncta: A Reappraisal'. *Journal of Music Theory*, XVII (1973), 86-109

Fallows, David. *Dufay*. London: J. M. Dent and Sons Ltd, 1982

Federhofer, Hellmut and Federhofer-Königs, Renate. 'Ein anonymer Musiktraktat der Stiftsbibliothek Fiecht'. E. Fässler, ed., *Festschrift Walter Senn zum 70. Geburtstag*. Munich: Katzebichler, 1975, pp. 36-52

Federhofer-Königs, Renate. *Johannes Oridryus und sein Musiktraktat (Düsseldorf, 1557)*. Beiträge zur Rheinischen Musikgeschichte 24. Cologne: Arno Volk-Verlag, 1957

—. 'Johan(nes) Vogelsang und sein Musiktraktat (1542)'. *Kirchenmusikalisches Jahrbuch*, XLXIX (1965), 73-123

Ficker, Rudolf von. 'Beiträge zur Chromatik des 14. bis 16. Jahrhunderts'. *Studien zur Musikwissenschaft*, II (1914), 5-33

Bibliography

Finscher, Ludwig. 'Zu den Schriften Edward E. Lowinskys'. *Die Musikforschung*, XV (1962), 54-77

Fischer, Kurt von. 'Eine wiederaufgefundene Theoretikerhandschrift des späten 14. Jahrhunderts (Chicago, Newberry Library, Ms. 541. - olim Codex cujusdam ignoti bibliophili Vindobonensis)'. *Schweizer Beiträge zur Musikwissenschaft*, I (1972), 23-33

Fox, Charles Warren. 'Accidentals in Vihuela Tablatures'. *Bulletin of the American Musicological Society*, IV (1938), 22-4

Frerichs, Elly. 'Die Accidentien in Orgeltabulaturen'. *Zeitschrift für Musikwissenschaft*, VII (1924-5), 99-106

Gallo, F. Alberto. 'La tradizione dei trattati musicali di Prosdocimo de Beldemandis'. *Quadrivium*, VI (1964), 57-84

— . 'Citazioni da un trattato di Dufay'. *Collectanea Historiae Musicae*, IV (1966), 149-52

— . 'Alcune fonti poco note di musica teorica e pratica' in Gallo, ed., *L'ars nova italiana del trecento: Convegni di studi 1961-1967*. Certaldo: Centro di Studi sull'Ars Nova Italiana del Trecento, 1968, pp. 49-76

— . 'Marchetus in Padua und die "franco-venetische" Musik des frühen Trecento'. *Archiv für Musikwissenschaft*, XXXI (1974), 42-56

— . 'Beziehungen zwischen grammatischer, rhetorischer und musikalischer Terminologie im Mittelalter'. D. Heartz and B. Wade, eds., *International Musicological Society. Report of the Twelfth Congress Berkeley 1977*. Kassel: Bärenreiter, 1981, pp. 787-90

Godt, Irving. 'A Lesson in *Musica Ficta* from Guillaume Costeley and Le Roy & Ballard, 1570-1579'. *The Music Review*, XXXVIII (1977), 159-62

Gümpel, Karl-Werner. 'Das Tastenmonochord Conrads von Zabern'. *Archiv für Musikwissenschaft*, XII (1955), 143-66

— . *Die Musiktraktate Conrads von Zabern*. Mainz: Verlag der Akademie der Wissenschaften und der Literatur, 1956

— . 'Zur Frühgeschichte der vulgärsprachlichen und katalanischen Musiktheorie'. *Spanische Forschungen der Görresgesellschaft*, XXI (1968), 257-336

— and Sachs, Klaus-Jürgen. 'Der anonyme Contrapunctus-Traktat aus Ms. Vich 208'. *Archiv für Musikwissenschaft*, XXXI (1974), 87-115

Gushee, Lawrence A. 'Questions of Genre in Medieval Treatises on Music'. W. Arlt, E. Lichtenhahn and H. Oesch, eds., *Gattungen der Musik in Einzeldarstellungen. Gedenkschrift Leo Schrade*, vol. I. Berne and Munich: Francke Verlag, 1973, pp. 365-433

— . 'Musica enchiriadis'. *The New Grove Dictionary of Music and Musicians*, XII (1980), 800-2

Gysin, Hans Peter. *Studien zum Vokabular der Musiktheorie im Mittelalter. Eine linguistische Analyse*. Zurich, 1959

Haar, James. 'Roger Caperon and Ramos de Pareia'. *Acta Musicologica*, XLI (1969), 26-36

— . 'Zarlino's Definition of Fugue and Imitation'. *Journal of the American Musicological Society*, XXIV (1971), 226-54

— . 'False Relations and Chromaticism in Sixteenth-Century Music'. *Journal of the American Musicological Society*, XXX (1977), 391-418

Hammerstein, Reinhold. *Diabolus in Musica. Studien zur Ikonographie der Musik im Mittelalter*, Neue Heidelberger Studien zur Musikwissenschaft 6. Berne and Munich: Francke Verlag, 1974

Hanen, Martha K. *The Chansonnier El Escorial IV.a. 24*. Musicological Studies 36. Henryville, Pa.: Institute of Mediaeval Music, 1983

Harden, Jean. '"Musica Ficta" in Machaut'. *Early Music*, V (1977), 473-7
Harrán, Don. 'The Theorist Giovanni del Lago: A New View of the Man and his Writings'. *Musica Disciplina*, XXVII (1973), 107-51
—. 'New Evidence for Musica Ficta: The Cautionary Sign'. *Journal of the American Musicological Society*, XXIX (1976), 77-98. See also *ibid.*, XXXI (1978), 385-95; XXXII (1979), 364-7
—. 'More Evidence for Cautionary Signs'. *Journal of the American Musicological Society*, XXXI (1978), 490-4
Haydon, Glen. 'The Case of the Troublesome Accidental'. B. Hjelmborg and S. Sørensen, eds., *Natalicia musicologica Knud Jeppesen septuagenario collegis oblata*. Hafniae: Wilhelm Hansen, 1962, pp. 125-30
Herlinger, Jan W. 'A Fifteenth-Century Italian Compilation of Music Theory'. *Acta Musicologica*, LIII (1981), 90-105
—. 'Fractional Divisions of the Whole Tone'. *Music Theory Spectrum*, III (1981), 74-83
—. 'Marchetto's Division of the Whole Tone'. *Journal of the American Musicological Society*, XXXIV (1981), 193-216
Hibberd, Lloyd. '*Musica Ficta* and Instrumental Music, c. 1250-c. 1350'. *The Musical Quarterly*, XXVIII (1942), 216-26
Hirschfeld, Robert. 'Notizen zur mittelalterlichen Musikgeschichte. (Instrumentalmusik und Musica Ficta)'. *Monatshefte für Musikgeschichte*, XVII (1885), 61-7
Hirshberg, Jehoash. 'Hexachordal and Modal Structure in Machaut's Polyphonic Chansons'. J. W. Hill, ed., *Studies in Musicology in Honor of Otto E. Albrecht*. Kassel: Bärenreiter, 1980, pp. 19-42
Honegger, Marc. 'La tablature de D. Pisador et le problème des altérations au XVIe siècle'. *Revue de musicologie*, LIX (1973), 38-59, 191-230; LX (1974), 3-32
Hoppin, Richard H. 'Partial Signatures and Musica Ficta in Some Early 15th-Century Sources'. *Journal of the American Musicological Society*, VI (1953), 197-215
—. 'Conflicting Signatures Reviewed'. *Journal of the American Musicological Society*, IX (1956), 97-117
Hughes, Andrew. 'Some Notes on the Early Fifteenth-Century Contratenor'. *Music and Letters*, L (1969), 376-87
—. 'Ugolino: The Monochord and *Musica Ficta*'. *Musica Disciplina*, XXIII (1969), 21-39
—. *Manuscript Accidentals: Ficta in Focus 1350-1450*, Musicological Studies and Documents 27. N.p.: American Institute of Musicology, 1972
—. 'Musica Ficta'. *Die Musik in Geschichte und Gegenwart*, XVI (1979), 1308-14
— and Bent, Margaret, eds. *The Old Hall Manuscript*, Vol. I, Part 1, Corpus Mensurabilis Musicae 46. N.p.: American Institute of Musicology. 1969, pp. XVIII-XXV
— and Gerson-Kiwi, Edith. 'Solmization', *The New Grove Dictionary of Music and Musicians*, XVII (1980), 458-67
Huglo, Michel. 'L'auteur du "Dialogue sur la musique" attribué à Odon'. *Revue de musicologie*, LV (1969), 119-71
—. 'L'auteur du traité de musique dédié à Fulgence d'Affligem'. *Revue belge de musicologie*, XXXI (1977), 5-19
Jacobs, Charles. 'Spanish Renaissance Discussion of Musica Ficta'. *Proceedings of the American Philosophical Society*, CXII (1968), 277-98
Jacobsthal, Gustav. *Die chromatische Alteration im liturgischen Gesang der abendländischen Kirche*. Berlin: J. Springer, 1897

Bibliography

Jeppesen, Knud. *Der Kopenhagener Chansonnier*. Copenhagen: 1927
—. 'Eine musiktheoretische Korrespondenz des früheren Cinquecento'. *Acta Musicologica*, VIII (1941), 3-39
—. *The Style of Palestrina and the Dissonance*, 2nd edn Copenhagen: E. Munksgaard, 1946
Johnson, Martha. 'A Study of Conflicting Key-Signatures in Francesco Landini's Music'. *Hamline Studies in Musicology*, II (1947), 27-40
Kaufmann, Henry W. *The Life and Works of Nicola Vicentino (1511-c. 1576)*. Musicological Studies and Documents 11. N.p.: American Institute of Musicology, 1966
Kottick, Edward L. 'Flats, Modality, and Musica Ficta in Some Early Renaissance Chansons'. *Journal of Music Theory*, XII (1968), 264-80
Kristeller, Paul Oskar. 'Music and Learning in the Early Italian Renaissance'. *Journal of Renaissance and Baroque Music*, I (1946), 255-74
Kroyer, Theodor. *Die Anfänge der Chromatik im italienischen Madrigal des XVI. Jahrhunderts*. Leipzig: Breitkopf und Härtel, 1902
—. 'Zum Akzidentienproblem im Ausgang des 16. Jahrhunderts'. *Internationale Musikgesellschaft, III. Kongress, Wien, 25. bis 29. Mai 1909*. Vienna and Leipzig: Artaria and Breitkopf und Härtel, 1909, pp. 112-24
Lange, Georg. 'Zur Geschichte der Solmisation', *Sammelbände der Internationalen Musikgesellschaft*, I (1899-1900), 535-622
Lange, Helmut K. H. 'Ein Beitrag zur musikalischen Temperatur der Musikinstrumente vom Mittelalter bis zur Gegenwart'. *Die Musikforschung*, XXI (1968), 482-97
Lenneberg, Hans H. 'The Critic Criticized: Sebastian Virdung and his Controversy with Arnold Schlick'. *Journal of the American Musicological Society*, X (1957), 1-6
León Tello, Francisco José. *Estudios de historia de la teoria musical*. Madrid: Instituto Español de Musicologia, 1962
Levitan, Joseph S. 'Ockeghem's Clefless Compositions'. *The Musical Quarterly*, XXIII (1937), 440-64
—. 'Adrian Willaert's Famous Duo *Quidnam ebrietas*. A Composition which Closes Apparently with the Interval of a Seventh'. *Tijdschrift van de Vereniging voor Nederlandse Muziekgeschiedenis*, XV (1939), 166-233
Levy, Kenneth J. 'Costeley's Chromatic Chanson'. *Annales musicologiques*, III (1955), 213-63
Lindley, Mark. 'Early Sixteenth-Century Keyboard Temperaments', *Musica Disciplina*, XXVIII (1974), 129-51
Lockwood, Lewis. 'A Dispute on Accidentals in Sixteenth-Century Rome'. *Analecta Musicologica*, II (1965), 24-40
—. 'Computer Assistance in the Investigation of Accidentals in Renaissance Music'. D. Cvetko, ed., *International Musicological Society. Report of the Tenth Congress Ljubljana 1967*. Kassel: Bärenreiter, 1970, pp. 444-9
—. 'A Sample Problem of *Musica Ficta*: Willaert's *Pater Noster*'. H. S. Powers, ed., *Studies in Music History: Essays for Oliver Strunk*. Princeton: Princeton University Press, 1968, pp. 161-82
Lowinsky, Edward E. 'The Goddess Fortuna in Music, with a Special Study of Josquin's *Fortuna d'un gran tempo*'. *The Musical Quarterly*, XXIX (1943), 45-77
—. 'The Function of Conflicting Signatures in Early Polyphonic Music'. *The Musical Quarterly*, XXXI (1945), 227-60
—. *Secret Chromatic Art in the Netherlands Motet*. New York: Columbia University Press, 1946

—. 'On the Use of Scores by 16th-Century Musicians', *Journal of the American Musicological Society*, I (1948), 17-23
—. [Review of Gombert, *Opera omnia.*] *The Musical Quarterly*, XXXVIII (1952), 630-40
—. [Review of Brumel, *Opera omnia.*] *MLA Notes*, X (1953), 312-4
—. 'Conflicting Views on Conflicting Signatures'. *Journal of the American Musicological Society*, VII (1954), 181-204
—. 'Adrian Willaert's Chromatic "Duo" Re-Examined'. *Tijdschrift van de Vereniging voor Nederlandse Muziekgeschiedenis*, XVIII (1956), 1-36
—. [Review of Clemens non Papa, *Opera omnia.*] *MLA Notes*, XIII (1956), 677-8
—. 'Matthaeus Greiter's *Fortuna*: An Experiment in Chromaticism and in Musical Iconography'. *The Musical Quarterly*, XLII (1956), 500-19; XLIII (1957), 68-85
—. 'Early Scores in Manuscript', *Journal of the American Musicological Society*, XIII (1960), 126-73
—. *Tonality and Atonality in Sixteenth-Century Music*. Berkeley and Los Angeles: The University of California Press, 1961
—. 'Foreword'. H. Colin Slim, ed., *Musica Nova*. Monuments of Renaissance Music 1. Chicago and London: The University of Chicago Press, 1964, pp. V-XXI
—. 'Renaissance Writings on Music Theory (1964)', *Renaissance News*, XVIII (1965), 358-70
—. 'Introduction'. H. Hewitt, ed., *Ottaviano Petrucci, Canti B*. Monuments of Renaissance Music 2. Chicago and London: The University of Chicago Press, 1967, pp. V-XVI
—. 'Echoes of Adrian Willaert's Chromatic "Duo" in Sixteenth- and Seventeenth-Century Compositions'. H. S. Powers, ed., *Studies in Music History. Essays for Oliver Strunk*. Princeton: Princeton University Press, 1968, pp. 183-238
—. 'The Musical Avant-Garde of the Renaissance or: The Peril and Profit of Foresight'. C. S. Singleton, ed., *Art, Science and History in the Renaissance*. Baltimore: The Johns Hopkins Press, 1968, pp. 111-62
—. '*Secret Chromatic Art* Re-Examined'. B. S. Brook, E. O. D. Downes, and S. Van Solkema, eds., *Perspectives in Musicology. The Inaugural Lectures of the Ph.D. Program in Music at the City University of New York*. New York: Norton, 1972, pp. 91-135
—. 'Music in Titian's *Bacchanal of the Andrians*. Origin and History of the *Canon per Tonos*'. D. Rosand, ed., *Titian: His World and His Legacy*. New York: Columbia University Press, 1982, pp. 191-282
Markovits, Michael. *Das Tonsystem der abendländischen Musik im frühen Mittelalter*. Publikationen der Schweizerischen Musikforschenden Gesellschaft II.30. Berne and Stuttgart: Paul Haupt, 1977
Martinez, Marie Louise. *Die Musik des frühen Trecento*. Münchner Veröffentlichungen zur Musikgeschichte 9. Tutzing: Schneider, 1963
Martinez-Göllner, Marie Louise. 'Marchettus of Padua and Chromaticism'. F. A. Gallo, ed., *L'Ars nova italiana del trecento. Secondo convegno internazionale 17-22 luglio 1969*. Certaldo: Edizioni Centro di studi sull'Ars nova italiana del trecento, 1970, pp. 187-202
Massera, Giuseppe. *La 'mano musicale perfetta' di Francesco de Brugis dalle prefazioni ai corali di L. A. Giunta, Venezia, 1499-1504*. Historiae Musicae Cultores 18. Florence: Leo S. Olschki, 1963

—. 'Musica inspettiva et accordatura strumentale'. *Quadrivium*, VI (1964), 85-105

—. 'Suggestioni teoretiche nel *Lucidarium* di Marchetto da Padova: dai "Generi" alla "Musica Colorata"'. M. D. Grace, ed., *A Festschrift for Albert Seay*. Colorado Springs: The Colorado College Music Press, 1982, pp. 1-20

McGary, Thomas J. 'Partial Signature Implications in the Escorial Manuscript V.III.24'. *Music Review*, XL (1979), 77-89

Meier, Bernhard. 'Die Handschrift Porto 714 als Quelle zur Tonartenlehre des 15. Jahrhunderts'. *Musica Disciplina*, VII (1953), 175-97

—. 'Eine weitere Quelle der Musica Reservata'. *Die Musikforschung*, VIII (1955), 83-5

—. *Die Tonarten der klassischen Vokalpolyphonie*. Utrecht: Oosthoek, Scheltema & Holkema, 1974

Mendel, Arthur. 'Devices for Transposition in the Organ before 1600'. *Acta Musicologica*, XXI (1949), 24-40

—. 'Pitch in Western Music since 1500: A Re-Examination'. *Acta Musicologica*, L (1978), 1-93, 328

—. 'The Purposes and Desirable Characteristics of Text-Critical Editions'. E. Olleson, ed., *Modern Musical Scholarship*. Stocksfield: Oriel Press, 1980, pp. 14-27

Michels, Ulrich. 'Der Musiktraktat des Anonymus OP: ein frühes Theoretiker-Zeugnis der Ars nova'. *Archiv für Musikwissenschaft*, XXVI (1969), 49-62

—. *Die Musiktraktate des Johannes de Muris*. Beihefte zum Archiv für Musikwissenschaft 8. Wiesbaden: Franz Steiner, 1970

Miller, Clement A. 'The *Dodecachordon*: Its Origins and Influence on Renaissance Musical Thought'. *Musica Disciplina*, XV (1961), 156-66

—. 'Gaffurius's *Practica Musicae*: Origin and Contents'. *Musica Disciplina*, XXII (1968), 105-28

Myers, Joan Wallace. *Spanish Musica Ficta According to Juan Bermudo*. M.A. thesis, Stanford University, 1966

Niemöller, Klaus Wolfgang. *Nicolaus Wollick, 1480-1541, und sein Musiktraktat*. Beiträge zur Rheinischen Musikgeschichte 13. Cologne: Arno Volk-Verlag, 1956

Noblitt, Thomas. 'Chromatic Cross-Relations and Editorial *Musica Ficta* in Masses of Obrecht'. *Tijdschrift van de Vereniging voor Nederlandse Muziekgeschiedenis*, XXXII (1982), 30-44

Oesch, Hans. *Guido von Arezzo. Biographisches und Theoretisches unter besonderer Berücksichtigung der sogenanten odonischen Traktate*. Publikationen der Schweizerischen Musikforschenden Gesellschaft II/4. Berne: Paul Haupt, 1954

—. *Berno und Hermann von Reichenau als Musiktheoretiker*. Publikationen der Schweizerischen Musikforschenden Gesellschaft II.9. Berne: P. Haupt, 1961

Palisca, Claude V., ed. *Hucbald, Guido and John on Music: Three Medieval Treatises*, trans. W. Babb. New Haven: Yale University Press, 1978

Paulsmeier, Karin. 'Akzidentien im Codex Bamberg'. *Schweizer Beiträge zur Musikwissenschaft*, II (1974), 21-46

Perkins, Leeman L. and Garey, Howard, eds. *The Mellon Chansonnier*, 2 vols. New Haven and London: Yale University Press, 1979

Pirrotta, Nino. 'Marchettus de Padua and the Italian Ars Nova'. *Musica Disciplina*, IX (1955), 57-71

—. ed. *The Music of Fourteenth-Century Italy*, vol. III. Corpus Mensurabilis Musicae 8. N.p.: American Institute of Musicology, 1962

Bibliography

Pogue, Samuel F. *Jacques Moderne: Lyons Music Printer of the Sixteenth Century.* Travaux d'Humanisme et Renaissance 101. Geneva: Librairie Droz, 1969

Powers, Harold S. 'Mode', *The New Grove Dictionary of Music and Musicians*, XII (1980), 376-450

—. 'Tonal Types and Modal Categories in Renaissance Polyphony', *Journal of the American Musicological Society*, XXXIV (1981), 428-70

Preussner, Eberhard. 'Solmisationsmethoden im Schulunterricht des 16. und 17. Jahrhunderts', H. Hoffmann and F. Rühlmann, eds., *Festschrift Fritz Stein zum 60. Geburtstag überreicht von Fachgenossen, Freunden und Schülern.* Braunschweig: Henry Litolff, 1939, pp. 112-28

Randel, Don Michael. 'Dufay the Reader'. *Studies in the History of Music*, I (1983), 38-78

Reaney, Gilbert. 'Musica Ficta in the Works of Guillaume de Machaut'. *Les Colloques de Wégimont*, II (1955), 196-213

—. 'Accidentals in Early Fifteenth-Century Music'. J. Robijns, ed., *Renaissance-Muziek 1400-1600. Donum natalicium René Bernard Lenaerts.* Leuven: Katholieke Universiteit, Seminarie voor Muziekwetenschap, 1969, pp. 223-31

—. 'Accidentals and Fourteenth-Century Counterpoint in England'. *Quadrivium*, XII (1971), 195-208

—. 'Transposition and "Key" Signatures in Late Medieval Music'. *Musica Disciplina*, XXXIII (1979), 27-41

—. 'The Manuscript Transmission of Hothby's Theoretical Works'. M. D. Grace, ed., *A Festschrift for Albert Seay.* Colorado Springs: The Colorado College Music Press, 1982, pp. 21-31

Reckow, Fritz. 'Clavis', H. H. Eggebrecht, ed., *Handwörterbuch der musikalischen Terminologie.* Wiesbaden: Fritz Steiner, 1971

Riemann, Hugo. *Verloren gegangene Selbstverständlichkeiten in der Musik des 15-16. Jahrhunderts. Die musica ficta; eine Ehrenrettung.* Musikalisches Magazin 17. Langensalza : H. Bayer, 1907

—. *History of Music Theory. Books I and II. Polyphonic Theory to the Sixteenth Century.* Lincoln: University of Nebraska Press, 1962

Rifkin, Joshua. 'Pietrequin Bonnel and Ms. 2794 of the Biblioteca Riccardiana'. *Journal of the American Musicological Society*, XXIX (1976), 284-96

Ripin, Edwin M. 'A Re-Evaluation of Virdung's *Musica getutscht*'. *Journal of the American Musicological Society*, XXIX (1976), 189-223

Routley, Nicholas. 'A Practical Guide to *Musica Ficta*'. *Early Music*, XIII (1985), 59-71

Ruhnke, Martin. 'Lassos Chromatik und die Orgelstimmung'. H. Hüschen and D.-R. Moser, eds., *Convivium musicorum. Festschrift Wolfgang Boetticher zum sechzigsten Geburtstag am 19. August 1974.* Berlin: Verlag Merseburger, 1974, pp. 291-308

Rumbold, Ian. 'The Compilation and Ownership of the "St Emmeram" Codex (Munich, Bayerische Staatsbibliothek, Clm 14274)'. *Early Music History*, II (1982), 161-235

Sachs, Curt. 'Chromatic Trumpets in the Renaissance'. *The Musical Quarterly*, XXXVI (1950), 62-6

Sachs, Klaus-Jürgen. *Der Contrapunctus im 14. und 15. Jahrhundert. Untersuchungen zum Terminus, zur Lehre und zu den Quellen.* Beihefte zum Archiv für Musikwissenschaft 13. Wiesbaden: Franz Steiner, 1974

—. 'Die Contrapunctus-Lehre im 14. und 15. Jahrhundert'. F. Zaminer, ed., *Die mittelalterliche Lehre von der Mehrstimmigkeit.* Geschichte der Musiktheorie 5. Darmstadt: Wissenschaftliche Buchgesellschaft, 1984, pp. 161-256

Bibliography

Schlecht, Raymund. 'Über den Gebrauch der Diesis im 13. und 15. Jahrhundert'.
  Monatshefte für Musikgeschichte, IX (1877), 79–88, 99–108
Schmalzriedt, Siegfried with Mahlert, Elke and Sunten, Bernd. 'Clausula'. H. H.
  Eggebrecht, ed., *Handwörterbuch der musikalischen Terminologie*. Wies-
  baden: Fritz Steiner, 1974
—. 'Kadenz'. H. H. Eggebrecht, ed., *Handwörterbuch der musikalischen
  Terminologie*. Wiesbaden: Fritz Steiner, 1974
Schmid, Manfred Hermann. *Mathias Greiter. Das Schicksal eines deutschen
  Musikers zur Reformationszeit*. Schriftenreihe des Heimatmuseums Aichach 2.
  Aichach: Mayer und Söhne, 1976
Schmidt, Anton Wilhelm. *Die Calliopea legale des Johannes Hothby. Ein Beitrag
  zur Musiktheorie des 15. Jahrhunderts*. Ph.D. diss., Leipzig University. Leipzig;
  Hesse und Becker, 1897
Schoop, Hans. *Entstehung und Verwendung der Handschrift Oxford Bodleian
  Library, Canonici misc. 213*. Publikationen der Schweizerischen Musikfor-
  schenden Gesellschaft II.24. Berne and Stuttgart: Paul Haupt, 1971
Schrade, Leo. [Review of Lowinsky, *Secret Chromatic Art in the Netherlands Motet*.]
  Journal of Renaissance and Baroque Music, I (1946), 159–67
Schwartz, Rudolf. 'Zur Akzidentienfrage im 16. Jahrhundert'. *Internationale Musik-
  gesellschaft, III. Kongress, Wien, 25. bis 29. Mai 1909*. Vienna and Leipzig:
  Artaria and Breitkopf und Härtel, 1909, pp. 109–12
Seay, Albert. 'The *Dialogus Johannis Ottobi Anglici in arte musica*'. *Journal of the
  American Musicological Society*, VIII (1955), 86–100
—. 'Florence: the City of Hothby and Ramos'. *Journal of the American Musicol-
  ogical Society*, IX (1956), 193–5
—. 'The "Liber Musices" of Florentius de Faxolis'. *Music and History. Leo Schrade
  on the Occasion of His Sixtieth Birthday*. Cologne: Arno Volk Verlag, 1963,
  pp. 71–95
—. 'The 15th-Century *Coniuncta*: A Preliminary Study'. J. LaRue, ed., *Aspects of
  Medieval and Renaissance Music. A Birthday Offering to Gustave Reese*.
  New York: Norton, 1966, pp. 723–37
—. 'The Beginnings of the Coniuncta and Lorenzo Masini's "L'Antefana"'. F. A.
  Gallo, ed., *L'Ars nova italiana del trecento. Secondo convegno internazionale
  17–22 luglio 1969*. Certaldo: Edizioni centro di studi sull'Ars nova italiana del
  trecento, 1970, pp. 51–65
Skei, Allen B. 'Stefano Rossetti, Madrigalist'. *The Music Review*, XXXIX (1978),
  81–94
Smith, F. J. '"Accidentalism" in Fourteenth Century Music'. *Revue belge de musicol-
  ogie*, XXIX (1970), 42–51
Smits van Waesberghe, Joseph. 'The Musical Notation of Guido of Arezzo'. *Musica
  Disciplina*, V (1951), 15–53
—. *De musico-paedagogico et theoretico Guidone Aretino eiusque vita et mori-
  bus*. Florence: Leo S. Olschki, 1953
—. 'Les origines de la notation alphabéthique au moyen âge'. *Anuario musical*,
  XII (1957), 3–16
—. *Musikerziehung. Lehre und Theorie der Musik im Mittelalter*. Musikge-
  schichte in Bildern III 3. Leipzig: VEB Deutscher Verlag für Musik, 1969
Stevenson, Robert. *Juan Bermudo*. The Hague: M. Nijhoff, 1960
—. *Spanish Music in the Age of Columbus*. The Hague: M. Nijhoff, 1960
Thibault, Geneviève. 'Instrumental Transcriptions of Josquin's French Chansons'.
  E. E. Lowinsky, ed., *Josquin des Prez*. London: Oxford University Press, 1976,
  pp. 455–74

Bibliography

Tischler, Hans. 'Musica Ficta in the Parisian Organa'. *Journal of Music Theory*, XVII (1973), 310-19

—. '"Musica Ficta" in the Thirteenth Century'. *Music and Letters*, LIV (1973), 38-56

Toft, Robert. 'Pitch Content and Modal Procedure in Josquin's *Absalon, fili mi'*. *Tijdschrift van de Vereniging voor Nederlandse Muziekgeschiedenis*, XXXIII (1983), 3-27

Tucher, Georg von. 'Zum Musikpraxis und Theorie des 16. Jahrhunderts, V: Accidentien und Musica Ficta'. *Allgemeine musikalische Zeitung*, VIII (1873), 1-6, 17-21, 33-7, 49-54, 65-9, 81-4, 129-33, 161-5, 177-82, 193-6, 209-12

University of Illinois Musicological Archives for Renaissance Manuscript Studies, The, comp. *Census-Catalogue of Manuscript Sources of Polyphonic Music 1400-1550*, 3 vols. Renaissance Manuscript Studies 1. N.p.: American Institute of Musicology, 1979-84

Vogel, Martin. 'Boethius und die Herkunft der modernen Tonbuchstaben'. *Kirchenmusikalisches Jahrbuch*, XLVI (1962), 1-19

—. 'Musica falsa und falso bordone'. L. Finscher and C.-H. Mahling, eds., *Festschrift für Walter Wiora zum 30. Dezember 1966*. Kassel: Bärenreiter, 1967, pp. 170-6

Wiora, Walter. 'Zum Problem des Ursprungs der mittelalterlichen Solmisation'. *Die Musikforschung*, IX (1956), 263-74

Wolf, Johannes. *Geschichte der Mensuralnotation von 1250-1460*, vol. I. Leipzig: Breitkopf und Härtel, 1904

—. 'Die Akzidentien im 15. und 16. Jahrhundert'. *Internationale Musikgesellschaft, III. Kongress, Wien, 25. bis 29. Mai 1909*. Vienna and Leipzig: Artaria and Breitkopf und Härtel, 1909, pp. 124-5

Woodley, Ronald. 'Iohannes Tinctoris: A Review of the Documentary Biographical Evidence'. *Journal of the American Musicological Society*, XXXIV (1981), 217-48

Wulstan, David. 'The Problem of Pitch in Sixteenth-Century English Vocal Music'. *Proceedings of the Royal Musical Association*, XCIII (1966-7), 97-112

Index

I. NAMES AND TITLES

Index